P9-BXY-714

Voluntary Associations in Tsarist Russia

VOLUNTARY ASSOCIATIONS IN TSARIST RUSSIA

Science, Patriotism, and Civil Society

JOSEPH BRADLEY

HARVARD UNIVERSITY PRESS
Cambridge, Massachusetts
London, England
2009

Printed in the United States of America

Library of Congress Cataloging-in-Publication Data

Bradley, Joseph.
Voluntary associations in Tsarist Russia : science, patriotism, and civil society / Joseph Bradley.
p. cm.
Includes bibliographical references and index.
ISBN 978-0-674-03279-8 (alk. paper)
1. Associations, institutions, etc.—Russia—History.
2. Civil society—Russia—History. I. Title.
HS71.R8B73 2009
369.0947'09034—dc22 2008047153

To Chris

Contents

Preface

MANY YEARS AGO the editors of a volume on late-imperial Russian cities asked me to write the entry on Moscow. In the first draft of my article I utilized the demographic, economic, and sociological approach of my first book, *Muzhik and Muscovite.* The editors sent my article back and asked me to add a bit on cultural and intellectual life in order to round out what was supposed to be a broad survey of the city. While I had done some general reading in these areas, I had never pursued this dimension of Moscow's history. Considering the request to be a reasonable one, I began to look over my notes as well as at some new material.

While reading up on topics less familiar to me, such as Moscow University, the city's schools, the publishing world, and the world of art and art patronage at the turn of the twentieth century, I was struck by one particular feature of Moscow's culture—the number and variety of clubs and societies that dotted the city's landscape. I read that Moscow had a flying club, an automobile club, a racing club, a vegetarian society, an Esperanto society, a lawn tennis club, and a fox terrier and dachshund society. I had never particularly noticed, much less paid attention to, these kinds of organizations. Having spent years researching chiefly the city's peasant migrants and the urban poor, I wondered what I had been missing. Not much, I thought at first: such clubs were no doubt for the city's small upper crust and even smaller cultural and artistic elite. They could hardly have touched or cared about the city's factory districts, multifamily tenements, and Khitrov Market, the city's main skid row.

However, as I read on, other kinds of organizations caught my eye—temperance societies, literacy committees, technical societies, medical societies (and separate ones for new, specialized areas of medicine). To be sure, in my first book I had examined the city's overall welfare infrastructure, but my focus had been on state and municipal relief, not on private charity. Curious, I checked a few city directories of the era and saw that indeed Moscow had a sampling of Victorian-era civic organizations, organizations whose missions, I surmised, were to ameliorate this or that aspect of city life. I noticed also that many organizations, especially the science and other learned societies, had extensive publications, including *Izvestiia (News), Zapiski (Notes), Trudy (Proceedings),* and so forth. According to the city directories, the societies held meetings at particular venues and had officers. Some sponsored expeditions, organized exhibitions, and founded museums.

But we don't think of Russia as a nation of joiners, so what were these Victorian-type organizations doing in Moscow (and in St. Petersburg as well)? Were they, perhaps, hollow imitations of European organizations? How did they get started? What were they trying to accomplish? What was their relationship to the government? In Europe and North America, historians often regard voluntary associations as incubators of middle-class values. Did their existence mean that the prevailing judgment about a small and ineffectual Russian middle class has been misleading? Likewise, in Europe and North America, historians often regard the existence of civic organizations as evidence of a sphere of life outside the control of the state. Did their existence in Russia mean that the autocratic state had loosened its grip on public life? I decided that while I might not be able to address all dimensions of Russia's associations, their existence merited analysis. Moreover, it seemed then that few historians were looking at this dimension of Russian life.

If by the end of the nineteenth century Russia's big cities had borrowed the typical Victorian-era voluntary associations from Europe, then, I reasoned, I had better learn more about the European originals. Reading the comparative literature on nongovernmental organizations took me into new historiographical fields—the middle class, history of science, urban culture—in other countries. It was beginning to seem to me that while the experience of association was never entirely the same in different countries, there were many shared traits. I found immensely stimulating *The Peculiarities of German History* by David Blackbourn and Geoff Eley, which challenged the idea that Germany developed along a separate path from the one followed by the rest of Europe. Russia, of course, has had its own *Sonderweg.* Its experience of voluntary association differed from that of Great Britain and the United States. But the more I read about European and Russian associations and even about the relationship between state and society, the more similarities I saw, especially when Russia is compared to continental Europe. Although differences between Russia and the West certainly stand out, insufficient attention has been paid to commonalities.

The beginning of my interest in the topic took place in the late 1980s. One of the features of the era of glasnost and perestroika in the Soviet Union was the rapid appearance of new forms of voluntary organizations. They were grassroots and unofficial, or, as they were called in Russian, *neformaly*. Sociologists counted and studied them, and the newspaper *Komsomol'skaia Pravda* wrote about them—no doubt, because the unofficial organizations appeared to be drawing young people away from the Komsomol. Private initiative, long suppressed or channeled by Soviet official bodies, seemed to be enjoying its springtime. Historians at the time, in the Soviet Union and abroad, were seeking "alternatives," or a "usable past," as ways to revive dimensions of the past that had long been suppressed or ignored, dimensions that clustered around alternatives to Stalinism and alternatives to Leninism. Could there have been alternatives to tsarism, I wondered, in prerevolutionary grassroots civic activities, which were later swept away by war, revolution, and the party-state?

This was also a time when the concept of "civil society" was enjoying a rebirth. Beginning in the late 1970s, the East Europeans began to use civil society, a "parallel polis," in the words of the Czech dissident Jan Benda, to conceptualize a field of thought and action that was an alternative to the party-state and, on a deeper level, an alternative to the pervasive étatism of authoritarian regimes. In other regions experiencing a "transition from authoritarian rule"—southern Europe, Latin America—the concept of civil society found receptive adherents. In western Europe and North America, theorists from both the Left and Right framed discussions of political culture in terms of civil society or in terms of a closely related concept popularized by Jürgen Habermas, the "public sphere." On the Left, civil society became a useful category of analysis of social change that loosened rigid Marxist categories of class and class struggle and shifted focus to the realm of culture and citizen initiatives. On the Right, civil society evoked the localism of Burkean "little platoons" and directed attention away from the modernizing state and to the actions of private individuals. By the late 1980s, Soviet political scientists, sociologists, and philosophers were using the term civil society *(grazhdanskoe obshchestvo)* as a way to frame a discussion of rights, private initiative, and the rule of law, still largely an imagined, though perhaps, it seemed then, a realizable, community.

But what did theorists in the West and nonstate actors in the East understand by civil society? Was it the relatively homogeneous political community of the ancients? Was it the private battleground of competing interests that ushered in the modern world, described by the thinkers of the Scottish Enlightenment and theorized by Hegel? Was it the site of "intermediary bodies" admired by Montesquieu and Tocqueville, of self-rule that defended the individual from the centralizing state? While much writing about civil society was eclectic, to say the least, in its most general sense civil society promised a community independent of the state. But under the conditions of authoritarian and totalitarian rule, which denied autonomy from the state and its agents, such a community was highly contested and to a significant degree still imagined.

Late-tsarist Russia had also embarked on a "transition from authoritarian rule," even if the transition was fitful and contested by autocracy. Although voluntary associations were an important part of that movement, historians have underappreciated their role. The world of bylaws, meetings, and annual reports was a world of choice, community, and new public identities. The story of Russian voluntary associations was the story of the self-organization and initiative of dedicated Russians, the story of myriad projects to spread scientific knowledge and improve life, the story of collaboration and partnership with government officials and state agencies. Fatefully, it was also the story of increasing conflict with political authority. In short, associations were a critical part of the development of civil society that was struggling to limit the scope of arbitrary autocratic and bureaucratic authority.

It would not be possible to tell this story had it not been for the material and intellectual assistance of a long list of institutions and individuals. In the early stages I benefited from a summer fellowship and a Travel to Collections grant from the National Endowment for the Humanities, as well as a fellowship from the National Council of Soviet and East European Research. Visiting teaching positions at Ohio State University and Georgetown University helped me conceptualize the project in its early stages, and I am grateful to my short-term colleagues and students for these opportunities. Being a guest one summer of the history faculty at Moscow State University at the invitation of Yuri S. Kukushkin allowed me to embark on archival research. I would also like to thank the Kennan Institute for Advanced Russian Studies for a travel grant, which helped in the final stages of manuscript preparation. At all stages, the Office of Research at the University of Tulsa has provided research support.

I have benefited from the work of the staffs of many Russian archives and libraries, working under the difficult conditions of the 1990s. I am especially grateful to Zinaida Ivanovna Peregudova and the staff at the

State Archive of the Russian Federation in Moscow for helping me find police reports of the public activities of associations. Likewise, Serafima Igorevna Varekhova and the staff of the Russian State Historical Archive in St. Petersburg helped me find government reports as well as materials of the organizations themselves. I thank the directors for admission to the Central Historical Archive of Moscow, the Russian Archive of the Academy of Sciences, the Moscow Society of Naturalists, the Museum of the History of Moscow, and the Russian Geographical Society. The staffs of the reading rooms and the manuscript divisions of the Russian State Library in Moscow and the National Library of Russia in St. Petersburg and of the reading room of the State History Library in Moscow filled untold orders of published and unpublished material. For the reproduction of pictorial material I am grateful to the State Archive of Documentary Film, Photographs, and Sound Recordings (St. Petersburg); the State Museum of the History of St. Petersburg; the State Polytechnical Museum in Moscow; and the Library of Congress.

Closer to home, on numerous occasions I have benefited from the extensive collection and reference service at the University of Illinois Champaign-Urbana; Helen Sullivan and Larry Miller have always taken interest in the project and helped me to find sources. Research for this book was also conducted at the Library of Congress and facilitated by the staff of the European Reading Room. I also want to thank the Davis Center for Russian and Eurasian Studies for facilitating the use of several of Harvard's libraries—the Widener Library, the Law School Library, the Medical School Library, the Museum of Comparative Zoology Library, and the Tozzer Library. The Interlibrary Loan Office at the University of Tulsa filled countless orders expeditiously. Finally, a number of research assistants have helped me find sources or compose bibliographies over the years, and I am grateful to Heath Henry, Rachel Kunkel-Bodziak, Irina Kissina, David Morse, Aleksei Shapiro, and Sergei Terekhov.

I have presented my work in a variety of venues, and I want to thank the organizers and participants of conferences and workshops for their invitations: the Midwest Russian Historians' Workshop meetings at the University of Chicago, the University of Illinois Champaign-Urbana, and Indiana University; the Conference on Russian *Obshchestvennost'* at Purdue University; the Conference on Reforming Eras in Russian History at the Kennan Institute; the Conference on Civil Society and Democratization at the University of Warwick in the United Kingdom; the Conference on Cultures of the City at the European University in St. Petersburg; the History Faculty at Moscow University; the Conference on Science and the Russian Intelligentsia at the University of Georgia; and the History Departments at the

University of Illinois Champaign-Urbana, the University of Kansas, and Texas Tech University.

Passages from two of my published articles appear in chapters one, four and the conclusion: "Subjects into Citizens: Societies, Civil Society, and Autocracy in Tsarist Russia," *American Historical Review* 107, no. 4 (October 2002): 1094–1123, and "Pictures at an Exhibition: Science, Patriotism and Civil Society in Imperial Russia," *Slavic Review* 67, no. 4 (Winter 2008): 934–966.

I have used the Library of Congress system for the transliteration of Russian words throughout. All dates are according to the Jullian calendar.

I have benefited greatly from the encouragement and criticism of many individuals. In the early stages, Fred Starr, Richard Stites, and Allan Wildman gave me encouragement. André Liebich as well as my colleagues at the University of Tulsa, Eldon Eisenach and Paul Rahe, gave me valuable feedback on civil society in western political thought. Zhenya and his family, Lena, Sergei, Natasha, and other friends in Moscow and St. Petersburg provided companionship over the years. Laura Engelstein, Gary Hamburg, and Gary Marker shared their views of Russian civil society with me; their probing queries helped me to sharpen my argument. Katia Dianina, Cathy Frierson, Jörg Hackmann, Guido Hausmann, Blair Ruble, Anastasiia Tumanova, Galina Ulianova, and Claudia Weiss read parts of earlier versions. Harley Balzer and Bill Wagner read an earlier draft of the manuscript and offered me detailed comments and suggestions. I am also grateful to Kathleen McDermott, my editor at Harvard University Press, for guiding the manuscript through various production stages and to the press's anonymous readers for their valuable suggestions. Any shortcomings that remain are my own. Finally, the discerning judgment of Chris Ruane, fellow Russian historian and my wife, has been invaluable at all stages of this project. She and my stepson, James Ruane Hinshaw, have lived with Russian voluntary associations for many years, and their love and support have helped me see the book through to the end.

Illustrations

Voluntary Associations in Tsarist Russia

Introduction

Russian Associations

By the beginning of the twentieth century, Russia, not known as a nation of joiners, had by rough estimate, ten thousand voluntary associations. Private associations, sanctioned by the government, entered the public realm with a breathtaking number and variety of missions and projects. Societies were everywhere—St. Petersburg and Moscow, the capitals of the non-Russian regions of the empire, the major provincial centers, and even small towns. The range of these groups included learned societies, small-town charitable and agricultural societies, and clubs for recreation and sport. On the eve of World War I Russia had the largest number of cooperative societies in the world.[1] The rapid growth of associations in the second half of the nineteenth century both caused and reflected fast-paced social, economic, and cultural changes. Although severely circumscribing public action, an understaffed government could not keep up with the expansion of associations, many of which it had encouraged in the first place. Associations enabled Russians to take initiative, organize themselves, and work together to achieve common goals. They were a focal point of a contradictory political culture: on the one hand they fostered a state-society partnership; on the other hand they were a critical element in the effort to emancipate society from a personalized autocracy and arbitrary officialdom.

Yet despite the startling ubiquity of associations, historians have neglected this seemingly anomalous feature of Russian political culture. There is not a single published history in English—and a small number in Russian—of

Russia's major societies, let alone of myriad lesser organizations. Although many scholars have used materials generated by Russian societies to tell other stories—of farming, of imperial exploration, of charity, of education, of public health, of the professions, for example—no one has studied associations collectively as a coherent phenomenon. This book is an attempt to rescue Russian associations from historiographical oblivion. But it is more than an attempt to fill in a gap in our knowledge. By placing associations in their political and social contexts and by focusing on the contested sphere of private initiative, I will examine the meaning of associational life and the role of associations in the development of civil society under the imperial regime. I will suggest alterations in the map of public life in tsarist Russia by giving agency and voice to the long forgotten founders, officers, and members of private associations. This book will document the possibilities, as well as the limitations, of public life under autocracy, and the cooperation as well as confrontation with political authority.

In the prevailing view of Russian political culture, there are, of course, reasons for the absence or, at best, weakness of the spirit of association, civil society, and an autonomous public. An all-powerful and repressive state deprived its subjects of civil rights. Not brought into existence by a "contract," the state acted, while a politically immature, passive, and fragmented society was acted upon. Since the state, the artificer of the Russian nation, created for its own purposes society's corporate institutions, Russia's estates had no claim to "ancient rights," the language of noble resistance to monarchies in western Europe. Although it granted privileges, almost to the bitter end autocracy denied Russian subjects rights—freedom from personal dependence and arbitrary domination, inviolability of person and domicile, the rule of law, civil and property rights—as well as some sort of parliament or assembly of the estates. A fragmented society was incapable of, and prohibited from, the self-organization necessary to stand up to the tsarist leviathan. Unwilling to allow individual rights to be invoked against it, the state prevented the institutionalization of civil society. By the time the ideas of constitutions and limited government finally emerged in Russia in the early nineteenth century, they were vigorously resisted by autocracy and, later, were overshadowed by radicalism, which was no less suspicious of civil and property rights. Autocracy took special care to swaddle associational activity in the public realm: "To allow intermediary bodies to develop as representatives of this embryonic civil society was tantamount to an abdication of authority by the sovereign."[2] Thus, the hypertrophy of the state and atrophy of society were entwined in a "double helix" of Russian political culture under the Old Regime.[3] The radical intelligentsia dismissed the "small deeds" of voluntary associations, especially those sanctioned by the state, in favor of the grand struggle against autocracy. Finally, the tragic fate of civil society and private initiative, rocked by war and revolutions and eradicated by totalitarianism in twentieth-century Russia, as well as the authoritarian and oligarchic development of post-Soviet Russia, has only cemented the prevailing view that the development of civil society was doomed. In the pithy, oft cited, but misleading words of Antonio Gramsci, "In Russia the state is everything and civil society is primordial and gelatinous."[4]

To be sure, historians occasionally concede that, by the end of Catherine's reign, "the blueprint for a civil society in Russia was ready"; by the end of the reign of Alexander I, "the growth of civil society proved to be irreversible."[5] It has been argued that "an organized society capable of acting independently of the state and placing limits on its powers," appeared in the nineteenth century, though it is not clear when.[6] Similarly, the Great Reforms created the framework for a civil society that was "of sufficient size and autonomy to challenge the regime's monopoly on political authority" and that was "generally hostile to the existing regime," a civil society that finally emerged at the end of the nineteenth and beginning of the twentieth century.[7] Historians of the 1905 Revolution and of Russian labor attach great significance to Russia's first revolution in mobilizing opposition to autocracy and launching the development of civil society and of a plebeian public sphere.[8] But the overall negative characterization of Russian political culture is not in dispute. Despite the misleading picture of the absence of associations and of an autonomous public, the dominant interpretation of Russian political culture does contain an indisputable truth. Contested by the autocratic state, the very existence of voluntary associations and their works, not to mention civil society and an autonomous public sphere, did not develop smoothly and could not be taken for granted in tsarist Russia.

However, the ability of the tsarist regime to suppress civil society and to thwart the impulse to associate is frequently exaggerated. "Censors and police patrolled society," one historian states, "restricting intellectuals *to private discussions*" and channeling the public expression of ideas *largely to literature and art,* thereby stifling "*a broad civil society of autonomous organizations* and interest groups."[9] This view has been put even more strongly: "Autocracy *destroyed or crippled all autonomous institutions* . . . as useless or even inimical to its purpose. *No middle ground of spontaneous non-governmental public activity was left,* alas, to mediate between an extreme absolutism and anarchy."[10] One of Russia's most prominent historians declared that due to the absence of a civil society, "Russia has not escaped totalitarianism before or since 1917 . . . The state monopolized every activity, and no autonomous society existed apart from its all-pervasive scope . . . An omnipotent state means subjects deprived of initiative."[11] It is small wonder that such essentialist views of Russian political culture are reproduced outside our field as well. To take but one example, at a conference devoted to Jürgen Habermas, Geoff Eley observed that "nineteenth-century Russia provides an excellent counterexample for the growth of the public sphere. It displayed the *absence* of all those processes—particularly the *emancipatory impulse of free associational initiative*."[12] Historians from a variety of historiographical schools and political preferences are in remarkable consensus. The prevailing Russian essentialism reflects an "axiomatic negativism," and thus Russian political culture is a history of failures, weaknesses, fragmentation, backwardness, and lost opportunities.[13] Public action has been ill fated, primitive, amorphous, confrontational. The story of late-imperial Russia is fundamentally a story of what did *not* happen.

But if the autocratic regime had so crippled autonomous organizations, if the tradition of voluntary association had been so weak, then how could so many associations have existed in nineteenth-century Russia? Were they, perhaps, merely lackeys of the imperial regime? If the police had successfully confined debate to private discussions of literature and art, how could Russian subjects have staked a claim to the scrutiny of public policy? If Russia had no middle ground of spontaneous nongovernmental public activity, where did Russians acquire the capacity for individual initiative and the methods by which talent was mobilized for public purposes, civic cooperation, and interest-group articulation and representation? If society had no "capacity for action independent of the state," how can we explain the sudden appearance of an organized political public at the turn of the twentieth century? If Russia never had a civil society, then how do we account for the fact that in the nineteenth century the Russian security apparatus regarded it as a formidable foe? The origins of the seemingly sudden appearance of an organized political public must be sought not in dramatic events at the turn of the twentieth century but in the prepolitical mobilization of countless Russians that had been quietly proceeding for several generations.[14]

The need for more work on Russian civil society has been recognized, and work on public life and associational activity is now promising.[15] There are signs that Russian historiography is turning away from the story of an all-powerful state and a primitive civil society, away from the study of the decline of tsarist Russia as it inexorably headed toward revolution.[16] Historians are examining what kept tsarist Russia together rather than simply reaffirming what broke it apart. Rather than focus exclusively on failure, on the "social basis" of great confrontations between state and society, historians recognize small achievements in alternative channels for gradualism and reform. The Great Reforms of the 1860s coupled with economic growth, mobility, urbanization, and advances in education and communication, fostered the development of organized structures that mediated between the individual and the state. A lively nonrevolutionary civic life emerged in the largest cities as new professional, entrepreneurial, artistic, and scientific elites aspired to create new public identities. By the end of the nineteenth century, bureaucratic service to the state or visionary service "to the people" no longer defined the concept of public duty. Studies of Russian Freemasonry, the Great Reforms, local and municipal government, charity, liberal academics, professionals, the press, popular reading habits, and even civil rights show that educated Russians could increasingly engage in practical, purposive, civic activity directed by, and at, structures "between tsar and people."[17]

In slighting the development of associations, traditional views bury other dimensions of political culture under an authoritarian essentialism that prevents us from drawing an adequate map of nineteenth-century public life. If we focus on Russia's autocratic ways, we emphasize the differences between Russia and Europe, the enervating consequences of a monolithic autocracy, and the inevitability of revolution. However, the concept of civil society permits exploration of new lines of inquiry. So, if we venture into the less-explored terrain of Russia's emerging civil society, we may find a rather different picture of public life. One thing we are sure to find: voluntary associations, always under the watchful—both benevolent and suspicious—eye of autocracy.

I SHOULD STATE my usage of the concepts "voluntary associations" (also frequently called civil associations) and "civil society." Civil associations may be defined as "autonomous institutions, capable of making their own statutes and by-laws; outside the direct control of some higher political body, such as a government agency; with their own peculiar or internal aims; and with the capacity to manage their own affairs."[18] Historians generally have in mind modern, secular, nonprofit, and self-regulating philanthropic, educational, cultural, and learned civil associations that, according to the authority on nineteenth-century French associations, offered new forms of organized sociability and self-definition. Membership was voluntary rather than compulsory, appointed, or ascribed. Members governed their activities with written rules, they held regular meetings, they owned and disposed of property, they elected their officers, they pursued limited goals, and they selected their own membership. Straddling the border between private life and collective public action, associations were entities chartered by political authority and obliged to submit to the laws of the state.[19] No less important than civil associations, though not a subject of this study, were political associations—organs of local self-rule, municipal corporations, and some sort of parliament or assembly of the estates—that mediated between civil associations and the state.[20]

The legal status of civil associations often gave official sanction to a variety of public projects and to the articulation and pursuit of interests in the public realm, actions that take on special meaning in the context of authoritarian political regimes. Where their existence cannot be taken for granted, associations endeavor to create the social infrastructure of nonbureaucratic, nonmarket-based relations and to provide venues for participation in the public sphere, thereby combating the individual isolation in repressive regimes. Modern associations have been a way to mobilize, coordinate, publicize, and honor individual efforts to come up with solutions to practical problems, and even associations that collaborated closely with the state have fostered individual initiative, a conviction of the efficacy of public action, and a sense of duty to others. Associations have pursued tasks that were beyond the means of individuals and that were fulfilled incompletely by official agencies: the diffusion of useful knowledge, the popularization of science, the preservation and promotion of the national heritage, and the advancement of education, among others. In this way, the leaders of associations played a role in civic life analogous to that of entrepreneurs in the market. As gatherers and distributors of information about the realm, associations have been critical nonstate entities that enabled the political community to frame issues and learn about itself. In a constant striving for utility and improvement, the twin pillars of the Enlightenment, associations have assisted the state in the mobilization of natural and human resources for the purposes of national prosperity and prestige.[21] Associations have indicated the potential for the self-organization of society. By examining the role of associations in patriotic projects of improvement and social reform, we may explore the opportunities for private initiative and civic engagement under autocracy.[22]

The term "civil society" is more elusive. It is an abstraction that has been used by various philosophical traditions, and different breeds of civil societies have existed under a variety of regimes. Moreover, the term is used as an analytical tool both to describe an existing political configuration and to posit a desirable state of affairs. It may be briefly defined as the network of human relationships and institutions outside the direct control of the state that structure individual action and allow private persons, unconnected by personal attachments, to manage their affairs. According to John Gray, civil society is "the domain of voluntary associations, market exchanges, and private institutions within and through which individuals having divergent conceptions and diverse and often competitive purposes may coexist in peace."[23] Philosophers of the Scottish Enlightenment, such as Adam Ferguson, David Hume, and Adam Smith, as well as Hegel, theorized a sphere or "irregular topography" of human relationships, institutions, and associations of private persons that satisfied needs and pursued (enlightened) self-interest through work and exchange. This sphere of human relationships—what eighteenth-century philosophers called civil society—enabled individuals to define and differentiate themselves, to gain recognition from others, to recognize the needs of others, and to attain a sense of community.[24] In one strand of Enlightenment thought, philosophers accentuated the separation between civil society and sovereign authority and contrasted the former with tyranny as a way to conceptualize largely secular institutional and moral attempts of citizens to limit the scope and abuses of monarchical and ecclesiastical power. In an equally important strand more important for my purposes, other philosophers regarded civil society and the state as overlapping realms of mutuality and accentuated their partnership and the subservience of the former to the latter. Cameralist philosophers, for example, states Isabel Hull, "founded civil society on obligation, not rights."[25]

By the mid-nineteenth century, "society" largely replaced "civil society" as a concept, an indication that in western Europe propertied and educated men were secure in civil society. In the twentieth century the Marxist Antonio Gramsci detached civil society from the capitalist economy and made civil society a contested arena of cultural institutions that mediated between the economy and the state and that transmitted a "bourgeois" ideology, thereby permitting the bourgeoisie to achieve "hegemony."[26] In the 1970s and 1980s, east European intellectuals, then experiencing a different species of hegemony, used the concept of civil society as an antonym to the totalitarian state, the command economy, and an atomized society. Theories of civil society more and more began to emphasize fluid processes rather than institutional products.[27]

A particularly important component of civil society, and an equally elusive conceptual cousin in much of the literature, is the "public sphere" *(Öffentlichkeit)*, which may be defined as the domain of civil society where private people, freed of duties and obligations to the ruler, come together voluntarily as a public to represent interests, deliberate matters of common concern, and voice opinions. The public sphere is also usually understood to be "bourgeois," but if lacking a basis in private property, it may also be "plebeian." It emerged under royal absolutism in the self-organized network for communicating information. According to the preeminent theoretician of the public sphere, Jürgen Habermas, voluntary associations constitute the institutional core of the social infrastructure of civil society.[28] Key members of such associations were the various groupings of a nonentrepreneurial bourgeoisie, "whose scientific, literary, artistic and religious pursuits put them at odds with state power but also at odds with the selfish pursuit of private interests and privileges."[29] Because authoritarian regimes closed the channels of representative politics and made it difficult for their subjects to act freely in concert, voluntary associations frequently substituted for and preceded constitutions and representative bodies. In this way, the "practitioners of civil society" gained confidence to make claims for political representation and power.[30] Yet, most theorists agree that civil associations, by themselves, cannot create a strong civil society or protect it from the encroachment of the state. This is especially true in polities lacking constituted intermediary bodies, sometimes termed political associations, such as organs of local self-rule, municipal corporations, some sort of parliament or assembly of the estates, and, later, political parties.[31]

A tension has always existed between civil society's universalist ideals and its exclusionary practices. Classical social theorists commonly understood civil society to be of the educated and propertied, or "bourgeois" *(bürgerliche Gesellschaft)*. Nineteenth-century civil societies and public spheres were considered to be associations of free and propertied men, and insofar as most women—like many men, as well—were not legally free in their person, property, or labor, they were not considered fit for membership. Yet in the same way that it subjects the state to pressure, the public sphere has been used as a vehicle of empowerment by groups, such as women and the propertyless, excluded from participation in bourgeois civil society. Thus, while civil society can legitimate the existing order in the Gramscian manner, it can simultaneously constitute the arena in which that order may be contested, acting as a "crucible in which citizenship is forged."[32]

In order to probe the role of voluntary associations in the formation of Russian civil society, I will examine the nature, founding, functioning, self-organization, and self-definition of a selected group of associations, mainly learned societies. I have selected these associations for several reasons. The learned societies were sanctioned and patronized by the state, and government officials were prominent charter members. Legal recognition, imperial patronage, and a system of rules and bureaucratic practices gave a certain tutelary protection to them. The learned societies were only the leading edge of a budding private initiative that also included the Masonic lodges of the eighteenth and early nineteenth centuries, many faith-based charitable societies, and the literary and philosophical salons and circles of the 1830s and 1840s. Accelerating during and after the era of the Great Reforms, private initiative founded associations to promote technological development and economic growth, to improve public health and education, to foster a market for art and music, to pursue sport and recreation, and to assert ethnic identity in a multinational empire. Through associations, physicians, teachers, engineers, and lawyers, among others, often in collaboration with organs of local self-government, developed a professional consciousness, and fashioned a new ideal of public service.[33]

The rapid growth and ubiquity of associations, of course, helps me make the argument that their neglect in history is incompatible with their significance in life. At the same time, it complicates any attempt to analyze them. I make no claim that the organizations I have selected were typical or representative of all of Russia's learned societies, let alone of all associations. Many types of organizations—academies and universities; trade- or profession-based guilds, corporations, trade associations, cooperatives, and unions; secret societies; political parties; churches, sects, and other religious associations; informal and ephemeral salons and circles; and associations for the pursuit of recreation, sport, and artistic production and performance—already have or will have their own historians. Likewise, this is not a detailed microhistory of societies' internal lives or of the relationships among members. Neither is it a sociological inquiry or a study of Russia's allegedly "missing" middle class; issues of members' class and status, religion, and ethnicity must wait another historian.[34] The learned society was preprofessional, and although some issues, such as the use of scientific knowledge and the relationship between scientists and the state, are similar, this study is not about professionalization.[35] Since the societies I am using were headquartered in St. Petersburg and Moscow, provincial associations, let alone those representing the many national minorities in the empire, are beyond the scope of this book.

My scope is limited in other ways as well. Civil societies in eighteenth- and nineteenth-century Europe were considered to be associations of free men. As a historian of gender relations in Germany puts it, the constitutions of the patriotic societies "did not explicitly prohibit women, artisans, workers or servants among their membership. However, it seldom occurred to anyone to admit persons of these categories into their numbers."[36] With few exceptions, not only did the pursuit of science and learning exclude women; the "performance of science" was a site of "masculine self-fashioning." This was especially true of Russia's learned societies: academicians, professors, government officials, and, by the end of the nineteenth century, professionals—in careers not open to women—

dominated the membership of these privileged and exclusive bodies. I am aware that if associations were its institutional core, a civil society so constituted, as it was in Europe as well, was exclusionary. Although there are important gender, class, and ethnic issues, how associations excluded certain groups must be the subject of another book.[37]

Despite the fact that the civil society project and its universalist ideals concealed exclusionary practices, we should not slight the significance of civil associations in an authoritarian regime such as tsarist Russia, where everyone was excluded from citizenship. This book will show that despite their limitations in scope and membership, the learned societies were significant because they envisioned the capacity of citizenship for at least a few. Based on the legal right to represent their households, men in associations later claimed to represent larger constituencies and even the nation as a whole. In staking out a domain of self-definition, self-organization, and action, learned societies instigated processes that later were used by other groups to pursue their own agendas and to imagine a world of individual autonomy and limited political authority. Moreover, despite these limitations in coverage and scope, the major Moscow and St. Petersburg learned societies possessed the longevity, formal and legally constituted relationship with political authority, extensive paper trail, stature, and public missions that allow us to problematize associational life under autocracy.[38] In particular, certain key moments in the life of learned societies—their founding and aims, their relationship to the state, and the realization of public projects—allow us to reconstruct the broader social, intellectual, and institutional framework in which associations operated. Many associations quite self-consciously provided a national networking for members as well as conveyor belts in the efforts to disseminate useful knowledge. By exploring the capacities of individual and group self-definition and initiative, this study will give voice to organizations whose voices have thus far been muted in the historiography of a country not known to be favorable to interest-group articulation.

The learned societies fostered three defining developments in imperial Russia: an interest in science, education, and the diffusion of useful knowledge; patriotism and public service; and the public sphere of civil society. Each of these thematic areas had its analogue in Europe and North America; indeed, they are paradigmatic of modern public life since the Enlightenment. Each thematic area allows us to explore the changing opportunities, and the limitations, for private initiative and collective action under autocracy.

The story of science in modern Russian history is well known in its general outline. Peter the Great utilized science and technology to gain access to the commercial world of northern Europe and to attain military strength and great power status. Peter began a process by which natural knowledge and technical expertise served state interests and national prestige in the mission to overcome Russian backwardness. In his fascination for the collection and display of objects of the natural world, Peter began the use of science in Russia as a tool to forge an eventual demystification of the world and the westernization of Russian culture. Government patronage of the advancement and diffusion of secular knowledge was one of the most powerful instruments of modernization and westernization in the emperor's toolbox and in that of his successors. But Russian monarchs were inconsistent in their application of this instrument. On the one hand, needing expertise to build a modern Russia, the monarchy sanctioned and nurtured the production and dissemination of useful knowledge through an infrastructure grounded in civil society. At the same time, the state was unwilling to surrender control over the directions that useful knowledge might take.

Science became a process as well as a product. By providing new models of moral and cultural authority and by claiming to eradicate superstition and ignorance, science everywhere in Europe fostered the development of public opinion. When Russian monarchs chartered the Academy of Sciences and the universities, when they sent Russians abroad for scientific training, they created bodies of natural knowledge, communities of independent thought, and networks of communication. In order to rule for the benefit of their subjects and to utilize human and natural resources for productive ends, Russian monarchs, like the enlightened monarchs of Europe, needed information about their subjects and about the realm. This gave impetus to the cultivation of expertise and the accumulation of positive knowledge. Patterns of scientific inquiry spread throughout the realm—observation, accurate measurement, record keeping, mapping, documentation, collection, inventory, reports, publicity, and criticism. Thus from the beginning, the pursuit of science became a model of state-society partnership in pursuit of common objectives: patronized by the state, this enterprise coordinated and systematized otherwise random efforts across the vast Russian empire for the purpose of national betterment.

The monarch's patronage of science and the service of science to state and monarch were endeavors wrapped in the rhetoric of patriotism and public duty. The ethos of service to the state launched by Peter I is well known. National progress and prosperity by means of the application of science to the study of natural and productive resources fit the twin Enlightenment projects of utility and improvement. To be useful and to improve was to be patriotic. Russian monarchs encouraged their subjects to take initiative in assisting the state; thus patriotic duty could be willing and voluntary, not just commanded. The rhetoric of patriotism and usefulness to state and fatherland imbued private endeavors well into the nineteenth century. Useful work for the glory of the fatherland stirred national consciousness, pride, and self-esteem; it also stirred a new identity of self-worth and mission. To study a vast *(neob"iataia)* Russia, to preserve its cultural patrimony, and to inform the world of its treasures were all patriotic duties. But the pride and patriotism that peaked after the victory over Napoleon was soon counterbalanced by government reaction and obscurantism at the end of the reign of Alexander I and during that of Nicholas I. The reaction, coupled with a growing awareness of Russia's problems, drove dedicated Russians to redefine patriotism and service. Service to the monarch and to the state was soon overshadowed by a desire to serve Russia and the Russian people, and an ethos of service to the people that was first glimpsed in the latter part of the eighteenth century became full blown in the middle of the nineteenth century. This was the patriotic motor that drove a movement to educate, reform, and improve. And in this context, the continuing dependence of science on the Russian state and on Europe became less and less tenable.

One way to lessen this dependence was the spread of education and the popularization of natural knowledge. Indeed, for a long time the state took the initiative in education, an investment in "conservatively managed change."[39] Needing to train government officials, the tsarist state scored notable achievements at the "high end" of the education ladder—the Academy of Sciences, the universities, and a small number of high-priority technical institutions. The state also offered educational opportunities to young men of humble origins; but it did not want any other body to provide this kind of opportunity. Like investment in economic growth, large-scale investment by the tsarist regime in education infrastructure took a backseat to the maintenance of military power. As a result, primary and vocational education suffered from inattention and, as did many other areas of public life, from inconsistent and contradictory government policies. This began to change after the death of Nicholas I in 1855. During the era of the Great Reforms, liberal economists and government officials recognized that modernization now meant a skilled population and a more productive labor force and was, in short, an investment in human capital. Emperor Alexander II himself stated that education "guaranteed the future well-being of Russia."[40] The government realized that the participation of society in the provision of education was desirable. But the dissemination of secular knowledge about the natural world as well as the solicitation of society's participation carried risks. Society desired to expand the scope of its activities to disseminate useful knowledge, and the government became even more fearful of losing control of the process.

In its endeavor to popularize science, inculcate patriotism, and patronize education, the state had an eager "junior partner," the learned society. Because such societies championed the dissemination of learning, they, and their projects, were created or enabled by the state, beginning in the eighteenth century. And because the learned societies promised to contribute to the state-sanctioned project of national renewal beginning in the era of the Great Reforms, the state gave the green light to an explosive growth of private initiative. As one government official recalled, at the beginning of the era of the Great Reforms, "All at once there appeared a striving toward private initiative."[41] Thus sanctioned, associations carved out a space not completely under state control. Increasingly throughout the nineteenth century, associations championed the initiative *(samodeiatel'nost')* and autonomy *(samostoiatel'nost')* of Russian science and the diffusion of useful knowledge in patriotic service to Russia. Such institutions offered new forms of sociability, self-definition, and self-organization. In this way, scientific and learned societies enabled men to display distinction and gain recognition from others for their experience, talent, expertise, self-mastery, cultural stewardship, and civic leadership. The promise of a mastery over nature also further distinguished civil society from the state of nature, and the fusion of learning and public service, with both state and voluntary associations acting as the catalyst, spurred the growth of civil society.

In most of Europe civil society evolved from a state-enabled, state-protected, and often state-guided entity to one dominated by private initiative. Russia, too, followed this trajectory, albeit later and more haltingly. Beginning in the reign of Catherine II, the first seeds of Russian civil society had already begun to sprout, and the era of the Great Reforms provided the favorable conditions for their growth and the context in which associations operated. The judicial statutes of 1864 embodied the legal (if not the constitutional) principles of civil society—the notions of the individual legal person, equality before the law, trial by jury, judicial immunity, publicity, and legal representation in court. Despite setbacks to the principle of government of laws in the wake of the assassination of Alexander II in 1881 and the continuing arbitrariness of the Russian bureaucracy, the judicial reforms fostered the development of legal consciousness and injected legalism into the relationship between associations and the state. Despite their restricted autonomy, by the end of the nineteenth century, Russia's zemstvos and city councils, created in 1864 and 1870, were responsible for considerable progress in public health, veterinary medicine, education, fire prevention, famine relief, and information gathering. Moreover, they planted the seed of political representation that zemstvo men cultivated as the leaders of the liberal movement at the beginning of the twentieth century.[42] Publishing and the press also spearheaded the growth of the public sphere of Russia's civil society. In 1865 the government eased prepublication censorship restrictions. While this did not create freedom of the press, it enabled a rapid growth in the expression and circulation of information and ideas that the government was unable to suppress.[43] More than any other component of civil society, publishing and the press were institutions where public opinion could be expressed; in providing information and publicity, they were essential for the undertakings of voluntary associations.

By examining the role of voluntary associations in the formation of civil society, we may see from a different angle how Russian political culture worked, a view often obscured in discussions of state institutions and revolutionary politics. Indeed, we cannot understand fully the relationship between state and society without understanding the emergence, projects, and mission of associations.[44] In many ways, of course, Russian civil society was the creation of the state, albeit a state inconsistent in its goals and policies. The state patronized the learned societies and granted them certain privileges. Throughout imperial Russia, the boundaries between the "official" and "unofficial" were poorly fortified and easily transgressed. Most Russian associations, and certainly the august learned societies, saw their role as collaborating with the authorities and assisting the state in the achievement of mutual objectives. In their internal affairs (meetings, selection of members, election of officers, formulation of goals), associations were private *(chastnye obshchestva)*. But in the means selected to achieve their goals, associations inexorably entered public life, which autocracy considered its prerogative. In so doing, the members of associations realized that public discussion, especially on patriotic projects such as the dissemination of learning for the greater good of Russia, was imaginable, even under autocracy, that nonstatist solutions to problems were feasible in a country with a long statist tradition. The association was a critical ingredient in the lengthy process by which Russians, to borrow Kant's definition of the Enlightenment, were gradually released from tutelage.

By studying the learned societies, we may also see how the relationship between associations and the state evolved from cooperation and collaboration to confrontation. From the beginning, the state was of two minds in its treatment of private initiative, and there was a tension between the patronage and nurture of the state on the one hand and government restrictions on the other. The government wanted the contribution of private initiative to the modernization project without political side effects. Along with support for the achievement of mutual goals, officialdom engaged in a tutelary scrutiny of the public activities of associations, to make sure they did not enter forbidden territory, that is, policy and politics. In the public sphere of an emerging civil society, associations asserted the right to an autonomous existence and agency against an autocratic regime unwilling to recognize institutional limitations to its power. By the end of the nineteenth century, the relationship between associations and the state became much more contested and politicized, as many associations became de facto pressure groups and the proliferation of projects forced officialdom to regulate more closely their activities. Although no single act was directed against associations, the spirit of the counterreforms of the 1880s and 1890s—the hostility to the zemstvo, attempts to turn back judicial independence, restrictions of university autonomy, among others—worsened the tension between civil society and the state by century's end.[45] By examining government attempts to control and confine public initiative and the resulting conflict between the tsarist bureaucracy and educated society over the autonomy of associations, we can evaluate the meaning of associations and civil society in autocratic Russia.

Russia had far too many associations to write a comprehensive history. Rather than a seamless narrative, the chapters of this book are "moments," in a series of stories about Russian associations set in the overall analytic framework of the development of science, patriotism, and civil society. The Free Economic Society—Russia's oldest association, founded by a group of nobles, officials, and academicians and chartered by Catherine II in 1765—and the Moscow Agricultural Society were established in an age preoccupied with agricultural improvement by means of the application of science and the dissemination of useful knowledge. Their appearance marks the beginning of a process whereby a public sphere and associational life were sanctioned under autocracy, and these private associations became public forums for a discussion of, and dissemination of views on, a wide range of scientific and economic matters. The Russian Geographical Society, the chief locus of the broadening scholarly and public interest in the Russian nation and empire as well as the locus of government support for science under Nicholas I, not only accumulated geographic and ethnographic knowledge but helped define and articulate a Russian national identity. Thus the Free Economic Society, the Moscow Agricultural Society, and the Russian Geographical Society popularized science and, through corresponding memberships and branch societies, began to draw the public into the patriotic endeavor of gathering information about the realm.

In the second half of the nineteenth century, more and more societies of science and natural history regarded their mission to be the dissemination of scientific, medical, and technical literacy. Using the early years of the Moscow

Society of Friends of Natural History, Anthropology, and Ethnography (OLEAE in its Russian initials) as a case study, I examine private associated initiative to popularize science in Russia's second city during the era of the Great Reforms. In order to accomplish these objectives, OLEAE created meeting places, exhibitions, and a museum where scientists and nonscientists could interact and where the public could not only satisfy its curiosity about the natural world but also develop its capacity for self-instruction and the rational use of leisure. Most important, OLEAE had a patriotic mission—to make science Russian and to train Russian scientists.

Private associations also promoted industrial development and technical education. The borrowing, domestication, and generation of industrial technology were regarded as Russia's key to progress, the linchpin of which was the dissemination of applied science and technical education. The Russian Technical Society ran a variety of enterprises to develop Russia's human and material resources for industrial purposes. Such civic activism challenged the tutelage of the authorities, as we see in an examination of two sets of scientific congresses—the congresses of naturalists and the congresses organized by the Pirogov Society of Russian Physicians—that became new forms of communication, dissemination of knowledge, and publicity. By the late nineteenth century, an increasingly active public sphere of debate that included advocacy and representation was no longer in doubt in tsarist Russia. Thus well before the Revolution of 1905, the groundwork was laid for the participation of private associations in the public arena.

CHAPTER ONE

European Societies and the State

Russia in Comparative Perspective

To many educated Russians, European civil societies presented the idealized, successful "other"—successful states and successful societies—that failed in late-imperial Russia. As the following chapters will show, the legal status and political environment of Russian associations were precarious and to a great degree determined by an autocratic state and arbitrary officialdom. A budding Russian civil society lacked the support of imtermediary powers available in Europe. Yet certain social, cultural, and political circumstances favoring the development of successful civil societies and voluntary associations in Europe were complex and conflict ridden. As the institutional core of civil society, voluntary associations existed in the political and legal boundaries and traditions of individual states, all of which had distinctive legal, political, and cultural traditions. Recent research, especially by historians of France and Germany, allows us to get a broader view of the place of associations in the state-society relationship as well as the role of associations in the development of science, in the diffusion of useful knowledge, and in the impulse to improve and reform. Before we examine associations in Russia, it behooves us at the outset to sketch briefly what initiative meant for associations in Europe and how it was achieved. We may thereby see that the differences between Russia and Europe were less than commonly assumed and that in the practice of association the Russian case was part of a broader European phenomenon. We may understand the Russian experience—the possibilities as well as the limitations—better if we place it in a larger perspective.

Many European historians who use the concepts of civil society and the public sphere adopt, self-consciously or not, the idea of the "limited fit," that is, the idea that "real-life, historical civil societies may not have a perfect fit of all the theoretical elements of civil society."[1] Recently historians from a variety of national fields have examined the role of voluntary associations in the constitution of individual and group identities, the relationship between the individual and the state, reform movements, the construction of citizenship, and the realms of public and private life in ways that are suggestive for Russia. This new literature, according to Philip Nord, is "centered less on structures than on voluntary action, on the dynamics by which democratic institutions can be made to sprout on the seemingly inhospitable ground of authoritarian rule." Nord notes that "ordered, nonclandestine, and collective activities," the building blocks of civil society, start with "dense and intertwined networks of communication and sociability and an informed citizenry, neither deferential nor defiant, which is committed to making public institutions work."[2] Because authoritarian regimes closed the channels of representative politics and made it difficult for their subjects to act freely in concert, associations indicated the potential for the self-organization of society. Recent research explores the question, felicitously posed by Daniel Gordon of ancien régime France, "How do people living in an authoritarian regime maintain their sense of dignity?" By examining voluntary associations, we may explore Gordon's answer to his own question: "to invest seemingly insignificant areas of life that the authorities do not control with the maximum amount of meaning."[3]

Associations and the State in the Eighteenth and Nineteenth Centuries

In Old Regime Europe, Roman law had established the principle that no association could be established without the permission of the sovereign; likewise, it was unlawful for persons to assemble without authorization. As the more centralized territorial state grew in size and power in the seventeenth and eighteenth centuries, sovereigns, wary of challenges to their power, claimed the sole authority to confer, or "concede," to associations a legal existence. That such a concession from the sovereign was necessary in each case underscored the fact that associations existed by privilege only. Because associations could be, and were, established for purposes inimical to state order, the state considered it necessary to supervise them. According to a Parisian police spy of the 1740s, "All association is always dangerous to the state."[4] In the view of Thomas Hobbes, associations threatened order and peace and posed the danger of treason. Highly suspicious of any spontaneous public initiative that might contradict state goals, absolute rulers repressed the intrusion of seemingly harmless associations of private persons into realms, such as religion and politics, considered to be the domain of the state or the established church. In the view of one monarch, "Associatons are hurtful to the state, for they enlighten the people and spread liberal ideas."[5] Nevertheless, the actual regulation of associations under political absolutism was haphazard.[6]

Beginning in the eighteenth century, continental monarchs enabled and even purposefully created societies in order to encourage, patronize, and protect scientific, charitable, and cultural activities that could further national progress and demonstrate their enlightened reigns.[7] Sympathetic local officials often initiated or facilitated the creation of learned societies. Government officials in large numbers joined scientific and philosophical societies, whose meetings and projects offered a forum to present ideas in an unofficial capacity. Aspiring to assist and advise the sovereign in the collection of knowledge and improvement of the natural and human world for the public benefit, learned societies assiduously cultivated the membership of officials and notables as a sign of recognition, approval, and protection. Such approval could come in the more concrete forms of subsidies for expensive projects, meeting space, free postage, awards for prize competitions, and government printing privileges. The authorities considered societies to be fulfilling social or cultural functions and therefore tolerated them as long as they did not turn into political societies. Paradoxically, such service to the public good and the attendant close relationship to the state fostered a sense of individual self-worth and collective autonomy.[8] Thus, on the European continent, state and society fostered an ethic of mutuality, and civil society grew alongside the centralizing national state.

Once established, however, voluntary associations helped create an autonomous zone of associated public life, separate from and at times at odds with the state, a zone that emerged during the Enlightenment and continued through the first half of the nineteenth century. By the nineteenth century, the principle of freedom of association spread as part of the idea of the freedom of the individual from the limitations of the traditional authorities of state, church, and family. In practice authoritarian states were often unable to control the lives of private associations, but they did not readily surrender institutionalized autonomy to such bodies. Even in Great Britain, fear of the French Revolution prompted government measures to suppress associations thought to be subversive and to monitor the affairs of many more.[9] We may get a better sense of the opportunities as well as the limitations of associations if we turn to France and Germany.

France

Because, as Daniel Gordon has stated, "everyone besides the king was officially powerless in the public sphere," civil society was neither autonomous nor strong under the Old Regime.[10] In 1629 an edict of Louis XIII forbade any kind of league, association, or assembly that formed without royal permission. Until the Revolution, associations existed only as bodies given the privilege to exist by the monarch. Prepublication censorship and royal control of the printing trade going back to the age of Cardinal Richelieu reflected the Old Regime's suspicion and passion for secrecy, and voluntary associations were watched by the police and treated, as one historian states, "as if they constituted a permanent threat of subversion and a threat to national security."[11] One of the results of such royal tutelage was a fragmented society. Philosopher and statesman Anne-Robert Turgot stated, "[France is] an aggregate of different and incompatible social groups whose members have so few links between themselves that everyone thinks solely of his own interests; no trace of any feelings for the public weal is anywhere to be found."[12] Tocqueville picked up the argument. The central power in ancien régime France, he argued, "held all Frenchmen in tutelage" and "had succeeded in eliminating all intermediate authorities." Nobles, bourgeois, and peasants were "split up into a number of small groups almost completely shut off from each other . . . Nothing [had] been left that could obstruct the central government, but, by the same token, nothing could shore it up."[13] As one historian aptly puts it, the French state's struggle against its opponents was "a struggle for the life of the regime; the government could not allow the opposition to use the weapon of associations."[14]

Royal restrictions imposed obstacles but did not suffocate the movement to associate, and a public sphere emerged under royal absolutism in what Jürgen Habermas has called the "network for communicating information and points of view"—the institutions and practices of market capitalism, new forms of urban sociability (the clubs, salons, cafés, coffeehouses, stages, arenas, and academies of London and Paris), and a lively print culture.[15] A Habermasian public imagined that it could comment on the affairs of state, expose abuses of power and privilege, and supervise the actions of officials, forcing a monarchy one historian has called "powerless to forbid public debate" to "explain, persuade, and seek to win approval"—in short, to be accountable.[16] By compelling the state to legitimate itself before public opinion, a voluntarily constituted and self-organized public based authority on reason rather than tradition and force. To paraphrase Keith Baker, the public sphere asserted that there was a public apart from the person of the king.[17] Thus, in the second half of the eighteenth century, despite—or perhaps because of—the best attempts of sovereign authority to prevent it, the French public sphere not only appeared but became politicized. A discourse of society against the state, emerged during the Enlightenment as a way to conceptualize institutional and moral attempts to limit the scope of state power.[18]

During the French Revolution, the Jacobins were suspicious of organizations that divided the "popular will." Similarly, in Napoleonic and Restoration France, according to Maurice Agulhon, the French authority on associations, the state was hostile to the right of association, hostile not so much to associations per se but to freely formed associations, for which the population was allegedly ill prepared.[19] As the Swiss economist Simonde de Sismonde put it, "The usages, opinions, and customs of the French do not render them fit to enjoy a degree of liberty of which the English preserve peaceful possession."[20] The "habit of surveillance" that, according to Tocqueville, animated the supervision and regulation of both the ancien régime and postrevolutionary governments, was "almost an obsession with the central government," an obsession that lasted to the end of the nineteenth century.[21] Article 291 of the 1810 penal code required government permission, conferred by the local prefect and by the minister of the interior in Paris, for "any association of more than 20 members meeting regularly for any purpose."[22] The authorities scrutinized the bylaws, membership lists (including names, addresses, and occupations), and verbatim minutes of meetings. Nonpolitical associations were regarded with the same suspicion as political ones. The bylaws of associations prohibited the discussion of religion and politics at meetings, an obligation that demonstrated the intrusion of the state into the internal affairs of associations as well as the threat such discussions posed to the state. If an association deviated from its stated goals, it could be closed. Finally, article 293 of the penal code provided punishment to anyone who made available without prior permission meeting space, even to members of an approved association.[23] To combat those associations allegedly circumventing the 1810 penal code by subdividing, a law of 1834 subjected associations divided into small groupings to the restrictions of article 291, extended the penalties for participation in illegal associations, and left the government to distinguish between legal and illegal associations.[24] After a brief moment of freedom in 1848, the Second Empire restored the authority of article 291 and abandoned the distinction between political and nonpolitical associations. Even the Third Republic required all associations, as Carol Harrison notes, "to submit to government scrutiny."[25] Although liberalization of the restrictions on associations was debated under the Third Republic, it was not until the law of 1901 *(contrat d'associations)* that an association could be formed freely without prior authorization of the local prefect, whose regulatory powers were also diminished. Although associations could form without prior authorization, such associations did not have legal rights, such as the right to own property. An association's registration with the authorities continued to include a copy of the bylaws and detailed information on the organization. Despite the liberalization of 1901, "any association with unlawful purpose or dangerous to the republican form of government" was prohibited.[26]

What was the significance of such restrictive legislation? To some contemporaries it was indeed ominous. Eloquent and highly influential were the observations of Tocqueville. The Frenchman feared the centralizing tendency of and the encroachment on local and intermediary powers by a modern government that renders "every day private independence more weak, more subordinate, and more precarious . . . In all matters of government the state tolerates no intermediate agent between itself and the people . . . and acquires more and more direct control over the humblest members of the community."[27] A despotic state atomizes its subjects: "Despotism, which by its very nature is suspicious, sees in the separation among men the surest guarantee of its continuance and it usually makes every effort to keep them separate. A despot easily forgives his subjects for not loving him, provided they do not love one another. He does not ask them to assist him in governing the state; it is enough that they do not aspire to govern it themselves."[28] When Tocqueville wrote that "wherever at the head of some new undertaking, you see the government," he had in mind not tsarist Russia but statist France.[29] One reason why Tocqueville was so struck by associations in America was their limited existence in France: "Any independent group, however small, which seemed desirous of taking action otherwise than under the aegis of the administration filled it with alarm, and the tiniest of free associations of citizens, however harmless its aims, was regarded as a nuisance."[30] Referring directly to article 291 of the 1810 penal code, Tocqueville mused, "What strength can even public opinion have retained when no 20 persons are connected by a common tie, when not a man, nor a family, nor a chartered corporation, nor a class, nor a free institution, has the power of representing or exerting that opinion and when every citizen, being equally weak, equally poor and equally isolated, has only his personal impotence to oppose the organized force of government?"[31] Equally ominous to Tocqueville was the uncertainty and arbitrariness created by the legislation and the difficulty in distinguishing authorized from unauthorized associations: "When some kinds of associations are prohibited and others allowed, it is difficult to distinguish the former from the latter beforehand. In this state of doubt men abstain from them altogether, and a sort of public opinion passes current which tends to cause any association whatsoever to be regarded as a bold and almost illicit enterprise."[32]

But was the spirit of association paralyzed? Might custom and practice have allowed what laws did not? Absolute monarchy did not squelch the impulse of association; indeed, the monarchy was forced to sanction associations in order to enlist public support in efforts to strengthen the realm. Even Tocqueville acknowledged that "though the government had absolute control of public affairs, it was far from having broken the spirit of individual Frenchmen."[33] Moreover, Tocqueville's pessimistic views have been challenged, and several historians have noted the impressive growth of associations despite the legal obstacles.[34] In nineteenth-century France, cooperation rather than conflict was the norm, as one historian notes: "Members of associations and representatives of the state did not usually see one another as antagonists . . . While prefects and mayors meticulously verified the political reliability of associations, they also cultivated their bourgeois members, men whose cooperation could help their administrative functions run smoothly." Official surveillance was counterbalanced by "official attention."[35] Large groups of the population resented the state's arbitrary impositions, yet more and more of them jumped through the administrative hoops to create associations and make them effective. A constitutive assembly of members could draw up a society's charter. A relatively free press allowed a society to proclaim its opening and its aims, to announce future agendas and to report on past meetings, and to get publicity in the way of editorials, advertisements, correspondence, and coverage of jubilees and other festive occasions. A public physically far removed from the personal interaction of association members could thereby be drawn into the missions, agendas, and daily life of many voluntary associations. By the end of the century, improved transport and communications enabled ordinary persons to experience associational life far from home. Indeed, Agulhon notices an association boom beginning twenty years before the granting of freedom of association in 1901. Thus France provides the example of a statist political culture underlying several regimes—monarchy, empire, republic—that was hostile to freely formed associations and provided a high degree of intrusive regulation and supervision of associational life. At the same time, Maurice Agulhon and Carol Harrison argue, the state tolerated the existence of myriad societies and by and large did not prevent its citizens from founding or joining them.[36]

Germany

In the German states and, later, the German and Austro-Hungarian empires, associations existed in an equally complex and contradictory environment. As many German historians have observed, a philosophical tradition, articulated by Hegel, dictated that the state guided and supervised society; voluntary associations did not have an autonomous existence outside the state. The emphasis on individual rights, prominent in Anglo-American and French political thought, was absent in Germany. The state itself fostered and nurtured associations, and societies collaborated with the state in many enterprises, such as the provision of charity and the dissemination of new farming techniques. Over time, of course, the activities of associations broadened the scope of civil society. Nevertheless, Daniel McMillan states, "Even the most determined liberals abhorred conflict between the state and civil society and sought not so much the autonomy of civil society from the state, but rather a harmonious collaboration between the two . . . Harmony between the state and civil society was considered the norm, not adversarial relations."[37]

The fear of political societies cast a shadow over all forms of association during and after the French Revolution. The formation of any association had to be approved by the government, and the Prussian Law Code of 1794 barred associations whose purposes and activities were deemed "contrary to the general peace, security, and order."[38] One local official in the age of Metternich stated, "It is not only senseless, but also unlawful for private persons to think themselves, either individually or in league with others, competent to take a hand in Germany's affairs of state."[39] In the early nineteenth century, according to one historian, repressive governments "forced associations to be private affairs. The forming of associations was severely repressed or did not evolve at all." The fear of revolution in Vormärz Prussia, a tutelary bureaucracy, and "the dogma of the limited faculties of the subjects," as Thomas Nipperdey puts it, meant that "there was no free, public, political or institutional life which allowed the development of interests, opinions or activity on the part of the individual or groups, still less the evolution of responsibilities."[40]

As did France, the German states enjoyed a brief moment of freedom of association in 1848, but subsequent constitutions and laws reintroduced restrictions and controls. Although the 1850 Prussian Association Law conceded more autonomy to nonpolitical associations, the authorities continued to scrutinize all associations that appeared political, as well as public meetings. The authorities could prohibit or close any association that pursued undesirable (that is, political, often religious) goals. Moreover, the

1850 Prussian Association Law and, later, the 1867 North German Confederation required that associations submit to the authorities copies of their bylaws, all publications, names of members, and agendas of meetings, as well as restricted the membership of minors and women and forbade collaboration or correspondence between associations in order to keep societies local and prevent any kind of national federation.[41] Later, the newly created political police conducted surveillance of associations and their meetings; in some German states, such as Saxony, the political police attempted to micromanage associational life. The police had the power to attend meetings and, if they deviated from their professed agenda, shut them down.[42] After the association law of 1867, the Austro-Hungarian government, one historian states, "grudgingly tolerated most associations, with the understanding that they would remain far from politics and would strictly adhere to their stated goals . . . Wary of even the slightest sign of political activity, the authorities at times sent police informants to associations' meetings and used the royal censors to keep societies from publishing even harmless announcements, bylaws, and memberships lists."[43] At last, after fourteen years of debate and only a decade before the collapse of imperial Germany, the German Association Law of 1908 granted the rights of association and assembly. After 1908, according to one historian, "the serious liabilities of political associations which were so visible in the nineteenth century all but disappeared."[44] Even so, on the eve of World War I, the public "complained constantly about police action against associations and assemblies."[45]

Paternalistic authoritarian states in Germany and Austria, alarmed by the idea of freedom of association and assembly, scrutinized associations and attempted to keep all associations from forming without authorization, discussing public issues, and creating a national federation. Because German states prevented organized society from participating in political matters, seemingly innocuous activities acquired political implications; what began in the eighteenth century as tutelage and collaboration by the 1840s increasingly became rebellion against authoritarian rule.[46] Thus, in the German states, by the late eighteenth and early nineteenth centuries, an emerging public sphere—though divided by occupation, class and confession—became a medium of communication and what Richard van Dülman has called "a breeding ground for initiatives of reform of absolutism."[47] According to Alfons Hueber, associations were in a legal limbo—"nowhere were they completely free and nowhere were they completely prohibited"—this, in the exemplar of the Rechtsstaat.[48] Associations offered a substitute for popular representation in an effort to "unseat the state as the arbiter of the public good." Conversely, as in France, as political absolutism retreated during the second half of the century and as associational life became more complex, more and more associations were able to operate despite government restrictions and scrutiny.[49]

But how could dissidence enter associations under political absolutism, especially when most were not organized with the intent to engage in politics, let alone to dissent? The most provocative answer comes from Margaret Jacob's examination of an alternative political culture of Enlightenment-era associations. Continental associations, Jacob argues, "emulated British practice and therefore emulated British forms of governance and the environment of constitution, legislation, representation, assembly and voting," even as these associations retained traditional hierarchical and patriarchal values and did not directly challenge political absolutism. Charters were founding documents written in what Jacob calls "the new language of constitutionalism," by which members represented and governed themselves.[50] In absolutist regimes such civic responsibility of private individuals acting through voluntary associations not only conferred upon members a sense of dignity and empowerment but also created the perception that they were acting independent of the state or the authorities. Such associations taught self-governance, the skills of which included submitting to rules; electing officers and new members; calling, running, and attending regular meetings; planning projects, mobilizing the public and generating publicity; paying dues, raising funds, and managing money; speaking and debating in public; and working with others and judging others' activities. At stake was full participation in public and political life, that is, citizenship. What threatened states (and not just absolutist states) was the capacity of self-representation and initiative that came with participation in associations. The result, Jacob boldly argues, was self-confidence, a civic consciousness, a new self-organized political culture, and a micropolity separate from the state. Thus, Jacob states, "modern civil society was invented during the Enlightenment" in "the new zone of voluntary associations" that "looked away from the passivity of the subject, toward the activity of the citizen, away from absolutism and oligarchy, toward more representative forms of government."[51]

The complicated political and legal relationship between continental states and an emerging critical public has important implications for a study of Russia. The existence of political absolutism, intrusive government regulations and supervision, censorship, along with the absence of freedom of association and assembly and of representative government in western and central Europe has generally not been regarded by theorists and historians as incompatible with the appearance, growth and functioning of civil society. Almost every generalization made about the deficiencies of tsarist Russia—the power and suspicion of the authorities, the tutelary role of the state, the weakness and fragmentation of society, the obstacles to private initiative—has at one time or another been made by contemporaries or by historians about ancien régime Europe. This is not to say that there were no differences between Russia and, say France, or that the two countries had a common heritage. But it is to say that the differences can be exaggerated. It is easy to place European associations outside historical time and to idealize their strength, autonomy, and role in movements to constitute liberal democratic regimes. The reality is more complicated. Monarchs and states promoted and permitted associations through the concession system, and associations were regarded as a privilege. Associations took advantage of royal privilege and were more likely to grow in scope when they avoided political activities that directly challenged absolutism. Voluntary associations rarely achieved total autonomy and were always subject to state restrictions. At the same time, restrictive laws did not prevent the formation and growth of associations; however restrictive, a system of laws and rules gave a certain tutelary protection to associations. Even associations that collaborated closely with the state fostered a participatory mentality. But although monarchs encouraged sociability to enhance their prestige and to enrich the realm, they were wary of the political uses to which associations might be put. There was a constant tension between societies eager to be independent and governments that, not without reason, feared disorder and subversion. As the protracted discussion of freedom of association in late nineteenth-century France and Germany suggests, not only conservative officials but also liberals and republicans could be wary of the misuse of association. Although many historians point to imperial Russia's fragmented society and its weak bourgeoisie, this observation has been made about all countries on the European continent; countries without a strong bourgeoisie could still foster the associational impulse. As the training ground for civic engagement in public affairs, such "institutions of civil society building" were especially important in authoritarian regimes unwilling to recognize institutional limitations to their power.[52]

Science, Public Service, and Reform

The Russian associations that constitute the core of this study were all in one way or another science societies. The study of science and, more important, its application and diffusion for the betterment of Russia were their common public service. The state, too, was a patron of science and encouraged the establishment of science societies and patronized many of their projects. Before we turn to the Russian case, it is important to examine briefly the role of science and public service in associational life in western and Central Europe. Governments and private individuals and, later, municipalities and the business community joined in the pursuit of science; new forms of sociability and civic identity; and the spread of technical education, vocational training, and other projects for improvement and reform. In case after case, the motor of public science was the voluntary association. The experience of science societies in the eighteenth and nineteenth centuries reveals a very complex relationship between cultural institutions, the state, and the individual, as well as the meaning of association, especially in absolutist regimes.

Historians of science and philosophy concur that by the second half of the eighteenth century, natural philosophy had transformed the worldview from a religious to a secular one; from qualitative analysis to mathematical, mechanical, and empirical analysis; and from the idea of an immutable nature to one of a temporal, changing nature. By repudiating the dogmas of religion and Aristotelian philosophy, natural philosophy claimed to be a new authority, which promised the mastery of nature, a new method to reach moral and natural truths. Essential to the creation of empirical knowledge was sensory experience, and through observation and experiment, knowledge of the natural world could be attained. Collecting, naming, classifying, and cataloging held the keys to natural history. Finally, natural philosophy came to be linked to what the economic historian Joel Mokyr calls the "knowledge revolution," or the "industrial Enlightenment," the aims of which were utility, improvement, progress, and the public good.[53]

But science was not simply a product, the accumulation of empirical knowledge; it was, as Mary Terrall puts it, "a process of producing, evaluating and representing knowledge." This inexorably led to the development of the collective enterprise of public science, the chief vehicle of which was the science society.[54] Princely dynasties, enlightened monarchs, and state officials first patronized science in order to improve the strength the realm. State- or princely supported academies, which had their origin in Renaissance Italy and entered the modern era via seventeenth- and eighteenth-century France, replaced personal with institutional patronage. In the absolute monarchies on the European continent, state-financed academies, whose members were paid civil servants, were akin to agencies of government. Learned societies, among the most important of which were scientific, philosophical, and nature societies, were legal entities chartered by a sovereign authority, legal entities that appeared first in England and then spread to the Continent. Although they were often dependent upon the patronage of the wealthy and powerful, private science societies were voluntary and self-organized alternatives to the official study of science in universities and academies. By pooling and distributing resources, by disseminating scientific work, and by popularizing and publicizing scientific inquiry, the learned societies acted as promoters and entrepreneurs. Although scientists were everywhere relatively small in number, societies of science extended their reach.[55]

The science society was the linchpin of a set of institutions that, in Mokyr's terms, served "useful knowledge, the scientific method, and the application of science" in order to accomplish the twin Enlightenment goals of utility and improvement. The science society was the premier way through which the public could unlock the secrets of the natural world by experiment and observation, the key elements of the scientific method. For nonscientists—the audience and the patrons of science—science societies facilitated access to the Enlightenment or, in economists' terms, reduced "access costs" to useful knowledge. In order to extend their patronage and to promote industrial enlightenment and improvement, societies of science fostered informal networks and patterns of communication, vital to the exchange of information. To make useful knowledge public, societies built "bridges," as Mokyr calls them, of "catalogued and ordered information" between the natural world and the human environment—observatories, agricultural research stations, museums, libraries, public lectures, technical schools, and botanical and zoological gardens. Essay competitions, expeditions, networks of corresponding members, and other outreach projects mobilized volunteers in collaborative scientific enterprises and popularized natural knowledge.[56] Such enterprises capitalized on and, in turn, fostered an awe of nature as well as an intense "curiosity about the remote and unusual" among a public that was everywhere allegedly thirsting for knowledge.[57] Learned journals, encyclopedias, dictionaries, textbooks, and manuals, where "knowledge was codified and described in technical writings and drawings," made it easier to "look things up." Sharing the processes of creating and diffusing useful knowledge with the public was a way to validate the scientific enterprise. Perhaps more important, the diffusion of applied science, combining utility with entertainment, created a public.[58]

Like other new settings—salons, cafés, literary clubs, and Masonic lodges—the philosophical and scientific societies nurtured new forms of sociability that stressed reciprocal, egalitarian, and polite communication. Societies of naturalists offered to both specialist and amateur the direct experience of natural phenomena; indeed, by emphasizing that anyone could be a naturalist, the goal of such societies was to draw in the public. Just as they sought order in nature, the leaders of science societies imposed on their fellow members internal order, self-definition, and written rules, all publicized by meetings and publications.[59] In the words of Margaret Jacob, "the web of voluntary associations and informal sociability" was "the lived experience" that "undergirded a new mental universe," and provided "an ideal setting for cultural and intellectual advancement."[60] The pursuit of science (or literature or philanthropy) was based on the shared interests and commitments of otherwise isolated individuals in common pursuits, perhaps accounting for the reverential tone, the sense of fellowship that pervades the reflections of members themselves. As Lorraine Daston puts it, "the intensity of commitment to improvement mattered more than the specific object of improvement."[61] Scientific knowledge and the presentation of observations or the results of experiments before peers and patrons—sometimes called the "performance of science"—enhanced individual self-image, self-confidence, and autonomy. By means of dramatic and crowd-pleasing displays of modern life and the wonders of applied science, public lectures and demonstrations and, later, museums and exhibitions displayed visions of progress through the division of labor and the cooperation of science, industry, private associations, and governments, all in service to the public. Thus propertied and educated men displayed distinction and gained recognition for their experience, talent, expertise, stewardship of learning and culture, civic leadership—in short, they became "public somebodies."[62] In this process, while men of science undoubtedly acted for personal and professional interests, they also acted in the name of the public or the nation; that is, they claimed to represent it.

The authority of science to order nature began to spill over into claims to authority for the rational, that is, "correct," organization of society and self-governance. The mastery over nature promised mastery over human nature. The practice of science as a tool for the public good promised practical solutions to a wide range of economic and social problems. By the nineteenth century, popular education and individual moral improvement were believed to hold the key to progress. Literacy, education, and the spread of secular knowledge to the common people were designed to foster a thirst for positive knowledge, the rational use of leisure, and a belief in material and moral progress.[63] The appearance of numerous organizations, clubs, and societies, as one historian notes, "provided an important focal point of, and forum for, a progressive and reformist discourse and activity" designed to democratize learning and create an educated and productive citizenry. To the degree allowed them by law, the attitude of the state, and their own energies and means, members of associations pursued many goals of individual and social reform and mobilized a public for reform causes. Among the individual values transmitted by associations were many commonly associated with the middle class: hard work, respectability, independence, self-help, and self-improvement.[64] Although historians and social scientists have connected many reform projects with the bourgeoisie, a wide spectrum of liberal landowners, professionals, and government officials, especially on the European continent, championed education and individual improvement. In any event, recent studies have challenged the existence of the bourgeoisie as a unified and dominant political and economic class.[65] It was believed that education would bring about "a striving for independence, either individually or on the basis of associations and self-governed initiatives," to participate in an autonomous public life.[66] In this way, it was hoped, the poor could leave the state of nature in which they were commonly regarded as living and enter civil society. Thus the association was an important component in what George Stocking calls a "Victorian cultural ideology," in that association presented modern European civilization as the high point of evolutionary progress, respectability, rational self-improvement, and mastery over external and internal nature.[67]

The Old Regime and the new associational sociability existed in a relationship of compatibility and mutuality, and cooperation between science societies and the state was the rule rather than the exception.[68] The societies of science and philosophy did not directly challenge political absolutism, and in many ways they profited from its privileges. Scientific and philosophical societies did not oppose monarchy but, as Daniel Gordon argues, tried "to establish a determinate mode of interaction within it."[69] States initiated, patronized, sponsored, and funded many of the important projects of applied science of the nineteenth century. In Central Europe, the state was an activist partner in the projects of education and reform, and government officials were a significant contingent of association membership. Service to the monarch enhanced the scientist's stature as well as the prestige of the monarch. For private men who needed public activity under a monarchy, the philosopher Condorcet observed, "The study of science can only represent . . . an immense vocation with enough glory to content their pride and enough usefulness to give satisfaction to their spirit."[70]

Experimental science required a collaborative effort to achieve common goals as well as an extensive allocation of resources that only monarchs or governments could provide. In addition, applied science fostered a collective endeavor to study and improve the natural and human resources of the realm, thereby helping to create a sense of national identity and to build an empire. States and scientists alike regarded the creation and diffusion of knowledge as patriotic. Approved by sovereign authority, national progress and prosperity were goals often explicitly stated in association publications and by members themselves. Of the many manifestations of this impulse, three may be mentioned briefly. First, associations were in the forefront of a statistical movement to investigate the realm, including all forms of economic activity, and to study the utilization of human and natural resources for productive purposes. In this patriotic endeavor, private associations of science and learning could also, as James Scott says, "see like a state" in the project to measure, count, map, classify, and educate the realm. Second, later in the nineteenth-century many associations believed they could assist the state by facilitating the cooperation between science and industry through technical publications, industrial exhibitions, research, and what today would be called feasibility studies. Finally, in order to create a more productive and, often, more moral citizenry, associations provided their expertise to the quintessential project of improvement—the spread of education, in particular, primary and vocational education.[71]

But associations of amateurs and informed laymen and learned societies, both of which carved out a relatively autonomous sphere of activity relatively free from state interference, were more and more drawn into public affairs. Because they functioned as "learned assemblies" that tirelessly emphasized cooperation and collaboration to achieve common, self-defined goals, even ostensibly apolitical learned societies came under the watchful eye of continental authorities, who feared, rightly, that such associations would be drawn into politics. Theodore Hamerow has noted the importance of nonpolitical associations in political life under absolute monarchy. A government suspicious of its subjects' political activities drove reform efforts into the

> guise of scholarly, professional, economic, or even musical and athletic associations . . . Interest in public affairs was often channeled into organizations which were ostensibly nonpartisan or nonpolitical. Meetings of historians, naturalists, jurists, physicians, teachers, singers, etc., began to perform a quasi-political function. All the civic organizations were symptoms of a political life. A congress of civic activists was more than just a congress of certain specialists; it was the preparliament which leads to the real parliament. Organizations . . . exercised a powerful influence over public affairs on the basis of property, status, and education.[72]

Even cultural and scientific associations were not immune. As Klaus Tenfield notes, "the government and police needed to know the intentions of associations and would send spies to find out."[73]

At the same time that the science of the Enlightenment era enjoyed a cooperative relationship with political authority, science also was a powerful weapon of intellectuals who wanted to challenge the authority of monarchs, churches, and states. This was most true in the area of popular education, regarded as a prerogative of state direction. Advocacy of universal, secular education was at the heart of the French anticlericalism and republicanism during the second half of the nineteenth century. Officials of the Second Empire were concerned that education projects camouflaged political activity. Liberals and republicans in the opposition were forced to develop their ideas clandestinely, as Janet Horne says, "within an interlocking network of clubs that met under the guise of philanthropic organizations, *sociétés savantes,* Masonic lodges, or public lecture groups."[74] Labor and industrial organizations, benefit societies, and scientific, literary and artistic associations sprang up; though not officially authorized, some associations were tolerated and existed in a legal limbo. After republican forces consolidated their power at the end of the nineteenth century, the state gained more control, not less, over popular education, and in 1904 religious orders were forbidden to operate schools.[75] In paternalistic political cultures on the European continent, education remained a prerogative of the state, and voluntary associations claiming to enhance national betterment through the dissemination of secular knowledge were carefully scrutinized.

States and established churches with a monopoly in education were suspicious of unsupervised private efforts to spread learning, especially to the mass of the population. The French state, according to François Guizot, was the "natural protector of intellectual activity," and the Ministry of Public Instruction "the natural tutor" of learned societies.[76] Since the projects of popular education were synonymous with republicanism and anticlericalism, during the Restoration and Second Empire, the government did not trust even those education societies "created in the spirit of accord with the government" and was hostile toward any educational activity "outside regular channels." Victor Duruy, minister of education from 1863 to 1869, feared that "the emperor's enemies would exploit elementary and vocational education for their own political ends" and accordingly believed that it was dangerous "to grant an association extended powers and a general character." Because the "tendencies displayed by its members necessitated vigilant surveillance," the French Society for Elementary Education could do little more than "discuss classical books, present medals, and hear an annual oration." One such "extended power," the establishment of public libraries, came under particular scrutiny. "Popular libraries, school libraries, communal libraries," according to the Bishop of Orleans, represented a "horrifying diffusion of skepticism." In 1864 a circular of the French Ministry of the Interior called to the attention of prefects the public libraries sponsored by voluntary associations: "As much as it may be appropriate to support and facilitate efforts to moralize and instruct people, so much is it indispensable to preserve them from the disastrous effects that anti-social doctrines and troublesome books will produce upon them." The local prefects were responsible for selecting or approving the public libraries' officers as well as examining their catalogs annually to make sure they contained "only useful, professional books, belonging to that body of wholesome literature proper to elevate and educate."[77]

THIS DISCUSSION MERELY touches on a vast literature stretching across many national historiographies. The historical experience rarely fits perfectly into theories of civil society and the public sphere, even in western Europe. It is often not clear whether a given civil society already exists or is in the process of becoming, or how a given polity progresses from the absence of civil society to its presence. But for the historian interested in understanding the development of voluntary associations and the dynamics of civil society in autocratic polities, certain moments in the European experience should be suggestive.

At the outset, a word of caution is in order. Societies' jubilee editions emphasized internal effectiveness and external influence. But the impact of associations, even in western Europe, was often less in practice than it was in the visions and laudatory publications of associations themselves. Societies were often divided by personal quarrels, and officers worked long hours pro bono.[78] Associations of science and learning typically relied on the state for material support, and the literature contains more than enough examples of struggles to survive financially. Many problems, coupled with an allegedly indifferent populace, limited the accomplishments of most societies, and they were often perceived to be ineffective in the public eye. Even in England, where the barriers to associational activity were fewer than in most other countries, as one historian notes, "there is no evidence that the efforts [of moral reform societies] had any lasting effect on social and moral disorder in the capital or elsewhere."[79] Moreover, in the eighteenth century many continental societies imported from England an associational model having a "constitutional" structure. That is to say, an associational model from a limited constitutional monarchy held accountable by Parliament was imported to the culture of political absolutism. Recognition of the inherent limitations of associations themselves and of the importation of certain associational models from foreign political cultures is particularly important when assessing the limitations of Russian associations. The failure of Russian associations to accomplish all they intended—or claimed—to accomplish cannot be explained solely by the failings of Russian traditions, institutions, and social structure or by the grafting of foreign forms onto an inhospitable host.

The voluntary associations of civil society had their growing pains in Europe. They were not born full bloom, strong and autonomous, during the Enlightenment; it took a century or more for them to develop. They developed at a different pace in different countries; associational networks were thinner in Germany and France, for example, than in England and Scotland. The relationship between civil society and the state, especially in continental Europe, was ambivalent, and the status of voluntary associations unstable. The boundaries between the state and civil society were frequently porous, and collaboration and cooperation were just as likely as confrontation to define the relationship. Associations were nurtured by monarchs and by government officials; almost without exception, associations, especially learned societies, were willing to take advantage of their privileged status under political absolutism. The diffusion of useful knowledge was a collaborative effort of governments, municipalities, business, associations, and private individuals, and associations existed in a relationship to political authority that was largely one of mutuality and cooperation. We shall see that, as in western Europe, science in Russia provided the tools to legitimate the established order of privilege, funding, and status emanating from the government, academies, and universities. But at the same time science undermined the established order by asserting a new form of authority. Although it has been common to emphasize an autonomous civil society and public sphere, separate from and often antagonistic to the state, civil society has rarely achieved complete autonomy. The state has always regulated and even repressed the activities of the public sphere of civil society, and civil society has been more likely to grow in scope when it has avoided political activities that directly challenge central political authority.

Most theories of civil society presuppose the existence of civil rights guaranteed by a state based on law; likewise, the public sphere requires a certain degree of publicity regarding affairs of state and of access to the public arena.[80] By these criteria, only a few polities of western Europe and North America spawned robust civil societies. Elsewhere, notably in continental Europe, rights were more contested and acquired more recently. The institutional core of civil society constituted by voluntary associations frequently preceded or developed in tandem with constitutions and representative bodies. The mixture of nurture and suspicion on the part of the authorities, the concession system and the requirement of government permission and registration for an association to have a legal status, the fear that seemingly innocent activities were a cover for politics, and the monitoring of societies' activities by the police—all were Europe-wide features of eighteenth- and nineteenth-century associational life.

Despite these limitations, in authoritarian regimes the practice of science as a tool for the public good and the dissemination of education created for associations a semiautonomous, semipublic, secular space outside the state and systems of aristocratic patronage. These spaces, these "institutions of civil society building," were explored and eventually settled by intrepid adventurers in the realm of civic action and "outreach" projects of philanthropy and cultural stewardship. Societies of science, philosophy, and philanthropy, as Michael Sonenscher puts it, allowed "those living under an intrusive government and an otherworldly church to endow areas of life that the authorities did not control with greater amounts of meaning."[81] Claims Margaret Jacob, "The shared sense of the importance of their activity, reinforced by dues, ceremonies, ornaments, decorations, as well as by libraries purchased and lectures attended, or . . . by nature observed and thus engaged in ways that promised control—this made some men and a few women different." By providing new models of moral and cultural authority, the dissemination of science, Jacob continues, had "emancipatory potential," particularly under political absolutism. This was especially true of experimental science and natural history that "addressed nature directly" and "depended upon open inquiry among communities of scientists free from clerical control and tied into international networks of communication," in "a space in civil society not directly under the control of an absolutist monarch."[82]

Moreover, according to Jacob, under political absolutism in seventeenth-century Britain, experimental science was "connected to the emergence of constitutional, representative systems of government."[83] In the course of the eighteenth century, normative laws "govern[ed] these private societies in ways that made them capable of being transformed into microscopic, and contractually founded and constitutionally governed, civil societies," complete with constitutional self-government and laws, elections and representatives, majority vote and committees. The rhetoric of representation and equality was then spread to the Continent's monarchies.[84] Despite dependence on wealthy patrons or on the state, the members of associations asserted their capacity to manage their own affairs, that is, their capacity for self-governance, a capacity often referred to as citizenship. In this new public sphere, propertied and educated men acted freely and became, in Daniel Gordon's felicitous phrase, "citizens without sovereignty."[85]

The experience of European associations suggests that Russia was less exceptional than commonly supposed. Russians borrowed the voluntary association from Europe, and in their relationship to the state Russian associations followed a trajectory similar to that of their European counterparts, albeit later in time. Likewise, when placed in a European context, the response of the Russian government to private associations was less singular, though at the time it seemed unique to the Russian intelligentsia, who were unfamiliar with the tutelage of European states. Russian officialdom did not have to reach back to ancient traditions of patrimonialism or Muscovite absolutism; the experience of eighteenth- and nineteenth-century Europe was more relevant. Russia had to deal with associations just as European governments had to—and the tsarist government dealt with them in many of the same ways. Although autocracy maintained a legendary suspicion of the organized activity of its subjects, it is often overlooked that political authority in Europe, especially on the Continent, was equally vigilant. To be sure, ruling over a vast and sparsely settled empire and facing a dearth of intermediary bodies to check its power, Russian autocracy was a more formidable and arbitrary adversary than French or even Prussian absolutism. Nevertheless, as we will see, associations, especially those whose mission was the dissemination of useful knowledge and popular education, offered areas under autocracy where men alongside and outside officialdom could claim the right to participate in public life.

CHAPTER TWO

The Application of Science

The Free Economic Society and the Moscow Agricultural Society

The Beginnings of Russian Associations, 1765–1855

The public sphere and associations of civil society were the product of a fitful process that began in the age of "enlightened" absolutism under Catherine the Great (ruled 1762–1796) and her eldest grandson, Alexander I (ruled 1801–1825). Although it is customary to omit the "enlightened" when discussing the absolutism of Catherine's youngest grandson, Nicholas I (ruled 1825–1855), and to focus on the repression of associations in the wake of the Decembrist revolt in 1825, in fact, the impulse to associate survived. Indeed, as will be discussed in this and the following chapter, formal associations continued to exist and in some areas, notably those that promoted science and "official nationality," even flourished. Thus, during the century before the era of the Great Reforms, two important components of civil society—a public sphere and associational life—emerged in Russia, as in western and Central Europe, under political absolutism. But what kind of civil society and associational life emerged in late eighteenth- and early nineteenth-century Russia? We can better understand the later evolution of Russian associations if we understand the intellectual and political framework in which they emerged.

Russia's enlightened absolutism was guided by German natural law philosophy and the paternalistic practices of the German states, practices that emphasized obedience to the authorities, social responsibility, and duty to the community. Not motivated by personal or dynastic interests, an enlightened monarch was the chief modernizing and "civilizing" force to improve the prosperity of the realm and of his or her subjects. Monarchs sponsored and encouraged the development of private initiative on the part of loyal servants of the state and of the institutions by which private initiative could be collectively realized; that is, they encouraged the development of civil society. An orderly and disciplined society thus framed by political absolutism would help state and monarch to administer effectively and thereby bring progress and civilization to a vast realm. Consequently, a civil society so constituted was hardly independent, let alone adversarial; rather, it was in a relationship of mutuality with the state, a partnership in the civilizing process.[1]

The emphasis on obligations, obedience, and duty was reflected in many philosophical and educational tracts of the age. In 1783, for example, Catherine publicized the virtues of service and obedience in a translation, which she edited, of *The Duties of Man and Citizen,* a catechism of morals and conduct by Johann Ignaz von Felbiger, author of textbooks and teaching manuals that were influential in the Habsburg empire. "All members of civil society," von Felbiger posited, "must do their utmost for society's well-being, assist willingly in whatever the supreme authority instructs, and honor all its institutions . . . If any subject has any useful intention or suggestion by which the society can profit or [by which] harm can be avoided, then he ought to submit his suggestion to the high authorities."[2] Thus, the monarch's subjects were encouraged to take the initiative in assisting the state by "any useful intention or suggestion." In theory the spirit of duty summoned in this educational tract would be willing and voluntary, not commanded. In short, such duties were patriotic.

Like Central European monarchs of her time, Catherine II sanctioned and even created a space where a partnership in the civilizing process could exist and flourish. Technically, of course, Catherine's unfortunate husband, Peter III, took the first step in this process when he freed the nobles from obligatory state service in 1762. This was one of the greatest "enabling" acts of Russian history, for as Isabel de Madariaga argues, it created a sphere of private initiative, a society separate from the state, thereby putting "the Russian noble at last on a par with the gentry and nobility of other countries."[3] Catherine attempted to stimulate initiative and promote public activity and public opinion. One example is the Legislative Commission of 1767. By creating a partnership between sovereign and society and the semblance of public consultation, Catherine sanctioned a quasi-independent and controlled public opinion that would serve the dual task of bringing progress and prosperity and of generating support for government policy.[4] Second, Catherine also promoted, for a time, a less-controlled stimulus to public opinion—a lively print culture. On 15 January 1783 the empress authorized private printing establishments. Although thirteen years later Catherine reversed herself by closing the private printing presses and creating a government censorship office, the semiautonomous publication and self-censorship of the Academy of Sciences and of Moscow University were untouched. (In any event, in 1802 Alexander I legalized again private printing presses.) Such independent publishing, argues Gary Marker, helped bring "intellectual life to a point where it could sustain itself outside of—if not necessarily in opposition to—the government."[5] In sum, Catherine's actions, according to Madariaga, fostered a more differentiated and pluralistic society, reduced the relative significance of the court as the center of cultural life, and marked "the coming of age of Russian intellectual life."[6]

Catherine's desire to stimulate local initiative, to foster the sense of obligations not only to the state but also to society, and to promote the public good can be discerned in the birth of voluntary (or "free") associations to pursue various goals such as learning, the arts, and useful knowledge. Guided by an enlightened ruler, associations could compensate for the dearth of the spirit of enterprise. In this, Russia followed the path of Central Europe. Not only did *The Duties of Man and Citizen,* for example, emphasize obedience to the state; it also provided a justification for the citizen's duties to others: "Because of many obstacles people cannot acquire for themselves all the necessities and advantages of life without the help of others . . . We must, whenever possible, do a good turn and be useful to others and thus seek their well-being together with them."[7] During the eighteenth century, Central Europe witnessed, in Richard van Dülmen's words, the beginning of "private initiatives by private individuals wishing to form associations outside the existing forces of authority such as the court, church and the estates . . . [and] to stimulate patriotic consciousness."[8] Catherine II and Alexander I encouraged private associations and displayed varying degrees of tolerance toward their activities, and many "patriotic" literary, philosophical, scientific, and charitable societies, modeled after similar associations in the German states, were founded. Thus, during the half century of the reigns of Catherine II and Alexander I, according to Marc Raeff, a new sense of identity and mission to assist the state and to help the nation emerged among the "cultivated members of civil society," the "Decembrists without December." As we will see below, Russia's first associations were imbued with the rhetoric of patriotism, the public interest, and contribution to what Raeff calls "the spiritual and material progress of the nation," a rhetoric that only intensified after the triumph over Napoleon in 1812. In this way, Raeff notes, "the blueprint for a civil society in Russia was ready."[9]

Because of its ethos of service, Freemasonry was a particularly important form of new sociability in eighteenth- and early nineteenth-century Russia. Even though its heyday was short lived, the lodges were centers of intimacy and friendship based on the urge to do good. Freemasonry was infused with the rhetoric of patriotic service to the fatherland and, equally important, to fellow human beings. Masons engaged in a civilizing mission that combined self-improvement with the improvement of society. As Douglas Smith argues, by drafting bylaws, electing officials, and holding regular meetings, the Masonic lodges were "laboratories for civic culture," laboratories that cultivated the capacity of self-government. Not surprisingly, as we will see below, Masons were prominent among the founders and active members of Russia's earliest societies. The Masonic lodges were part of a new sociability that utilized public spaces and public assemblies—such as the English Club in Moscow and St. Petersburg, various salons and circles, and the spaces near Moscow University—to discuss philosophical and social problems as well as to establish connections and networks and to cultivate a spiritual self-fulfillment. Many of these gatherings were ephemeral and left little documentary record.[10] Thus, at the beginning, civil society and associational life were not defined in opposition to the state. On the contrary, most associations regarded their relationship with sovereign authority as mutual and stressed the harmony and cooperation between civil society and the state.

Several types of association were founded. One type of society promoted the literary language and correct Russian usage.[11] Another type was the secular charitable society, which was animated by Russian Orthodoxy and gave organizational framework to private philanthropy. For a time, the problems of charity and need, issues that came close to government policy, were discussed at public meetings; reports were published on charitable activities in Europe. As Adele Lindenmeyr points out, by providing information on the activities of European charitable societies, Nikolai Novikov and other Russian pioneers in Russian charity "wrote primers for creating voluntary associations in Russia." Because government officials were prominent as founders or members of the board of many charitable societies, some of which had imperial patronage, "the boundaries between official and public spheres, state and civil society, were blurred and permeable."[12]

In 1802 Alexander I granted to the universities the right to sponsor learned societies for the diffusion of knowledge and culture. In the historiography, their existence has been overshadowed by the imperial academy of sciences, by the literary salons and circles, and by the Masonic and other secret societies.[13] Between 1804 and 1811, four learned societies were founded at Moscow University: Society of Russian History and Antiquities, the Physics and Medical Society, the Society of Naturalists, and the Society of Friends of Russian Literature. Foreign scientists played an important role in these first societies of learning and science. Invited to Russia in the eighteenth and early nineteenth centuries, they brought with them the idea of the significance of learned societies to science and education. For example, as superintendent of the St. Petersburg School District, Count S. S. Uvarov recruited foreign scientists for the new St. Petersburg University. A supporter of enlightened monarchy, Uvarov believed that the autocrat should guide modernization and "protect the resources of national wealth," including the human capital of an educated elite. Later, as president of the Academy of Sciences and as minister of education under Nicholas I, Uvarov wanted to raise the image of Russia as an enlightened empire and to make the Academy a "showcase of Russian contributions to modern scientific thought."[14] Moreover, science societies championed the idea of the usefulness of science to the prosperity of the realm. As a result, such associations, David Wartenweiler has noted, "soon developed into vital structures for debating new ideas and inventions . . . In the absence of a positive right of association, this was an important breach in the state's quasi-monopoly of public organizations."[15]

Throughout Europe, absolute monarchs took a paternalistic attitude toward associations of private persons, and the legal status of associations reflected this. In France, for example, a charter provided the legal basis for the state to supervise the activities of independent, or free, societies *(sociétés libres)*.[16] In his study of government regulation of Russian voluntary associations, Nikolai Anufriev used the analogy of the concession system, a common means by which absolute monarchs, especially Russian monarchs, enabled and encouraged, through privileges, private individuals to develop industry and commerce. As in Europe, a charter *(ustav)* gave legal status to societies. This document combined a constitutive charter as well as the society's rules and procedures for self-governance (its bylaws). Although we may think of a charter as a document written by monarchs or their servitors and granted to private persons, in fact the founding members of Russian societies drew up their own constitutive document. The charter was approved on a case-by-case basis by the authorities, often by the monarch personally. In the early years of the reign of Alexander I, the government devolved approval from the emperor to the Committee of Ministers. The charter was the basic legal document governing all aspects of an association's existence. Unlike associations for business and commerce regulated by civil or commercial law, Russian associations of private persons were regulated by administrative (or police) law.[17]

In the era of the French Revolution, no government was indifferent to private societies; associations were treated with a mixture of nurture and repression. Russia's first associations had to contend not only with a nurturing state but with a suspicious and capricious one as well, one that restricted the autonomy and the scope of their activities. Like the other absolute monarchies of Europe, Russia had no law on associations. The regulations governing voluntary associations were codified, if that is the word, in the Police Code *(Ustav blagochiniia)* in 1782. This statute distinguished between legal associations and secret societies, which were forbidden. As in Europe, no society could be founded without prior permission of the government. Any society approved by the government was assured of its patronage and protection, while any "gathering or assembly for deliberation or action detrimental to peace and tranquility" was prohibited. Since only those associations requesting particular privileges, such as ownership of land, free postal privileges, or government subsidies, were required to submit their charters for approval, many other associations existed legally without explicit government permission. Thus, in the early stages, private associations in Russia were "free" (or *vol'noe,* literally, "possessing its own will," the word commonly used at the time); that is, once recognized by the authorities, their existence was rather loosely regulated. In fact, the Police Code did not really provide "order" to public activity. Although it did distinguish associations whose bylaws had imperial approval from those which did not, in Anufriev's opinion, the regulatory state was "less interested in establishing clear procedures for founding and legalizing associations than in establishing active administrative supervision over them."[18]

Such administrative supervision, the bane of Russian political culture and a source of civil society's weakness throughout the imperial period, opened the door to arbitrariness and repression. Catherine herself feared a leadership that exhibited too much independence of action or that appeared to flirt with subversion. In 1797 Emperor Paul forbade the use of "obshchestvo" (society) and "grazhdanin" (citizen).[19] The story of reaction and obscurantism, the military colonies and the Holy Alliance, in the last decade of the reign of Alexander I and continuing into the reign of Nicholas I has been told often. Although societies began to flourish under Alexander I, after 1815, according to Raeff, the emperor returned to a policy of "prohibition and prosecution of worthwhile civic organizations . . . Public issues were declared out of bounds for private individuals and made a monopoly of the state."[20] From 1817 to 1824, the reactionary Prince

Alexander Golitsyn headed the dual ministry of education and religious affairs. His successor, Admiral A. S. Shishkov, believed that Russia had gone too far in emulating western Europe and needed to preserve its own soul. Two of his protégés, Michael Magnitskii and Dmitrii Runich, led the attack on Russian universities. In the wake of the mutiny in the Semenovskii regiment and the Metternich-inspired reaction of conservative monarchies to secret societies, a decree of 1822 shut down the Masonic lodges, banned secret societies, forbade organization of any unchartered association, and required all prospective associations to submit their bylaws for government inspection and approval. In 1825 a circular of the new minister of education, Admiral A. S. Shishkov, required all learned societies to submit a report of their activities at the moment of their founding and annual reports for all subsequent activities.[21] The more meticulous regulations that associations faced by the end of the nineteenth century came about gradually; as the government was forced to face new contingencies, ad hoc restrictions eventually became codified. And, after the reign of Alexander I, new societies no longer called themselves "free" *(vol'noe)*. Thus the era of relatively ad hoc and loose government regulation came to a close.

Nevertheless, the story of reaction is not so simple. Government regulation, even increasing and more repressive regulation, did not herald the death of civil society and associational life. Although Raeff claims that "only strictly private groups such as literary salons and circles were tolerated and even these were subjected to close scrutiny by the police," Russia's most prominent learned societies continued to function, and Alexander I gave his stamp of approval in 1819 to the Moscow Agricultural Society. More detached from sensitive issues of politics, education, and religion, these learned societies applied science in patriotic service to monarch and fatherland. Alexander Martin captures the nuances of the age, noting that even the reactionary Shishkov founded an association, the Symposium of Lovers of the Russian Word, to disseminate ideas of national pride and patriotism. Thus, even conservatives, in Martin's words, "promoted the development of a civil society involved with public affairs . . . and strengthened Russia's sense of cultural identity."[22]

The way to understand the beginnings of Russian associations is to go back to the origins of two of the empire's oldest voluntary societies and to examine in greater depth their goals and projects and their relationship with the state. Founded in 1765, the Free Economic Society was the empire's oldest voluntary association. Enjoying the patronage of Catherine II herself, it was close to the Russian court without being an appendage or agency of state. From its establishment in 1819, the Moscow Agricultural Society was led by some of the empire's greatest landowners, whose ties were closer to Moscow than to the imperial court. Voluntary associations, although always under the watchful, nurturing, but often suspicious eye of autocracy, became the institutional core of an emerging civil society.

A "Patriotic Society for the Encouragement of Agriculture and the Economy in Russia"

The Free Economic Society and the Moscow Agricultural Society were established in an age preoccupied with progress in agriculture. Improvement and progress by means of the application of science to the study of natural and productive resources was one of the most important goals of the European Enlightenment. By bringing the benefits of science to agriculture, nature itself could be improved and made more productive. No less important, agriculture's human component could also be improved by "break[ing] the cycle of tradition, inefficiency, and ignorance and replac[ing] it with improvements and scientific methods."[23] To further the increase and dissemination of useful knowledge and the popularization of scientific, or "rational," farming, in the second quarter of the eighteenth century, agricultural societies were founded in Scotland, Ireland, England, France, the German states, and Switzerland. In France, nineteen agricultural societies opened between 1757 and 1789, most in the 1760s.

That so many societies were founded in eighteenth- and early nineteenth-century Europe to improve agriculture suggests a widespread assumption that without the intervention of scientific and landowning elites and often the state, traditional farming techniques would not have been likely to change. Agriculture was a precarious human endeavor, and crop failures periodically threatened rural life and, accordingly, the wealth of the realm. Agricultural societies existed in a variety of formal and informal institutional arrangements. The existence of a few "improving landlords" in the realm meant that in Britain the crown could play a secondary role. Nevertheless, the Royal Society of the Arts, founded in 1754, the Royal Dublin Society, founded in 1731, and the Royal Agricultural Society, founded in 1838, depended on the patronage of the crown. Agricultural societies in Scotland linked economic progress with patriotism and national improvement.[24] Not unexpectedly, on the Continent states and monarchs played a more activist role. Most French agricultural societies were founded by state officials and existed only by government patronage and subsidies. Considering local initiative wanting, the government tried to prime the founding of agricultural associations by organizing a national agricultural council in 1819 as a "forum providing for exposure to the agricultural enlightenment"; local prefects organized branches of the council.[25] In Prussia and the other German states, according to Marion Gray, princes "without exception" promoted economic growth, agricultural innovation, and the betterment of rural life. Accordingly, most eighteenth- and early nineteenth-century agricultural societies, also called "patriotic societies," were "founded at the rulers' behest," were supported by the government, and numbered many officials in their membership. Not surprisingly, such agricultural societies aspired to play an advisory role to the state in agricultural improvement and chose their projects accordingly; their meetings and projects were a convenient venue to present ideas in an unofficial capacity.[26]

The experience of European societies of science and economic improvement, especially those on the Continent, are an important background to our understanding of Russian associations. Russia's earliest societies were born in a Europe-wide context of paternalistic rulers, state-society partnership, and "patriotic" assemblages dedicated to progress and prosperity. Monarchs encouraged the networking and communication of dispersed farmers for the sake of technical improvements in agriculture. Across Europe, associations welcomed state approval, recognition, and protection and assiduously cultivated government officials for their patronage and provision of large grants for expensive projects, awards for prize competitions, and printing and franking privileges. A mixed membership consisting of private landowners, scientists, and government officials made the boundary between "state" and "society" indeterminate. When regarded in the European context, Russian government supervision of associations and state-society mutuality to achieve common objectives are less exceptional than they seem at first glance.

The Origins of the Free Economic Society

As in Central Europe, the traditional purpose of the manorial estate was not the exploitation of nature but the exploitation of serf labor. But in the 1750s and 1760s a few government officials, such as Nikita Panin, began to realize the benefits of improvements in Russian agriculture and estate management. Furthermore, they connected improvement to an ethic of usefulness among the nobility, a curtailment of the abuses of serfdom, and a more efficient and humane economic and political system. Although German cameralism was better known in Russia, the ideas of the physiocrats and those of Adam Smith regarding the virtue of private initiative and economic enterprise in promoting the wealth of the nation were published in official journals and widely discussed. At the same time, middling provincial landlords, influenced by European ideas of rationalized agriculture, had begun to take more interest in, as one historian puts it, an "administrative order on their estates that would promote the moral and economic welfare of the peasants while making their own incomes more secure." This "burgeoning spirit of self-improvement," or "enlightened seigneurialism," grew slowly and steadily from 1765 on.[27] In 1764 Catherine II, interested in land reform in Livonia, traveled to the Baltic provinces. Although her true intentions have long been disputed, there is evidence to suggest that the empress wanted, as Robert E. Jones says, "to mitigate the evils of serfdom without arousing excessive expectations among the serfs or hostility among the nobles," by creating a "climate of opinion in which the nobles might agree to reforms to improve the life of the serfs."[28]

As in the rest of Europe, a body designed to study agriculture and to exchange information seemed to be the most efficacious institutional mechanism for creating such a "climate of opinion." Catherine and her advisers considered three institutional strategies. The first was to create an agricultural division within the Academy of Sciences. However, Mikhail Lomonosov, the scientist, philosopher, and poet, opposed this plan on the grounds that the academy was dominated by foreigners, who would not be interested in or familiar with rural Russia. In 1763 Lomonosov advocated a second institutional strategy, the creation of a government department, a prototype of a "ministry of agriculture."[29] In a 1764 memorandum to the empress on the state of Russian agriculture, Jacob Johann Sievers (see figure 2.1), governor designate of Novgorod, recommended a third strategy—a private agricultural society that could collect, translate, and disseminate information about the most applicable of foreign advances in agriculture and the arts. Sievers spoke with some authority. Son of an estate manager in Estland, he favored the "Baltic method" of leasing estates, a variant of which Catherine regarded as a strategy for the gradual elimination of serfdom. Sievers advised Catherine on many matters of provincial affairs, and the empress instructed her loyal servant to gather information on local economic conditions and customs and to promote agriculture. Perhaps more pertinent, while serving in the Russian Embassy in London, he became acquainted with the Royal Society of the Arts, a private society promoting science and useful knowledge, well patronized by the English crown.[30] A private or independent ("free") society held several additional advantages over a government department. It bore resemblance to European institutional arrangements. Moreover, it was organized privately by men who "on the basis of voluntary consent had decided to establish an assembly among themselves." Situated in a network of personal patronage, the deliberations of an independent society did not carry the expectations of

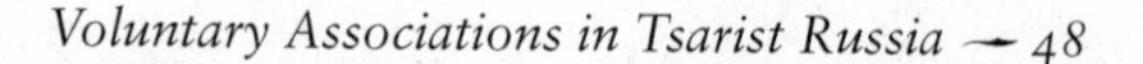

Figure 2.1 Jacob Johann Sievers, one of the founders of the Free Economic Society. (*Russkie Portrety XVIII i XIX vv.* St. Petersburg, 1905–1909.)

policy response. Catherine could easily permit discussion, even public discussion, and at the same time dissociate herself from it when advantageous to do so.[31]

In 1765 Ivan I. Taubert, court librarian and president of the Academy of Sciences, drafted an organizational plan, along with a charter and bylaws, for such a private society, one independent of government *(vol'noe)*, a "patriotic association for the encouragement of agriculture and estate management." Thus was born Russia's first association, the Free Economic Society. The Free Economic Society was a radical departure from current practice in that the Russian government did not control it. There is no doubt that the society, while independent of government, benefited from Catherine's political and material support, and its charter and bylaws were approved quickly. Catherine conferred on the society "separate" (or personal) patronage and permitted it to use a government printing press and the imperial coat of arms. The society's own logo (see figure 2.2) was a drawing of bees bringing honey to a beehive—which was commonly associated at the time with religious, moral, and economic virtues of industriousness and cooperation for the benefit of all—bordered by the inscription "useful" *(poleznoe)* along with symbols of farm labor, plentiful harvests, and imperial patronage.[32]

This inscription reflected, in Joel Mokyr's words, the "urge to create institutions that would serve useful knowledge, the scientific method, and the application of science," institutions "where useful knowledge was preserved, diffused, and augmented."[33] As in the case of many European associations of the age, especially on the Continent, such pursuit of useful knowledge was also patriotic. Given the interest of the society's imperial patron in bringing progress, enlightenment, and order to her adopted land, it is not surprising that the members would regard the encouragement of agriculture and economic progress as their patriotic duty. They found, as their model, the "beneficial measures" and the "wise solicitude" of the government.[34] To be sure, the need to solicit and maintain patronage from state and monarch no doubt inflated the rhetoric of service to the fatherland. This explicit link between enlightened self-interest, independent public action, and patriotic duty helped an absolute monarch give her blessings to what amounted to a public experiment.

A Charter under Autocracy

During its 150-year existence, the Free Economic Society was governed by a charter. Simultaneously acting as its bylaws, the charter was drawn up by the society (and periodically renewed) and approved by the monarch. The charter stated the goals and scope of activity of the Free Economic Society, while the bylaws contained the rules by which it managed its own affairs. In their letter to Catherine proposing the establishment of the society, the charter members expressed their desire for self-governance, stating, "Our society would be governed in its endeavors by its own obligations and bylaws and this is why it should be called the Free Economic Society."[35] The charter and bylaws became a template for subsequent associations.

The founding members established their own goals, the means to attain them, and internal rules and regulations—hence, its name "free," or voluntary. A body of members who had "united by voluntary consent" was, ap-

Figure 2.2 Logo of the Free Economic Society, on the title page of the society's chief serial publication, *Transactions (Trudy)*. (Photocopy courtesy of the State Public History Library, Moscow.)

propriately, the society's highest decision-making body. The members' meetings, or general assembly *(obshchie sobraniia),* by majority vote elected officers by secret ballot, selected new members, and approved projects and a budget. Later, many meetings were open to the general public. The bylaws spelled out what we would today call term limits, and initially the presidency rotated every four months. (In 1782 this was changed to an annual term.) A board *(sovet),* consisting of a president, vice president, secretary, treasurer, and, later, chairs of divisions and committees, planned the society's activities and set the agenda for the general assembly. The society could create ad hoc committees and commissions as it saw fit, and the various departments and committees had considerable autonomy to set their own agendas. Like the Academy of Sciences and Moscow University, the Free Economic Society acted as its own censor; the power to approve items submitted for publication in the society's *Transactions (Trudy)* rested with the general assembly. In addition, the society could import foreign publications duty free and uncensored. Finally, in any dispute over the interpretation of the charter, or in any activity not anticipated by the charter, the society could appeal to higher authorities, up to and including the monarch.[36]

Such a document gave associational life a special meaning in tsarist Russia. The charter explicitly or implicitly, granted certain rights and privileges as well as considerable autonomy to the society to manage its own affairs. The charter functioned as a microconstitution jealously defended by the society's members. Like the Prussian agricultural societies, sanctioned and patronized by an autocratic monarch, the Free Economic Society was governed by the principles of voluntary association of members and self-governance that suggested the political milieu of western and Central Europe. Indeed, these principles were what made the society "free." The founding members of the Free Economic Society wrote their own bylaws in the language of representation. To be sure, the charter had to be approved by the government, and there is no doubt that its provisions were constrained by an understanding of what was acceptable. Nevertheless, in drawing up its own charter and bylaws, the society was actively engaged in the process of self-definition and proclaimed the capacity of self-governance. The power of members to select new members created a bond of trust and mutual respect in the achievement of common goals; moreover, the government neither appointed nor validated the officers. Although the society was dependent on government subsidies and its fundraising activity was closely supervised, the government did not dictate how the society should spend its money.[37]

In providing a legal grounding for a voluntary association, the charter illuminates certain features of Russia's nascent civil society and its relationship to the state. On the one hand, the rights and privileges, the autonomy and self-governance, and the language of representation were a breach in autocratic power. On the other hand, shortcomings present at the outset foreshadowed later conflict with the government. Although the Free Economic Society had considerable autonomy to manage its own internal affairs, the charter was ambiguous about its freedom of external action. Later statutes and, worse, secret government circulars imposed more and more regulation by requiring the permission of the authorities in order to fulfill the society's public mission. Although the society had the right to appeal decisions of the authorities, in autocratic Russia such an appeal could not be directed to the independent adjudication of the courts but only to officialdom and the monarch. Nevertheless, for more than a century, the society's partial autonomy in the framework of a relationship of personal patronage, as well as the society's many opportunities for collaboration with the state, suited the Free Economic Society's members and its undertakings.

Members and Meetings

Although a Habermas-influenced historiography regards the eighteenth-century public sphere as a product of the bourgeoisie, noble proprietors and civil servants as well as members of the emerging free professions constituted the membership core of the eighteenth-century learned societies all over Europe. This should not be surprising in the agricultural societies. In Britain wealthy landowners dominated agricultural associations, making them, as one historian puts it, "clubs for a new class of gentlemen who [were] in the habit of agricultural experiment." The dukes and earls who often were the officers of British agricultural societies were "valued for their tone and solidity."[38] In France, "privileged bearers of essentially a classical culture"—civil servants, members of the free professions, gentlemen farmers, and, especially in provincial societies, the clergy—constituted the majority of the members. In Central Europe, government officials and scientists dominated the membership of agricultural societies. The charter members were always presented as "zealous," "enlightened," "honorable," "notable," "patriotic," "distinguished," and "men of good will." The motives for joining and participating in the activities of societies included a mixture of "local patriotism" and "local ennui," vanity, reputation, as well as a "taste for research and scientific debate." But perhaps above all was the desire for the "company and fellowship of like-minded men." Bastions of masculinity and privilege, learned societies excluded women from membership.[39]

More often than not, men did not take advantage of their self-proclaimed superiority, and the commitment of many members was disappointing.

Many contemporary accounts describe irregular or declining attendance at meetings, apathetic or indifferent members, waning enthusiasm, financial difficulties—in short, a precarious existence. British agricultural societies allegedly existed for the benefit of only a "few science-minded country gentlemen." According to Peter Clark, "membership was important more for the social, political, and cultural gains of the landowners." Few non-London members of the British antiquarian and archaeological societies "could afford to visit the metropolis regularly," and many members did not participate in activities. As Philippa Levine says, "It was a committed core of enthusiastic men and women who offered up their leisure hours gratis to the administrative business of the societies." Despite the presence of men "with a good deal of capital," as Kenneth Hudson notes, it often took a "man of exceptional energy and public spirit," extensive contacts, and vision to guide associations in their early years.[40] Certain observations about French societies became a dreary refrain: "no longer functions," "exists only on paper," "kept going only by the zeal of the secretary," and "the agricultural society dissolved due to lack of interest." The most active members of French societies were called "the locomotives"; without their initiative and perseverance, as Jean-Pierre Chaline notes "some [French] learned societies would not have been created or sustained." An American authority on French science considers that a few energetic individuals constantly had to "breathe life into the societies of agriculture."[41] Composed chiefly of professionals, scientists, and government officials, German societies, according to Henry Lowood, "lacked a membership base in the countryside where the peasants and farmers [plied] their trade." Those few members who lived in the countryside resisted reforms. Moreover, most of the "farmers" listed on the rolls of agricultural societies were large landholders, village officials, or clergy and thus not intimately connected with the everyday rhythms of farming.[42] Keeping in mind that the membership of European agricultural societies failed to live up to its potential will help put similar accusations of Russian associations in comparative context.

Among the charter members of the Free Economic Society, there was no shortage of notable, patriotic, and distinguished men. The society's fourteen original members included luminaries of the "enlightened" and high-ranking nobility, such as Count Grigorii Orlov, Catherine's "favorite" at the time; Count Roman I. Vorontsov, senator and father of one of Catherine's close friends, Princess Ekaterina Dashkova, herself elected to membership in 1783; Count Ivan G. Chernyshev, friend of Nikita Panin and chief procurator of the Senate, member of the Admiralty College, and special ambassador to England; and Baron Aleksandr I. Cherkasov, president of the Medical College. Charter membership also included court officials such as Ivan I.

Taubert, member of the Academy of Sciences and imperial librarian. In addition to Taubert, other scientists were Andrei A. Nartov, son of a mechanic under Peter I and member of the Academy of Sciences, director of the School of Mining, and one of St. Petersburg's most prominent Freemasons; Timofei I. Klingstedt, member of the Academy of Sciences and also vice president of the College of Justice for Estonia, Latvia, and Finland; Johann Gottlieb Lehmann, a chemist and member of the Academy of Sciences from Leipzig; Khristian Pekken, scientific secretary of the College of Medicine and author of Russia's first popular medical book; the Swedish-born physician and naturalist Johann Peter Fal'k, director of the Botanical Gardens; Henry Jacob Ekleben, court gardener; and Johann Georg Model', member of the College of Medicine. Several prominent founders were Masons—Sievers, Vorontsov, Orlov, Chernyshev, and Nartov; this brought to the Free Economic Society the ethic of improvement and duty to mankind as well as the sense of brotherhood that were nurtured in the microsocieties of the Masonic lodges. Moreover, the many members of foreign birth or foreign ancestry brought what has been called the "Baltic Enlightenment" to Russia: according to Lisbet Koerner, civil servants of German-Scandinavian origin, who believed that science held the key to catching up with western Europe, applied European science to Russia, in A. I. Khodnev's words, "to bring an immediate benefit to the country that had become for many of them a new fatherland."[43]

The rights and duties of membership, as stated in the bylaws, did not recognize distinctions of class and rank. In the early years, as we have discussed, it was not hard to adhere to this principle. At the same time, the bylaws followed European practice in specifying membership categories, which were later emulated by many subsequent learned societies. "Active" members, who constituted the residential core of the society, had demonstrated activity in economic affairs and were required to contribute three compositions per year to the society's chief organ, the *Transactions (Trudy).* Corresponding members reported their observations, the results of experiments, and local agricultural developments. Auditors translated useful foreign works. Bestowing honorary membership added luster to the society, and several well-known European scientists were honorary members, among them Arthur Young, the most prominent popularizer of the application of science to agriculture. Moreover, bestowing honorary membership to members of the imperial family secured continued patronage and donations. The original bylaws also admitted without election provincial governors as non-voting members; the bylaws of 1824 extended the same privilege to government ministers and women. Before election to membership, a candidate had to be presented to the Free Economic Society by three active members who could vouch for his or her qualifications. From fourteen in 1765, the number of members rose to over one thousand by 1860.[44]

Weekly meetings created the opportunity for discussion and disagreement. Decisions were voted on openly, with those in favor of a proposal standing in place, or by secret "ballot," with members dropping either a white ("yea") or black ("nay") billiard ball into an urn. While encouraged, debate was to be kept within bounds. Following European practice, the Free Economic Society emphasized decorum in its deliberations. "Recognizing that concord is the strongest protection of any Society," read the 1765 bylaws, "the members of this economic assembly promise to observe common decency among themselves and to shun anything that would violate good will and concord." The president was responsible for maintaining order, and according to the 1859 bylaws, he had the authority to ring a bell to restore order and, if that failed, to close the meeting.[45]

Despite a dose of self-mythologizing regarding the equality of members, rank and status did divide members of the Free Economic Society. The society's leaders came from the wealthy and "enlightened" landlords and notables close to the court. One of the charter members, Timofei Klingstedt, proclaimed, "Our society consists only of those personages who have not the slightest intention of receiving personal aggrandizement or vainly showing off their abilities; their only desire is to be useful to the Fatherland."[46] However, this usefulness was not always realized. Eager to be illuminated by the empress, many of the great magnates were not about to forsake the glitter of the capitals for the life of a country squire personally involved in estate management; for them, membership was largely ceremonial.[47] Alongside the great magnates were lower-ranking provincial nobles as well as the men of science and learning, many of whom were Baltic Germans. Despite rhetoric about service to progress and scientific agriculture, the views of the Society's members were conservative. In his examination of nobles of the era, Jurij Lotman claims that

> during the Alexandrine period educated, Europeanized noble society led a dual existence. In the sphere of ideas and "philosophical speech," society had assimilated the norms of European culture that had grown out of the Enlightenment. The sphere of ordinary behavior—of everything related to everyday preoccupations, custom, the real conditions of estate management, and the real circumstances of the civil service—was not open to "philosophical" interpretation. From the point of view of ideas, it was as good as nonexistent . . . This pluralism of behavior—the ability to choose behavioral style according to situation and the duality arising from the division between the "practical" and the "philosophical"—characterized the progressive Russian nobleman of the early nineteenth century.[48]

Endemic in Russian culture, the discrepancy between ideals and reality pervaded the Free Economic Society as well. The leaders and the rank-and-file members of the society could discuss modern agricultural techniques and even peasant property rights in the abstract. At the same time, they declined to apply this discussion to their own estates or to their own peasants.

That many members of the Free Economic Society were highly placed meant that collaboration with the government was the natural state of affairs, as it was in the analogous German agricultural societies. The society continued to enjoy patronage at the court and in the ministries well into the nineteenth century. For more than a century, the society cultivated close ties with government agencies, from which it asked assistance and received subsidies. Notables and government officials mingled with some of Russia's most prominent academic scientists and scholars, including the chemist Dmitrii Mendeleev, the geographer P. P. Semenov, the botanist A. N. Beketov, and the economist Ivan Vernadskii.[49] These members, along with prominent landowners, made up the "old guard," in the terminology used at the end of the nineteenth century by officialdom and liberal members of the society alike. Officers and members approached their activities in the role of patrons of agriculture, industries *(remesla),* and science. In this, the Free Economic Society defined its role as one of complementing and assisting the government in the pursuit of mutual goals—bringing progress and prosperity to the nation. In order to assist the government most effectively, the society had been accorded certain privileges and independence of action, which were supported by members and officialdom alike. The "old guard" saw to it that the society's privileges were not abused. Although its privileges were contained in its bylaws, the actual conduct of the society was governed less by the bylaws than by the temperament of its core members.[50]

THE FREE ECONOMIC SOCIETY's links with government set a pattern for reciprocal and mutually beneficial and collaborative relations between Russia's voluntary associations and the state, a pattern that prevailed until the end of the nineteenth century. The society had imperial patronage, accepted members of the royal family as office holders, received what we might call today government grants, and petitioned government offices for favors and privileges, such as free postage. Like many future associations in the nineteenth century, the Free Economic Society was called on to assist the government in the study of a variety of problems and in implementation of policy. In this, a "patriotic society for the encouragement of agriculture and the economy in Russia" was fulfilling its patriotic duty. Until the 1890s, there is little evidence that the government compromised the principle of voluntary membership, internal integrity, or autonomous self-management of the society's affairs.

At the same time that the Free Economic Society unavoidably had a very close relationship with autocratic power, it also established and cultivated ties with foreign societies and prominent individuals. Many members, especially in the early years, were Baltic Germans, who helped to disseminate information about Baltic farming practices. At the beginning of the nineteenth century, the society established connections to the German agriculture societies of Hamburg, Saxony, Braunschweig, and others, thereby providing its members with descriptions of improvements, drawings and models of new technology, and compositions on estate management. Although Arthur Young's views were too partial to economic freedom to be published in Russia, historian S. A. Kozlov claims that enlightened landowners knew about his work: "This was important for the development of free thinking on economics and society in Russia and subverted the ideas of despotism."[51] Thus, even while the necessity of a close relationship with the government no doubt circumscribed the society's autonomy, the appearance of Russia's first nongovernmental (but government-approved), western-style association was a singular moment. This is perhaps what the improving landlord and memoirist A. T. Bolotov sensed when he saw a copy of the society's first publication in 1766: "As I already had a certain understanding of economic societies in other countries and of all their institutions, I almost jumped with joy when I saw from this book that the same kind of thing had been set up in our country and even named and taken into her particular patronage by the Empress herself. I . . . began to read everything in it with great enthusiasm and attention."[52]

The Free Economic Society marked the beginning of a process whereby independent public initiative was sanctioned under autocracy. The spread of agricultural societies in nineteenth-century Russia provides an example of this process at work. Like French and Prussian government officials, the Department of Rural Economy in the nineteenth century encouraged nobles to found agricultural societies. N. S. Mordvinov, president of the Free Economic Society from 1823 to 1840, helped to create other agricultural societies. When more Russian agriculture societies began to appear in the second quarter of the nineteenth century, most out-of-town members of the Free Economic Society were also members of another, "local" agriculture society. Under Nicholas I, fifteen agricultural societies were founded; they included the important Agricultural Society of Southern Russia, founded in Odessa in 1829, as well as societies in Kazan', Iaroslavl', Kaluga, Estland, Kurland, and the Caucasus. By 1898 there were more than two hundred agricultural societies in the empire.[53] But oldest of these and most comparable in size and national importance to the Free Economic Society was the Moscow Agricultural Society.

The Moscow Agricultural Society and the Resurgence of Patriotism

In 1818 a Baron Rozen, a corresponding member of the Free Economic Society, proposed creating economic societies in every province of the empire. In the same year at a private meeting of landowners of Moscow and vicinity, several nobles discussed ways "to activate the material forces of fertile Russia, reduce the obstacles to improved farming, instill into farming practices knowledge and science, and spread improvement from the heart of Russia to the borders of the world's largest country."[54] Chaired by Prince Dmitrii Vladimirovich Golitsyn, "a respectable Russian gentleman" and governor general of Moscow Province from 1820 to 1843, the meeting was attended by great magnates, such as Count P. A. Tolstoi; Stepan Stepanovich Apraksin, owner of fourteen thousand serfs; and Nikolai Nikolaevich Murav'ev. Prince Sergei Ivanovich Gagarin, owner of five thousand serfs, suggested that "from such random and short-term assemblies should be created a permanent society" to exchange information on agriculture. Thus was born the Moscow Agricultural Society, approved by Alexander I in 1819 and opened in 1821.[55]

The timing of the founding of Russia's second agricultural society illustrates the contradictory approach of autocracy toward private initiative and nongovernmental associations. It was founded in an age dominated by the Holy Alliance, Metternich, and the obscurantism of Alexander Golitsyn, Shishkov, Magnitskii, and Runich at the end of Alexander's reign. The authorities feared secret societies, and associations in the sensitive areas of politics, religion, and education, such as the Masonic lodges and the Bible Society, were closed. At the same time, the Moscow Agricultural Society, like the Free Economic Society and other learned societies at Moscow University, escaped the crackdown against education and science. Both agricultural societies promised the application of science for national betterment within the existing political and social structure. Perhaps more important, both had eminent patrons at the court and among Russia's wealthiest and most pedigreed landowners. In 1825 the Moscow Agricultural Society was placed under the protection of Nicholas, soon to be tsar of Russia.[56] Founded following the Napoleonic Wars, the Moscow Agricultural Society began its existence in the wake of the first of three great nineteenth-century surges of Russian patriotism, and, as will be shown in this section, the rhetoric of fervent patriotism and desire to work for the fatherland permeated its mission.

In contrast to the Free Economic Society, large private landowners rather than notables at the court played the most important role in the founding of the Moscow Agricultural Society. During the years 1818–1860, 621 of its 770 active members were landowners, and 211 owned five hundred to one thousand serfs. Its first two presidents, Prince D. V. Golitsyn from 1818 to 1844 and S. I. Gagarin from 1845 to 1859, were among the nation's greatest landowners and pedigreed families. In its early years, its membership also included sixty-five professors (including professor of medicine and agriculture Mikhail Grigor'evich Pavlov, professor of zoology Karl Frantsovich Rul'e, professor of veterinary medicine Khristofor Grigor'evich Bunge, and professor of agriculture Iaroslav Al'bertovich Linovskii); agricultural notables (such as A. T. Bolotov, who became an honorary member in 1820 at age eighty-two; F. V. Samarin, father of the prominent Slavophile; Vladimir Aleksandrovich Cherkasskii, later a member of the Editing Commission on the eve of the Great Reforms; Count S. S. Uvarov, a "modern" landowner who believed in scientific farming, machinery, and efficient agricultural methods); as well as a smattering of Moscow manufacturers and even Decembrists and Decembrist sympathizers. Although the landowners took conservative sociopolitical positions, in general they sought "a harmonious fusion of west European improvements and native traditions *(na pochvennicheskikh ideinykh pozitsiiakh)*."[57]

The preamble of the charter of the Moscow Agricultural Society, having in mind the practice of Europe, noted, "Everywhere agriculture societies have been created by the direct patronage of governments . . . Agriculture already constitutes Russia's greatest source of wealth. Its improvement promises [Russia] an inexhaustible treasure beneficial to each and everyone as well as to the state as a whole." The society's main goal was to "test by experiment the laws of agriculture that have been recognized as useful in other countries and apply them to the soil, climate, and local conditions of Russia." Other goals were testing new machines and implements, publicizing observations and discoveries, and investing in agricultural education. As Prince D. V. Golitsyn put it in his first address to the society, the mission of the Moscow Agricultural Society was the "augmentation of our knowledge in agriculture and its dissemination in our Fatherland."[58]

When Alexander I approved the charter and bylaws on 4 January 1819, he bestowed upon the Moscow Agricultural Society certain privileges. The society could amend its bylaws as needed to achieve its goals; it had the privilege of free mailing up to one *pud* (thirty-six pounds); it could create branches in the provinces; it received an annual government subsidy; and it had the right to use the imperial seal and to select its own logo, which three years later became *"ora et labora" (molis' i trudis').* For these privileges the society was obliged to submit an annual report to the Ministry of Internal Affairs. The bylaws also spelled out the categories, selection, and obligations of members, which closely resembled those of the Free Economic Society.[59] The bylaws provided for specialized divisions in the society, and in the early years these were four: scientific (or theoretical), agriculture and animal husbandry (or practical), mechanical, and educational. A board that met weekly consisted of the president, vice president, secretary, treasurer, and heads of the four divisions. The professors of the scientific division wrote articles and translations for the society's publications. Active members of the division of agriculture and animal husbandry were obliged "every year to submit reports of experiments conducted on their estates, or descriptions of the advantages of one system of cultivation over another, based on experiment, and in general, anything pertaining to farming." The engineers and mechanics of the mechanical division tested improvements, implements, and innovations. The bylaws obliged members to hold a monthly general meeting, to which guests of both sexes could be admitted with a special ticket; there was also an annual meeting at which a report was presented.[60]

The relative autonomy granted the new society amid obscurantism reflected the importance attached to the dissemination of useful knowledge. It was also a product of the ethos of patriotic service that pervaded the self-definition of a Russian association. After Russia's victory over Napoleon, a resurgence of "ardent love of the fatherland" fostered the recognition that the empire could be served best by the combined efforts of persons dedicated to improving agriculture. As Stepan Maslov noted, "A civic consciousness awakened among many nobles, and this fostered action for the commonweal."[61] The rhetoric of service to the fatherland and not just to state or monarch motivated its members and infused every undertaking of the society. In his address at the society's twentieth anniversary celebration in 1840, Prince D. V. Golitsyn expressed gratitude to the society's "wise government, whose paternal solicitude [*otecheskaia zabotlivost'*] anticipate[d] everything that could possibly benefit Russia and generously nourishe[d] this main branch of wealth everywhere." Likewise, in lobbying for more government assistance for agricultural improvement, Count Mordvinov celebrated the close ties between the society and the state: "Hail the unity strengthened by the harmonious yearning for the good of the Fatherland and for the good of Russia, for she is our mother." Members were inspired by "patriotic feelings of love of Russia," and by a "zeal for the good of the Fatherland," to be "useful to [their] compatriots" and to "promote the common good."[62]

The professed commitment to "patriotic duty" helped create a new sense of identity, self-worth, and mission for the noble who wanted to serve the nation as well as the monarch. Given the difficult conditions under which they operated, the earliest Russian societies gave their members a sense of importance in the community. P. M. Preobrazhenskii, a teacher at the school of the Moscow Agricultural Society in the 1840s, stated "The farmer [*sel'skii khoziain*] is first and foremost the motor . . . that brings life to the inert forces of the land. Without his efforts, there can be neither prosperity of the nation nor wealth of the state."[63] In a letter to D. V. Golitsyn, the society's president, Prince N. G. Viazemskii, marshal of the nobility in Kaluga, expressed the sense of self-worth brought about by the commitment to agricultural improvement: "In a state such as ours, the noble landowners are in essence the chief champions of agricultural improvement. This enlightened estate is more capable than any other of new and useful enterprises. Possession of property and permanent residence on their estates obliges them to consider the most felicitous arrangement [*blagoobdumannyi poriadok*] of agricultural labor to study assiduously nature and its gifts . . . The efforts of this society mediated by the landowners over time can affect improvements in the agriculture of even the most simple farmer in every corner of Russia."[64]

The Agricultural Societies and their Projects

The goals of eighteenth- and nineteenth-century agricultural and scientific societies in Europe were the patriotic acts of increasing and disseminating useful knowledge and popularizing scientific, or "rational," farming. Perhaps the most common method used to attain these goals was the publication of journals and treatises that catered to and stimulated a fascination with publicizing the results of experiments linking scientists to improving landlords. In so disseminating useful knowledge, such formal institutions invariably created informal networks and patterns of communication and interaction, the "invisible colleges" vital to the exchange of information.[65] The voluminous publications, "the showcase of a society's activities," reveal a "capacity to contribute to science" and "the opportunity to demonstrate [members'] learning and usefulness to the community." The various bulletins and minutes of meetings likewise disseminated important information about the societies' projects and personnel, albeit in a pompous style of mutual celebration and "a predilection for pointillist detail."[66] Other projects included maintaining libraries and scientific collections; organizing exhibitions, public lectures, and demonstrations of innovations and implements; conducting statistical surveys; advocating agricultural education and founding schools; and establishing model farms and experimental stations. Societies also sponsored essay competitions to demonstrate the service of applied science to important issues of the day. Such competitions generated public interest in matters of economic improvement; offered solutions to concrete problems; gauged or mobilized public opinion; and provided a "low intensity" public input into policy without committing governments or institutionalizing the process.[67] All of this outreach activity was presented and publicized at regular meetings, at which correspondence and various reports were read and discussed, new members were elected, and project proposals were generated and evaluated. Annual meetings, often open to the public, were more ceremonial and, frequently in the presence of the appropriate officials and patrons, included a president's address, an annual report of the society's activities, the awarding of prizes, and homage to the great deeds of a member or patron.[68]

At the same time, the secondary literature suggests that the many projects did not achieve all their intended results and that European countries by and large did not see significant improvements in agriculture attributable to the efforts of agricultural societies by themselves. We have already seen that many European agricultural societies led a precarious existence. According to Peter Clark, the work of the Royal Dublin Society, was branded "marginal," and "failed to achieve any important increase in Irish agricultural output." Allegedly, few farmers read the publications of British agricultural societies, and the publications' immediate impact was only on "a tiny minority of farmers."[69] French agricultural societies were accused of emphasizing theory over practice. The print runs of their scientific publications were limited to a few hundred. In Arthur Young's opinion, one society was like any other: "They meet, converse, offer premiums and publish nonsense. This is not of much consequence, for people instead of reading their memoirs, are not able to read at all." Even if societies could reach farmers, reformers, who did not hold the ordinary farmer in high regard, were "skeptical that many farmers would listen."[70] Keeping this in mind will help put the performance of Russian associations in comparative context.

The Free Economic Society

Like the missions of European scientific and agricultural societies, the mission of the Free Economic Society was the increase and dissemination of useful knowledge. To achieve this goal the society chose means common to the age, among which were publications, essay competitions, data collection, and projects to advance public health and education. At one of its first meetings, the members decided to establish the *Transactions (Trudy)* as a permanent organ to publish articles of the members, compositions submitted to the society, and the minutes of meetings. As one of its charter members stated, "It has been known for a long time that periodic compositions greatly facilitate education and the diffusion of useful knowledge."[71] From 1766 to 1794, Catherine herself subsidized this major source of information on economic conditions in the empire. During its first quarter century, Russia's first private learned journal disseminated to the general reading public "healthy" ideas on farming—improving fodder, tools, crop diversification and rotation—as well as on estate management, public health, and descriptions of the latest European innovations. In addition, the society published descriptions and drawings of agricultural implements and machines; agricultural manuals; and "instructions," collections of orders and regulations landlords gave to their stewards. In the more liberal intellectual climate after 1801, the articles in the *Transactions* touched on the social aspects of rural life as well.[72] Of course, it was difficult for the many treatises on agriculture and political economy to bridge the gap between theory and practice and to reach a large public. In no small way, this was due to fluctuation in print runs and difficulties in distribution.[73] Nonetheless, the treatises and the reports from far-flung correspondents forced the members to record and measure accurately observations and experiments, to provide scientific documentation, to maintain scientific journals, to compile agricultural data, and to catalog techniques—all essential components in the diffusion of useful knowledge.

Designed to stimulate public interest and encourage improvements in Russia, publication was an interactive process between the society and the public. Readers of the first volume of the *Transactions* were invited to submit their observations and discoveries. At the society's meetings, reports of observations and experiments of correspondents all over Russia were read and later published in the *Transactions*. Members were asked to perform experiments, test innovations, and evaluate the results of experiments submitted to the society. Seeds of new strains of plants were mailed as a supplement to the *Transactions;* the editors encouraged members to plant and record their observations as well as to distribute the seeds in their region.[74]

The privilege of using the society's own censors put the journal in an unusual position in an autocratic empire: being exempt from the prepublication censorship of the state and church and free from direct government supervision and interference. To be sure, self-censorship considered the opinions of powerful patrons. Yet all evidence suggests that Catherine herself left publication decisions to the members of the Free Economic Society. Items submitted for publication in the *Transactions* had to be approved by an editorial board consisting of the president, two secretaries, and three members appointed on a rotating basis, as well as by a majority vote of members.[75]

No sooner had the ink dried on the Free Economic Society's charter than the empress herself turned this august group of landowners, officials, and scientists into something more than a disseminator of useful knowledge. Not satisfied with the advice she was getting on the peasant question, Catherine raised the issue of peasant property rights under the auspices of the Free Economic Society. At Catherine's prompting, the society launched its first essay competition by posing this provocative question: "What is more useful to society, that the peasant should own land or merely movable property, and how far should this right extend?" In other words, what is the best form of landholding, private or common? Essays were solicited abroad as well as in Russia, and indeed of 162 submissions, only 7 were from Russians, suggesting that the question may have been too hot to handle.[76] Taken together, the essays expressed a considerable range of opinion. A majority of the essays favored peasant landownership, and a few went so far as to advocate peasant freedom. First prize, a gold medal worth 250 rubles, was awarded to Bearde de l'Abbaye, doctor of civil and canon law at the University of Aachen. The winning essay advocated peasant landownership but in small amounts and on a gradual basis, so that the peasants would still be forced to rent land. Moreover, the author proposed that the landlords, not the government, be given full powers to solve the peasant question. No doubt, this preservation of landlord dominance, both economic and juridical, was the essay's "winning" quality in the eyes of the Free Economic Society. Other essays that were well received by the society, as V. I. Semevskii notes, "either reflected ripening views among a certain number of educated persons, or were at least accessible to many in society."[77]

Views that were "ripening" were one thing. However, views that were ready to be picked were quite another, and the Free Economic Society found itself in the thick of one of the hottest issues of political economy and state policy. The Legislative Commission had started its deliberations, during which the issues of freedom, property rights, and serfdom were openly debated. In this context, it could not be guaranteed that the publication of essays that exposed the abuses of serfdom would not provide ammunition for the advocacy of more far-reaching legislative measures. The society's members were not uniform in their views, and sixteen of twenty-eight members opposed publishing Bearde de l'Abbaye's essay. However, this majority deferred to a more powerful minority, which included two Orlovs, Roman Vorontsov, Count A. S. Stroganov, and Count Ivan Chernyshev. Thus the first-prize essay was translated into Russian and published in the society's *Transactions* in 1768.[78]

An article by a Tver' landowner published in the *Transactions* during the latter portion of the reign of Alexander I may illustrate the self-censorship of the society, at a time when the authorities suppressed any alleged deviation from religion and morality and carefully watched discussion of the peasant question and serfdom. In 1819 N. V. Zubov submitted a composition about his plan to divide and consolidate some of his fields and transfer them to his serfs as their private property; the composition was published in the *Transactions* in 1821, the decision to publish generated considerable retrospective disagreement within the society. The society, after all, was not monolithic in its opinions, and members had different views about what to publish. Some members thought that in publishing an article that touched the issue of landownership, the society had entered political and legal areas beyond its competence. One member framed his opposition to publication as follows: "The purpose of the Free Economic Society is the improvement of agriculture and estate management; these are appropriate subjects for the society. But to consider the disposal of the landlord's land is to touch a sacred right granted by God only to our most gracious sovereign. [The society] has no authorization to examine existing laws and property rights." Pavel Sumarokov, a writer and member of the Senate, thought that the article should be removed from the *Transactions:* "The Economic Society is called 'free' due to the exclusive right to discuss and print free of censorship its innovations and advice only about estate management and not about statutes and political matters. This exceptional trust thus imposes upon our corporation an exceptional caution far exceeding that of other dependent [*podchinennye*] writers."[79] Thus *pace* Sumarokov, the government permitted the first public discussion of political issues such as landownership and the value (moral as well as economic) of serfdom on the pages of the society's journal. By the narrow vote of 11–10, the society decided to leave the article untouched.

However, most compositions and competitions were less controversial. The 1809 competition asked whether *obrok* (quit-rent) or *barshchina* (corvée) was the more advantageous fulfillment of the serf's obligations to the landlord, while that of 1812 asked whether serf or free labor was more profitable. Other competitions touched on strip farming, land consolidation, and education. Competitions were also announced for inventions and improvements, as well as for tests of innovations. Sometimes, even peasants entered the competitions.[80] Several essay competions had patriotic overtones. For example, in 1783 a competition was announced for the best answer to the following question: "How can a Russian [*rossianin*] of the middling station in life content himself solely with rude [*neobdelannye*] Russian products?" One composition published in the *Transactions* claimed, "It is necessary that every inhabitant of the empire give preference to products of his own country and use only those absolute necessary foreign items which his own land either does not make or makes in an insufficient quality and quantity . . . A patriot will replace a foreign article with a native one."[81]

To maximize the publicity for the essay competions, announcements and the questions to be answered were published not only in the *Transactions* but also in other periodicals, such as *Moskovskie vedomosti.* To ensure objectivity, authors submitted their entries anonymously but marked by a sign *(deviz)* of their choosing; a separate envelope contained the authors' name, address, and sign. The society's jury read the compositions and declared the winning entries before opening the envelopes to determine authors' identity. Altogether there were 243 competitions during the society's first century and 235 prizes awarded. But one half of the competitions solicited no entries at all, and not all entries were deemed prize worthy. For example, the announcement of a prize for the best composition on local economic conditions that accompanied the 1790 survey prompted only one entry during the next ten years. During the society's first half century, prizes were offered by the royal family and highly placed persons at court or in officialdom. However, from 1816 on, prize money came mainly from the society's endowment, though it was often augmented by the royal family or by private donations. Semevskii claims that the competitions were frequent topics of conversation in St. Petersburg and "an educational experience for contemporaries." He noted, "The peasant question was raised, and raised quite loudly." The essay competitions on peasant property rights and serf relations "provided the public with a discussion of the master-serf relationship from a wide variety of viewpoints."[82] They provided a filter, and a government-approved filter at that, through which European ideas could be openly discussed and through which Russian ideas on such vital areas of national policy could be formulated outside official channels.

The Free Economic Society aimed to increase the amount of information available on local economic conditions, primarily, but not only, those of agriculture. The society was founded at a time when governments, academies, and private bodies in Europe eagerly gathered statistical material to quantify useful knowledge about the realm. In her "instructions" to the Legislative Commission, Catherine observed, "I prepared the

Manifesto calling up the deputies from the whole Empire, in order that I might learn more about the situation in each area."[83] In Russia, reliable data on local economic conditions had always been and would continue to be the bane of a vast empire and an autocratic government. In the 1760s, the Academy of Sciences organized expeditions to study the countryside and the state of agriculture, industry, and commerce. But it was the Free Economic Society that undertook to compile some of the first systematic survey data anywhere by means of questionnaires sent out in 1766 and 1790. The first volume of the *Transactions* solicited information on sixty-five "economic questions." For each of the empire's regions, the surveys compiled data on the natural resources, soil, and climate; cultivation, livestock, farming techniques, and harvests; the state of the rural economy and the living and working conditions of the peasants; and the state of transport, handicrafts, women's work, poverty, health, diet, and leisure. The means of compiling information in different years reflected the gradual increase in direct contact between the society and the public. At first, the society did not have full control over the operation and had to rely on the government apparatus—primarily the local governors—to collect data. But in 1804, when the society received one of the most coveted privileges of any modern organization—free postal service—it was able to contact individual landlords directly. Finally, during the reign of Nicholas I, the society adopted the practice of English, German, and Scandinavian agricultural societies of compiling regional data from the observations of correspondents and traveling members.[84] Despite obstacles, peasants responded to the questionnaires, often with the complaint that under current conditions they could not follow the useful advice on farming; needless to say, these observations were never published. Later, in the nineteenth century, the society undertook major statistical studies, based on responses to published questionnaires, of the grain trade, the peasant commune, and farm prices. In the words of a nineteenth-century authority on Russian agriculture, these surveys were thereby presented "for the judgment of the public [*na sud publiki*]."[85]

One of the best-known correspondents was Andrei T. Bolotov (see figure 2.3), a self-educated middling nobleman, natural philosopher, writer, and publisher committed to estate improvement and individual moral self-perfection. While visiting Moscow in 1766, Bolotov discovered the Free Economic Society when he bought a copy of the *Transactions* on the street:

> And my satisfaction grew even greater when I saw that, following foreign examples, all the nobles living in the province along with other people of every rank had been invited to communicate their economic observations to the Society and to pave the way for this, 65 questions were appended at the

Figure 2.3 A. T. Bolotov, a reforming landlord and member of the Free Economic Society and the Moscow Agricultural Society. (*Russkie deiateli v portretakh* St. Petersburg, 1886, p. 75.)

> end of this book, of such a kind and concerning such matters, to which it could not be complicated or difficult for anybody to answer, provided that he understood something of provincial life and agriculture and knew how to write and possessed a pen.[86]

Bolotov responded to the questions with information on his native Kashira district of Tula Province, and his first published work appeared in the second volume of the *Transactions.* In 1767 he was invited to join the society. Later the publisher of *Sel'skii zhitel'* (1778–1779), editor of *Ekonomicheskii magazin* (1780–1789), and author of *Derevenskoe zerkalo, ili Obshchenarodnaia kniga* (1798–1799), Bolotov became one of Free Economic Society's most active members.[87]

Over time the activities of the Free Economic Society became vast in scope (*obshirnaia zadacha,* in Pakhman's words). In his centenary history, A. I. Khodnev, a chemist from Khar'kov University trained by the German Thaer, noted that although most people considered the Free Economic Society to be an agricultural society, in fact it was an all-purpose economic and technical society that extended to public health and well-being.[88] It built many "bridges to reduce access costs to knowledge." The most visible "bridge" activities were in the fields of public health and education—a smallpox vaccination program, an agricultural school, book distribution, and exhibits of agricultural specimens and implements. Beginning in 1824, the society founded vaccination committees in twenty-six provinces, dispatched vaccination information and instruction brochures, published western literature, trained vaccination personnel, and provided the vaccine. By 1837 more than 10 million infants had been vaccinated and ten thousand trained to administer the vaccine.[89]

From the beginning, the Free Economic Society took the initiative in Russian agricultural education. One of the society's first essay competitions in 1767 suggested public education as a preparatory step to freeing the serfs, and the society routinely gave prizes to competitions on the best ways to spread "useful knowledge." In 1789 Count F. E. Argal't, president of the society and also chief of the Army Corps of Noble Cadets, introduced agricultural lessons into the training of cadets. Beginning in 1825, the society participated in the funding and operation of an agricultural school on the Novgorod estate of one of its members, Countess Sof'ia Vladimirovna Stroganova, sister of Prince D. V. Golitsyn, president of the Moscow Agricultural Society. The purpose of the school, to be discussed further below, was to train orphans and children of poor nobles and government officials to be estate managers. Later, another member, V. Ia. Shvittau, opened a school near Gatchina.[90]

Almost immediately upon its founding, the Free Economic Society began to acquire a library. When funds did not permit the acquisition of foreign books in 1769, the members decided to organize a pledge drive for the purpose; frequently, the collection was augmented thanks to private donations. To facilitate the diffusion of useful knowledge, the society managed the free distribution of the members' publications. In the 1820s the society began to distribute books to provincial libraries, schools, and seminaries; a decade later it began to publish primers. In 1830 N. S. Mordvinov, an admirer of Adam Smith and a society member since 1778 and president from 1823 to 1840, donated thirty-five thousand rubles to establish a public library in order to disseminate useful agricultural information. Not content merely to send books to libraries, in the 1830s the society began to help provincial governors in Orel, Pskov, Tula, and elsewhere to open public libraries, and Mordvinov proposed to the Ministry of Internal Affairs a network of provincial libraries. In the 1840s several distributions numbered over 10,000 books, including one in 1844 of 63,000 books and treatises on agriculture and industry, to all parish schools and seminaries. Khodnev likened this in scale to the distributions by the British and Foreign Bible Society. When in 1827 the society decided to catalog its collection, the library owned 3,464 books and treatises (834 in Russian and 2,630 in foreign languages). By 1857 the collection totaled almost 12,000 books. The library was open to nonmembers, but as Khodnev admitted, the six-ruble fee limited its use mainly to members; in 1836 it became open and free to all; that is, it became public.[91]

The society publicized Russian and foreign improvements, by means of collections, exhibitions, museums, and lectures. The society's work in collection, cataloging, and display evolved over many decades. Private persons and members sent minerals, soil samples, plants, models, machines, and objects of peasant industries to the society; members often bequeathed their private collections. Begun as a private accumulation of specimens sent to the society by private donors for use by its members, this "cabinet of nature" was opened for limited public viewing in 1803 (for one day a week) and expanded in scope, system, and accessibility steadily thereafter to include innovations and implements. In the nineteenth century, the society donated objects to other associations. In 1824 the society opened a workshop to make machines from the prize-winning designs submitted in competitions. In 1845 a merchant member, I. S. Vavilov, donated a collection of various wares of peasant industries to form the basis of the Museum of Folk Industry. In 1853 the society founded the small Museum of Applied Natural History as well as the Museum of Designs and Machines, to display models of tools and agricultural implements the society had been acquiring over the years, chiefly for tests.[92]

The Free Economic Society contributed to a relatively new means to disseminate knowledge—the exhibition—by organizing displays of agricultural implements and new farming techniques and by providing judges and medals to validate the efforts of other organizations and individuals. Members began to discuss organizing livestock exhibitions in the early nineteenth century. The first large agricultural exhibition was held in Odessa in 1842, organized by the Agricultural Society of Southern Russia. By midcentury, the Free Economic Society regularly organized in many Russian cities exhibits of plant specimens, livestock, agricultural machines and implements, and peasant industries. In 1850 the society organized the first National Agricultural Exhibition in St. Petersburg. The processes of both collecting and viewing were a means to solicit public participation.[93] Like the descriptions and drawings in the society's publications, such collections and exhibits acquainted the curious with innovations in agricultural implements and farming techniques. Displays of out-of-date agricultural implements became silent witnesses to technological progress, a goal that was at the heart of so many societies of the period. Exhibitions had the added functions of determining the current state of Russian agriculture and, it was hoped, "encouraging emulation among landlords and thereby improving agriculture."[94] Indeed, an article in the *Transactions* claimed that exhibitions in Russia were even more important than in, say, Germany, whose farmers had a higher literacy rate: "Exhibitions can transform productivity and direct millions of people from rude, irresponsible labor to rational and modern labor and by exposing them to a world of wonders, about which they have no doubt, double or triple productivity . . . Agricultural exhibitions can awaken a strength of will and this awakening will be the most salutary and solemn triumph over our chief ills."[95]

A final example of outreach activity sponsored by the Free Economic Society was the public lecture. Pupils at Stroganova's school were required to attend lectures sponsored by the society. Lectures on agriculture began in 1832 but soon began to cover a wide range of topics in science, trade, and industry. In 1835 the Free Economic Society began organizing public lectures; that members went out of town to deliver lectures was considered a novelty. Lecturers were professors at St. Petersburg University and the Medical-Surgical Academy, as well as teachers, officers, physicians, merchants, and "even ladies." Lectures were accompanied by visual aids such as printed programs, seeds, and demonstrations and experiments, making them, according to Khodnev, "well known" in St. Petersburg.[96]

The founding of the Free Economic Society marked the beginning of efforts to popularize the scientific study of agriculture in Russia—the study of land use, crop diversification and rotation, seeds, soil science, fertilizers, animal husbandry and beekeeping, flax cultivation, and the continued testing of new implements and techniques. The society undertook major statistical studies that often involved the cooperation of local authorities and were disseminated among government officials in St. Petersburg. In order to improve agriculture, the author of a study of pre-reform agriculture societies opined, "There must be an entity that could combine differing views and propositions of individuals, in which every innovation could be tested, and which could stimulate new ideas and discoveries." According to Pakhman, "Intercourse, that invincible force for the rapid, all-around and rational development and improvement of man and humanity, offers every important enterprise undoubted assistance. The union of differing views, information, experience, and talents makes possible that which seems hopeless for one person or for many working separately and without a common plan. There is hardly any branch of human activity that would not be to one degree or another indebted to the intercourse and free effort of many persons. Science, which has for a long time received the benefit of sociability, has stimulated the creation of numerous and various learned societies and companies."[97]

The Moscow Agricultural Society

Not satisfied with meetings as the primary means to spread useful information, the founders of the Moscow Agricultural Society immediately took an active, "outreach" role, primarily through publications, efforts to spread literacy, and sponsorship of agricultural research. Its chief publication was the *Journal of Agriculture (Zemledel'cheskii zhurnal),* which commenced publication in 1821 and was Russia's first journal devoted exclusively to agriculture; Nicholas I was one of its most avid readers. Given that the Free Economic Society's *Transactions* appeared only intermittently from 1821 until the 1840s, for a while the *Journal of Agriculture* was Russia's only agricultural journal. The journal's mission was to publish articles by landlords working on their estates, in the hopes that this would, in Prince D. V. Golitsyn's words, "prompt private persons to report their useful observations and encourage readers to offer their comments and ideas about agriculture." Soon reports were coming in "all the way from Siberia," and "everyone wanted to publish information about their experiments and observations." The *Journal of Agriculture* published original compositions, translations from foreign journals, reports on experiments and observations, and business and correspondence of the society. A newspaper that the Moscow Agricultural Society started publishing in the early 1830s, the *Agriculture Gazette (Zemledel'cheskaia gazeta),* contained articles intended for a peasant readership; an increasing number of peasants subscribed. In its periodicals and in separate publications, the society published data on agricultural conditions of the non-black earth provinces, as well as articles on the advantages of crop rotation, the introduction of clover, and numerous other farming innovations.[98]

The driving force behind many of the society's publications was its secretary, Stepan Alekseevich Maslov (1793–1879), in Chaianov's words, "a man of exceptional energy and vision," that is, one of the "locomotives" that Chaline viewed in French agricultural societies (see figure 2.4).[99] Son of a priest, Maslov was an active or honorary member of forty-five associ-

Figure 2.4 S. A. Maslov, secretary of the Moscow Agricultural Society. (B. E. Raikov, *Russkie biologi-evoliutsionisty do Darvina: Materialy k istorii evoliutsionnykh idei v Rossii* 4 vols. Moscow, 1951–1959, vol. 3.)

ations, including many foreign agricultural societies, and a Masonic lodge. In addition to numerous articles on farming and the promotion of Russia's sugar beet industry, in 1830 he translated the textbook of leading German agronomist Al'brekht-Daniel' Teer (Albrecht Daniel Thaer), *The Foundations of Rational Agriculture (Osnovaniia ratsional'nogo sel'skogo khoziaistva)* for which the Free Economic Society awarded him a gold medal. Influenced by Arthur Young, Thaer championed English methods of cultivation—crop rotation and the utilization of fertilizers and grasses—and was considered the father of agricultural science and rational agriculture. German agricultural practices were often a filter through which English innovations came to Russia, and from the 1820s through the 1850s, the Moscow Agricultural Society disseminated a wealth of information about them. A by-product of this information was knowledge about German agriculture associations and about agriculture education. Members of the society attended congresses of German farmers; Maslov went to Germany three times for this purpose.[100] Like the Free Economic Society, the Moscow Agricultural Society also published accounts of the activities of agriculture societies that lacked their own publications and, much later, of the zemstvos. This mediation through publications prompted Golitsyn to claim that by disseminating information among improving farmers scattered all over Russia, *Zemledel'cheskii zhurnal* performed "a great service to science." In his presidential address at the society's fifteenth anniversary celebration in 1835, Gagarin listed some of the most important publications of recent years and announced, "All these works had the sole aim of being useful to our compatriots and of raising agriculture to the level of a science."[101]

Not long after the founding of the Moscow Agricultural Society, Golitsyn spoke frequently of the need for estate managers, in the main peasants, to be literate. When a rudimentary school system was created in 1786 under Catherine II, rural schools were notable by their absence; the government took no responsibility for the education of privately owned serfs. Legislation in 1803 under Alexander I authorized the creation of parish schools for both state peasants and serfs. However, initiative was left to the clergy and landowners, and the government did not fund primary education. Under Nicholas I, the Church authorized clergy to establish parish schools. At the same time, several government ministries sponsored rural schools, though there is little indication that they reached a large number of peasants. Although the Ministry of State Properties, created in 1837, began to open rural schools, such schooling was available only to state peasants. The government was suspicious of private initiative in education, and the vast majority of landowners were indifferent to the schooling of their serfs.[102]

In meetings of the society, Golitsyn provided the example of his own estates, where peasant boys learned how to read and write. In 1833 the society heard a report on the improvement of morals of the pupils of a school of beekeeping, near the town of Baturin in Chernigov Province, run by one of its members, Peter Ivanovich Prokopovich, Russia's first apiarist. In 1844 the society heard a report by another one of its members, Nikolai Stepanovich Stremoukhov, about a school for peasant girls that he had opened in 1823 in the Sumy district of Khar'kov Province. The Moscow society awarded Stremoukhov a gold medal for his "concern for popular morality," which was allegedly "threatened by the removal of peasants from simple rural and agricultural life."[103] Stepan A. Maslov, the secretary and intellectual leader of the society, began to publish a series of articles and booklets advocating the dissemination among the peasants of literacy based on religious and moral principles. The booklets were dedicated and distributed to the Church hierarchy, and the literacy enterprise had the blessing of the imperial family, at the time imbued with the ideals of domesticity and the sanctity of the family. Support for the idea and testimonials of similar projects on private estates came in from all over the empire.[104]

In 1822 the Moscow Agricultural Society founded Russia's first agricultural school. The organizer and director of the society's school for the first sixteen years was Mikhail Grigor'evich Pavlov, an important agronomist of the time and one of Russia's first popularizers of agricultural science. In 1818, after becoming a doctor of medicine, Pavlov was sent to Germany, where he studied agriculture under Thaer. Upon his return in 1821, Pavlov became a professor of agriculture at Moscow University and taught the empire's first course on agriculture as a distinct discipline. He criticized usage of the three-field system and advocated crop rotation. The target pupils of the agricultural school were initially serf children sent and paid for by their masters. In 1835 nonserf graduates were accorded the same rights and privileges as those of provincial gymnasia: those who worked ten years on a private estate could become honorary citizens. Although some members of the society hoped that the agriculture school would produce a class of educated, self-interested, honest farmers, most graduates became managers or agronomists on private estates who had varying degrees of opportunity to apply their training, depending on the landowners. Other graduates entered state or local government service; a few began "dynasties" of peasant agronomists.[105] The Moscow Agricultural Society's agricultural school became a model for all of Russia's postreform agricultural schools.

In addition to its own school, the Moscow Agricultural Society facilitated the organization and administration of private schools founded by its members. Along with the Free Economic Society, it assisted in the administration of an agricultural school founded in 1825 by Countess Sof'ia Vladimirovna Stroganova (see figure 2.5), sister of Prince D. V. Golitsyn and a member of both societies, as well as one of the best educated women in Russia at the time. The school was jump-started when two graduates of the School of the Moscow Agricultural Society came to teach on Stroganova's Mar'ino estate in Novgorod province. The school was the first private agricultural school to get national attention. Landowners who sent their serfs to the school paid part of the fees, while the rest was paid from government money in the form of scholarships administered by the

Figure 2.5 Countess Sof'ia Stroganova, founder of an agricultural school administered by the Free Economic and Moscow Agricultural Societies. (*Russkie Portrety XVIII i XIX vv.* [St. Petersburg, 1905–1909].)

Free Economic Society. Nonserfs, largely wards of the Moscow Foundling Home, also attended. Stroganova's school contained a workshop to make agricultural implements and machines; beginning in 1839, the school trained veterinarians, offered courses in forestry, and opened a chemistry laboratory. It became too complicated and expensive for Stroganova to run, and shortly before her death in 1845 she ended her involvement; the school was taken over by the Moscow Agricultural Society.[106] In 1826 P. I. Prokopovich founded a beekeeping school; it remained in operation until 1879. By 1850 over 400 pupils had attended, and 393 were awarded diplomas; in later years, honors graduates received a three-year deferment from military service.[107]

These and other efforts to disseminate literacy and agricultural training to Russia's peasants are examples of the collaboration between state and society in the patriotic pursuit of national betterment. The leaders of the Moscow Agricultural Society viewed education not only as a way to disseminate new farming techniques. Education was also a way to support the existing social and moral structure, and the projects of private initiative quickly received government blessing. Stremoukhov, Golitsyn, and other creators of pilot projects, as well as their spokesmen, such as Maslov, were not proponents of free labor but of serf labor. They wanted to improve rural life by directing the debate away from the legal and economic plane to that of culture; they argued that the bane of rural Russia was not serfdom but ignorance *(nevezhestvo)*. Moreover, the government had been unwilling to take responsibility for the education of privately owned serfs. Since literacy, allegedly more than free labor, was "the foundation of progress in agriculture," Russian agriculture could not improve, the argument ran, unless its basic human component, the enserfed peasant cultivator, became a literate farmer.[108] Into the vacuum stepped the literacy committees. The society's various education projects culminated in the founding of the Committee for the Popular Dissemination of Literacy on Religious and Moral Principles, or the Literacy Committee for short, in December 1845. The purpose of the committee was to gather information and facilitate the acquisition of literacy by proprietary serfs.

The Literacy Committee not only assisted the state in the cultivation of a literate farmer within the context of serfdom but also gave meaning to the enterprises of its members. Maslov realized that private efforts of landowners on their estates were going unnoticed, and "their compatriots [were] deprived of the opportunity to witness their experiments and to express their gratitude and support." Private efforts scattered all across the empire needed publicity and, as it were, the moral support of both the public and officialdom. The function, then, of the Literacy Committee, indeed of the agricultural societies as a whole, was to publicize experiments, stimulate public discussion, and thereby facilitate the spread of literacy and progress. Just as individual landlords could receive proper credit and support, "the Moscow Agricultural Society [could] without fear stand before the judgment of contemporaries and its beneficiaries [*pitomstva*]." Maslov wrote, "Then at the fiftieth anniversary, when we will no longer be here, the next generation of members, having attained the goal of disseminating literacy, can say that the society had fulfilled its obligation and had not betrayed its motto, 'prayer and labor' [*ora et labora*]."[109]

The movement to educate Russia's serfs gives a twist to the common correlation of literacy, secular modernization, and gender. The impulse to create a literate serf was moral and religious. Maslov did not value knowledge and education for their liberating powers or for their perceived linkage to science, materialism, positivism, and progress. If anything, these values were contributing to an alleged decline of morals that, according to Maslov, threatened civil society. And, in Maslov's view, the existing "state of popular literature and the book trade" bore part of the responsibility. "Commercial interests" allegedly hawked "*Manuals, Gifts for Children,* and literature of that ilk at village fairs and markets." The challenge facing those who cared about the moral well-being of the Russian people was "to prevent the distribution of empty, useless, even harmful books [*knizhonki*] and replace them with books that [were] useful, instructive, and pleasant for the people." Maslov argued that the Moscow Literacy Committee could facilitate the distribution of an uplifting and low-cost alternative to the secular family books, thereby supporting the efforts of private landlords to educate their serfs in a religious and moral spirit. Indeed, just as provincial clerics were prominent in French agricultural societies, parish priests were an important contingent in the membership of the Moscow Literacy Committee. The committee recommended that every village school or church have a library stocked with "proper" books, supplied by the Ministry of Education and the Ministry of Internal Affairs.[110]

However, since the education of all serfs would not be feasible in the foreseeable future, which serfs should be targeted at the outset to receive education "in a religious and moral spirit"? Although it is commonly thought that young men are usually given preferential treatment in the acquisition of literacy and education in modernizing societies, in Europe the education of girls had been an important component in the practice of domesticity beginning in the late eighteenth century. Moralistic weeklies such as the *Spectator* promoted the idea that "reading was to improve women morally . . . by making them better daughters, wives, and mothers." Education would permit a woman's more successful execution of her family duties in a patriarchal society.[111] Such a strategy of domesticity appealed to the Russians. The key to education of the peasants, according to Stremoukhov, was the education of peasant girls, the future mothers of the empire's peasants. In 1847 the Archbishop of Vladimir and Suzdal', Parfenii (P. V. Vasil'ev-Chertkov), endorsed the projects publicized by Maslov: "The education of the people must begin with the education of mothers. The mother is the soul of the family; her daughters think her thoughts and utter her words. What a great good it will be if they will think and speak soundly and piously!"[112] The first of four booklets published by the Moscow Agricultural Society extolling the virtues of literacy based on religious and moral principles was devoted to girls' schools and the acquisition of literacy among serf girls on private estates.

Along with women's moral influence came certain practical advantages to educating girls, in the eyes of proponents of the project. First, since many fathers and sons were working away from home for long periods, the mother was in charge of children's upbringing. By imparting the ability to understand Church Slavonic *(tserkovnaia gramota)* to her children, the mother would be assisting the parish clergy, and it is no accident that parish priests and the ecclesiastical authorities alike endorsed the project. As Maslov stated, "No one can ignore the value and function of the mother in civil society."[113] Second, transmitting literacy through mothers would be a way to attain universal literacy without universal schooling. Finally, because girls' education was a lower priority than that of boys for the Ministry of Education and the Russian Orthodox Church, it was a project more feasible for private organizations, especially philanthropic societies. Efforts to educate Russian children, even serfs and even girls, were not new. But previous efforts had lacked an ongoing organizational framework outside officialdom and the Church. The significance of the movement launched by the Literacy Committee was that, for the first time, organized private initiative established a foothold in popular education.

The Moscow Agricultural Society also pioneered in sponsored agricultural research, primarily on its experimental farm. (As early as 1769 the Free Economic Society discussed the idea of an experimental farm, but the idea received little encouragement from government.)[114] At its first meeting, the Board of the Moscow Agricultural Society discussed such a venture, and in 1822 the society founded Russia's first experimental farm on leased marshland just outside of Moscow. The first director was Aleksandr Rogers, the son of an English farmer who worked for Count N. P. Rumiantsev, an honorary member of the Free Economic Society, whose suburban Moscow estate Kagul was known for its fine potatoes, "Kagul cream," and Rogers's plows and harrows. The experimental farm operated at a loss and had to be supported by government subsidies. Although it never became an effective model of consolidated farming for the majority of Russia's landlords, the experimental farm, like its parent organization, was successful in propagating certain advances in commercial farming (especially sugar beet cultivation) and sheep breeding. The experimental farm also boasted that by using science and rational management, it could guarantee greater productivity on marshland than the traditional three-field system could achieve on good land. Like the essay competitions of the Free Economic Society, though on a much more practical level, the Moscow Agricultural Society solicited proposals for crop rotation on the experimental farm. The farm also tested new agricultural implements, engaged in soil experiments, and tried various cultivation systems. Largely through the experimental farm, the Moscow Agricultural Society publicized the cultivation of potatoes and the use of stone buildings. In 1838, at a meeting to honor Professor Pavlov, who was retiring from the directorship of the experimental farm, president D. V. Golitsyn noted that before the founding of the society, no one in Russia thought that agriculture could be a science. But Professor Pavlov was the first "to illuminate by the light of science the common, ordinary labor on [Russian] fields." Golitsyn continued, "In rational agriculture, all production is illuminated by the light of knowledge . . . In this lies the destiny of rational agriculture that is conducted by the laws of science—not blind luck but calculated success."[115]

The society facilitated the dissemination of American tobacco in Russia by obtaining seeds in London as early as in 1826 and by offering a prize in 1832 for the best method of its cultivation. In response to constant requests for seeds of all kinds, the society in 1836 opened a seed depot that sold seeds at a moderate price. The maintenance of a mineral collection, collections of European agricultural implements, an agricultural library, and the organization of agricultural exhibitions and, later, congresses rounded out the activities of this energetic organization.[116] At the fifteenth anniversary celebration of the Moscow Agricultural Society in December 1835, Maslov noted that both the monarch and officials had stated that "agriculture was the most important topic of government and [that] it was time to pay it special attention." This being the case, Maslov reasoned, only by elevating agriculture to the level of a science would it get the attention of monarch and government. Five years later, in an address at the society's twentieth anniversary celebration, Golitsyn reflected on the progress of agriculture as a science: "Members who attended the inaugural meeting of the society can remember how immature was our notion of agriculture . . . Gentlemen, I am pleased to credit the successes of the science of agriculture in our Fatherland in part to the efforts of our society, and to the harmonious work of its enlightened members." During the past twenty years, Golitsyn added, the Moscow Agricultural Society had "shed the light of science on Russian agronomy, heretofore only in the hands of blind practice."[117] The leaders of the Moscow Agricultural Society not only applied science to Russian agriculture but also turned the study of agriculture in Russia into a science.

The Significance of the Agricultural Associations

How may we assess the meaning of the first century of the life of Russia's first two independent associations of science, political economy, and agriculture? What was the significance of their activities during a period when they were among Russia's few chartered nongovernmental organizations? It must be readily acknowledged that both contemporaries and historians have criticized the societies for failing to accomplish many of their goals. But in assessing the contribution of Russia's two oldest and most prominent agricultural associations, historians may have been looking at the wrong criteria. It is worthwhile to examine from a different perspective the meaning of two of Russia's oldest societies, whose record of public service set a precedent for others to follow.

Historian Michael Confino and others argue that the Free Economic Society failed to confront the nation's most serious economic, legal, and political issues and to solve the more technical problems within its competence. Similarly, the agricultural societies failed to bring prosperity to the countryside or to ameliorate the abuses of serfdom, much less abolish it. Neither association transformed the habits of the majority of noble landlords, let alone those of peasant cultivators.[118] Members' views on political economy were conservative, and most members flinched at the thought of any realignment of Russia's political institutions and system of landownership. Given the magnitude of Russia's agricultural problems and a pervasive and entrenched serfdom, according to the conventional view, the efforts of the societies seem halfhearted, the scale of activities completely inadequate, and the results disappointing.

To be sure, historians concede that the agriculture societies faced many obstacles over which they had little control and that it would have taken far more than their efforts to bring about agricultural improvement on a large scale. Even European agricultural societies, most of which operated under more favorable institutional, economic, and geographic conditions, have been found wanting in their performance. In addition to the vested interests and habits of their members, as well as the discrepancy between ideals and Russian reality, the agricultural societies faced government treatment that vacillated between negligence and petty tutelage, as well as the indifference, if not resistance, of the peasant commune. Apathy, isolation *(zamknutost')*, and deference to the autocratic power of Russia's landowners were legendary, and there is no shortage of evidence in the records of the two agricultural societies to support this view. In an address to the members, Golitsyn deplored "the indifference of the best landowners who could enrich the society with their advice, observations and experiments. Instead, their agricultural experience remains unknown and their silence deprives the society and all landowners of useful observations."[119] Since the Free Economic Society, in particular, was called on to assist the government in the study of a variety of problems and in implementation of policy, a degree of subservience to monarch and state was unavoidable. As one historian notes, the Free Economic Society "could be circumspect, even obeisant, in its behavior. One of its goals was always to survive."[120] Because of the conditions in which Russian agricultural societies lived, it would be remarkable if they had been able to transform rural life.

However, the influence of Russian agricultural societies appears negligible only at first glance. Recently, historians in Russia have been rethinking the standard Soviet interpretations of the development of capitalism in Russia as well as seeking the successful blending of tradition and innovation in the past that might inform the present. In the judgment of the first Russian historian of the twenty-first century to investigate the problem of agricultural improvement and to challenge the pessimistic view of agricultural performance, Russian historiography has focused excessively on the negative results. The lack of large-scale results, argues Kozlov, should not detract from the achievements of those who strove to improve Russian agriculture or from evidence of "a slow but steady trend toward more rationalization of agriculture in the central non-black earth provinces . . . Agricultural improvements slowly but surely changed Russian agrarian life."[121] This change was in no small way due also to the efforts of the Moscow Agricultural Society, "the main center of the theory and practice of the rational agriculture movement of the pre-reform era" and the main promoter of "market-oriented thinking and profit maximization."[122] Binding their significance to performance or failing to place Russian agricultural societies in a broader context easily allows the historian to point to failure or to Russian exceptionalism. The institutional, economic, and geographic obstacles to agricultural improvement in Russia, as well as the mixed assessment of the performance of European agricultural societies, suggest that the historian must not seek the significance and meaning of Russians' early efforts at independent associations in performance alone. The significance of the Free Economic Society and, later, of the Moscow Agricultural Society, lies less in any particular product they did or did not, could or could not, deliver. To the members, to paraphrase Jurij Lotman, every action of an association was regarded as being significant and worthy of remembrance and embodying a higher meaning, even if the concrete results fell short of expectations.[123] The significance of the Free Economic Society and its offshoots lies in their contribution to three of the most important projects of the European Enlightenment—the application of science and the diffusion of useful knowledge, patriotic service to state and society, and the creation of the public sphere of civil society.

The founding of the Free Economic Society marked the beginning of the popularization of the scientific study of agriculture in Russia. The leaders of the two agricultural societies were patrons of science, and service to and promotion of science and the diffusion of science in Russia were their self-conscious missions. But implicit in the self-definition of members was not only the task of bringing science to Russian agriculture but also the endeavor of accomplishing the complementary task of elevating Russian agriculture to a science. Both societies funded applied research, the dissemination of knowledge, and the gathering of data. They disseminated Western ideas and improvements as well as cultivated relationships with foreign scientific and agricultural organizations by exchanging publications and by publishing accounts of the activities of foreign societies. They were "communities of knowledge" that diffused useful data and also created informal networks and patterns of communication and interaction for the exchange of information. Members assiduously cultivated the methods of science as well as built "bridges" between "knowledge and the human environment."[124] Although agricultural improvement took a backseat to the exploitation of serf labor on many estates, one historian has nevertheless credited the Free Economic Society with being the "midwife of Russian capitalism."[125]

In his *Catechism for Good Patriots* in 1790, Jean-Antoine Chaptal, a chemist and factory owner in revolutionary and Napoleonic France with influence in the Ministry of the Interior, wrote, "A *savant* finds his calling in the enlightenment of his country in matters agricultural and industrial."[126] At this starting point in the development of Russia's voluntary associations, a "patriotic society for the encouragement of agriculture and the economy" served not only state and monarch. Service to the fatherland was one of the driving forces behind the Free Economic Society and the Moscow Agricultural Society from the beginning. The members of the Free Economic Society "wished to contribute to economic growth and to cooperate with its dear fatherland." The society drew up a plan to study "a huge and vast [*neob"iatoe*] fatherland," an enterprise that "appealed to national pride" because it "fully satisfied the feeling of national self-awareness of the inexhaustible wealth of the Russian empire . . . Russia has everything [*Chego net v Rossii*]," including, apparently, scientific societies.[127] Like traditional forms of patriotic duty, this new form of service also brought glory and honor. In organizing and gathering information about the empire, for example, the members of the Free Economic Society, according to Khodnev, "burned with the desire to exalt the honor and glory of the society." Khodnev noted that "in the pursuits of science, the arts, and citizenship" the members "bound the laurels of victory together with the laurels of peaceful prosperity."[128] Thus a by-product of such service to monarch and nation was the creation of a new sense of identity, self-worth, and mission for the patriotic noble.

The Free Economic Society and the Moscow Agricultural Society directed their efforts at natural and productive resources, the study of improvements abroad, and the translation of foreign works. In their projects to disseminate useful knowledge and spread literacy, both agricultural societies invested considerable effort in Russia's human resources. All the while, the ultimate goal of improvement was the betterment of Russia: applying foreign improvements to Russia; making foreign works available to a Russian readership; collecting data on Russian agriculture, industry, and commerce; and facilitating contacts among landowners, government officials, and scientists. In the last decades of the eighteenth century, no Russian institution was as self-consciously focused on Russia as was the Free Economic Society.[129] In its mission to serve the nation, the Free Economic Society pointed in the direction of a new generation of societies, whose mission, as we shall see in the following chapter, was the study of the Russian people.

The appearance of the Free Economic Society marks the beginning of a process whereby a public sphere and associational life were sanctioned under autocracy. A pioneer on terrain undefended by the freedoms of speech, association, and assembly or by a government of law, the Free Economic Society was one of the few associations untouched by government repression in the wake of the French Revolution. In the late eighteenth and early nineteenth centuries, the impulse to associate stemmed from an increased acquaintance with the independent public initiative possible in Europe, the absence of which had been a perennial bane of Russian political culture. To be sure, public initiative under autocracy could not appear overnight. But as the proponents of associational life never tired of repeating, associations provided the framework for initiative, combined resources, unified otherwise dispersed efforts, and enabled the many to accomplish what the individual could not.[130] The association supported the public self-affirmation of the individual and thereby laid the foundations for the formation of a future civil society.

In associations, argues Mokyr, knowledge about the natural world became increasingly "non-proprietary, and scientific advances and discoveries were freely shared with the public at large."[131] The Free Economic Society and the Moscow Agricultural Society were public forums for a discussion of and dissemination of views on a wide range of scientific and economic matters. By becoming the first public forum for a discussion of and dissemination of views on economic policy, the Free Economic Society sowed the seeds of participatory public dialogue, civic consciousness, and citizenship.[132] This created a precedent, however tentative, to the representation of interests, a precedent that, as we shall see, was to be followed later by other groups denied citizenship. Legitimized public representation promoted a sense of self-respect and individual dignity. At the same time, the capacity to represent others carried with it the willingness to be judged by others, and not only by the government. "Whether our efforts should be rewarded," Prince Golitsyn addressed the members of the Moscow Agricultural Society in 1825, "whether the principles guiding the society to attain its goals will work, this is to be judged by our fellow compatriots."[133]

Born in the age of enlightened despotism, these principles continued even in the age of the "arch reactionary," Nicholas I.

CHAPTER THREE

The Quest for National Identity

The Russian Geographical Society

As early as the late eighteenth century, the mission of Free Economic Society was to serve and study the nation and empire. In the nineteenth century such a mission permeated many other Russian societies, including, as we have seen, the Moscow Agricultural Society. As is well known, educated Russians became obsessed with national identity and with Russia's place in Europe and in history. They explored the realm and "discovered" the life of the common people. The origins of this interest in nation and empire lie in the influence of European, especially German, ideas and in the policies of "official nationality" under Nicholas I. "Official nationality" had its counterpart in an "unofficial" nationality situated in the projects of the Academy of Sciences and Russian learned societies during the first half of the nineteenth century, most prominently in the Imperial Russian Geographical Society (RGO). By the middle of the century, Russian learned societies had not only begun to study imperial expansion and national identity but to create Russia's national heritage. This chapter will highlight the first steps in this process. After placing the study of national heritage in a European context, I will briefly discuss the early efforts of the Society of Russian History and Antiquities to study the Russian past. The rest of this chapter will focus on the Russian Geographical Society—its founding; disputes in the early years over organization and mission; and two divisions most concerned with the study of the empire's human resources, the Ethnographic Division and the Division of Statistics and Political Economy. These two divisions also demonstrate the ambivalent attitude of the authorities toward associational activity: while both received government sanction and support, the colloquiums sponsored by the Division of Statistics and Political Economy prompted close government scrutiny. We may thereby see the opportunities—as well as the limitations—of private initiative in imperial Russia and the Geographical Society's contribution to the development of Russian civil society.

Many historians have noted the "Victorian fascination with the past," a fascination that predated Queen Victoria and was not limited to Great Britain. Romanticism and historicism emanating from Germany provided philosophical justification for an emphasis on the cultivation of the self and the study of natural history, the "historicizing of the earth," in Roy Porter's felicitous phrase. The study of the history, customs, and ways of life of distinct and cohesive groups of people—"fast-disappearing ways of life," to use the formulaic phrase—spurred efforts not only to preserve the cultural patrimony, the burial mounds and ruins "hidden in plain sight," but also to collect and record customs and beliefs that still survived in the countryside. As Peter Paret put it, the "effort to put oneself in the place of people of another age . . . encouraged the search for the specific, the time-bound, and the unique."[1] As "the casual observations of the curious" shifted to the discipline of scholarship and science, new professional elites, civil servants, and scientists became stewards of the national heritage. Such patriotic endeavors required a wealthy, leisured elite, and if that was in short supply, the patronage of monarchs and government officials. Scientific collections and observations were stimulated by naval exploration in, as a study of the naturalist Joseph Banks puts it, "an area where the goals of empire and the enlightenment could meet in happy accord."[2] The new obsession with the national heritage was not simply nostalgia for an idealized rural past or a reaction against modern technology and utilitarianism. Improvements in communication and literacy and the beginnings of leisure travel increased the amount of data on natural history and geography available to the public while also accelerating the perceived pace of change. As John Stuart Mill observed, "the idea of comparing one's own age with the past could only become popular at a time when everyone had become conscious of living in a changing world." Studying the past reflected an acceptance of progress and gave continuity to a changing present. The antiquarians, according to Philippa Levine, "were not the tail end of a Romantic movement fleeing from utilitarianism but the proud expression of the predominantly acquisitive culture in which they flourished. Their possessions—symbolized by artifacts and manuscripts which graced the showcases of their museums—were knowledge and the nation's memory."[3]

The vehicle that mobilized the study of natural history and the stewardship of the national patrimony was the voluntary association. The Victorian-era antiquarian societies, the societies of naturalists, and geographical societies "cultivated the capacities of curiosity [and] acquisitiveness" as well as awe of nature and of the abundance of nature.[4] The geographical societies came about due to naval exploration and imperial expansion. The founding of the antiquarian and naturalist societies, in contrast, is often depicted as an act of spontaneous generation, as if by nature itself—a gradual germination from an informal group of persons linked by fellowship to a formal organization. Like the study of agriculture, the study of natural history, geography, history, and archaeology, was conducive to a cooperative effort. Moreover, the practice of collecting and "the performance of science" were gendered: collectors and naturalists, almost exclusively men, demonstrated mastery over knowledge as well as social prestige for their "display of taste, distinction, and discernment."[5] Societies brought together and coordinated the observations, classifications, and curiosity of otherwise disparate explorers, amateurs, travelers, and civil servants, thereby building up a repository of useful knowledge. Scientists of relatively new disciplines, such as archaeology, anthropology, and ethnography, capitalized on and promoted this public interest as a way to overcome resistance to their inclusion in the curriculum at universities. Such systematized, codified, cataloged, and disseminated knowledge facilitated a process—the experience of scientific inquiry, "learning by doing"—and contributed to a product.[6] As we have seen, not only did agricultural societies collect plants and run experimental farms; they also studied local customs and peoples. Geographical associations mapped the realm, and many societies borrowed ends and means from the study of the natural world—the accumulation of positive knowledge by means of expeditions. Natural history societies founded botanical gardens, zoological parks, mineral collections, and laboratories. Historical, antiquarian, and archaeological societies linked present and past by discovering, preserving, and publishing documents and records, studying genealogies, describing prominent churches and buildings, and preserving ruins. All societies published their findings, maintained libraries, and initiated contacts with other societies.[7]

Because the search for national identity and the study of the realm was an act of pride and patriotism, the professed goals of associations and states were one and the same. Monarchs founded societies, museums, and even branches of government—the Royal Society in England, the Kunstkammer of Denmark, and the Antiquaries College in Sweden, for example—to assemble natural historical artifacts and curiosities, often a by-product of naval expeditions, and to help implement royal policy. Such artifacts, as one historian has said, "validated imperial expansion and national cohesion."[8] Societies, even seemingly apolitical, neutral antiquarian societies, needed state permission to exist and to pursue their activities. Many associations had to rely on governments for membership, for financial subsidies, and for facilitated contact with local officials, and everywhere in Europe there was a close relationship between geographical societies and governments. According to Susan A. Crane, "Associations of northern and central Germany relied on the Prussian government for more than an annual donation; they existed only insofar as they could prove to officials that they had no political agendas and were organizations for 'purely scholarly purposes.'"[9]

The Society of Russian History and Antiquities

As many historians have noted, the first few decades of the nineteenth century witnessed under the stewardship of prominent Russians in and out of government a budding interest in the origins and distinguishing features of the Russian nation and empire.[10] The origin of the study of this national heritage is commonly credited to a circle led by Count Nikolai Petrovich Rumiantsev and labeled "the nest of Russian Slavistics." After retirement from a stellar career that included a tour as foreign minister (1808–1814), Rumiantsev launched a second career as a passionate collector and publisher of old Slavic and Russian manuscripts and as a patron of Slavic studies. Members of Rumiantsev's circle included scholar and Metropolitan of Kiev Evgenii (Evgenii Bolkhovitinov), author of numerous histories and descriptions of monasteries, bishoprics, and localities; the German-born philologist, Aleksandr Khristoforovich Vostokov (né Ostenek); the philologist, archaeographer, and collector of rare manuscripts Konstantin Fedorovich Kalaidovich; P. I. Keppen; and P. M. Stroev. Rumiantsev's collection of rare books and manuscripts became the basis of the museum that bore his name. The historian and literary critic Aleksandr Pypin suggests that Rumiantsev was a rather paradoxical promoter of the study of Russian antiquities and national "self-awareness," in that he was an archetypal westernized nobleman: educated in France, he was a Francophile and even an admirer of Napoleon, himself an occasional collector of antiquities.[11] However, the paradox is more symbolic than substantive. It was precisely a westernized nobleman whose expression of Russian identity would have been framed in the European fascination with antiquities, collecting, and the national heritage.

Also familiar with European practices were civil servants such as Petr Ivanovich Keppen, a key figure in the development and promotion of Slavic studies in Russia. The son of a physician brought to Russia from Germany by Catherine II, Keppen attended the University of Khar'kov. There he heard lectures on Russian history, ethnography, and statistics by Professor G. P. Uspenskii. Influenced by Evgenii (Bolkhovitinov), Uspenskii believed that "it is more important for each nation to know the history and modern condition of its fatherland than that of foreign countries. To not know the features that distinguish one's own from other lands is to be a foreigner at home."[12] After his graduation in 1814, Keppen worked in the postal department in St. Petersburg. He was one of the founders of the Free Society of Friends of Russian Literature in 1811 and a member of Rumiantsev's circle. In his travels to the Austrian empire, Keppen studied archaeology, history, literature, and ethnography; visited various Slavic lands; and in Vienna and Prague met scholars such as Iosif Dobrovsky, the doyen of the budding Slavic movement, who were studying Slavic antiquities and national culture. Upon his return to Russia, Keppen entered government service under the conservative advocate of true Russian education, Admiral Aleksandr Semenovich Shishkov, then minister of education. Once in government service, Keppen suggested that Russian universities teach Slavic languages. In 1825 Keppen began publishing *Bibliograficheskii listok* [*Bibliographical Newsletter*], which contained information about Slavic antiquities and the scholarly activities of contemporary Slavicists.[13]

When antiquarianism and the desire to study the natural history of the locality spread from Europe to Russia, the "local" became "Russia"—the boundless *(neob"iataia),* understudied Russia—and the relationship between Russia and Europe approximated that between the "local" in France and Britain and metropolitan Paris and London. The interest in Russian national heritage first received institutional expression as early as 1804, when the Society of Russian History and Antiquities (known by its Russian initials as OIDR) was founded at Moscow University. The goal of the society was to collect, edit, and publish with commentaries old Russian documents, such as princely charters and Yaroslav's *Russkaia pravda,* as well as to collect manuscripts, coins, and other artifacts of the past. During the first decades of the society, its leaders were amateur antiquarians: retired major P. P. Beketov, professor of mineralogy and estate management A. A. Prokopovich-Antonskii, and retired major general A. A. Pisarev. Their interests lay more in numismatics, archaeology, and iconography than in what we would today call history. Irregular publications, irregular financial support, apathy, and lack of direction made the achievements of the society in its first decades modest; in 1810 it was even shut down temporarily by Alexander I for its inactivity.[14]

Nevertheless, Russia's first antiquarian society made an important contribution to the process by which the country's national heritage was created—the concept of patriotic service to the nation by means of the collective effort of private individuals and national expeditions. In an address in 1811, P. P. Beketov, the society's second president, pronounced that someday the readers of its publications would say, "They loved their fatherland and worked for its welfare and glory." The society was also important in the origin of Slavic studies: "Already in the modest activity of the Moscow Society of History and Antiquities . . . we see the vital scholarly interest in Slavic studies [*slavianstvo*] and in its past."[15]

The collective efforts of private individuals and national expeditions were boldly argued in a talk by the famous historian and member of the Rumiantsev circle Pavel M. Stroev at a members' meeting of OIDR on 14 June 1823. Stroev presented what was everywhere becoming a formulaic justification for voluntary societies: collective efforts could accomplish far more than the efforts of single individuals, however well intentioned and executed. Learned societies were like trading companies *(obshchestva torgovye)* in that they pooled resources and knowledge—that is, in Stroev's strikingly modern-sounding words, intellectual capital *(kapitaly uma)*—in order to accomplish great goals. And, indeed, Stroev had goals in mind that were far more ambitious than the publication of a few primary chronicles. Stroev claimed that owing to the work of the writer Nicholas Karamzin and the manuscript-collection efforts of Count Rumiantsev, interest in history was greater than when the society was founded. If OIDR limited its mission to the publication of a few primary chronicles, Stroev argued, this would limit it to a "decorative" existence. Instead, the society ought to cast its net much more broadly and "construct [*soorudit'*] the historical record [*pamiatnik*] worthy of our life." Gathering the national heritage ought to be a national endeavor:

> Let all of Russia become one big open library. We should not define our work in terms of a few hundred well-known manuscripts but in terms of an infinite number: in the vaults of monasteries and cathedrals . . . in archives . . . in cellars and warehouses . . . scattered over a vast territory from the White Sea to the Ukrainian steppes and from Lithuania to the Urals.[16]

Realizing that the mission to "discover Russian history" *(privesti v izvestnost' Rossiiskuiu istoriiu)* would take the society far beyond a few Moscow collections, Stroev proposed to launch three expeditions, each of which was to be followed by reports, evaluations, catalogs and inventories. Stroev thus injected features of the scientific method into the previous randomness *(sluchainost')* of collecting the historical record. Stroev's bold and sweeping plan to expand the mission of OIDR exceeded the society's financial and professional capabilities and was not approved by the members. It was not until the 1840s that OIDR, under the leadership of one of Russia's first Slavicists, O. M. Bodianskii, began to pursue historical subjects more systematically. Although not completely realized by OIDR, this concept of patriotic service to the nation left a legacy more effectively imitated by many other organizations. The project was taken up six years later by the Academy of Sciences, when Stroev himself led the first Achaeographic Expedition. And, one generation later, two new societies, the Archaeological Society and the Russian Geographical Society, returned to the idea of expeditions as part of a more vigorous effort to explore the empire and create its national heritage.[17]

The Origins of the Russian Geographical Society

The broadening scholarly and public interest in the Russian nation and empire through study in a variety of disciplines—history, literature and linguistics, geography, ethnology, and natural history—as well as government support for science under Nicholas I and Uvarov came together in the 1840s with the founding of the Imperial Russian Geographical Society. Still located in St. Petersburg, the Geographical Society is one of the oldest continually existing societies in the world. During the last years of the reign of Nicholas I, the Geographical Society was the most active private organization of the empire. It brought together scientists, government officials, explorers, and intellectuals to study social and economic questions. It is one of the few Russian societies that has been extensively studied, both before and after the Revolution. The society's "progressive role" in the formation of Russian thought and science was viewed favorably by Soviet scholars, who were attracted to its interest in the Russian nation and its harboring of youthful radicals in the 1840s and 1850s. Moreover, to Soviet scholars the Geographical Society was the institutional expression of the social type of the Russian explorer. Not a conqueror, not a freebooter (nor, of course, in service to conquerors and freebooters), not an exploiter of weaker peoples for the sake of gathering data, the Russian explorer was a *prosvetitel'*, bringing the light of knowledge and truth to mankind.[18]

Fedor Petrovich Litke (1797–1882) and Karl Ernst von Baer (1792–1876) represent two types of *prosvetitel'*. Litke (see figure 3.1) was an explorer-*prosvetitel'* whose scholarly and administrative career spanned half a century of service to three sovereigns. Litke's Baltic German family was

Figure 3.1 Admiral F. P. Litke, explorer and first vice president of the Russian Geographical Society. (P. P. Semenov, *Istoriia poluvekovoi deiatel'nosti Imperatorskogo Russkogo geograficheskogo obshchestva, 1845–1895*. St. Petersburg, 1896, vol. 1.)

so Russianized that he was a native speaker of Russian and learned German only at school. In the 1820s and 1830s, Litke took part in naval expeditions of the Arctic, White Sea, and Kamchatka regions. In 1832 he became tutor to Grand Duke Konstantin Nikolaevich and observed experiments in wireless telegraphy. Later in his career Litke was appointed vice admiral in 1843 and became a member of the State Council in 1855; he received the title of count in 1866; and in the 1860s and 1870s he became president of the Academy of Sciences. But the position he was most proud of was his appointment in 1845 as the first vice president of the Russian Geographical Society, that organization's highest executive officer.[19] One of "Uvarov's scientists," the naturalist and polymath Baer (see figure 3.2) was a scientist-*prosvetitel'*. The founder of comparative embryology, who began his career in Koenigsberg, Baer understood geography broadly: "The earth reveals not only the distribution of organisms but also the fate of peoples." He was an advocate of science: "Natural history must become a subject of general education and not remain valuable only to the few . . . The study of natural history is the key to the knowing of other sciences of nature." While in Koenigsberg, Baer took an active part in the German Society, the Physics-Mathematics Society, and the Medical Society. Eventually, his broad scientific interests and experience in association turned him into a leader in a community of men dedicated to the study of Russia's natural resources.[20]

The details of the origins of the Geographical Society have been told in many, and slightly differing, published accounts and need detain us only briefly. According to longtime secretary P. P. Semenov, "the founding of the Society quite fortuitously came in the 1840s, when Russian national feelings had started to awaken among Russian young people, when, in harmony with signs from above, progressive young people began to work not only on the rebirth of the Russian ethnic group but also on the liberation of the Russian people from servitude, and when the primary task of each and all was thought to be the study of the native land and its people."[21] While Uvarov was president, the Academy of Sciences sponsored seventy expeditions to study the Russian empire's geography and natural history. As early as 1825, Baer wrote to Litke of his plan for a natural historical study of the Arctic coast. In 1843 Baer joined a group of statisticians and explorers to discuss economics and statistics; this group was led by Keppen and included N. A. Miliutin, A. P. Zablotskii-Desiatovskii, and N. I. Nadezhdin. Baer also gathered acquaintances at his home for discussions of geography and natural history.[22] In his history of the Geographical Society, Semenov identified distinct groups of what in the British or American context might be called gentlemen scholars and what in Russia may be called government scholars, which converged to share a common interest in geography. As was the case of the Royal Geographical Society, founded in 1831—whose leaders were naval officers, government officials, and aristocrats and whose patron was King William IV—explorers, navy men, and general staff officers were prominent founders of the Russian Geographical Society: Litke, I. F. Kruzenshtern, Baron F. P. Vrangel', P. I. Rikord, F. F. Berg, M. P. Vronchenko, and M. N. Murav'ev. They were joined by the "Uvarov" academics Baer, Friedrich Georg Wilhelm Struve, G. P. Helmerson,

Figure 3.2 K. E. Baer, naturalist and one of the founders of the Russian Geographical Society. (B. E. Raikov, *Karl Ber, ego zhizn' i trudy* [Moscow, 1961], opposite p. 320.)

and Keppen and the independent scholars (that is, those from "society" and of Russian ethnicity, as Semenov noted) K. I. Arsen'ev, A. I. Levshin, P. A. Chikhachev, and V. I. Dal'.[23] At one of Baer's gatherings in the winter of 1843–1844, Litke and Arsen'ev suggested organizing a geographical society "to gather and guide the best young people of Russia for a broad study of the native land." One year later, a banquet at the Academy of Sciences honoring A. F. Middendorf, a zoologist at Kiev University who had just returned from a highly publicized expedition to the Amur region, demonstrated that the thirst for geographical knowledge was not limited to the Baer "circles" but was widespread in the St. Petersburg naval, academic, and civil service communities. At the suggestion of Vladimir Dal', who was the personal secretary to L. A. Perovskii, the minister of internal affairs, in whose domain resided the field of government statistics, Litke,

Baer, and Vrangel' decided in the spring of 1845 to approach that ministry with their project. Later that year they drew up bylaws that were quickly approved by Perovskii and by Nicholas I.[24]

In a memorandum to Perovskii dated 1 May 1845, Litke, the "patron" of the society, made the case for a national geographical society. Demonstrating an awareness of institutional turf, disciplinary changes, and international prestige, Litke anticipated one major objection, no doubt expressed verbally in one of the many St. Petersburg gatherings. Several government departments, including the Topographic Depot and the Oceanographic Department as well as the Academy of Sciences, already conducted research in physical geography. Because the presence of another organization would lead to competition and disperse scarce human and financial resources, the government was loath to sanction the existence of an allegedly superfluous private society. Although he conceded that other bodies in Russia already conducted geographical research, Litke argued that that was not their exclusive function; moreover, government research was not always appropriate for, let alone accessible to, scholarship. Litke pointed out that other enlightened countries had geographical societies but, as yet, Russia did not. Such a national geographical society could consolidate, coordinate, and disseminate the great amount of private and seemingly random collection of geographical information, that is, make geography a science. Otherwise, Litke feared, potentially valuable geographical knowledge would otherwise be lost.[25]

Lost? Mountains and oceans lost? Litke's arguments signify changing definitions of the nature and function of geography occurring throughout Europe. By the time the Russian Geographical Society was born, the modern science of geography had broken away from the narrow boundaries of physical geography. In the early nineteenth century the German geographer Karl Ritter, whose work was widely known in the Russian scholarly community, broadened the concept of geography to include the study of the land *(Erdkunde, zemlevedenie)* and its inhabitants, as well as the more traditional study of physical features. Thus, geography began to include anthropology, archaeology, ethnology, literature and linguistics, folklore, statistics, and political economy. Litke argued that geography included natural history, and as a new science, it was not covered thoroughly by the established disciplines in the Academy of Sciences. It was not Russia's lakes Litke feared losing but its legends. This point must be kept in mind when we discuss the manifestations of "nationalism" in the Geographical Society below.

Litke repeated the case for establishing the society in an address to its inaugural meeting in October 1845. The geographical societies of Europe placed the study of their own country in second place behind the study of general, or world, geography. This posed a dilemma to the new geographical society of Russia. Due to Russia's size, the variety of geographical features and human populations, the inaccessibility of much of the country, and the fact that Russia was an understudied region of the world, the study of national geography took on greater importance. Because undertaking a thorough study of both world and national geography would exhaust the resources of even the largest geographical society, the purpose of the Russian Geographical Society was the study of Russia. From this followed a very public agenda. Not only would the geographical society disseminate information at home and abroad and thereby inform the world about Russia. It would also have an even more significant educational and patriotic mission: to spread in Russia itself a taste and a love of geography, ethnography, and statistics, to "recruit the best forces of the land to work for the benefit and glory of our precious Fatherland."[26] As the author of a jubilee history of the first twenty-five years of the society in 1871 put it, the Russian Geographical Society promoted the study of the native land *(otechestvovedenie)*.[27] The founding of the Geographical Society marked the beginning of the popularization of what today might be called Russian area studies.

Before turning to a discussion of the goals, leadership, and internal organization of the Geographical Society, one last glance at its founding may be suggestive. The Soviet historians T. A. Lukina and N. G. Sukhova unearthed correspondence between Litke, Baron Vrangel', and Baer in the years immediately preceding and following the opening of the society. The trope of birth, as well as the precariousness of pregnancy, birth, and infancy, occurs frequently. In May 1845 Baer, the founder of comparative embryology at the beginning of his career, wrote to Litke, "It wouldn't be a bad idea if all the founders of the society—you, Vrangel' and myself—could talk a bit more about the embryo." In order to bring in Struve, Baer wrote, "Admiral Litke has requested me to ask whether, if you are in town today, you would drop by Litke's in the evening in order to participate, as a midwife, in the birth of the geographical society."[28] Transgressing species boundaries, Baer used the metaphor of birth in an ironic way. In the spring of 1845 he learned of Dal's suggestion to make the seventeen-year-old Grand Duke Konstantin Nikolaevich president, an honorary office, of the new society. Somewhat surprised, and clearly amused at this no doubt shrewd suggestion, Baer wrote to Litke, "For this to work, the brood hen must have wide and warm wings to incubate the egg, and she must bring the embryo the kind of big dowry they give to princesses." (Baer was right: the Geographical Society received an annual government subsidy of ten thousand rubles, a "dowry" far bigger than that of any other Russian scientific society of the day.) Later, Baer recalled the founding of the society in a letter to Litke: "The baby appeared and although he had three fathers, this, however, was not to his advantage."[29]

The precariousness of childbirth and infancy was also on the mind of the founders. Soon after the society opened, Baer and Litke had to leave St. Petersburg on business simultaneously. Baer wrote to the new vice president, "I am very sorry . . . that you had to leave your baby—the Geographical Society—an orphan." Abroad on a mission with the grand duke and unable to attend the meeting of 9 April 1846, Litke heard of dissension and disorder. Litke wrote Vrangel', "We will be sorry if our baby (as we may call the Geographical Society) suffocates in the fumes of discord."[30] Concerned about unity within the organization as well as order and decorum at its meetings, Litke added, "If the habit of argument takes root the way it did at that meeting, then the development of science will surely be smothered and in its place, parties will be born." When he approved the temporary bylaws of the society, Minister Perovskii of Internal Affairs expressed this very concern to Litke. Litke cautioned, "We must take measures to avoid a hubbub at the May meeting, and by hubbub I mean the kind of debates that have no place at a general meeting."[31]

The gendered language in this correspondence is not accidental. The maternal instinct to protect an infant suggests a position of weakness and subordination in the face of forces over which the mother has no control. As in the state of nature, the infant is in danger not only from its own weaknesses but also from predators, who are just as likely to be within the family as without. The maternal language also suggests domesticity, nurture, the creation of life—a life that is in need of strong (male) protectors. Finally, it is important to note what this language is *not:* the masculine language of the military, expeditions commissioned by the government, exploration, and subjugation. Recently, gender historians have argued that new definitions of masculinity—sometimes labeled bourgeois masculinity—tried to situate manly behavior in the voluntary associations of civil society. In France, for example, bourgeois men, made insecure by an exclusionary state, a vicissitudinous market, and an increasingly feminized home, established dominance in the public sphere. This process worked somewhat differently in Russia: efforts to participate in the public sphere began to redefine masculinity, but as the metaphors above suggest, this new identity was much more precarious than in Europe.[32]

The founding of the Russian Geographical Society began the popularization of geography in Russia. The society funded applied research, disseminated knowledge, gathered data, and facilitated contacts among explorers, government officials, and scientists, all in an effort to popularize the study of the people and places of the empire. The founders of the Geographical Society were patrons of science, and service to and promotion of science and the diffusion of science in Russia were their self-conscious missions.

Not only was the task of bringing science to Russian geography implicit in the self-definition of members; they also set out to elevate Russian geography, in its broadest usage, to a science.

Like all of Russia's learned societies, the Geographical Society issued voluminous publications. The society was granted the right to request privileges from the sovereign, one of which, free postal service, it received in 1845. The first volume of the society's *Zapiski* [*Notes*] came out in 1846. But unlike the scholarly journals of many of Russia's learned societies of the day, the *Zapiski* were published in Russian. The first issue quickly sold out and had to be reprinted three years later. Not wanting to limit itself to scholarly publications and at the same time wanting to popularize the study of geography, the Geographical Society in 1848 began publishing the popular *Handbook for the Amateur Geographer (Karmannaia knizhka dlia liubitelei zemlevedeniia),* which sold out its first print run of twelve hundred copies. The society soon added the *Newsletter (Geograficheskie izvestiia),* which contained shorter items and announcements. According to Semenov, Baer's articles about anthropology and ethnography enchanted readers and recruited many to the study of ethnography.[33]

The Politics of the Russian Geographical Society

No sooner was the baby born, as Baer might have put it, than family squabbles rocked the infant's cradle. Temporary bylaws, modeled after those of the Royal Geographical Society in London and in force for four years, defined the new Russian society's organizational structure and mission. But questions of membership, the mission statement, and internal governance divided the society's founding members. In addition, participants and historians have woven into the society's decisions what we might call today "identity politics," which have been explained by the seemingly rapid change in the composition of the Geographical Society and by the conflict between the "Russian party" and the "Germans," a conflict that paralleled a similar divide in the German-dominated Academy of Sciences.[34] The focus of much of the disagreement was the draft of permanent bylaws by a special commission appointed for that purpose on 3 December 1847 and chaired by Litke and sent to all members for comment. Dmitrii Miliutin, joined by Nikolai Miliutin and V. S. Poroshin, a statistician and professor of political economy at the University of St. Petersburg, submitted their opinions on a number of matters in a separate report. The nature of these disagreements as well as the arguments presented draw a revealing picture of the society's first few years and of the views of its leaders. The arguments tell us much about institutional politics, imperial awareness, and changing intellectual and scholarly agendas. These issues are important because a nongovernmental organization was working out its own its goals, self-definition, and the principles and procedures by which it would conduct its business. In the absence of a bureaucratic chain of command or orders from a minister, notable at court, or the tsar himself, the Russian Geographical Society had to sort out these things by deliberation. Participants in the debate represented themselves and certain views of the ends and means of the new organization. This is certainly not to say that reasoned opinion drove out passion and patronage. But it was significant that in autocratic Russia, the disagreements proceeded without heavy-handed efforts of the government to dictate what goals were appropriate for the society, how it should choose its members, and how it should govern itself.

To begin with, the membership of the society changed markedly in the first year of its existence. For some, of course, membership in this, as in other high-profile private associations everywhere, was an honorific. According to the statistician K. S. Veselovskii, "for anyone who considered himself an educated person, whether or not he was interested in geography, it was all but obligatory to have the title 'member of the Geographical Society.'"[35] But patriotic service to the cause of the study of Russia was also taken very seriously. At the suggestion of Admiral Rikord and V. I. Dal', Litke appointed A. V. Golovnin, the twenty-four-year-old son of Admiral Golovnin, Rikord's former superior, to be the society's secretary. Golovnin used the secretariat and his connections in the Ministry of Internal Affairs to recruit progressive officials and intellectuals—in Dmitrii Miliutin's words, "to enliven the Society and to encourage support for it among the Russian public."[36] In the Russian manner, the secretariat proved to be a powerful tool for changing the membership and even initiating policy changes. In a separate report of the bylaws commission, Dmitrii Miliutin, Nikolai Miliutin, and V. S. Poroshin urged that the society draw more members into its activities in order to "benefit science." From 51 members by the end of 1845, the society grew to 510 in 1850. Soon the society's membership included A. K. Girs, I. P. Arapetov, Iu. A. Gagemeister, A. N. Popov, M. Kh. Reitern, and A. P. Zablotskii-Desiatovskii, all future members of the Editing Commission under Alexander II, as well as the westerner jurist, historian, and publicist K. D. Kavelin and the political economist Vladimir Miliutin. The Miliutin brothers were the center of a circle that included Arapetov, Zablotskii-Desiatovskii, and Count Ivan P. Tolstoi. This circle, later called the "Russian party," was responsible for a recalibration of the Geographical Society's mission. Despite the importance Litke attached to the study of Russian geography, the draft of the permanent bylaws stated that the chief activity of the Russian

Geographical Society was the study of general, or world, geography. However, many members objected to the new draft, and in a revision suggested by the board that received little opposition, the permanent bylaws privileged the study of Russian geography.[37]

In the absence of command from above, how the society should manage its own affairs was another divisive issue. In the debate over the drafting of permanent bylaws, the majority of members supported several changes in organization and internal governance that reflected judgments about the distribution of power within the society—the composition of the board and the election of officers. According to the temporary bylaws, a board *(sovet)* chaired, in name only as it turned out, by Grand Duke Konstantin Nikolaevich regulated the overall activity of the society and acted as the patron of geography in Russia and an intermediary between the society and the government. The board's members were elected at the general members' meeting.[38] In the discussion of the permanent bylaws, some members wanted the board to acquire the right to appoint its own new members. However, as D. A. Miliutin recalled it, the board, dominated by the same scientists who had founded the society, "regarded the rest of the Society as a public, there to contribute money and attend general meetings." The younger generation sought to create a less hierarchical organization by subordinating the board to the authority of the general meeting and by shifting the power to elect new board members to the general meeting. In this view, the board would be no more than an administrative organ to carry out decisions made at general meetings or by the society's divisions. Despite the fact that Nikolai Miliutin "brought an element of passion" into the debate, the Miliutin "opposition" (the Miliutin brothers, joined by Zablotskii-Desiatovskii and Poroshin), as it was called, was not entirely successful. In a compromise, it was decided that new members of the board would be chosen at a general meeting from a slate of two candidates nominated by the board. However, the Miliutins were able to exact a provision that the general meeting had the right to nominate additional candidates from the floor (see figure 3.3).[39]

The Miliutin opposition fared better on a second issue of internal governance—the election of the vice president and secretary. The president being a figurehead, the real director of the society was the vice president, who appointed a secretary to carry out the day-to-day administrative affairs of the society. The temporary bylaws stipulated election by the general meeting from a slate of three nominees presented by the board. Litke and several other charter members wanted to change this so that the board alone would elect the vice president and secretary. To Litke and many other charter members, "unrestrained elections," that is, elections by the members' meeting and not by the board, would be "harmful at present and dangerous in the future." It posed the threat that "the choice might be a person not known or

Figure 3.3 A meeting of RGO in its headquarters in St. Petersburg. (*Niva*, no. 16 [1890]: 433; courtesy of the Library of Congress.)

not trusted by the government. While the board could propose candidates in good faith, no one would be responsible for elections at the general meeting, conducted and sometimes even prepared in obscurity."[40] By a narrow majority, the society voted to elect the vice president and secretary in the same way that the members of the board were elected, that is, at a general meeting from a slate of two candidates nominated by the board. As one reviewer of Semenov's jubilee history noted, a half century later, Litke's fear was uncalled for: "It is typical that our scientists and in general all organizers of useful institutions do not trust the rest of the society and doubt that others hold as dear those intellectual interests that excite them. Civil society had no voice and therefore was an enigma; uniting in groups for common tasks was difficult and poorly developed. Therefore, the mistrust of the charter members in the regular members [*k masse*] while not excusable was at least understandable, *especially in those long ago times.*"[41] The issue of elections illustrates not only generational issues but also concerns about decorum, connections, and patronage that were important in the early years of a private association. As we will see, over time the leaders of Russian societies came less and less from an elite of notables close to the government or the court.

A final matter of internal governance was the procedure for choosing the heads of the four divisions. The four original divisions were World Geography, Russian Geography, Statistics, and Ethnography. (One immediate organizational consequence of the focus on Russian geography was a shake-up in the original divisional structure. The Division of World Geography was disbanded, and the Division of Russian Geography was split into the Physical and Mathematical divisions.) In these autonomous divisions was situated the society's scholarly work and the mentoring of young persons on the road to a scientific career. Such a role was arguably more significant in Russia than in other countries, where geographical societies could count on more widespread individual initiative in research and scientific expeditions. In his jubilee history, Semenov describes the role of the autonomous divisions:

> With the free entry of anyone interested in the successes of Russian geography, the divisions were turned into the kind of laboratories where ideas are exchanged, where the initiative for public enterprises to advance science are inspired, where research strategies are discussed, where completed work is evaluated and prizes are awarded, and where the results of private investigations are assembled and published.[42]

In addition, within a few years, the society opened chapters in Tiflis (the Caucasus chapter, 1850), Irkutsk (the East Siberian chapter, 1851), and in

Vilno (the northwest chapter, 1851). The chapters became a meeting point for the metropolitan and provincial intelligentsia not only to further scientific inquiry, but also to spread an interest in the society's activities and to draw in a provincial public:

> By gathering and uniting provincial intellects, the chapters of the Geographical Society serve as a shelter for people who have been seeking in intellectual occupations a relief from provincial boredom and the false authority that reigns in the salons of Petersburg idlers. The provincial chapters encourage the modest amateurs by creating for them an attractive life compared to the deathly monotony of life around them.[43]

But should the heads of the divisions be appointed by the board or elected by the general members' meeting? If the Miliutin "opposition" had been a consistent force for democratization, as it has sometimes been portrayed, one might expect that it would have favored the latter. In fact, it favored, and eventually won, a third method: election of the division heads by the members of their respective divisions. Thus democratization within an even smaller unit combined with a desire to protect expert authority to create complete divisional autonomy within the Geographical Society. Society members were free to join the division of their choice and within those divisions to hold their own meetings, to determine their own agenda, to elect their head, to appoint commissions, and to publish their own papers.[44] This divisional autonomy was to be a lasting feature of Russian voluntary associations. The learned societies studied in this book were all "big tent" organizations, housing a variety of members and scientific agendas. In the Russian Geographical Society, the explorers and naval officers could organize their expeditions while, as the following two sections will show, members with other agendas could flourish on their own. A big tent led by notables in society and government and patronized by the imperial family sheltered activities that might have been more problematic, from the point of view of the authorities, on their own.

Unlike serving on governing boards, writing mission statements, and voting in elections, mapmaking is part of the geographer's trade. Given that cartography is an important means by which states and publics understand national identity and assert imperial control, this, too, became entwined with identity politics. In the auditorium of the society hung an English-made map on which all of European Russia, including St. Petersburg and Moscow, was shaded gray and marked *Asia*. "England has cleverly driven us from Europe," a report of the Third Section, the political police created by Nicholas I, laconically noted. European maps such as this offended Russian self-definition as a nation and as an imperial power alongside its European neighbors. Thus, when Litke commissioned a map of central Asia from mapmakers in Munich rather than Russian mapmakers, it not only reminded Russian patriots of British efforts to keep Russia out of central Asia but also appeared to be an injudicious unilateral act on the part of the vice president without consultation of the membership. The more the empire spread and the more Russia expanded in Asia, the more European Russia became, or believed it was becoming.[45]

The election of officers in 1850 reflected many of the disagreements of the previous years. To cap the many changes in organization and internal governance, the divisions elected four new division heads, and young Russians were elected to eleven of seventeen positions on the editorial board of *Zapiski,* the society's most important research organ. According to Semenov, at the very first elections the Miliutin "opposition" "tried to replace the ubiquitous non-Russian names with more popular Russian ones," and only four (Struve, Berg, Baron E. K. Meyendorf, A. K. Girs) of the society's sixteen-member board had non-Russian names. Finally, in the important election for vice president, Litke was defeated by one vote in a "palace coup" by M. N. Murav'ev, former governor and former head of the Office of Land Surveys. According to a report of the Third Section, most surely based on the views of an informer within the Geographical Society, Litke, "as an honest and noble man" noted for his "feats as an explorer and scholar," was regarded as more worthy than Murav'ev to hold the office of vice president. Yet Litke was thought to prefer foreigners. Murav'ev, one of several notables who had recently joined the "opposition" within the society, allegedly manifested more "Russian spirit."[46]

The argument of the "young progressives" in the debates on the bylaws—that the Russian Geographical Society should be more "Russian" in its membership and leadership—struck a responsive chord within the society. Indeed, many of the new Russian members recruited by Golovnin did not see eye to eye with the scientific establishment that controlled the Geographical Society at the outset. Charter members such as Litke, Baer, Struve, Keppen, and Vrangel' were "Uvarov" scientists of Baltic German origin, at the peak of their careers, and members of the Academy of Sciences. They were explorers and naval officers who made their reputations by "blockbuster" explorations of faraway coasts. The new members, grouped around the Miliutin brothers, were less interested in far-off expeditions and felt that the Baltic Germans did not express enough sympathy with, as Semenov put it, "their pet national projects." Soviet historians, such as Litke's biographer, have also emphasized that "the Miliutin party of ultra patriots" believed that the geographical establishment was insufficiently patriotic and only weakly defended the national agenda within Russian geography.[47]

However, the role of ethnicity or national allegiances of the society's leaders in institutional politics can be exaggerated. The Baltic German charter members had no lack of patriotism. Even Semenov later wrote, "This entire generation of renowned scientists, who raised the banner of Russian science despite their German names and a bit of cliquishness [*zamknutyi partikuliarizm svoego kruzhka*], was truly loyal to Russia."[48] E. M. Murzaev, a post-Soviet authority on the organization, argues that many founding members from the Baltic provinces were second, third, or even fourth generation Russian born. They wrote in German in order to spread knowledge of Russia among the world scientific community:

> They dedicated their lives to the development of Russia's economy, culture and science. If so, then it is doubtful that there was a serious 'struggle against a German group' . . . One can hardly charge Baer, Kruzenshtern, Keppen, Litke, and Struve with anti-Russian attitudes and actions. They worked for the glory of Russia and actively promoted the establishment of our science.[49]

Litke's own account of his defeat in 1850 omits direct references to the issue of Russian national identity. Litke was more concerned about the viability of the organization; he viewed the Russian Geographical Society much as a captain would a ship. He wanted to steer it on a safe course and prevent unforeseen events. He was skeptical of the younger generation and perhaps had a better sense of the precariousness of the society's existence. He worried that internal bickering and a lack of decorum might bring about government interference.[50] Indeed, reports of the Third Section referred to a "democratic movement" and "communists in the Geographical Society" and claimed that many members were also closely connected with the Petrashevtsy, the circle gathered around M. F. Butashevich-Petrashevskii for the study of humanitarian and reform projects and utopianism. This group allegedly included the Petrashevets A. P. Balasoglo, V. S. Poroshin, V. A. Miliutin, N. A. Mordvinov, P. P. Semenov, and the government official and statistician E. I. Lamanskii, all of whom authored government reports about the internal conditions of Russia. The Third Section reported, "Everyone says that this society should have been made part of the Academy of Sciences which has an accurate summary of all meetings and speeches, so that members are always under the scrutiny of the government. They are less likely to discuss Russian geography here than the current political situation in Europe and its immediate consequences."[51] But perhaps more important, it would appear that Litke, fearful that the younger generation was trying to take over the organization, worried more that passions and parties would destroy the society from within.

> This effort which promises an unhappy future for the society cannot but disappoint all those who wish the Geographical Society success. From this moment it ceases being a geographical and learned [society], but what will it become? And the nastiness of a certain party in achieving this goal will shame the society so that it will almost be embarrassing to be a member. What a great pity![52]

As Litke's account hints, more important than ethnicity or national allegiances were generational changes, institutional patronage, and the imperatives of new scholarly agendas. Even in accounts that stress the national factor, the language of "new people" and "young scientists" is pervasive. The young scientists grouped around the Miliutins strove for originality and scholarly independence, which, at this moment, meant a focus on Russia. As Bruce Lincoln claims, in the late Nicholaevan period, progressive officials and intellectuals sheltered independent minds in the Ministry of Internal Affairs and sought to "seize control of the one institution outside the bureaucracy and academy amenable" to the "new thinking" of the day.[53] As in the Academy of Sciences, the issue had less to do with ethnicity and more with a perception that the scientific establishment was insufficiently committed to applied science and, more to the point, to science applied in Russia, an issue that will be explored more in the following chapter.

What lay behind the rather rapid recalibration of the society's organization, internal governance, and mission? What agendas were embedded in the institutional politics? There is more to it than personal rivalries, generational differences, burgeoning Russian radicalism, and sense of national pride. Running throughout the accounts of the first years of the society's existence is the need to study Russia and, first and foremost, the Russian people. We can see better the shift in the scholarly agenda of the society, as well as its key role in creating a sense of national identity, if we look more closely at the division that practiced the Russian variant of the "new geography"—the Ethnographic Division.

"Buried under the Volcanic Ash of History"

The scholarly agenda of RGO took place in the context of interest in national heritage and educated society's discovery of the Russian common people, who allegedly embodied the spirit of the nation. The pages of journals of the time contained travel accounts and descriptions of natural history and ancient folk customs and rituals, particularly of Siberia, allegedly long since forgotten among the educated classes of European Russia. At a meeting of the Moscow Society of Friends of Russian Literature (Obshchestvo liubitelei Rossiiskoi slovesnosti) in 1822, Ivan Snegirev, future professor of

Roman antiquities and Latin at Moscow University as well as ethnographer and archaeologist, delivered a paper on the woodcut *(lubok)* as the quintessential expression of folk wisdom, morals, and artistic creativity.[54] Educated Russians were starting to discover a geographic and cultural "other" within the borders of the empire. As in Europe, the "other," according to Mark Bassin, defined how Russians "perceived the outside world" and also became indispensable in an attempt to establish their own identity.[55] The impetus to study the nation and empire was more an affirmation of Russia's present progress and its place in Europe than it was a repudiation of both.

Litke's memorandum to Perovskii of 1 May 1845 outlining a plan to create a geographical society also made the case for a division of ethnography. Litke began his memorandum with a familiar rationale for the creation of institutional expression of a new scholarly field in Russia: while ethnographic societies already existed in Germany, France, and England, Russian ethnography was barely developed institutionally before 1845. The European societies originated in the perception that the distinctive features of nationality were everywhere being rapidly erased from memory. Litke wrote, "This creates the danger that historical information and events, which are important for the study of the nation, and which can still be preserved today, will in the course of a few decades perish forever." Moreover, the country with the richest "endangered" material—Russia—was the least studied. By providing information useful to government and public alike, Litke argued, the Geographical Society could perform a valuable patriotic service.[56]

The first head of the Ethnographic Division was the naturalist Baer. He expressed his views of ethnography in general and the practice of ethnography in Russia in particular at a general members' meeting of 6 March 1846. Baer regarded ethnography from the point of view of anthropology and natural history and believed in the influence of the natural environment on the national character of a people. At several moments in his address, he made the common argument of the day, that to study peoples living in remote parts of the empire was to study peoples who had long since disappeared, that is, to see before one's very eyes the past:

> Besides, we see that the life of peoples, and their corresponding character, is more and more being driven out by western progress. For this reason, it is all the more urgent to preserve for posterity, in accurate descriptions, the special features of folk life before it is too late.[57]

Like a dean arguing for a larger piece of the budget for his or her college, Baer skillfully framed a common argument in terms of committing resources to the study of ethnography. His address opened in a way to get attention:

> If a rich donor who wanted to leave a memorial to his love of learning and his love of Russia asked me how to do it, I would say to give us the means to study Russia for several years and to compile and publish a complete ethnographic description of its people.

But Baer appealed not just to this hypothetical rich donor's love of learning and of Russia: he also appealed to the desire to be remembered forever, that is, to vanity: "This way you will leave behind a work which can never be revised or improved and which will be used far into the future the way we search for information in the writings of Herodotus."[58] Baer showed how the new science of ethnography could compete with other scholarly fields to get resources. Owing to the continual specialization of knowledge, Baer claimed, fewer and fewer people in the future would remember a project in the natural sciences, depriving it of eternal recognition. A history project, along the lines of Rumiantsev's collections, would never be able to recapture the entire past; moreover, other institutions had been doing this for years. But an ethnographic project was completely different; it had urgency: "The materials for ethnographic research are diminishing as we speak [*s kazhdym dnem*] because the spread of progress [*prosveshchenie*] is erasing the differences among tribes. Peoples are disappearing and are leaving behind nothing more than their names."[59] Of course, this hypothetical donor was the Geographical Society itself. If it wanted to undertake a project that could never be superseded, it would wisely invest in ethnographic research, whose materials would otherwise soon become extinct, never to be created again.

But the agenda of the Ethnographic Division did not immediately privilege the study of ethnic Russians. Indeed, during the Ethnographic Division's first year, Baer authorized several expeditions to the north Urals and even Africa, as well as expeditions to study Latvia and the Finnish tribes around St. Petersburg. However, new Russian members were much more interested in studying Russian folk life than in studying anthropological geography or exotic non-Russian tribes. Dal', Nadezhdin, the philologist I. I. Sreznevskii, and the orientalists P. S. Savel'ev and V. V. Grigor'ev constituted what Semenov labeled the "Russian national school" of ethnography and changed the direction of the division. Baer tolerated this school, but it must have made him uneasy. Claiming that his insufficiency in the Russian language prevented him from effectively leading the division (his important 1846 address was written in German), he stepped down at the end of 1848, to be replaced by N. I. Nadezhdin.[60]

Among the key figures who shaped the development of institutional ethnographic studies in Russia, perhaps the most important was Nikolai Ivanovich Nadezhdin (1804–1856; see figure 3.4). The son of a village priest, he finished Moscow Theological Seminary in 1824. He was tutor to Yuri Samarin and in the 1820s participated in S. T. Aksakov's literary circle. Later, as professor of Russian literature, art, and archaeology at Moscow University, Nadezhdin argued that Russian culture needed a synthesis of the classical and romantic aesthetic. More important, Nadezhdin worked out a theory of the ennobling function of literature, a theory that influenced the critic Vissarion Belinsky and suggested that literature must be "a mouthpiece of national self-awareness and one of the most powerful forces leading the people along the path of historical development."[61] Expelled from Moscow University in 1832 because the authorities disapproved of his play *Dmitrii Kalinin,* which was critical of serfdom, Nadezhdin continued, paradoxically, to be a school inspector for the Ministry of Education. Meanwhile, in 1831 he began publishing the magazine *Telescope,* which again ran him afoul of the authorities when it published Peter Chaadaev's "Philosophical Letter" in 1836. The magazine was closed and Nadezhdin was exiled to Vologda, where he seemingly underwent a career change. As he later wrote, "The recent catastrophe tore me away once and for all from aesthetics and archaeology. I turned my studies to the fields of geography and ethnography . . . I turned to history in general and to our history [*otechestvennaia*] in particular."[62] Nadezhdin founded local institutes of geographic and ethnographic research and, as if to answer Chaadaev's damnation of Russia for its lack of civilization, began to seek the wellsprings of Russian civilization in the people.

Nadezhdin's career, his personal and professional contacts, and his views illustrate the intellectual crucible of Moscow in the 1820s, 1830s, and 1840s and the difficulty in attaching the labels "westerner," "Slavophile," and "official nationality." Through membership in a student circle in the 1830s, Nadezhdin was close to Timofei Granovsky and Nikolai Stankevich; he also influenced the archetypal westerner Vissarion Belinsky. At the same time, he was tutor to Yuri Samarin, an associate of Konstantin Aksakov, and came to glorify the Russian people. His circle included V. I. Dal', V. V. Skripitsyn, I. P. Sakharov, and the orientalists V. V. Grigor'ev and P. S. Savel'ev, many of whom were later active in the Russian Geographical Society. The editor exiled for publishing Chaadaev's critique of Russian civilization became, six years later, the editor of a government serial, the *Journal of the Ministry of Internal Affairs,* which he edited until his death. Like many Slavophiles, he was a monarchist who believed in an egalitarian society. He believed that while Russia should not "replant the fruits of the European Enlightenment," it should adopt the methods of European education, culture, and science. Although his views also suggest an affinity with official nationality, he ran afoul of the authorities too often and never held a high government position.[63]

Figure 3.4 N. I. Nadezhdin, writer, critic, and head of the Ethnographic Division of RGO. (*Russkie Portrety XVIII i XIX vv.* [St. Petersburg, 1905–1909].)

No sooner had he joined the new Russian Geographical Society in 1846 than Nadezhdin delivered a major address outlining his views of ethnography, and in 1850 he became the head of the Ethnographic Division. Speaking before the members on 29 November 1846, in a talk titled "The Ethnographic Study of the Russian People," a longer version of which was published in the society's *Zapiski,* Nadezhdin made his case for Russian area studies. While Baer had earlier prioritized the study of extinct peoples and the non-Russian tribes of the Russian empire using the methods of natural history and anthropology, Nadezhdin privileged a study of the Russian people, to explore "what makes Russia Russia, that is, the Russian."[64] However, this was not a simple replacement of one object of scientific study for another. Nadezhdin had a broader scholarly and moral agenda, to make the Russian Geographical Society the center of a Russian national ethnography.

In his 1846 address Nadezhdin justified in different terms from that of Baer the institutional expression of a new scientific discipline in Russia. Ethnographic material did not constitute ethnography and Russian ethnography would be a science only if and when existing ethnographic material was passed through the "crucible of strict and discriminating criticism" in order "to satisfy the existing needs of popular self-understanding [*narodnoe samopoznanie*]." In order to satisfy these needs, Nadezhdin placed the Russian common people at the heart of a Russian ethnography: they allegedly had preserved the way of life, national characteristics, and legends of a distant past, as if this knowledge had been "buried under the volcanic ash of history," to borrow Semenov's brilliant metaphor. In addition, Nadezhdin, reflecting the influence of Slavistica noted at the beginning of this chapter, advocated the study of the seemingly "Russian" traits among other eastern Slavs, or "the Russian element [that] bursts through from the mouth of the Neman to the mouth of the Danube."[65]

Assuming that the distinguishing features and original character of the Russian nation were most likely preserved in the simple folk—and, if buried under "volcanic ash," these features were perfectly preserved—in 1847 Nadezhdin drew up an ambitious program of empirical study. The "crucible of strict and discriminating criticism" was, of course, provided by RGO, the vehicle that would transform random ethnographic material into a science. The Geographical Society sent out seven thousand questionnaires all over Russia, with elaborate instructions about what and whom to look for. The groups presumed to be the repository of Russian national character were, in addition to the "simple country folk," the middling classes of the city—tradesmen, merchants, and people of various ranks. The material to gather was grouped in six categories: (1) physical features, especially distinctive features of body build and appearance; (2) language, especially local slang and dialects and local pronunciation patterns; (3) domestic life, including dwellings, utensils, food, dress, customs and rituals, in which "in all probability the ancient heritage of original morals and customs of the people have been preserved"; (4) remnants of social life such as customary law and the village gathering, where "time has not erased the original organizations of popular life"; (5) intellectual and moral capacities and differences "to the extent that nature and the development of the folk spirit, and not external borrowings and imitations, is still visible"; and (6) folk legends and memories, "that living and impartial history in which people express themselves as they are without any pretense or self-delusions."[66] By 1852 the Geographical Society had more than a thousand manuscript replies to the questionnaires, with the greatest response coming from the Orthodox clergy. The material, which was used widely in the six volumes of the *Etnograficheskii sbornik,* in the Geographical Society's ethnographic atlas, and in scattered other publications of the Geographical Society, constitutes a rich lode of local descriptions. Nadezhdin followed this ethnographic data with a collection of Russian geographical terms and in 1852 with a questionnaire that was designed for the non-Russian peoples of Kamchatka and that for the first time posed the question of popular aesthetics: did the public have "the capacity to appreciate the refined, the popular type of beauty, especially female, and the preferred forms, proportions and colors?"[67]

The significance of this enterprise is difficult to overestimate. As a result of Nadezhdin's efforts, the greater part of the "gold reserve" of Russian folklore, according to M. K. Azavodskii, was based on materials collected by the Russian Geographic Society. The classic works of the collector of folk legends, myths, and Slavic antiquities A. N. Afanas'ev, the philologist L. N. Maikov, the collector of folktales D. N. Sadovnikov, as well as collections of Russian fairy tales were all connected with the Geographical Society. The same holds true for reference works of Dal' and I. I. Sreznevskii. In fact, Dal' was already working on his collection of aphorisms when the data and observations began coming in to the Ethnographic Division. The ethnographic data also made possible the large number of everyday words and usages in Dal's dictionary of the living Russian language.[68]

More important for my purposes, the enterprise was a combination of direction from above and initiative from below. As happened with the analogous societies in Europe, descriptions of localities had started coming to the Geographical Society soon after its creation. The society decided to utilize this spontaneous enthusiasm in drawing up its research program, and "the zeal of volunteers in the service of learning exceeded all expectations." In turn, the questionnaires stimulated a broad public interest in ethnography and local studies and, no less important, publicized the Geographical Society. The Ethnographic Division thereby acquired and mobilized a significant number of amateur researchers outside the capital and flicked on the switch of a constant flow of "important and curious observations" about the far corners of the empire to the society's headquarters in St. Petersburg. At a time when nongovernmental studies of provincial life were regarded with suspicion, the Ethnographic Division, under the "big tent" of RGO, was able to gather valuable data. In this way, the Geographical Society nurtured private initiative, facilitated the networking of like-minded persons and organizations, and directed scientific research projects that involved the public.[69]

Under the leadership of the Ethnographic Division, the project passed through the "crucible of strict and discriminating criticism," as Nadezhdin put it, that is, the methods of scientific inquiry. As in other voluntary societies, the many, working together to achieve common objectives, could achieve what isolated individuals could not. As its spokesmen and proponents never tired of pointing out, the Geographical Society combined resources and gave direction to otherwise dispersed efforts. The society imposed order on those random efforts that "continually poured in from the outside, changing in their composition and diverse in their combinations." It built a base of empirical data, created an ongoing system of questionnaires and instructions, and provided a center for the collection and processing of material. In this way, the otherwise random ethnographic observations could stand alongside the more ordered written documents as evidence of the past; more important, they became a science. The Geographical Society could thereby make that lasting contribution to posterity, about which Baer had spoken, "for only a learned society in the Slavic lands could obtain materials that would be sought in vain in other countries." Thus, the Ethnographic Division hitched "the needs of popular self-understanding" to the development and popularization of a new scientific discipline.[70]

The enterprise of the Ethnographic Division spread news about the society all over Russia. Though perhaps the best publicized, the efforts of the Geographical Society to create a national heritage and national identity were not isolated. For example, the Russian Archaeological Society, founded in 1846, followed the same trajectory as the Geographical Society in the process of defining its mission. Because the field of Russian archaeology was not yet developed—most archaeological discoveries pertained to classical antiquity—most charter members of the society were foreigners; and the serial publications of the society as well as compositions presented to the society were in French or German. During the first few years of its existence, the Russian Archaeological Society focused its attention on the study of classical archaeology and numismatics. However, interest in Russian archaeology soon developed, and in 1851 a division of Russian and Slavic archaeology was created. As was noted at the fiftieth jubilee, this "pointed the society in a new direction: to study predominantly Russian archaeology." As they had done in the Geographical Society, younger members, such as Ivan E. Zabelin, redefined the canon and placed study of Russia's national heritage at the forefront of the Archaeological Society; their lasting achievement was the Alexander III Historical Museum, founded in 1872.[71]

Thus, in the 1840s, as the cosmopolitan and educated upper classes sought a bond with the common people, the Russian Geographical Society was at the center of a quest for national identity and a national science. It was at the center of a movement that privileged the study of all aspects of peasant life. It wanted to study the people in order to preserve them, and to do so it helped develop the science of Russian geography. The result of this "unofficial nationality" was a Russian ethnography. However, the Ethnographic Division was not the only division of RGO occupied with the study of the empire's human resources. The vast amount of information about the empire's social and economic institutions also required the "crucible of strict and discriminating criticism"; that is, it needed to be quantified and processed. The loci of this work in the Geographical Society were in its Statistical Division and, later, in a short-lived Committee of Political Economy. The government sanctioned this work and commissioned much of it. At the same time, the work of the Statistical Division touched government economic policy and, in doing so, came under close government scrutiny. A brief examination of statistics and political economy in RGO will show the opportunities as well as the limits of associations in mid nineteenth-century Russia.

Statistics and Political Economy

At the founding of the Geographical Society, the state of Russian statistics was no better than the study of Russian ethnography. Lincoln suggests four shortcomings of Russian statistics in the late eighteenth and early nineteenth centuries: the lack of any single government agency responsible for compiling statistics; the poor communications between the center and the provinces; the incompetence and fear of local officials; and the secrecy surrounding the collection and holding of information. As a result, government statistics were largely unavailable, even to policy makers; those that were available, especially those not compiled for fiscal purposes or compiled by the police or local authorities, were unreliable. In some critical areas (landholding and harvests, for example) no statistics existed.[72] Of course, there was another dimension to all of this. In those days, and not just in Russia, statistics were regarded as an important tool in studying social and economic life; as such they were part of political economy. As James Scott argues, measurement was an act of power relations that created reality more than reflected it. Statistics were thought to hold the key to theories of the development of national wealth and prosperity and, thus, to be in the proper domain of government. Indeed, according to Michael Cullen, "underlying much of the work of the nineteenth-century statistical movement lay the belief that the work was properly one for central and local governments which had devolved upon private societies and individuals by default." Regarded as part of a process of "improving" society, the efforts to record, measure, and classify were frequently "a prelude to action and reform," and thus many associations willy-nilly became involved in politics.[73] But, of course, in Russia information gathering was a delicate subject and could lead to criticism of the existing order. Accordingly, the government, and particularly the censors, were suspicious of any investigations of economic and social life. Semenov narrates the tale, perhaps apocryphal, of the censor, shaky in his understanding of foreign terms, who confused "sociology" with "socialism," and "demography" with "democracy." At the same time, according to Alexander Herzen, who briefly had an insider's view, "the Ministry of Internal Affairs had at that time a craze for statistics."[74]

The recognition of the importance of statistics was reflected in the original name proposed for the Geographical Society—the Geographical-Statistical Society—and in the creation of the Statistical Division as one of its divisions. At its inception, the mission of the Statistical Division was premised on the fact that government statistics collected only for administrative purposes were not usable for scholarship. The Statistical Division scrutinized the official sources that were the basis of government statistics with an eye to analyzing their shortcomings and devising methods to correct them, it publicized the existence of statistical materials in those areas where data were incomplete and fragmentary, and it promoted and published private initiative in statistical work. As in the field of ethnography, the Geographical Society aspired to found a national science of statistics that would not be a random collection of numbers but the collection of descriptive statistics "of all measurable elements of social life." Among the "measurable elements" sponsored or reviewed by the Statistical Division were collections of vital statistics, statistics on landownership, studies of the grain trade and domestic commerce, and statistics on crime and on the living conditions of workers in St. Petersburg. These studies created horizontal linkages with other communities, such as the Free Economic Society and the St. Petersburg merchant community; the report on living conditions was publicized in the daily *St. Petersburg News*. Members of the society strongly believed that statistics not only were necessary for policy making but were an exercise in public service and patriotism, and many RGO statistical studies paved the way for the Great Reforms.[75]

Several of Russia's best-known statisticians of the time were members of the Geographical Society. Two representatives of the "first generation" of Russian statisticians were P. I. Keppen and K. I. Arsen'ev. A member of the Academy of Sciences, professor of statistics, and a charter member of the Geographical Society, Keppen led the project to compose an ethnographic map of the empire. Like many of his era who were in and out of government service, Keppen hitched national statistics to the well-being of the fatherland. Critical of the shortcomings of periodic government inventories of the tax-paying population, better known as revisions *(revizii)*, Keppen campaigned for a national census (as it turned out, an idea a half century ahead of its time), permission for which was denied in the atmosphere of heightened fear of "inappropriate" ideas in 1848. Son of a parish priest, Konstantin Ivanovich Arsen'ev in 1819 became adjunct professor of geography and statistics at the University of St. Petersburg. However, two years later, in the Magnitskii-Runich crackdown at Russian universities, he was removed allegedly "for teaching in a spirit contrary to Christianity and subversive of the social order." As if to prove the irrationality of that social order, two years later Nicholas I named Arsen'ev to be the tutor to the future Alexander II, in history and statistics. In 1835 Arsen'ev was appointed chief of the new Government Statistical Administration, a post he held until 1853. As one of the charter members of the Geographical Society, Arsen'ev mentored young Russians who wanted to collect statistics as a means for the study of political economy and whose activism was grounded in government and nongovernment institutions.[76]

After the Crimean War, the anarchist and RGO member Peter Kropotkin wrote in his memoirs, "everyone in Russia talked of political-economy; lectures on free trade and protective tariffs attracted crowds of people."[77] Led by V. P. Bezobrazov, editor of *Vestnik Geograficheskogo Obshchestva* [*News of the Geographical Society*] as well as the journal of the Ministry of State Properties, and I. V. Vernadskii, professor of political economy at the University of St. Petersburg and editor of the new weekly journal *Ukazetel' Ekonomicheskii* [*Economic Index*], a group of liberal economists in the Statistical Division gathered in St. Petersburg for "economic banquets" and organized public lectures on economic subjects. Among the participants were I. Ia. Gorlov, E. I. Lamanskii, P. A. Valuev, K. S. Veselovskii, A. P. Zablotskii-Desiatovskii, A. I. Levshin, N. A. Miliutin, F. G. Terner, and other "reformers." All were members of the Statistical Division; most held government posts, as high as current or future ministers, especially in Internal Affairs, Finance, and State Properties, or were members of the Editing Commission, drafting the legislation that emancipated the serfs in 1861. For example, Zablotskii-Desiatovskii, an opponent of serfdom, was the chief assistant to P. D. Kiselev in the Ministry of State Properties before becoming state secretary in the Economics Department of the State Council. As a member of the Statistical Division, in 1850 Zablotskii-Desiatovskii wrote a memorandum recommending a precise population count of every town, county, and province; along with K. S. Veselovskii, he prepared an economic atlas of the empire. G. P. Nebolsin prepared a study of foreign trade, and A. I. Levshin was a specialist on the Kirgiz Cossacks. E. I. Lamanskii, a specialist in money supply and the grain trade, was a member of the Free Economic Society, the secretary of the Geographical Society (1854–1855), and a longtime member of the Statistical Division. N. A. Miliutin acted as the group's patron and fed statistical materials compiled by officials in the Ministry of Internal Affairs to the Geographical Society.[78]

In February 1859, the liberal economists in the Statistical Division proposed the creation of the Committee of Political Economy, whose goals were to improve perceived theoretical and methodological shortcomings in the collection of Russian statistics by establishing contact with domestic and foreign statisticians, to apply political economy to Russian financial and economic problems, to increase public awareness of economic issues, and to prepare public opinion for changes in government economic policies. One of the society's statisticians, D. P. Zhukovskii, wrote, "The Geographical Society is different from other societies, whose members meet only to chitchat. The time has come to act."[79]

As an adjunct of the Geographical Society, the Committee of Political Economy did not have its own charter. It was intended to be a loosely structured body rather than a permanent organization, and indeed the word "committee" suggests a more formal structure than actually was the case. Given the large number of government officials and ministerial compartmentalization, the bane of Russian officialdom, the committee functioned almost like an ongoing interdepartmental seminar or colloquium *(beseda),* of the kind that are common in academic institutions. Members of the Geographical Society appointed members of the committee. The committee then elected its own chair and secretary; the latter became a non-voting member of the board of the Geographical Society. The committee drew up a set of rules *(pravila),* according to which it submitted a plan of its activities to the board of the Geographical Society and agreed to adhere strictly to its guidelines. Each member could invite a guest to meetings, and outside experts were regularly invited. An annual meeting, open to the public, heard, in addition to the annual report typical of all associations, a survey of the Russian and foreign economies for the past year. Convening every other Monday, the seminars of the Committee of Political Economy discussed a wide range of topics, including the money supply, Russia's commercial "crisis," colonization and peasant resettlement, postemancipation agricultural policy, tax policy, and financial policy and the state budget. Jointly with its sister organization, the Committee of Political Economy of the Free Economic Society (established in 1861), the Committee of Political Economy held additional seminars on Russian joint-stock companies, patents, factory inspection, and the sale of state properties.[80]

These seminars stood out on the St. Petersburg calendar in the early 1860s. At the height of planning for the Great Reforms, the seminars provided an opportunity for a mingling of liberal economists and officials, a mingling enhanced by the presence of guests and experts. Appropriately, practical questions of economics, finance, and administration predominated over theoretical. More striking, these nongovernmental seminars made policy recommendations—and the recommendations were of liberal political economy, such as financial *glasnost'* for the state budget and a tax on wealth rather than the capitation tax. Most important for my purposes, accounts of the meetings, many of which featured "lively debates," received considerable publicity. Minutes of the meetings were published in the *Zapiski* of the Geographical Society and summarized in the newspapers; the general press frequently gave coverage to the debates. By using the coverage in the press, as well as by establishing connections with other associations, the committee not only publicized the Great Reforms but also created a forum for an unprecedented sense of public participation in government policy.[81]

However, this public participation led, in the words of a writer for *Ukazatel' Ekonomicheskii,* to "a spirit of opposition that has awakened among the members of our societies."[82] Not all officials wanted the Committee of Political Economy encroaching on government turf. At a meeting of the Committee of Ministers on 21 December 1861, Alexander II himself raised the question of the influence of the committees of political economy in the Geographical and Free Economic societies. The emperor proposed a closer regulation of societies that were engaged in the study of political and economic issues. Several aspects of the matter troubled the Committee of Ministers. It appeared that controversial policy issues had driven out scholarly questions. In the midst of the high tension caused by the government entering uncharted waters, the Committee of Ministers considered undesirable any interference in or scrutiny of government policy-making. The unprecedented publicity of the committee's discussions allegedly whetted the public's appetite for more far-reaching changes in economic policy and administration; officialdom was concerned that this appetite might lead to a taste for the forbidden fruit of politics.[83]

On 5 January 1862, the Committee of Ministers decided to take measures to regulate more closely the special committees and commissions of learned societies that heretofore had been de facto independent associations under little supervision. In accordance with these measures, the continued existence of the Committee of Political Economy required the approval of the

Ministry of Internal Affairs. According to the rules *(pravila)* drafted by P. A. Valuev, the Committee of Political Economy was required to submit a plan of its meetings to the board of the Geographical Society. If the board had any doubts about the appropriateness *(svoevremennost')* of any topic, the vice president of the society would consult with the pertinent government department. In addition, the board was obliged to ensure that the committee did not exceed its established boundaries, that is, to ensure that the committee did not discuss topics of state administration. Valuev's rules were an attempt at a compromise: rather than place the supervisory powers in the hands of the Ministry of Internal Affairs, the rules left these powers with the board of the Geographical Society.[84] However, then came the troubling events of 1862—fires in St. Petersburg, the arrest of Nikolai Chernyshevskii, the crackdown on the journals *Sovremennik* and *Russkoe slovo,* the closing of the Sunday schools, agitation among the peasants, and growing unrest in Poland. A secret agent report on the committees of political economy made the Committee of Ministers more nervous. The report noted the increase in the size of the Geographical Society and the Free Economic Society. More disturbing, the committees were allegedly penetrated by "undesirable" persons who spread "antigovernment propaganda and the destructive ideas of communism, democracy, and atheism." Moreover, the large number of nonmembers at the meetings of the committees gave these learned societies the character of "an ancient assembly [*veche*] deciding the fate of the kingdom and people," holding "parliamentary debates on the most sensitive issues of state and law." This "idle talk," if unpunished, would distract "hot-headed young people" and "set against the supreme power an insurmountable barrier to the realization of the beneficial ideas." And because the Committee of Political Economy had high government officials as members, the educated public allegedly regarded it as a quasi-official body. The report recommended limiting the number of learned societies and shutting down the committees of political economy.[85]

Russian officialdom was not monolithic, and some representatives of state power were more sympathetic than others to the existence and activities of nongovernmental organizations. Unpublished minutes of the Committee of Ministers, which met on 16 and 30 October 1862 to determine the government's course of action, suggest that there was no unanimity in officialdom on this issue. Minister Valuev of Internal Affairs stated that, *pace* the secret agent report, the Committee of Political Economy had not become, nor had it tried to become, an official body. At the same time, because its work threatened to be "inconvenient" to the government, Valuev recommended that the number of nonmembers at meetings of the committee be reduced and that the Geographical Society's *Zapiski* be subjected to stricter censorship. In a dissenting opinion, the minister of education, A. V. Golovnin, argued that the committees of political economy, like any learned society, could not submit in advance a definite program of their meetings but only a preliminary one; moreover, by its nature political economy was difficult to limit to theoretical questions: "To restrict further the activities of this learned society that has been indisputably beneficial and well intentioned would be extremely unjust and insulting to the Geographical Society." Therefore, Golovnin proposed that approval of the preliminary program by the board of the Geographical Society ought to suffice; regular communication between the vice president of the Geographical Society and the minister of internal affairs could clear up any misunderstandings. In the end the Committee of Ministers accepted Golovnin's argument and instructed the Committee of Political Economy to submit a list of topics for its meetings to the board of the Geographical Society. The emperor penned in "sensible" *(del'no)* in the margins. Wary of unsupervised activity as the government was entering uncharted ground in legislating the Great Reforms, the Committee of Ministers warned both VEO and RGO that discussions of state policy and expression of opinion about government measures could not be allowed.[86]

As Golovnin predicted, RGO members were insulted. The Committee of Political Economy decided it could not submit a full program in advance for approval. Moreover, members believed that since the committee's rules conformed to the charter of the Geographical Society, the government had no right to demand changes. In any event, it was impossible to limit the committee's work to a theoretical study of political economy. This would lead the committee outside its proscribed sphere, and this could result in a grievous misunderstanding *(priskorbnoe nedorazumenie)* within the committee and between the committee and the rest of the Geographical Society. Finally, and most significantly, the committee decided that adhering to such rules, as well as to the supervision inherent in regular talks between the vice president of the Geographical Society and the minister of internal affairs, would deprive it of scholarly autonomy and the free discussion of important matters that would assist the government to undertake "healthy" policies. At a meeting of 26 November 1862, a meeting that was to be its last, the Committee of Political Economy, by a vote of 12 to 3, decided to disband.[87]

By refusing to sacrifice a certain degree of its autonomy, the committee stood up to political authority, no easy matter for individuals whose career paths had brought them in and out of government service. At a time when the government was encouraging public discussion *(glasnost')*, it also tried to control such discussion. Though short-lived as far as the Geographical

Society was concerned, this conflict showed the limits of public action and foreshadowed much more widespread conflict between state and society at the end of the century.

The Russian Geographical Society and Civil Society

What was the broader significance of the Russian Geographical Society for Russian intellectual life and political culture? In its quest to study nation and empire, the Russian Geographical Society, like the Free Economic Society and the Moscow Agricultural Society before it, aided the development of the public sphere of civil society. In so doing, it made a contribution to three of the most important projects of the European Enlightenment—the diffusion of applied science and the creation of a community of knowledge, patriotic service to state and society, and the establishment of a public forum, however limited, under autocracy.

The Geographical Society illustrates well the practice of "Baltic natural history," as historian of science Lisbet Koerner formulates the term. Many charter members were civil servants of German-Scandinavian origin, serving an empire on the fringes of Europe. Their voyages of discovery led to expeditions of a different kind—to study natural history, agricultural techniques, and finally ethnography. In "Baltic natural history," a "proto-romantic cult of the fatherland" created by "diaspora Germans" cultivated the "peasant as an object of scientific investigation." All aspects of peasant life appeared on the radar screen of Baltic ethnographers and statisticians—"customs, manners, dress, crafts, festivals, cooking, childrearing." Not only did the quest for an encyclopedic natural history produce imperial knowledge; it also promised self-knowledge of the nation.[88]

How did the Russian Geographical Society produce knowledge and self-knowledge? Like the Free Economic Society and the Moscow Agricultural Society, RGO strove to practice a public science in what Joel Mokyr calls a "community of knowledge." In associations, Mokyr contends, knowledge about the natural world became increasingly "non-proprietary, and scientific advances and discoveries were freely shared with the public at large."[89] Like the Free Economic Society, the Geographical Society was founded in an age of information, an age fascinated by the collection and cataloging of descriptions, observations, and artifacts about human and natural worlds. Like its predecessors, the Geographical Society built "bridges," to use Mokyr's term, of "catalogued and ordered information," the most important being printed materials that disseminated useful knowledge. But publication of the society's research did more than disseminate information about faraway places and the native land, as important as those were. As Mokyr suggests, the process of the diffusion of useful knowledge was just as important as the product. The Geographical Society strove to popularize geography and natural history. Its expeditions, compilations of data, and the reports from far-flung correspondents furthered the dissemination of the scientific method by obliging members and correspondents to record and measure accurately observations, to conduct experiments, to provide scientific documentation, and to maintain scientific journals. Furthermore, RGO contributed to the development of new scientific fields, such as ethnography and statistics. Through its projects it created a community not only for the intelligentsia of the capital but for officials and private persons across the empire, thereby helping to break down the sense of isolation of educated Russians, particularly important during the reign of Nicholas I.

In RGO's first jubilee history, F. R. Osten-Saken captured the spirit of early years. Osten-Saken noted not only the society's wide range of activity and its contribution to science and to a greater knowledge of Russia but also its outreach mission:

> From the very start, the Society was not a closed circle of learned specialists who emerged from their scientific collections [*kabinety*] to exchange ideas and inform each other of the results of their research. It threw open the door to all, without exception, who were interested in studying Russia, and summoned all her available and motley forces to independent action [*samodeiatel'nost'*] directed to that study.

The society united the activities of free and productive intellects, Osten-Saken continued, in "an enterprise of the human mind" that would have been impossible for individuals working alone. Moreover, like other "enterprises," RGO cultivated the habits of public as well as personal intellectual initiative, applied the principle of the division of labor, and provided a training ground for public or government work.[90]

As in western and Central Europe, the scientist or amateur who recorded observations and collected, classified, and ordered new knowledge in the collective company of peers was made to feel part of a national endeavor. The study of the nation did more than gather information on local customs and institutions: by promoting a sense of national identity and national self-esteem, it was patriotic.[91] The Russian Geographical Society was on the cutting edge of Russian area studies in service to the nation. Correspondents in far-off corners of Russia felt that by contributing their notes and observations, they, too, could do their bit to study Russia and to articulate

Russian national identity. In the fifteen years before the Great Reforms, no institution outside government more self-consciously focused on Russia than did the Geographical Society. By popularizing the study, in Osten-Saken's words, of "a huge and boundless [*neob"iatoe*] fatherland," the society not only appealed to but also aspired to act for the common good and for national pride. The society's members, allegedly "from the royal family down to the most modest provincial geographer," were infused with a "burning patriotism"—a desire to study the nation's productive forces and to facilitate its well-being, to serve Russia (and not just state or monarch) and to cement that "spiritual bond" that bound Russians "all together in the love for [their] native land."[92] In Semenov's somewhat self-mythologizing definition of the society's mission, "the Society was like a banner raised by progressive Russians with the consent of the crown." This banner united members "with the noble purpose of performing a lasting service to Russia, to promote with their selfless labor further knowledge of the Russian land and people and . . . those relationships which [would] hasten its further development and well-being." Most important, such patriotic service was undertaken not by command but "freely."[93]

As was true of European geographical societies of the era, especially in northern and Central Europe, patriotism and national pride fostered a collaborative relationship with the state. Because of their links to exploration, empire, and military (especially naval) operations, geographical societies everywhere were inherently close to governments. The Geographical Society's links with government continued a pattern begun by the Free Economic Society of reciprocal and mutually beneficial relations between Russia's voluntary associations and the state. In the first century in the development of Russia's voluntary associations, societies' goals and the state's goals coincided, and service to society joined service to state and monarch as a patriotic calling. It is not surprising that the members would regard the encouragement of an interest in Russian geography as their patriotic duty. From 1845 to 1861 the society's membership list contained numerous scholar-officials; almost all central government offices employed members of the Geographical Society. Like the Free Economic Society, the Geographical Society had imperial patronage, accepted members of the royal family as office holders, received government grants, and petitioned government offices for favors and privileges, such as free postage. Government departments commissioned many of its studies and were the primary consumer of the results. The leaders of the Geographical Society believed their mission to be of assistance to the empire in the execution of scientific work and the implementation of policy. As one historian notes, "this allowed the Geographical Society to conduct research and discuss financial and economic questions on a collegial basis . . . ; it permitted scholarly and practical recommendations to be translated into government policy." Even the Third Section recognized the benefit to the state when it reported, "[The society] organizes and guides research and local investigations equipped with those problems unresolved in work conducted by the government."[94]

The appearance of the Russian Geographical Society demonstrates the existence of a public sphere and an autonomous associational life even in the oppressive years of Nicholas I. At one of its earliest meetings, Vice President Litke suggested how the society could become a forum for the exchange of views:

> To give the meetings of the society more life and more significance, it would indeed be useful if . . . we started the practice of public debate during the meeting itself. The topic of these debates could be questions or observations . . . regarding a previously delivered paper, or regarding some information, thought, or proposal . . . One sensible speech will inspire another, one observation will follow another, and answer will follow question. Thus, that common exchange of opinions and information, that convergence among members, that participation in a common intellectual effort that constitutes the goal of our meetings will be born. In this way we will realize the idea of the society, for without these conditions there in essence will be no society.

This gave even the political police a favorable impression of meetings: "The meetings of the Society are for the presentation of papers and a discussion of all topics in its field of work. Special attention was paid to the discussions as a means of communication of useful information and exchange of opinions."[95] (See figure 3.5.)

However, a forum outside government in autocratic Russia existed on treacherous terrain. On the eve of the Great Reforms, the Geographical Society was a microcosm of an increasingly restless reading and discussing public. In becoming a forum covered in the press, the society became a vehicle of interest-group articulation and representation, one of the functions of the associations of civil society. By becoming a public forum for a discussion of and dissemination of views on many aspects of social and economic life, the Geographical Society framed the issues of participatory public dialogue, drew in the public, and cultivated civil consciousness. Litke himself walked a tightrope, for he was concerned about order and decorum at its meetings. Somewhat contradicting his support of public debate, Litke feared the politicization of a learned society, a politicization that could threaten the precarious existence of civil society. "If the habit of argument takes root," he later wrote, "then the development of science will surely be smothered and in its place, parties will be born."[96]

Figure 3.5 The Fiftieth Anniversary Meeting of RGO in the hall of the St. Petersburg City Council, 1896. (*Vsemirnaia Illustratsiia*, no. 1410 [1896]: 142; courtesy of the Library of Congress.)

The fate of the short-lived Committee of Political Economy was a sign of the precarious relationship between associations and the state in tsarist Russia. On the one hand, the government cooperated with associations and granted a rather surprising degree of latitude in their pursuit of scientific investigation and independent opinion. Despite Litke's concern, arguments over the society's charter proceeded among members openly without heavy-handed efforts of the government to dictate the society's policies, course of action, organization, or internal governance. On the other hand, when those investigations and opinions strayed into areas of government policy, the exclusive prerogative of the autocrat and officialdom, the government tightened its supervisory tethers. By the era of the Great Reforms, the Geographical Society was perhaps the most prominent society in the empire; it no longer needed to be worried that it might be smothered. As the following chapter will show, the era was a boon to the impulse to associate.

CHAPTER FOUR

Patriotism and Useful Knowledge

The Society of Friends of Natural History

DURING THE COURSE of the nineteenth century, more and more societies of science and natural history in Europe and the United States regarded their mission to be the popularization of knowledge of the natural world and the dissemination of scientific literacy, or what may be called "scientific capital." The leaders of science societies wanted the educated population to have a direct experience of the natural world through observation and experiment and to reduce access costs to useful knowledge. Broadening the appeal of science and demonstrating that natural knowledge can make a better world validated the scientific enterprise and the scientists themselves in the court of public opinion; thus, the argument ran, popularizing science was good for science. In order to accomplish these objectives, science societies engaged in education and outreach projects designed to create civic institutions and other meeting places where scientists and nonscientitsts could interact and where the public could not only satisfy its curiosity about the natural world but also develop its capacity for self-instruction and the rational use of leisure. Indeed, by emphasizing that anyone could be a naturalist, the societies of naturalists attempted to draw in the public and to disseminate learning and a love of science, and the mid nineteenth century was the heyday of popular natural history societies. Naturalist societies frequently had ties with the local community and often existed to record observations, collect artifacts, and engage in experiments about local phenomena of nature. In this way, amateurs, who often performed these tasks, could make valuable contributions to the scientific enterprise. Collections of scientific instruments allowed the nonscientist to watch and even conduct experiments, to learn by doing. Mechanics institutes and similar organizations held periodic competitions, planned exhibitions, organized lectures on subjects from art to physics, and commissioned designs. Thus, the demonstrations and displays of science, sometimes called the "performance of science," that combined utility and entertainment created a new audience for science; this new audience was no longer limited to the social or scientific elites and government officials but included amateurs who embraced a broad spectrum of the educated urban population.[1]

Among the many methods of popularizing science, industrial exhibitions, museums (often called "temples of science"), and botanical and zoological gardens were the most visible means for both the transmission of useful knowledge and the demonstration of the fruits of the modern world for an urban mass audience. Museums and exhibitions of science and industry fulfilled many functions. They fostered an awe of nature as well as an intense "curiosity about the remote and unusual" among a public that was everywhere allegedly thirsting for knowledge. Organizers wanted to draw teachers and pupils to the displays as well as to provide educational materials for classroom use. Museums operated in a network of sponsored activity—from art and music to excursions—to uplift the aspiring to lead wholesome lives by means of self-improvement, character building, and the rational use of leisure. Working- and middle-class publics could be brought together, and "the former could be exposed to the improving influence of the latter."[2] In the striking language of an anonymous British industrialist, quoted in the annual report of one association in 1852, "the Art Union of London [was] an enormous steam engine for the manufacturing of a love of art."[3] The international exhibitions, with the French leading the way, became part of movements for social reform and displayed the efforts of the middle classes to educate and meliorate the lives of working people. Cities sponsored exhibitions and built museums to enhance cultural life and cultivate civic and national pride, to show that city leaders could apply their vision and expertise in the service of civil society. By means of dramatic and crowd-pleasing displays of modern life and the wonders of applied science, museums and exhibitions displayed visions of progress through the division of labor and the cooperation of science, industry, private associations, and governments in service to the public. Indeed by disseminating useful knowledge in an entertaining way, museums and exhibitions helped create a modern public culture.[4] Finally, museums and exhibitions fostered a collective endeavor to learn about the nation and to promote native industry, thereby instilling a sense of national identity and self-esteem. Scholars have seen exhibitions, alongside museums of natural history, science, and industry, as central features of the bourgeois nation-state, as well as sites of modernity, where the modern ideas of progress and mastery of nature are staged and where identities are "manifested and experienced in public." In an age of patriotism, nationalism, and imperialism, exhibitions compelled nations to dramatize, even create, "conventionalized versions of their national images."[5]

Russia at midcentury was no exception to these trends. We have seen that the Free Economic Society, the Moscow Agricultural Society, and the Russian Geographical Society practiced a public science and that their corresponding memberships and branch societies drew the public into the national endeavor of gathering information about the realm. Nevertheless, science in these societies was in the main practiced by a small coterie. There was no institution in St. Petersburg or Moscow open to the public where the curious amateur could come and experience nature directly. Especially in the case of the Geographical Society, the chief consumer of the scientific enterprise was the state. In the Nicholaevan era, although the government patronized private societies of geography and economic improvement, the outreach projects of a more broadly targeted public science were not feasible. But the accession in 1855 of a new emperor to the throne began an era of reforms in Russian society. Using the early years of the Moscow Society of Friends of Natural History, Anthropology, and Ethnography (OLEAE in its Russian initials) as a case study, this chapter will examine private associated initiative in the roles of public outreach and stewardship of learning in Moscow during the era of the Great Reforms. The chapter will focus on this society's founding, organization, and mission, and on its two best-known projects of education and outreach, the Polytechnical Exposition of 1872 and the Polytechnical Museum. Although full discussion of the exposition and museum lies outside the scope of this book, their establishment illustrates the public mission of voluntary associations for national betterment in imperial Russia.

The Society of Friends of Natural History, Anthropology, and Ethnography

In the historiography of the era of the Great Reforms, the role of the reforming state and enlightened bureaucrats under Alexander II have overshadowed a dramatic rise of government-sanctioned private initiative. Following the death of Emperor Nicholas I in 1855, educated Russians felt a sense of optimism, energy, and renewal. "It is room, we need, room!" declared the writer N. A. Mel'gunov. "We need room as we need air, bread, the light of day! It is necessary for everyone of us, it is necessary for Russia, for her internal flowering, for her security and strength abroad."[6] The time came to be called the era of the Great Reforms, the most famous of which was the emancipation of the serfs in 1861. The reforms also included the creation of elected local self-government in 1864, the introduction of the jury system in 1864, the easing of prepublication censorship in 1865, and in 1874 the adoption of universal military service, then regarded in Europe as a source of military strength and national cohesion. During the reform era, the government sanctioned a great surge of public activity to mobilize support for its reform projects and to rejuvenate the nation. A report of the Ministry of Public Education noted, "Here, where the habit of relying on the government for everything and waiting for it to take the initiative is so deeply rooted, more than anywhere else, it is desirable to develop free associations established for the public good."[7] Legal scholar S. A. Muromtsev wrote, "The purpose of all the reforms of the present reign is to stimulate initiative [*samodeiatel'nost'*] in society."[8] As the history of the committees of political economy in the previous chapter has shown, the press began to carry an unprecedented state-sanctioned discussion of government policy, local conditions, and ideas for further betterment. The zemstvos and provincial press publicized local conditions, and there was a great variety of news, correspondence, and articles about the condition of different social groups, the local economy, and local culture. Russians then called this public discussion *glasnost'*. To be sure, the government was unwilling to permit any constitutional challenge to autocratic rule, and radicals resented the incompleteness of the reforms and the slowness of change; but for a while in midcentury, a spirit of earnest application of effort for national improvement prevailed, as the anthropologist D. N. Anuchin later recalled, "to point Russia on the path of European forms of citizenship."[9]

This spirit was perhaps most intense at the universities and among Russian youth. Russian universities were creations of the state, so the government had considerable power in their operation. In 1859 university admissions restrictions were eased, and students of modest means began enrolling in greater numbers. In 1863 the government issued a new charter giving universities more autonomy. One of the articles of this charter gave universities permission to organize their own learned societies, under the supervision of the university rectors and trustees, a privilege that had been granted in the first university charter of 1804 but circumscribed by that of 1835. The government devolved the authority to grant permission of associations to incorporate from the Committee of Ministers to individual ministries. The new learned societies were granted the right to gather to discuss the latest developments in various disciplines and to undertake projects on their own initiative: publication, organizing research expeditions, soliciting private donations, running laboratories, and building science collections. The Academic Committee of the Ministry of Public Education was charged with reviewing their charters and annual reports and providing material assistance. As a result, many Russian associations with a self-conscious public mission had their origins in the era of the Great Reforms. An official of the Ministry of Internal Affairs noted the flowering of new asscociations: "[There is] a general inclination toward the development of associational public activity in all forms and for all kinds of purposes."[10] In 1862 a censorship decree devolved the censorship responsibilities to the officers of the learned societies, a privilege previously enjoyed only by the Academy of Sciences and the Free Economic Society, thereby increasing the rapidity and volume of published scholarly work. For the budding provincial intelligentsia, the deliveries of journals from the capitals recreated the atmosphere of the universities; the journals were a "mail-order study group [*kruzhok*]."[11] Thus, during the era of the Great Reforms, the government gave the green light to relatively autonomous organizations to take the initiative in the roles of public outreach and the stewardship of learning. The government was even willing to tolerate public activity and public meetings. A report of the new Kiev Society of Physicians for 1860–1861 noted the change: "The fortunate idea of making meetings of the society more public [*glasnye*], both by publishing its minutes and by opening meetings to nonmembers, was realized this year and, we dare to say, was quite useful. By stimulating the members to greater activity, publicity [*glasnost'*] will also give them greater hope that their common efforts will not go unnoticed but, on the contrary, will help explain the unanswered questions of science."[12]

Russian youth believed that the study of science held the key to progress, and the late 1850s appeared to be a new dawn of science. The greatest passion was reserved for materialism, theories of evolution, Darwin, and, in Vladimir Solov'ev's words, "the cult of natural history." Russia's center of what might be called Darwin studies was the Moscow Society of Naturalists, a learned society at Moscow University. The Society of Naturalists (MOIP in its Russian initials) was founded in 1805 in order to gather knowledge about the natural history of Russia; to collect Russian scientific works about mineralogy, botany, and zoology; and to find new articles for Russian commerce. Although the focus of the society's scientific interests was natural history, MOIP had interests that stretched to industry, agriculture, and commerce on the one hand and physics on the other. The society having been founded in an age when native Russian science was virtually nonexistent, most members of MOIP were foreign or foreign descendents; its longtime president was the German naturalist G. J. Fischer von Waldheim, and its honorary members included Lamarck, Darwin, and Humboldt. In keeping with the cosmopolitan spirit of the age in which it was founded, MOIP kept close ties with foreign scientific societies and published most of its scientific papers as well as the proceedings of its meetings in French and German. It received an annual subsidy from the Ministry of Education. Despite the considerable fame of the Moscow Society of Naturalists, it was vulnerable to the criticism that it was a closed, guildlike association engaging in pure research and publishing in foreign languages; that is, it was an "ivory tower" inaccessible to the younger generation.[13]

The founding of Victorian-era natural history societies was often depicted as an act of spontaneous generation, as if by nature itself—a gradual germination from an informal group of persons linked by fellowship to a formal organization. So it also was in Russia. In 1862 a group of specialists, amateurs, and students affiliated with Moscow University began meeting regularly to share discoveries, results of experiments, and news from Europe. From these private gatherings, goes the foundation story, came the idea of the usefulness of an association of specialists and amateurs that would mobilize resources for the study of science. In the self-reverential tone to be found in the society's histories, the group "had no means other than a faith in their goal and in the existence of genuine friends prepared to help further a useful cause." In an age of greater and greater specialization and in a vast country that isolated scientists, the new society would fill a perceived need to be accessible to nonspecialists, to hold meetings open to the general public, and to publish in Russian.[14]

The guiding spirit of these discussions was Anatolii Petrovich Bogdanov (see figure 4.1), a zoologist and professor at Moscow University. Born in 1834 in a village in Voronezh Province, Bogdanov graduated from Moscow University in 1855. He taught for a year at an agricultural school run by the Moscow Agricultural Society and made several trips abroad to inspect zoological gardens and museums before joining the faculty of his alma mater in 1863.[15] In his effort to popularize science, Bogdanov found a kindred spirit in the geologist Grigorii Efimovich Shchurovskii (see figure 4.2). Born in Moscow in 1803, Shchurovskii spent a considerable part of his childhood at the Moscow Foundling Home. He received his schooling in the Foundling Home's school; on the board of trustees of this school was Fischer von Waldheim, president of MOIP. Having received encouragement from Waldheim, in 1822 Shchurovskii enrolled at Moscow University to study medicine, the subject area in which biology was traditionally taught. There one of his teachers was M. G. Pavlov, director of the Moscow Agricultural

Figure 4.1 A. P. Bogdanov, naturalist and one of the founders of OLEAE. (B. E. Raikov, *Russkie biologi-evoliutsionisty do Darvina* [Moscow, 1951–1959], vol. 4.)

Society's agricultural school and popularizer of agricultural science. Although he decided not to go into medicine, Shchurovskii supported further study in the natural sciences by giving private lessons; one of his pupils was Ivan Turgenev. In 1832 Shchurovskii joined the medical faculty as a lecturer in natural history. He was one of the first scientists in Russia to propose the teaching of anthropology and comparative physiology as independent disciplines. In 1835 he transferred to the new department of geology and

Figure 4.2 G. E. Shchurovskii, naturalist, one of the founders of OLEAE and president, 1863–1884. (*Iubilei G. E. Shchurovskogo,* published in *Izvestiia OLEAE* 33 [1885]; courtesy of the Library of Congress.)

mineralogy. In addition to his research and teaching duties, Shchurovskii organized geological excursions in the environs of Moscow and delivered many public lectures in an effort to popularize the study of science in Russia. He was a member of many other science societies, including the Mineralogical Society, MOIP, the Moscow Horticultural Society, the Moscow Agricultural Society, and the Society of Russian Physicians.[16]

Bogdanov wisely enlisted the support of the dean of the physics and mathematics faculty, Avgust Iulevich Davidov. Davidov, born into a Jewish family in Latvia, promoted science education, wrote many mathematics textbooks, and was an inspector of secondary schools. In a factionalized faculty, Davidov sided with younger scholars who valued scholarly autonomy and the right to criticize the existing order. He became a crucial patron of the group of young naturalists and petitioned the university to approve the new organization. In 1863 the Academic Council of Moscow University approved the charter of the Society of Friends of Natural History, Anthropology, and Ethnography and sent its recommendation to the Ministry of Education. The society's first president was Shchurovskii.[17]

The project of Bogdanov, Davidov, and Shchurovskii did not proceed unopposed. The patrons of established science considered the new organization to be a "scholarly secession," undermining the work of existing scientific centers and behaving in a demagogic manner to students. The youthful organizers were called enemies, not friends, of science *(ne liubiteli, a gubiteli).*[18] Opposition to the new association reached the Ministry of Education. In a letter of 24 January 1864, N. F. Levitskii, the inspector of the Moscow education district, recommended that, instead of a new society, a division or committee of the currently existing Society of Naturalists, MOIP, be created. Levitskii saw duplication of effort between the proposed new society and the older Society of Naturalists and argued that such duplication was a "needless luxury" that would stretch the limited resources for and interest in natural history too thin and thereby weaken MOIP. Although Levitskii claimed to see little difference between MOIP and OLEAE, he touched on a fundamental difference between the older society of naturalists and the newer one. To become a member of the former required substantial scientific work, while the latter required only the obligation to work on behalf of the society's goals. Members of MOIP regarded themselves as servants of science, of an abstract knowledge. Members of the newer society obliged themselves to work on behalf of the society's goals, that is, to put science in service to Russia.[19]

At a meeting of 11 February 1864, the Academic Committee of the Ministry of Education discussed the opposing recommendations of Moscow University and of the inspector of the Moscow education district. Although the Academic Committee acknowledged the views of Levitskii, in the end it sided with Moscow University over the ministry's own officials. The new society had an advocate on the Academic Committee, A. N. Beketov, professor of botany at St. Petersburg University. Beketov complemented his teaching and scientific research with public activism. He founded the University Botanical Gardens, taught at the Higher Women's Courses, was active in the early congresses of scientists and physicians, edited publications of the Russian Geographical Society and the Free Economic Society, and was later secretary of the latter organization. The Academic Council recognized that not all naturalists might be comfortable working with MOIP. If so, prohibiting the creation of a new society might hold back the development of science more than the duplication of effort feared by Levitskii. There was no need to contradict the views of those scientists who wanted to found a new organization, especially if the university's Academic Council endorsed this wish. This was especially true, argued Professor Beketov, because "a learned society is not an official corporation whose members are obliged to work for a common purpose. [A learned society] has freedom of action, and the forcible retention of certain members in one society will prevent that society from prospering . . . Regarding the alleged division, it is to be noted that MOIP has well-respected members, as one can only assume judging by the importance of their scientific achievements. It can in no way suffer from the formation of a new society; on the contrary, competition will appear among its members, the importance of which cannot be refuted both in scientific endeavors as in all human affairs."[20]

Criticisms of the new organization forced the founders of OLEAE to define the society's mission carefully. From the very beginning, the new society was highly self-conscious of having a patriotic and public mission—and of publicizing that mission. The naturalists Bogdanov and Shchurovskii embodied the opportunities for private initiative. In frequent addresses, Bogdanov and Shchurovskii fused their perception of public needs with the identity of the new society. Russian science was still in its infancy, Bogdanov and Shchurovskii maintained, and science was still considered a domain of Europeans: "We all know that not so long ago the Russian people were almost entirely limited to the study of western Europe . . . It was a rare Russian who believed that Russia offered as much as, let alone more, scientific interest than western countries." The large number of foreign words in Russian scientific vocabulary symbolized this attitude and "slowed the pace of public education and of science itself in Russia." Textbooks allegedly contained too much foreign material—"as if Russia was a small piece of the earth, its natural history of no interest." The study of Russia would gain scholarly legitimacy, Shchurovskii argued, if "the national in the study of nature replaced the universal and the general." Unlike learned societies founded to advance science, the goal of OLEAE was to advance Russia. While its mission was "not to separate Russia from Western science," it stressed the development of a self-sufficient *(samostoiatel'naia)* science in Russia, to "maintain the national character of Russian science," that is, "to make science Russian, native":

> In recent years we have seen a welcome turn from the West to the East, we have seen that enthusiasm [*zhivoi interes*] which has begun to appear in everything concerning Russia. Even better, we have begun to realize that the study of foreign lands can only be a supplement to the study of our own. What a welcome phenomenon![21]

The mission of learned societies, Shchurovskii concluded, was to leverage this thirst for knowledge about the natural world of Russia into the creation of a Russian science. To accomplish this goal, the founders of OLEAE envisioned a dual strategy—mentoring Russian scientists as they entered the community of scientists and popularizing applied science.

The charter members regarded OLEAE as an extension of the teaching function of the university, at a time of university expansion. The young organizers of OLEAE, some of whom were under thirty or who were students themselves, rejected the conventions and allegedly closed, guildlike nature of existing scientific organizations, with their particular privileges. The founders of OLEAE were critical of the fact that many of Russia's older scientific organizations, such as the Academy of Sciences and MOIP, published papers in foreign languages inaccessible to the growing Russian intelligentsia. OLEAE, like the Russian Geographical Society, was committed to publishing its material in Russian; the minutes of its meetings and scientific papers were published in a voluminous serial, *Izvestiia*. As Shchurovskii later reflected, the charter members admitted that they sought "to split the existing centers of science in Moscow, to gather around themselves a party having practical, not scholarly, goals, and to exert an influence over students."[22] The charter members all but admitted that they thought of themselves as a counteracademy.

To aid young scientists to do research and fieldwork and to present their findings to a community of Russian scientists and amateurs, OLEAE created a national network of corresponding members. Moreover, a decentralized organizational structure and considerable divisional autonomy provided by the society's bylaws offered more gateways for young scientists and amateurs to enter the community of Russian scientists, thus giving the country a generous supply of trained scientists. Like the Russian Geographical Society, OLEAE was held together less by administrative authority and hierarchy than by the recognition of the overall guidance of scientific disciplines in the structure of the society and by allegiance to the ideal of mutual interdependence, that is, a civil society in microcosm. The society's autonomous divisions mobilized and coordinated the work of amateurs in gathering data and observations about natural history and experimental science. The excursions and expeditions that became a regular feature of OLEAE, unlike the empirewide expeditions of the Geographical Society, prioritized the Moscow region and the provinces of European Russia.[23] Finally, the founders recognized that Russian science lagged behind European science, especially in Russia's deficiencies in the ancillary facilities then regarded as so important in science education—science collections, libraries, laboratories, instructional instruments, and textbooks. By building or augmenting the facilities and accoutrements of applied science and by making them more widely available, Russian scientists would not have to "go abroad to learn research methods and work in laboratories."[24] In the founders' view, just as the product was to be the democratization of science, the process was to be a democratization of the scientists. If the goal was to make science Russian, then the means were to train Russian scientists.

Privileging the study of Russia and mentoring Russian scientists, however, were missions directed at those who already possessed scientific knowledge. What about the many Russians who did not? The second strategy of OLEAE was to popularize science and spread an interest in applied science among the general population. The founders believed the society needed to keep up with the times and be accessible to the general public. Judging the creation of knowledge—theoretical research—already to be the turf of other institutions such as the Academy of Sciences in St. Petersburg, the charter members of OLEAE stated that what Russia needed most was the dissemination and popularization of science. OLEAE would "take knowledge from the collections [*kabinety*] of the scientist and make it the intellectual patrimony [*dostoianie*] of the whole population." Russia was deficient not in theoretical knowledge but, Shchurovskii boldly stated, "in the number of people who [could] use that knowledge." In the striking terminology of the charter members, OLEAE could make its greatest mark by spreading the "democratization of knowledge."[25]

At the time of OLEAE's founding, the premier means to popularize applied science and to display useful knowledge were the museum and the exhibition. "Experience has shown," noted Bogdanov, "that neither public lectures nor popular compositions" can inform the public as well as can collections on display.[26] The charter members of OLEAE decided that Moscow needed an institutional home for the display of materials as a means of educating the public and stimulating an interest in applied science and in Russian natural history. Moreover, a museum would be a means whereby a learned society, of necessity a small and selective association, could enlist the participation of the broader public in its projects. "Our museums by their very nature must be educational and, at the same time, Russian," claimed Shchurovskii—that is, patriotic in their prioritization of the study of Russia.[27]

The new Rumiantsev Public Museum, which had been transferred from St. Petersburg to Moscow in 1862 (a date selected to mark the millennium of the founding of Russia), provided the first opportunity to test these ideas. The founders of OLEAE quickly threw their energies into augmenting the new Dashkov ethnographic collection of the relocated Rumiantsev Museum.[28] In order to acquire a collection and to prepare the general public for the more scholarly and systematic nature of the science museum, Bogdanov proposed organizing an ethnographic exhibition, which was eventually held in 1867. Behind the rhetoric of dissemination of knowledge lay a desire on the part of the organizers to mobilize interest in new scientific disciplines and to publicize the existence of OLEAE itself. For its efforts on behalf of native science in organizing the Ethnographic Exposition, OLEAE was conferred the title "Imperial." Both the government and OLEAE wanted the Ethnographic Exposition to be a demonstration of Russia's might and the greatness of the empire.[29] However, the greatest legacy of OLEAE was the founding of the Moscow Polytechnical Museum. This project included, as part of the planning stages, the Polytechnical Exposition of 1872. The remainder of this chapter will be devoted to the organization of the museum and the exposition. We will hereby see how a private association acted as a catalyst for the pursuit—by the tsarist government, the city of Moscow, and the business community—of public science, civic pride, and patriotism.

Public Science in Moscow

Modern Exhibitions and Museums of Science and Industry

The founders of OLEAE borrowed museum practice from Europe, and Moscow's Polytechnical Museum was patterned after European museums of natural history, applied science, and industry. Private, princely, and ecclesiastical collections of objects, later called "cabinets of curiosities," dated from the sixteenth century. By the end of the eighteenth century, restricted princely collections gave way to institutions with state and philanthropic support; royal collections became national museums. After the French Revolution, museums such as the Conservatoire des arts et métiers, designed to disseminate useful knowledge, demonstrate progress, and promote the national identity of republican France, became sites of civic and industrial education. The first national exhibition of manufactured goods took place on the Champs de Mars in Paris in 1798, to commemorate the impending tenth anniversary of the French Revolution. European governments and publics strove to improve industrial design, as well the prestige and competitive position of each nation's manufactures. In the 1830s, the British Parliamentary Select Committee on the State of Arts and Manufactures decried an alleged decline of craftsmanship and proposed a system of schools of design as well as associations of industry and the arts. Exposing manufacturer and mechanic alike to objects of beauty and fine design, the argument ran, would inspire the production of higher-quality articles. At the same time, Mechanics' Institutes reached out to workers through libraries, natural history collections, experimental workshops and laboratories, and lectures and adult classes. Although the French had been toying with the idea of an international exposition, the first world's fair was, of course, the famous Great Exhibition in London, better known as the Crystal Palace, visited by 6 million in the summer of 1851. The grand exhibitions that followed were a merger of private and government initiative, patronage, sponsorship, and financial support.[30]

The Crystal Palace heightened in Britain the perception that the nation's displays were less refined than those of France and Germany. The Board of Trade decided that industrial design and workmanship, as well as public taste, could be improved not only by industrial education but also by the intervention of museums of industry and the arts. One of the organizers of the Crystal Palace Exhibition warned, "As surely as darkness follows the setting of the sun, so will England recede as a manufacturing nation, unless her industrial population become much more conversant with science than they are now."[31] The culmination of efforts to improve industrial design and a by-product of the Crystal Palace Exhibition was London's South Kensington Museum, later renamed the Victoria and Albert Museum. Founded by the British government, the South Kensington Museum mobilized the resources of government, private associations, and individuals in the cause of industrial education. With its collection of machines and display of "visible knowledge," the industrial museum became a center for research and scientific inquiry.[32]

But museums and industrial exhibitions did more than simply produce and transmit knowledge; they presented, in Steven Conn's words, "a positivist, progressive and hierarchical view of the world and they gave that view material form and scientific legitimacy." The sequential display of evolution from primitive to complex was inherently didactic, as was the obsession with classification and ordering of experience. An especially important purpose of such museums and exhibitions was education and the popularization of science, and ideas and cultural values were on display as well as the products of modern industry. The museum was an important component in what George Stocking calls a "Victorian cultural ideology," in that it presented modern European civilization as the high point of evolutionary progress, respectability, rational self-improvement, and mastery over external and internal nature.[33]

Science museums and industrial exhibitions had multiple goals and sent mixed messages. On the one hand, to their organizers and promoters they were "festivals of technical progress" that disseminated useful information, demonstrated the wonders of science and industry, and displayed visions of a better and increasingly urban world. They disseminated information about new products and improvements as well as the secrets of industrial processes. On the other hand, in their efforts to stimulate better industrial design, science museums and industrial exhibitions displayed a critique of modern mechanized industry. Despite the emphasis on the voluntary efforts of business and industry in the organization of the exhibitions, the state, especially in France, was indispensable to their success. Earlier and more-modest agricultural and manufacturing exhibitions promoted the direct experience of nature and the dissemination and mastery of new techniques. But the entertaining displays of modern life and the wonders of applied science in the grand exhibitions more and more promoted a passive consumption of entertaining science and useful knowledge. Finally, despite the rhetoric of interdependence of nations and peaceful competition, the international exhibitions more and more became sites of national self-promotion and imperial assertiveness.[34]

OLEAE and the Polytechnical Exposition and Museum

The idea of a Russian exhibition and museum of applied science was a fusion of several efforts to create a native infrastructure of science education, and OLEAE could draw on a half century of projects of various constituencies. As far back as 1791, members had been donating objects of peasant industries to the Free Economic Society. In 1803 VEO opened its collection, its "cabinet of nature," to the public one day a week. In 1853 the Free Economic Society discussed creating a museum of designs and machines from the models of tools and agricultural implements it had been sent over the years. In the 1820s Prince D. V. Golitsyn, president of the Moscow Agricultural Society, suggested an exhibition of agriculture and trade as a means of improving Russian productivity. In 1864 the Moscow Agricultural Society proposed founding an agricultural museum. Young Russian chemists who traveled to German universities beginning in 1857 attended student chemistry practicums and saw new chemistry laboratories, where they worked side by side with German chemistry professors and advanced chemistry students. When they returned to Russia, they petitioned the educational authorities for modern chemistry laboratories with facilities for both teaching and research. At the same time, government, business and education circles began to discuss the idea of founding a museum of applied science, modeled after newly opened museums of industry and the arts in Paris and London. In 1857 a group of Moscow manufacturers requested the Ministry of Education to open a department of engineering at Moscow University; such a department would include a laboratory and an industrial museum.[35]

All of these ideas had floundered on the difficulty of acquiring a significant collection and the anticipated indifference of the public. Moreover, the grand industrial exhibitions and museums were not without their critics in Russia. Some dismissed the expositions as "foreign concoctions" or were embarrassed by the modesty of Russian displays at the Crystal Palace. Others doubted whether such grand enterprises were in the capacity of a private association. Although the government did not dominate the public debate over Russia's participation in international exhibitions, conservative officials were suspicious of such public activity and of the motives of its organizers. Finally, D. A. Naumov, chair of the Moscow Zemstvo Executive Board and vice president of the Moscow Agricultural Society, and V. I. Butovskii, director of the Stroganov School of Design, argued in the daily press that exhibitions and museums did not aid industry and that money could be better spent in upgrading existing facilities and in improving industrial education in the schools. Exhibitions, in particular, with their overemphasis on consumption and entertainment, were allegedly too random and ephemeral to be of educational value.[36]

The era of the Great Reforms witnessed a surge of public discussion of a great range of issues bearing on science, education, and industrial policy. Two of Russia's most prominent liberal economists, Ivan Vernadskii and V. P. Bezobrazov, weighed in on the issue of industrial museums and exhibitions. Vernadskii and Bezobrazov, as discussed in Chapter 3, were members of the two committees of political economy of VEO and the RGO. In 1860 an editorial in Vernadskii's new journal of liberal economic thought, *Ukazatel' Ekonomicheskii,* made the case for a museum of science and industry. The editorial began by stating that in Europe museums were widely used as a method of education. Russia, in contrast, had few such institutions. Since they were not accessible or did not present knowledge systematically, Russian museums did not satisfy the current needs of society. The editorial recommended opening existing collections to the public, preparing systematic catalogs, offering guided tours on Sundays and holidays, and sponsoring public lectures in different areas of knowledge.[37]

One year later, the *Century* [*Vek*], a short-lived magazine founded in 1861 whose economics section was headed by Bezobrazov, advocated a ramping up of Russia's participation in industrial exhibitions. International expositions no longer showed the exceptional and the "freaks of nature," the editorial claimed, but tried to present an accurate appraisal of the current productive capacities of all nations. Therefore, Russian participation at world's fairs was valuable for business and commerce. Perhaps more importantly, expositions could help Russian merchants and industrialists become acquainted with their counterparts in foreign countries. The *Century* evoked the vision of a bourgeois civil society marked by the differentiation and interdependence of the market posited by the thinkers of the Scottish Enlightenment. Expositions "bring together business people in order that they may realize their mutual advantage and, on this basis, combine their capital, enterprise, and knowledge for the accomplishment of the great task of trade—to supply society with a given product in the greatest number at the least cost."[38]

In stepped OLEAE. Shortly after the Ethnographic Exposition closed, Shchurovskii appointed a commission chaired by A. P. Bogdanov to investigate the possibility of augmenting the university science collection and of organizing public lectures to familiarize the public with developments in physics and mechanics. Having received a grant of two thousand rubles from the Ministry of State Domains, Bogdanov and the physicist A. S. Vladimirskii toured physics and mechanics institutes in England, France, and Germany to acquire instruments and machines to be used in public lectures. At the same time, Shchurovskii proposed investigating the possibility of founding a natural history museum. At a meeting of OLEAE on 13 August 1868, the Bogdanov commission proposed to the members an exhibition of applied science that would provide the basis for a permanent collection as well as stimulate public interest in science, technology, and industry. The Bogdanov commission immediately became the Commission to Organize an Exhibition of Applied Science, chaired by Shchurovskii.[39]

The proponents of a museum of applied science claimed that the museum project could be jump-started by organizing an industrial exhibition. Although the instrumental conception of such an exposition remained constant, holding an exposition quickly became an end itself. Its planning ran parallel to and often ahead of that of the museum, and the most prominent proponents of the one were also proponents of the other. In both cases, OLEAE led the way. The Polytechnical Exposition of 1872 had its ancestors in trade fairs and various manufacturing exhibitions, both native and

European. The Russian government organized the empire's first manufacturing exhibition in St. Petersburg in 1829 and subsequent manufacturing and agricultural exhibitions for patriotic purposes, to promote native industry.[40]

Although the relationship between Russian government and society is often portrayed in terms of conflict, cooperation was more typically the rule. As we have seen, the tsarist state sanctioned and patronized Russia's science societies and many of their projects. For their part, most Russian science societies saw their role as collaborating with the authorities and assisting the state in the mutual pursuit of national betterment and prestige. The interests of state and society appeared to be shared interests, and state and society were willing to be partners. Government officials and scientists alike articulated the need for more Russian scientists and for a native science infrastructure. Thus, the members of associations realized that public discussion, especially on patriotic projects such as the dissemination of learning for the greater good of Russia, was imaginable, even under autocracy, that nonstatist solutions to problems were feasible in a country with a long statist tradition.

In order to gain stature and subsidies, as well as assistance in facilitating the exposition and the museum, OLEAE actively sought government support and participation. The Naval Ministry was the first government body to respond positively; it prodded other government departments to support and participate in the enterprise. Admiral Konstantin Nikolaevich Pos'et, tutor of Grand Duke Aleksei Aleksandrovich, as well as A. A. Zelenyi, minister of state properties, offered to intercede in an attempt to get imperial support.[41] One of the exposition's greatest supporters was the minister of war, Dmitrii Miliutin, and one of his aides, Adjutant General Nikolai Vasil'evich Isakov, was appointed chairman ofz the exposition organizing committee. A staunch monarchist and one of the masterminds behind the Great Reforms, Miliutin wanted to eradicate Russia's backwardness, educate the population, and modernize the army. On the eve of Russia's adoption of universal military service, Miliutin stated, "The public must be more closely linked to the army . . . and better acquainted with military matters." To critics in and out of government who grumbled that Miliutin's projects of military modernization were too costly, the minister of war argued that the exhibition would demonstrate that the large expenditures had been spent wisely. After Russia's humiliating defeat in the Crimean War, the realization that Russia was prepared for modern warfare would bolster national pride. In May 1870, the ministries of Finance and State Properties, already in frequent contact with OLEAE regarding planning an industrial exposition, approved the idea of using the exposition as the basis for a permanent industrial museum.[42]

At the same time that interest had been generated in Moscow for a museum of applied science and the affiliated exposition, government officials and the new Russian Technical Society in St. Petersburg (to be introduced in the following chapter) began discussing an industrial museum in the capital. Perhaps unaware of what had already been discussed in Moscow, the educator Nikolai Khristianovich Vessel' claimed, in an address before the Russian Technical Society in 1871, that the idea for a museum of applied knowledge originated at the Russian National Manufacturing Exhibition in St. Petersburg in 1870. One of the exhibition's visitors, Emperor Alexander II, expressed his satisfaction with the exhibition and especially with the pedagogical section, which had displayed schoolbooks and materials of the Ministry of War's Pedagogical Museum. The tsar gave imperial backing to the idea of creating a museum of industry and the arts, and the Ministry of Finance, in whose "domain" lay the development of Russian industry, appointed a commission to discuss the feasibility of founding such a museum. Aleksandr Butovskii, an economist of the Manchester School, author of a review of the Paris World Exposition of 1867, and director of the ministry's Department of Trade and Manufactures, chaired the commission. On the commission were officials from the ministries of Finance and State Properties, as well as members of the Russian Technical Society and of the Society for the Encouragement of the Arts, whose patron was Grand Duchess Maria Nikolaevna. The commission dispatched Vessel' to gather material about such institutions in Europe. In 1871 Vessel' presented material on the South Kensington and similar museums in Europe, and the commission decided to found a museum of industry in St. Petersburg. However, although it was impressed with the record of London's South Kensington Museum, the commission decided not to follow the South Kensington model—that is, the model of a monumental central, "national" museum—in St. Petersburg, because the public was allegedly not prepared for such a museum. The Butovskii commission, Vessel' later informed his Moscow colleagues, argued that the money needed to found a grand museum could be better spent in upgrading existing facilities and in improving industrial education in the schools. Accordingly, the commission proposed expanding an existing structure in the Solianoi Gorodok neighborhood and making this space available to the Museum of War's Pedagogical Museum and to the Russian Technical Society.[43]

It was still not clear whether the museum of the kind proposed by OLEAE would be built in St. Petersburg or Moscow. Not only had proposals to found new museums of industry in St. Petersburg and in Moscow both received government approval; they also got caught up in St. Petersburg–Moscow rivalry at a time of growing cultural assertiveness of the old capital, and among the issues under deliberation in government circles was whether to favor Moscow or St. Petersburg in this new project. In stepped OLEAE again. Realizing that times had changed and that support of the local community was an important ingredient in the success of such an enterprise, OLEAE shrewdly turned to Moscow's newly constituted representatives, the city council and the mayor. On 7 May 1870, Bogdanov, who managed to find time to be a member of the city council, informed the council of the proposals and of the discussion in government to found a new museum of industry. Believing that a national museum was important for Russian pride and that Moscow was the better location, Bogdanov suggested that the city council join the efforts of Moscow's learned societies and business community to bring such an enterprise to Moscow. The city council appointed a commission to study the matter; among the commission's members were Shchurovskii; I. N. Shatilov, president of the Moscow Agricultural Society; and V. K. Della-Vos, influential organizer and director of the Imperial Technical School. All were active in planning the Polytechnical Exposition and staunch advocates of a new industrial museum in Moscow.[44]

In its report, submitted to the city council on 25 August 1870, the commission supported, almost word-for-word, the arguments of prominent members of OLEAE for a national museum in Moscow. To be sure, the commission acknowledged, the predecessors of the 1870 city council had not embraced the idea of a science museum. As long as it had seemed to be a specialized museum, such as an agricultural museum, it was deemed outside the responsibility of the city government, especially a city government with limited means. Moreover, there were those in and out of government who doubted whether grand enterprises such as a museum and an industrial exhibition were in the capacity of a private association and who claimed that these enterprises were "a matter only for [national] governments."[45] At the same time, the city council commission capitalized on the reluctance in St. Petersburg to "think big." The commission argued that St. Petersburg was not the center of, nor did it represent, Russian industry. Furthermore, the commission's report quite cleverly claimed that if the purpose of such a museum was educational, little could be learned in St. Petersburg, where most leaders of industry were foreigners or were already educated (presumably, the report meant government officials). Finally, Vladimir Cherkasskii, the mayor of Moscow and a member of OLEAE, energetically argued before the city council that it was in Moscow's interests to have the museum.[46]

Indeed, patriotism and the popularization of science were the two dominant themes of the exposition and the museum. The Moscow museum project, claimed Bogdanov, would stimulate the private initiative needed by the government in the cause of public education. The exposition and museum could depict the "age-old struggle against external nature, . . . by showing the secrets of nature revealed." As Viktor Della-Vos put it later at the exposition inaugural banquet held at Moscow University, the purpose of the exposition was to emphasize education, to popularize science and technology, and to acquaint the public with "the basic principles of production." Process was to be more important than product. In an age of ever-increasing specialization in the sciences, displays could show the links between the sciences and, "in each branch of industry, a few examples of the latest technology and production processes."[47]

Just as important as the scientific and education goals were the patriotic; just as important as the "secrets of nature" were the secrets of Russia. By providing an opportunity to assess the state of Russian industries and to encourage native industry, the exposition and the museum would fulfill a public service function. The lectures and demonstrations accompanying the exposition and pitched at all Russian citizens would "summon, enlighten, and elevate the national moral feeling as well as the popular love and devotion to the fatherland."[48] In this connection, Nil Aleksandrovich Popov found a clever "hook" for both the exhibition and the museum. Director of the Ethnographic Division of OLEAE, Popov was a historian and Slavicist who had written extensively about Peter the Great. The exposition, Popov reasoned, not only would inform the public about current technological improvements but also would provide an opportunity to review the history of Russian industry. This would be especially important because of the impending bicentennial of the birth of Peter the Great. In order to honor the memory of the "great reformer" in the reign of another great reformer, Popov proposed postponing the exposition until 1872 and linking its agenda with Peter's bicentennial (see figure 4.3). Hitching the exposition to Peter's horse would have the added benefit, Popov concluded, of attracting more foreign displays and would thereby honor Peter's borrowing of foreign technology in order to modernize Russia. Thus, the exposition provided an opportunity the government could not suppress to continue Peter's work, and to demonstrate the greatness of Russia.[49]

The "victory" of Moscow was clinched in December 1870, when the mayor of Moscow, Prince Vladimir A. Cherkasskii, came to St. Petersburg to lobby personally on behalf of the "Moscow interests." A wealthy Tula landlord with ties to the Moscow Slavophiles, as well as a member of Grand Duchess Elena Pavlovna's salon, Cherkasskii was a prominent member of the editing commissions that drafted the Emancipation Act of 1861. As mayor

Figure 4.3 Polytechnical Exposition, 1872: A commemorative kerchief, made at the Danilov textile mill in Moscow, depicting Peter the Great and a map of the exhibition grounds in and around the Moscow Kremlin. (Courtesy of the Library of Congress, Prints and Photographs Division.)

of Moscow, beginning in 1868, he was a member of the commission that drafted the Municipal Statute of 1870. He was an admirer of Tocqueville and a champion of local authority with regard to central officialdom; in November 1870, he signed Ivan Aksakov's address to Alexander II, which called for greater civil liberties. However, neither his admiration of Tocquville nor the reprimand he received from Alexander II for signing Aksakov's address prevented him from lobbying to the central authorities. Not surprisingly, Cherkasskii supported the Moscow project. Emperor Alexander II approved the Moscow plan, and the Ministry of Finance appropriated a half million rubles for construction and, on 23 September 1872, appointed an organizing committee to plan the museum and, later, to run it.[50]

Arguments in favor of a Moscow museum are further evidence of the compatibility of economic development, scientific infrastructure, and patriotism observed by several scholars. The "merchant-Slavophile alliance," as Thomas Owen calls the Moscow business community and its literary allies, promoted native industry and economic self-sufficiency. They admired the technological progress of the West and, like the leaders of OLEAE, in Alfred Rieber's words, wanted to put "science in service to the nation." In their efforts to gain control of Russia's railroads over foreign companies in the 1860s, the merchant-Slavophile alliance demonstrated its public advocacy role.[51] Moscow, of course, stood for the happy merger of Russian distinctiveness and economic development. Although it might seem paradoxical that Moscow would honor the birth of the monarch who moved his imperial capital to St. Petersburg, in fact the anti-Peter rhetoric of the Slavophiles took a backseat to pragmatism. Asserting the centrality of Moscow in the development of Russian industry and scientific infrastructure was a more effective way to promote civic pride, demonstrate patriotism, and enter the public arena.

Planning and the Public

The planning process exemplifies the collaboration between state and society in pursuit of common goals. The honorary chair of the museum organizing committee was Grand Duke Konstantin Nikolaevich; its two cochairs were G. E. Shchurovskii and Adjutant General Nikolai Vasil'evich Isakov (see figure 4.4), who, as we have seen, also chaired the exposition organizing committee. Isakov played an important role in several education projects in midcentury and illustrates the overlapping of government and nongovernment public service. While curator *(popechitel')* of the Moscow education district from 1859 to 1863, Isakov studied foreign educational systems, organized teachers' courses, and initiated the relocation of the Rumiantsev Museum from St. Petersburg to Moscow. As superintendent of military schools beginning in 1863, Isakov helped found the Ministry of War's Pedagogical Museum and the Museum of Applied Knowledge in St. Petersburg. He was close to Viktor Della-Vos, a member of the organizing committee and director of the Imperial Technical School. Finally, Isakov was a member of numerous voluntary associations, including OIDR, MOIP, the Russian Technical Society, and the Russian Musical Society.[52]

Figure 4.4 General N. V. Isakov, educator and cochair of committees to organize the Polytechnical Exposition and the Moscow Polytechnical Museum. (*Niva*, no. 12 [1891]: 281; courtesy of the Library of Congress.)

The membership of the organizing committee was a mixture of government officials, municipal leaders, businessmen, and educators, many of whom were close to prominent Slavophiles and were involved in the 1867 Slavic Congress. Although the museum and exposition organizing committees were government appointed, following the French model, both had considerable autonomy in planning. They could select additional members, appoint directors of the various divisions of the museum and sections of the exposition, and invite consultants whose expertise was deemed necessary in particular aspects of planning. Finance subcommittees of both the exposition and the museum engaged in fund-raising, an important concession from a government that greatly restricted the opportunity of private associations to accumulate capital reserves.[53]

The planning of both exposition and museum was an example of collaboration between state and society. OLEAE received the moral, financial, and material support of the government. Indeed, in the early stages, because few believed that the exposition could be realized with private support alone, OLEAE got a grant of two thousand rubles as seed money from the Ministry of State Properties. At the same time, Alexander II charged the minister of education, D. A. Tolstoy, to ensure that the appropriate ministry approve all aspects of the exposition. The exposition organizing committee sought the assistance of central and local authorities to collect objects for display. This state of affairs conforms with the European practice, especially in France, of dual responsibility, whereby governments, while still holding ultimate supervisory control over expositions, allowed private bodies to organize them.[54]

Given autocracy's dominance over public life, the state's role in founding and planning the museum was hardly surprising. "It would be hard to imagine," an 1870 report of OLEAE admitted, "a museum created by private philanthropy or even by a municipality alone. As the experience of other countries has shown, only governments have the means . . . Museums, such as the proposed museum of education and applied knowledge, appear only as state institutions, founded and maintained by governments."[55] However, the Russian government played no more than a secondary role in the planning and administration of the Polytechnical Museum, a role at times limited to approving plans and providing subsidies. At the insistence of the organizing committee, the administrative structure was to be collegial and not the routinized government administration of an institution.

As Della-Vos argued, the new museum must be up-to-date and "apply, borrow or test any useful or instructive advances in foreign countries."[56] The exposition and museum organizing committees dispatched experts to study European exhibitionary and museum practice, to establish contact with European learned societies, and to acquire objects for display. Such trips *(komandirovki)* to the centers of European science during the era of the Great Reforms were part of a larger mutual project of state and society to borrow European practices in the dissemination of useful knowledge. The ultimate objective was to create a Russian scientific infrastructure that would obviate the need for such visits in the future. The president of the Moscow Architectural Society, N. V. Nikitin, a member of the committee, compiled an extensive report of his tour of European museums in 1873, which had been undertaken to apply the knowledge gained from an observation of European practice to solve problems in planning the polytechnical museum. Nikitin visited many exhibitions and museums, including the Vienna World Exposition of 1873, Kew Gardens, the Edinburgh Museum of Industry and the Arts, and even the Suez Canal panorama that had greatly stimulated public interest in the new canal project at the Paris World Exposition in 1867. He studied the model schools displayed at the Museum of

Natural History in Paris and the teaching section of the South Kensington Museum, as well as building design, lighting, heating, the organization of displays, the placement of objects, and the use of auditoriums. In Nikitin's opinion, the South Kensington Museum was a model in the application of the arts to industry and in the development of industrial arts education that other European museums strove to emulate. Museums such as the South Kensington "instill in the public that conviction in the power and importance of science and the arts, without which all methods to disseminate knowledge will never succeed." In addition, he also studied many other anthropological and ethnographic collections, specialized museums of industry, zoological and botanical gardens, and aquariums. Finally, he suggested that the Russian Society of Architects prepare guidebooks of Moscow as a way to attract the public, after observing that the Russian section at the Vienna World Exposition could have been "more attractive to the public" at a time when "museums and exhibitions [needed] to attract the public."[57]

The museum organizing committee spent considerable time discussing site selection and building design. The two designs then most common in Europe were the large, "monumental" museum building and the "garden" style of smaller pavilions, pioneered by the French and most frequently used for expositions. Pavilions allowed the simulation of a small town and emphasized the dual use of urban space for edification and leisure. And, as we will see in this chapter, the pavilions would evoke not just any small town but a Russian small town. Most committee members initially considered the garden style, the design pattern of Moscow's 1872 Polytechnical Exposition, more attractive to the public; moreover, the imperial court offered an attractive site on which to erect pavilions, the Aleksandr Gardens, which were adjacent to the Kremlin and the site of the 1872 exposition. After visiting the Kew Gardens, Nikitin announced, "The first result of my inspection of Kew was a strong desire to see something similar in Moscow." At the same time, however, the city council proposed to donate land on Lubianka Square, and for a while the organizing committee entertained the notion, advocated by Bogdanov, of splitting the museum collection into industrial and natural history components and building on both Lubianka Square and in the Aleksandr Gardens. However, because there was not enough money to launch simultaneous construction on two sites, the committee decided to build on Lubianka Square first; over the years, the enthusiasm for the garden design dwindled.[58]

Both exposition and museum organizing committees involved the public in planning, taking advantage of a new opportunity available to voluntary associations under autocracy. The exposition organizing committee sent brochures explaining the purposes of the exposition, brochures to be appended to issues of newspapers and magazines. It also sent letters to other organizations inviting them to participate. The Moscow Architectural Society organized competitions to design the pavilions; the Russian Music Society presented a music program; the Society of Russian Physicians helped organize the medical displays; the Association for the Dissemination of Technical Knowledge organized the photography display. The list could go on: before it ended, it would include the Russian Technical Society, the Russian Geographical Society, the Moscow Literacy Committee, the Moscow Horticultural Society, the Moscow Sailing Club, and the Society for Improving the Morals of Artisans and Workers. A representative of each of these associations sat on the relevant subcommittee, frequently alongside government officials. As one organizing committee member put it in October 1870, acknowledging that OLEAE had bit off more than it could chew, "All of Russia came to our aid."[59] The cooperation of a broad range of business, scientific, and philanthropic organizations demonstrated the fruit of private initiative; it also was evidence of the horizontal linkages between organizations characteristic of Russia's growing civil society.

The exposition organizers sought publicity, a quintessential feature of modern urban culture. The work of planning the exposition took place openly and was subject to public scrutiny in the press. The organizing committee familiarized the public with the progress of exposition and museum planning by publishing summaries of its meetings and budget reports in the metropolitan newspapers. Beginning one month before the Polytechnical Exposition opened and continuing through September, the organizing committee published a daily newspaper, *Vestnik Politekhnicheskoi vystavki,* "in order to give the public a faithful and complete account of the exposition." The newspaper also provided "other useful information and announcements"—government directives, wire service dispatches on political affairs, stock exchange and commercial news, correspondence from the provinces, feuilletons about Moscow life, and information about Moscow geared specially for Russian and foreign tourists.[60]

The museum organizing committee solicited the aid of the Moscow Architectural Society to hold a competition to design the building's facade. The committee then copied the European practice of making architects' designs available to the public. Architects' drawings were printed in the museum's *Materialy dlia istorii ustroistva,* published by OLEAE, and "these plans were exhibited to the court of public opinion" in the halls of the museum's temporary quarters. The opinions of different proposals were printed in the newspapers *Golos, Sovremennye izvestiia,* and *Russkie vedomosti.*[61] The organizing committee approved submissions favored by its honorary chair, Grand Duke Konstantin—a design for a facade submitted by I. A. Monighetti, the architect of the imperial court, and the overall building plan of architect and organizing committee member N. A. Shokhin. At this point the committee appointed a building commission, which worked closely with the city council and which divided into many different subcommittees.[62]

By 1870 the planning committee had expanded to 127 members divided into twenty-eight specialized subcommittees, each of which summoned expert opinion from members of the public. As Bogdanov told I. N. Shatilov, president of the Moscow Agricultural Society and chair of the exposition's subcommittee for planning the agricultural section, the organizing committee determined only the most general aspects of the exposition, leaving all other matters to be decided by the appropriate subcommittee. Collegial and decentralized administrative structures facilitated the participation of other learned societies and made both exposition and museum more responsive to the public.[63]

The 1872 Exposition

From May to September, 1872, more than 750,000 visitors viewed some 10,000 articles displayed in 90 pavilions in and around the Moscow Kremlin. An enterprise launched to provide the core collection of a museum of applied science transmitted knowledge about the natural world, employed science to entertain, and displayed technological innovations alongside Russian traditions. A full description and analysis of the 1872 Polytechnical Exposition is beyond the scope of this study. But brief mention of a few selected moments may suffice to suggest how OLEAE blended science, patriotism and entertainment and thereby enriched civic life.[64]

The inaugural banquet was an opportunity not only to reiterate the goals of the exposition but also to put a Russian stamp on a borrowed occasion and to prompt expressions of patriotism in front of dignitaries, which included Grand Duke Konstantin Nikolaevich and Moscow Governor General V. A. Dolgorukov. The decoration at the event invoked national triumph and national heroes: roses and garlands of laurel leaves adorned the main hall and corridors of Moscow University, and electric lights illuminated the bust of Peter the Great. By celebrating Peter the Great at Moscow University, the inaugural banquet, like the exposition as a whole, blended symbols of Peter's Russia with Moscow's Russia. In his oration, Viktor Della-Vos, director of the Imperial Technical School, stressed the obligation of every nation to participate in such international competition, thereby asserting Russia's arrival in that class of nations with the scientific and industrial capacity to hold such exhibitions. And private initiative, Della-Vos noted, enhanced that capacity: "Moscow, the center of Russian industry, demonstrated brilliantly that private initiative and energy in every useful undertaking is a force that can overcome the most difficult and, at first glance, insurmountable obstacles . . . The engines that switched on this major manifestation of private activity were government support, individual initiative, purity of motives, and national pride."[65] Rebutting arguments that Peter's reforms either were ephemeral or uprooted Russia, the historian S. M. Solov'ev, a member of the organizing committee, celebrated the Russia of Peter's creation—which confidently borrowed science and technology from the West to enlighten the nation. No less patriotic was OLEAE president Shchurovskii, who claimed that the exposition would promote native industry and help Russian industrial design overcome its dependence on foreigners.[66]

An especially important purpose of the world's fairs was education, and ideas and cultural values were on display as well as the products of modern industry. The dissemination of information about new products and processes, the sequential display of the evolution of industry from primitive to complex, and the obsession with classifying and ordering experience, were all didactic.[67] As Viktor Della-Vos put it in his address at the inaugural banquet, the purpose of the exposition was to popularize science and technology, to demonstrate the practical applications of science in everyday life, and to acquaint the public with "a few examples of the latest technology" and with "the basic principles and processes of production."[68] For example, along the Moscow River, the Navy Pavilion, a structure of iron and glass designed by I. A. Monighetti that resembled London's Crystal Palace housed a full-size merchant marine vessel as well as displays of Russia's growing maritime strength. Sections of applied science familiarized the Russian public with a dizzying variety of new technologies used in photography, mining, armaments, steel production, and railroad building, to name but a few. The agriculture section displayed not only the latest implements but also a model landowner's home, containing a library of reference works, dictionaries, encyclopedias, Russian atlases, and Russian history books, as well as several books on home economics, health, and child rearing—the fruits of the "industrial Enlightenment," to use the terminology of economist Joel Mokyr, that "reduced access costs" to modern useful knowledge. These books, as well as fiction (for the benefit of "someone who wants to read something besides the newspapers once in awhile"), suggest a model landowner already connected to a print public.[69] The village school, stocked with books supplied by the Society to Disseminate Useful Books, had a place for each pupil to store things: "in this way, the pupils without knowing it will get used to order and will learn to look after their property."[70]

At the same time, the transition to a new rural life that exemplified the "industrial Enlightenment" and respect for private property was made seamless by reminders of traditional Russian paternalism and wooden handicrafts. The agriculture section also displayed, the press noted, practical and inexpensive peasant-made wares, "not widely distributed due to their unfamiliarity," that would "satisfy the requirements of taste, order, convenience, and education."[71] In its display of peasant-made objects, the Moscow exposition was at the cutting edge of the promotion of the region's handicraft *(kustar')* industries at the end of the nineteenth century. As Wendy Salmond argues, the "collision of tradition and modernity" that characterized Russia in the latter part of the nineteenth century was accompanied by "an unprecedented revival and reassessment of native Russian traditions." Such "vernacular revivals," the Russian version of the arts and crafts movement, were an effort to assert an organic cultural identity and a sense of a distinct national past. However, utilized at an exhibition that stressed new practices and technologies, the prominent display of "unfamiliar" peasant handicrafts was not harnessed to influence industrial design but to publicize and market an image of Russia that the exhibition organizers reckoned would appeal to visitors. As Evgeniia Kirichenko puts it, the everyday and the prosaic were transformed into the artistic by the "poetics of exposition."[72]

Inside the pavilions, new technologies and the techniques of their display were borrowed from Europe and international exhibition practice; outside, the pavilions displayed wooden architecture and ornamentation borrowed from Muscovite churches and peasant handicrafts. Displays of applied science and modern empire were enclosed in wooden structures with elaborate decorative carving in the Russian folk style: modern science and empire were, quite literally, "at home" in Russia. The overall architectural integrity of the exposition bonded the visitor to the nation and to history. The building subcommittee, chaired by N. V. Nikitin, a proponent of the "Russian style" in architecture, created an architectural and aesthetic theme park that put pre-Petrine folk motifs in service to the needs of modern urban culture. The grand exhibitions of the day in Europe and North America captured the imagination and drew crowds by placing the visitor in a fantasy realm of the striking, the surprising, and the exotic. But while the European exhibitions found the exotic in other civilizations, most commonly the "Orient," at the 1872 Polytechnical Exposition the exotic was old Russia. The famous architect Viktor Gartman, a pioneer in the utilization of the elaborate lace- and embroidery-like decoration of folk architecture, designed a historical museum in ornamental Russian style for the Army Pavilion (see figure 4.5). The semicircular pavilion was topped by a "tent-roof" *(shatior)* reminiscent of sixteenth- and seventeenth-century Muscovite churches, especially the Church of the Ascension at Kolomenskoe, one of Peter the Great's childhood residences. Gartman's mobile folk theater, which also employed elaborately carved decoration, was inspired by the *balagan,* the temporary wooden stages of urban popular entertainments.[73] Although the stylized wooden architecture evoked long-ago Muscovite Russia, the use to which it was put looked forward to urban mass culture. As Evgeniia Kirichenko argues regarding the proponents of the Russian national style in architecture, "the influence of temporary wooden exhibition halls on the character of Russian urban architecture was immense . . . [It] gave a new impulse to the development of construction in wood in the Russian style . . . The 1872 Exposition became something of a manifesto and a demonstration of their artistic credo."[74] Moreover, although it might be tempting to see utilization of the Russian style in architecture as solely a nationalistic evocation of the Russian past, the organizers regarded aesthetic originality as a necessary way to attract visitors and increase ticket sales, the measure of success of modern exhibitions. Thus, the exposition organizers utilized the Russian-style aesthetic for the ultimate in modern purposes—marketing: the marketing of industrial development, national identity, and patriotism.

The Polytechnical Museum and the Audience for Science

Two months after the Polytechnical Exposition closed its gates for the last time, the Moscow Polytechnical Museum opened its doors in its temporary headquarters on Prechistenka Street; in 1877 the museum moved into its permanent quarters on Lubianka Square (see figure 4.6). During the first year more than 270,000 visitors attended, and from 1872 to 1885, the museum's attendance was 1,360,260. On Sundays, Thursdays, Fridays, and all holidays, there was no admission charge. Sales of publications, entrance fees, private donations, and government subsidies covered museum expenses. In addition, the museum made its collection, library, and auditorium and meeting rooms available to organizations such as the Society to Organize Reading Rooms and Public Readings, the Society to Disseminate Useful Books, the Higher Women's Courses, the Moscow Agricultural Society, and the Moscow Medical Society. By 1878 twelve learned societies

Figure 4.5 1872 Polytechnical Exposition: Army Pavilion, designed by the architect Viktor Gartman. (*Vsemirnaia Illiustratsiia*, no. 193 [1872]: 165; courtesy of the Library of Congress.)

Figure 4.6 Polytechnical Museum on Lubianka Square in Moscow, 1877. (Courtesy of the State Polytechnical Museum, Moscow.)

held regular meetings at the museum, thereby accomplishing one of the wishes of the Museum Committee—to make the museum a center of learned activity in the city.[75] Although a full discussion of the early years of this prominent Moscow institution is beyond the scope of this study, a brief glimpse at its education mission and at its most self-conscious attempts at outreach—public lectures and scientific demonstrations—will suggest the role of the association in creating a public.

The published record of the museum organizing committee and of meetings of OLEAE reveals the degree to which museum officials and members of its parent society had absorbed the ideals of progress through education and self-improvement. The museum was most proud of its role in adult education and the dissemination of learning, a role that it defined very broadly. Like the school, the museum carried a civilizing mission. In every country, claimed Della-Vos, "where the social structure rests on sober, rational principles and where the majority of the population recognizes the necessity of mental, moral, and material development, the dissemination of general education and specialized fields of knowledge must be regarded as a basic need." A museum that thus demonstrated its educational mission could mobilize the latent public support that OLEAE considered important to the enterprise's success. Later, proposing that OLEAE also found an anthropology museum, Bogdanov argued, "The experience of other large museums shows that these institutions are able to grow because they find major support in society, in the public."[76]

In its presentation of applied science, the Polytechnical Museum pursued multiple agendas. Perhaps befitting a creation of university scientists, the founders emphasized the museum's education functions. Again and again, museum reports emphasized that the collections of raw materials and machines documented manufacturing processes, demonstrated the division of fields of applied knowledge, and displayed the state of the art in all branches of science and industry. Using a common metaphor, one of its proponents, the critic Vladimir Stasov, defended the all-purpose museum as a different kind of educational experience, which provided the public with a "permanently open book" about industry, the arts, science, and technology.[77] The Division of Applied Physics, headed by A. S. Vladimirskii, set up not only a physics hall with demonstrations for lectures but also a physics laboratory where industrial research could be carried out. Moreover, museum organizers invited foreign manufacturers to display products, machines, and processes not yet common in Russia, in a special section of inventions and improvements. However, this created tension in a museum in the heart of Russian industry. The emphasis on process and "state of the art" did not favor the display of native manufactures. Shchurovskii spoke often on the need for Russian engineers to wrest control of industrial design away from foreigners, and, Professor I. P. Arkhipov argued that the museum should stimulate Russian manufacturers to develop native industry. The museum would thus mediate between manufacturers and the public by displaying the achievements of the former and sparking the curiosity and interest of the latter.[78]

The museum "public" for this sort of industrial education was that public assumed, everywhere in Europe and North America, to be at the ready to improve manufactures—and to improve themselves through education and the rational pursuit of leisure. One of many Russian reports of foreign museums noted that everywhere, especially in England, museums spearheaded the efforts to develop in the "industrial classes" a taste for the refined.[79] In his address titled "General Education and the Moscow Polytechnical Museum," Bogdanov opined that the museum would be most useful for "those who, by virtue of their education, . . . set themselves apart from the masses." Bogdanov continued, "In science today, it is not enough to have education in depth in one branch of knowledge; it is also necessary to have a well-rounded education . . . Everywhere, there are efforts to supplement the knowledge gained in schools."[80] A museum pitched at the ordinary working population promised "to provide to the class of people with modest means not only harmless but also useful ways to spend leisure time." Employing a common argument of the age, the economist A. I. Chuprov indicated that the museum's target audience was skilled artisans, who, "having acquired a storehouse of new ideas [from the museum], can introduce improvements in production and improve the quality of their labor and thereby directly improve their material well-being."[81]

To reach a wide audience, the Polytechnical Museum employed two closely connected means of diffusing natural knowledge at the time—public lectures and scientific demonstrations. Public lectures in the cities of western Europe and North America not only promoted a love of useful knowledge but also helped create a public. Their audience was predominantly the young and ambitious—apprentices, clerks, mechanics and artisans, skilled factory workers—who were attracted to tales of exotic travels and to demonstrations of the wonders of modern science and technology. The lecture might have been ephemeral and the audience local, but through publication and publicity the occasion could reach a larger public of shared learning. Moreover, the experience of organizing lectures and, even more, of appearing before a mixed audience of unfamiliar persons put organizers and speakers in the public eye and aided careers.[82] During and after the Great Reform era, many Russian associations sponsored public lectures. An annual report of the St. Petersburg Literacy Committee noted, "Public lectures are without a doubt one of the most powerful ways to disseminate education and scientific knowledge among the population, especially in a country like Russia." Indeed, despite government restrictions (or, perhaps, because of them), public lectures and readings were "wildly popular."[83] Although the following chapter will examine this phenomenon more closely, suffice it to say that the Polytechnical Museum began offering public lecture series on a variety of topics of popular science even while in its temporary quarters. During the first year, more than four thousand attended the lectures. Because the lecturers were paid an honorarium of fifteen rubles and because the lectures were free and open to the public, this aspect of the museum's activities operated at a loss. A report of the committee planning lectures at the 1872 Polytechnical Exposition in Moscow claimed that public lectures were one of the best means to disseminate popular scientific knowledge as well as to raise the population's "mental and moral level": "People will learn eagerly when they are explained things in a simple and accessible form—not when the lecturer imposes his own view but when he explains the connection between facts and lets the audience draw its own conclusions."[84]

Although many associations sponsored public lectures, the Polytechnical Museum played a singular role in staging scientific demonstrations. At the first meeting of OLEAE, on 14 May 1864, president Shchurovskii observed that the public eagerly visited the university collections, but the absence of guided tours and of proper preparation among the visitors detracted from the utility of such visits: "Museums are visited primarily by ordinary people—artisans, merchants, in general by those classes [*sosloviia*] who do not attend public lectures or even read popular treatises; for them our museums are the only way to become familiar with the objects of natural history." Shchurovskii stated that OLEAE could play an important role here not only by sponsoring public lectures but also by "organizing demonstrations [*ob"iasneniia*] of the most noteworthy objects and important and curious facts . . . which can be understood by the less educated."[85] The Polytechnical Exposition of 1872 showed to the museum planners the potential of demonstrations when visitors eschewed catalogs and written descriptions for the more visually rewarding, and entertaining, demonstrations. "They were particularly eager to visit only those sections of the exposition which offered demonstrations," Shchurovskii noted. He claimed, "This is not just a curious crowd; these are people who want to learn, who question each other, and who attentively listen to those who explain the objects in the museum."[86] In October 1877, the museum began a series of demonstrations of its collections on Sundays and holidays, pitched at schoolchildren and at a public with only the most rudimentary education. During the first year, an impressive number of twenty-three thousand—by all accounts, a very heterogeneous public—attended the Sunday demonstrations; up to five hundred to six hundred might be in the auditorium for any given demonstration. During the first ten years members of OLEAE used the museum collections to explain all manner of scientific and industrial processes ranging from the linen and wool industries to electricity and magnetism.[87]

There was considerable discussion within OLEAE about how to pitch the Sunday demonstrations to a general public. A review of the first year observed that if the demonstrations were well organized and lively, then the audience would be quiet and attentive, even when the topic was rather specialized, such as dairy farming, salt extraction, or the metric system. "However," the report noted, "if the speaker began to philosophize or use flowery language and demonstrate his erudition, then the audience would become agitated and show its boredom and even try to slip out of the room. But if the speaker came down to earth, the audience would again pay attention."[88] The "Sunday demonstrations," as they were called, were not without controversy. The governing boards of OLEAE and of the museum were aware of the view that drawing a large public into the museum for such demonstrations would simply encourage a holiday atmosphere, and the public would not take the museum collections seriously. But Bogdanov, Della-Vos, and others argued that it was better that the public spent its leisure time in the museum than elsewhere. Indeed, the museum board frequently discussed, as ways to make the museum more accessible to the general public, longer hours, days of free admission, guides, maps, signage, as well as the Sunday demonstrations.[89]

Differences of opinion within OLEAE and the museum board regarding the seriousness of the public lectures and Sunday demonstrations were not the only controversies in this form of outreach activity. As the following chapter will discuss in greater detail, Russian officialdom was reluctant to sanction unauthorized ventures into public education. Just as some on the museum board feared that the public lectures and especially the Sunday demonstrations were too general and not scientific enough, so too the Ministry of Education feared that a museum of applied science was presenting too much general knowledge. While acknowledging that public lectures were an important educational function of the museum, the Committee of Ministers insisted that the museum board needed to adhere to all existing regulations regarding public lectures. Each lecture, including lectures as part of museum fund-raisers, needed to be approved in advance by the Ministry of Education; lecture outlines and, for a course of lectures, syllabi also had to be submitted in advance for approval.[90]

To the museum founders, one thing that made hurdles of Russian officialdom worth jumping was the marvel at the heterogeneity of the museum's public. The heterogeneous public that filed past exhibits and sat in the auditorium had multiple meanings. Victorian institutions frequently trotted out the observation of heterogeneity in order to enhance the image of utility regarding their self-definition and projects, and Moscow's Polytechnical Museum was no exception. According to a review of the Sunday demonstrations, attendance changed from students and the well-off, when the museum was in its temporary quarters on Prechistenka, a quiet neighborhood inhabited largely by the nobility, to more ordinary people, when it moved to its permanent building on Lubianka Square, in the heart of Moscow's commercial district.[91] Thus V. A. Vagner, one of the museum guides in the 1870s, reminisced, "On Sundays crowds flocked to the museum straight from the bazaar strewn around the Nikol'skii gates: people in lower-class overcoats [*chuiki*] and in shawls who before had never heard of museums. The real Moscow street. But how well they listened, how interested they were!" In reminiscences written much later, Professor I. A. Kablukov claimed that "thanks to the Sunday demonstrations, which began at a time when public lectures, especially for ordinary people, were very difficult to organize, the Polytechnical Museum became Moscow's first university extension [*narodnyi universitet*]."[92] (Indeed, the auditorium became the primary site for lectures of the public university movement after 1905.)

After the opening of the Polytechnical Museum in 1877 and the Anthropological Exposition and Congress two years later, OLEAE seemed to need a rest from fifteen years of elaborate planning and organizational work. Shchurovskii had predicted that after a period of great enthusiasm and heightened activity, a time of quietude could easily set in. The remaining years of Shchurovskii's long presidency (up to 1884) and those of his successors, Professor A. Iu. Davidov (1884–1885), Professor A. P. Bogdanov (1886–1889), Professor V. F. Miller (1889–90), and Professor D. N. Anuchin (1890–1923), were characterized by an emphasis on the society's publications and the operations of its many divisions. Of the association's eight divisions and six commissions, nine published their own proceedings, and four published their own scholarly journals.[93] There were some signs, in the Physics Division, for example, that the society shifted emphasis away from applied knowledge and toward theoretical knowledge. At the turn of the century, the physics labs and lecture halls of the museum were the site of pioneering experiments in aerodynamics. At a meeting of the Physics Division in 1887, K. E. Tsiolkovskii reported on "a self-guiding long-bodied metal airship," a decade before a dirigible was realized by Count Zepplin. Later, N. E. Zhukovskii chaired a subcommittee on aviation and presented his experiments on aviation and wind tunnels.[94] But, on the whole, the practical mission remained uppermost.

OLEAE continued to assist university teaching by acquiring laboratory equipment (especially microscopes), making its facilities available for instructional use, awarding travel grants for research, and publishing dissertations. In conjunction with Moscow University and the Society of Acclimatization, OLEAE, again using the vision and organizational talents of Bogdanov, founded the Moscow Zoological Gardens. Although blockbuster exhibitions were no longer necessary to found science collections, more specialized exhibitions, such as the Anthropological Exposition of 1879, frequently in conjunction with scientific congresses, as well as regular excursions and expeditions characterized the 1880s and 1890s. Even though the society's courses in popular science were less singular by 1900 because many other institutions sponsored such programs, OLEAE continued to sponsor public meetings at which a variety of people (the writers Tolstoi and Briusov frequently came) heard lectures by famous scientists. At the century's end, the museum's auditorium had become a veritable civic center. By 1917 more than two thousand lectures had been delivered on an astonishingly wide variety of topics, which included a "recital" in 1913 by Vasilii Kamenskii, Vladimir Maiakovskii, and David Burliuk. "Dressed in a cocoa-colored suit trimmed with gold brocade with an airplane painted on his forehead," as Robert Wohl notes, Kamenskii lectured on "Airplanes and Futurist Poetry."[95]

At the first world's fairs, Russian displays were concentrated at the higher and lower end of the exhibitionary hierarchy—luxuries and raw materials. One generation later, at the Paris World Exposition of 1878, Russia had agricultural, technical, and natural history sections. OLEAE displayed instructional materials and, in general, the Russian collections were largely educational. According to the memoir account of one member, less than a generation after the society's founding, "Russian scientists showed that there was no need to go abroad to learn scientific research and work in laboratories."[96] What had happened? In one generation, science societies, in collaboration with the government, had launched major projects to popularize science, to make useful knowledge more accessible, and to develop an infrastructure of native science. Moreover, Russia had gained considerable experience in the modern exhibition and museum in no small part through the efforts of OLEAE. It is difficult to imagine a "primordial and gelatinous" civil society, Gramsci's oft-cited characterization of civil society in Russia, being capable of the conceptualization, organization, planning, and administration that lay behind the Polytechnical Museum. The efforts of OLEAE helped stimulate three features of modern urban culture—the diffusion of useful knowledge and a public science, patriotism and civic pride, and private initiative and civil society.

OLEAE created the infrastructure grounded in civil society for popularizing science, connecting tsarist officialdom, the new municipal government, the business community, the university scientists, and other private associations. By organizing blockbuster exhibitions and a grand museum of science and industry, OLEAE stimulated the production and consumption of natural knowledge. With its laboratories for future scientists; its displays of machinery, technical processes, and the useful products of the natural world; and its lectures and demonstrations pitched at a broader audience, the Polytechnical Museum was a key component in Russian society's rapidly developing scientific potential. It displayed the wonders of nature and demonstrated the use of natural resources for productive ends. Established by scientists who framed their projects in terms of a public, OLEAE used publicity to achieve its goals and thereby helped create a public. That public was, in the minds of the museum's founders, modern or could be persuaded to become modern, in that it allegedly aspired to self-improvement through education and a rational use of leisure. No doubt, it could be argued that such public science treated the public as a consumer of, even an audience for, science and, therefore, produced less independence of mind and judgment than its proponents believed. Of course, this, too, was modern, and, in any event, the founders of the museum believed that such public science was good for science. "Science thrives and takes root only where it is firmly linked with society," wrote Bogdanov, "when it is not excluded to an isolated caste of scientists . . . It gains strength where there are institutions which act as extensions of the schools, public polling stations, so to speak, of scientific interests . . . Science needs to speak in the vernacular."[97]

By speaking in the vernacular, OLEAE hitched public science to the mobilization of human resources in the service of patriotism and national prestige. Members of OLEAE obliged themselves to work on behalf of the society's goals, that is, to put science in service to the nation. In a claim tirelessly repeated by the society's officers, Russia needed to become independent of European science; Russia needed its own science and its own scientists. Less openly stated but implicit in OLEAE's mission, Russian science also needed to become less dependent on the Russian state and more capable of being sustained by an infrastructure grounded in civil society. The Polytechnical Museum was a vivid means of instilling in the visitor national pride *(natsional'noe samoliubie)*. Having such a museum, Shchurovskii claimed, would demonstrate to foreigners that "Russia [was] mentally and morally disposed to participate actively and independently in European civilization." But Shchurovskii was also addressing doubters at home: "Many think that Russians are not mature enough for such institutions . . . On the contrary, they have so matured that they now experience a genuine need for these kinds of institutions."[98]

The need for "these kinds of institutions" was allegedly acute in Russia's second city, Moscow. "Building a polytechnical museum," the critic Vladimir Stasov opined in 1871 during the early planning stages, "will honor our sleepy old lady Moscow and prove that she is alive and has awakened."[99] The exposition and museum were organized by a society whose members were professors at Moscow University, and they had the backing of the city council and the Moscow business and industrial elite. They enabled Moscow to display distinction and gain recognition for its talents, cultural achievement, and claims to importance in Russian industry. As Della-Vos put it, "Moscow, the center of Russian industry, demonstrated brilliantly that private initiative and energy in every useful affair is a force that can overcome the most difficult and seemingly insurmountable obstacles."[100] The romantic and Slavophile ideas of a Russian national identity and cultural distinctiveness centered in Moscow received their institutional expression during the era of the Great Reforms, in museums and exhibitions that displayed that identity in its most visual form. Like its European brethren, the Polytechnical Exposition and, later, the Polytechnical Museum, fostered a collective endeavor to learn about the nation, thereby promoting a sense of national identity and self-esteem. To assert its place in European civilization in an age of nationalism and imperialism, Russia had, paradoxically, to assert its Russianness—its cultural distinctiveness, patriotism, and imperial pride.

Moscow's scientific, business, and civic leaders believed they were appropriating Peter's legacy. In his address at the grand opening of the museum on 30 May 1877, Bogdanov referred to the famous Falconet statue of Peter, then observing its centenary: "In a new educational institution devoted to the natural sciences and technology, Moscow has built the monument that best corresponds to the spirit and goals of the reign of Peter the Great."[101] A century and a half after Peter, subjects of the artisan-tsar's successors operated in a different environment. Even a grand undertaking such as the Polytechnical Museum, like its cousins, the 1867 and 1872 expositions, was not the result of government decree but of private initiative. In the view of exposition and museum organizers and proponents, private initiative, "a new force in every endeavor," while heretofore "meager and bashful," was now "showing itself in full splendor . . . [A major undertaking] was carried out by private initiative without any kind of outside orders or interference from the government."[102] To be sure, this private initiative was sanctioned by a state that shared the goals of a private association. But to create such a center of useful knowledge took vision, considerable planning, organizational skills, and the mobilization of private persons. The museum was the result of a shared agenda and collaboration between private associations, the municipality, and the state. It was an example of a budding civil society in action and a model of state-society partnership.

CHAPTER FIVE

Government and the Public Trust

The Russian Technical Society and Education for Industry

DURING THE SECOND HALF of the nineteenth century, authoritarian regimes of Central and eastern Europe spearheaded rapid industrialization to catch up to the early leader, Great Britain, and to compete for national prestige and great power status. The application of science to industry and the effort to absorb and generate industrial technology became critical components of the drive to maximize the most efficient allocation of material resources and to invest in native human capital. Government officials, employers, and technical specialists recognized that the dissemination of applied science and practical knowledge in a competitive era of more complex technology and increasing specialization of labor required a greater investment in the technical training of the workforce. More and more white-collar experts intruded into traditional blue-collar structures of vocational training, and an alliance of government bureaucrats, employers, and engineers argued that schooling was the best way to train cadres for new industrial skills. By imparting literacy and general education as well as technical training, such schooling became part of a larger movement of education for citizenship and national strength, and Germany became the leader of state-supported industrial education. "The wars of the future," wrote an official of the Russian ministry of education, "will be won or lost in the technical and industrial schools." Through the intervention of experts, urban workers would be plucked out of the state of nature in which they were commonly regarded to reside and brought into civil society.[1]

The efforts of technical specialists were mobilized and organized by both governments and private associations. In their efforts to assist the state and employers in the development of modern industry, private associations disseminated information about new products and improvements as well as the secrets of industrial processes. More important for our purposes, they provided both forums and advocacy for the development of technical education. Developments in France may put tsarist Russia into perspective. Alfred Rieber has observed the affinities between the French and Russian engineering professions, especially the ethic of partnership between state and society, and the same may be noted regarding the approach to industrial education.[2] The Association Polytechnique was founded in Paris in 1830 to disseminate useful knowledge to the laboring population. In order to further adult and technical education, it later established branches in provincial France. In 1862 a combination of enlightened officialdom, Saint-Simonians, liberals, and republicans founded the Franklin Society as well as its many provincial branches, called "circles," which were "the driving force behind the public library movement," then regarded as essential for the broad dissemination of natural knowledge. The French Society for Popular Instruction, which in 1864 opened evening classes for workers to learn literacy, arithmetic, and accounting, and the League of Education, created in 1866, which sponsored technical schools, were part of a national movement for worker education by means of literacy classes, vocational training, and public lectures, a movement that exploded in the 1890s. Technical schools and public lectures operated in a network of sponsored activity to uplift the aspiring "to lead wholesome lives" by means of self-improvement, character building, and the rational use of leisure.[3]

In the second half of the nineteenth century, the import, domestication, and generation of industrial technology was regarded as Russia's key to progress, the linchpin of which was the dissemination of applied science and technical education. Beginning in the 1860s, private associations sought to assist the state and employers to develop Russia's human and material resources for industrial purposes. As it had nurtured public science since the eighteenth century, officialdom recognized that the state needed the technical expertise generated in civil society. Because private initiative helped the government to achieve its goals of bringing prosperity and prestige to the empire, the government encouraged private initiative. At the same time, the bearers of this expertise were becoming more and more independent of the state. They regarded themselves less as servants of the monarch or of the state; nor were they servants primarily of an abstract "science." Instead, more and more they were servants of the nation, of "the people."

The work of private associations may be examined through a case study of the Russian Technical Society, the most prominent of a generation of societies founded to promote industrial development and technical education. During the last fifty years of the imperial regime, the Technical Society ran a variety of enterprises, including vocational schools and classes, Sunday and evening schools, schools for children of factory workers, and public lectures. It became a resource center for vocational curriculum development and pedagogy and, eventually, an advocate of universal compulsory education. The Russian Technical Society organized congresses on vocational education and technical training, congresses that became a forum for a variety of public issues. Such civic activism challenged the tutelage of the authorities, and the efforts of the Technical Society to promote industry and industrial education received mixed signals from the government. Through its myriad projects, the Technical Society provided an example of what private initiative could do to study problems, facilitate solutions, and mobilize talent. In so doing, it endeavored to turn Russian education from an object of government tutelage into a trust held by the public.

The Founding of the Russian Technical Society

Several projects of the late 1850s and early 1860s may be regarded as the antecedents of one of Russia's largest and most influential private associations, the Russian Technical Society (RTO in its Russian initials). In and out of government, the time was favorable for the discussion of technological development, industry, and the labor question. New periodicals, such as *Ukazatel' ekonomicheskii* (Economic Index), founded by liberal economist Ivan Vernadskii, mediated public debate on economic questions. In a permissive spirit, the government sanctioned private Sunday schools, which for a brief period offered basic education to workers. St. Petersburg was also the site of several circles, public lectures, and symposia on technical subjects, events such as the "Chemistry Evenings" organized by Dmitrii Mendeleev and others. As we have seen, the new divisions of political economy of the Free Economic Society and of the Russian Geographical Society sponsored lively debates of government policy. They were also a haven for liberal economists such as I. V. Vernadskii, V. P. Bezobrazov, F. G. Terner, E. I. Lamanskii, M. Kh. Reitern, and N. Kh. Bunge, who, as

Harley Balzer notes, "shared a distrust of Russian industrialists."[4] At the same time, a dislike of excessive government tutelage predisposed them to encourage private initiative within civil society. Among the liberal economists was Evgenii Nikolaevich Andreev, a professor at the Forestry Institute and an official of the Ministry of Finance. A former government inspector of the St. Petersburg Institute of Technology, Andreev was dispatched to study technical education in Europe in 1856; later he reported on the London World Exhibition of 1862. Sensing a need of institute graduates, who were scattered across Russia, to keep connected, Andreev advanced the idea of founding a technical society for all engineers. Andreev was joined by the civil engineer M. N. Gersevanov, the architect P. P. Mizhuev, the mining engineer P. N. Alekseev, the naval engineer M. M. Okunev, the industrialist I. P. Balabin, the artillery engineer B. N. Bestiuzhev-Riumin, the naval officer N. I. Kaznakov, and the photographer A. V. Fribes. In 1864 they declared their intent to found a technical society in St. Petersburg to unite all engineering specialties under one umbrella organization. On 22 April 1866, the ministries of Finance and Internal Affairs approved the charter and bylaws, and the Russian Technical Society held its first meeting one month later.[5]

At this meeting Andreev spoke about the charter. Although the charter was commonly regarded as a document that indicated the limits of a Russian society's activities, Andreev encouraged a different interpretation. The organizational structure and administration outlined in the charter, Andreev argued, "[were] not the limits of the society but its rights, approved by a legal act, rights that [would] be the key to the society's success."[6] Although government ministers did not speak this way, it is significant that the society's guiding spirit framed his interpretation of the charter in the language of rights. Indeed, the charter outlined the most far-reaching approval yet by the government of a private association's public activity, a fact that underscores government support of private initiative when it was channeled in certain directions.

The highest decision-making body of RTO was the general meeting. The general meeting discussed and voted on proposals of the board, appointed commissions, approved a budget and annual program submitted by the board, and elected new members by secret ballot. Proposals to change the society's charter and bylaws required a two-thirds majority of the general meeting. Most of the society's income came from membership dues, supplemented by various donations, interest-free loans, and an annual government subsidy.[7] The general meeting elected the society's officers—a president, vice president, and secretary—who, along with the chairs of each division, composed the board *(sovet)*, which managed the society's affairs. The grandson of Nicholas I, Duke Nikolai Similianovich Leikhtenbergskii, a St. Petersburg industrialist, was the first chairman of the board. Presidents were customarily elected as much for their influence and access to upper officialdom as for their technical expertise. Such presidents included A. I. Del'vig (1866–1872), P. A. Kochubei (1872–1892), M. I. Kazi (1894–1896), and V. I. Kovalevskii (1906–1916). Baron Andrei Ivanovich Del'vig and Vladimir Ivanovich Kovalevskii provide examples of the cross-fertilization between officialdom and civil society facilitated by Russian associations. From 1861 to 1871 Del'vig was chief inspector of railroads; from 1867 to 1871 he was on the council of the Ministry of Transport. Kovalevskii worked under Sergei Witte in the Ministry of Finance and compiled reports on industry for various exhibitions. Kovalevskii left the ministry to become president of the Technical Society and concurrently was a member of the Geographical Society and the Society to Disseminate Commercial Education.[8]

From the beginning, the membership was heterogeneous; although dominated by the technical intelligentsia, it also included government officials (such as future ministers of finance Bunge and Ivan Vyshnegradskii), military officers, industrialists, and foreigners. Like most Russian associations, RTO offered different categories of membership. Honorary members were recognized for their special contributions to technology or for their usefulness to the society. Russian scientists such as Mendeleev joined foreigners such as Ferdinand de Lesseps, Thomas A. Edison, and Alexandre-Gustave Eiffel, along with many Russian government officials, as honorary members. Other membership categories included active members with expertise in some field of engineering, amateurs *(sorevnovateli)* interested in technology, and corresponding members living in other cities. RTO tried to establish contacts with the business community, and among the prominent St. Petersburg industrialists who were members were Vasilii Poletika, Ludwig Nobel, R. K. San-Galli, V. I. Butz, M. L. MacPherson, and N. I. Putilov.[9]

As stated in its charter, the goal of the new Technical Society was to facilitate the development of technology and industry in Russia. The society's seal contained the words "measures, weights, and numbers," and its slogan was "science and impartiality." By being a "universal" association, covering all branches of industry and engineering, RTO occupied, somewhat like OLEAE in Moscow, the same position in applied science as did the Academy of Sciences in the "pure" sciences. To accomplish its goals, RTO practiced what might be called "public technology"—the gathering and dissemination of useful knowledge for industrial purposes. RTO gathered and created useful knowledge by soliciting information about business and by studying factory materials, products, and work processes in Russia and abroad. The society sent every owner who joined an annual report of all inventions and innovations in various branches of industry. It also offered free technical consultation, appraisals of inventions and innovations, and assistance in the marketing of little-known products. It facilitated industrial research by establishing and funding technical libraries and engineering laboratories.[10]

To reach the broader urban community, the society operated information bureaus in St. Petersburg and in several branch chapters to provide technical, educational, and commercial reports; tested building materials, machines, and methods of production; and recommended local firms that could supervise various projects and draft proposals and that could keep accounts. The society facilitated the organization, presentation, and discussion of scientific research and awarded prizes and medals for the best solutions to technical problems. The St. Petersburg headquarters and each chapter published *Notes (Zapiski),* whose articles on domestic and foreign industry and technology, as well as descriptions of Russian patents, complete with technical drawings, made it the most important engineering journal in the empire.[11] In St. Petersburg, the society sponsored public lectures on industry and maintained a library, an engineering museum, a photography pavilion, and a large exhibition hall. The society and its chapters participated in or sponsored numerous Russian and international industrial exhibitions and congresses. For example, for the National Manufacturing Exposition in 1870, the Technical Society contributed collections, provided lectures, arranged factory tours, and organized a Congress of Russian Industrialists. The Electricity Division organized sensational exhibitions of electricity in St. Petersburg in 1880, 1882, 1885, and 1892 (see figure 5.1); later, at the suggestion of Dmitrii Mendeleev, the Division of Aeronautics played an important role in popularizing aviation. The society also sponsored exhibitions on photography, hunting weapons, fire prevention, and petroleum.[12]

RTO complemented its outreach activities with advocacy and the solicitation of government measures favorable to the development of industry and technology. The society's meetings were not only a source of scientific and technical information but also an arena for the discussion of policy questions. As an institutional base of support for scientific research, the society frequently backed requests for government funding as well as distributed unrestricted funds. The society submitted to various government offices reports on such topics as investment in native machine industry, the development of Russia's oil industry, railroad construction and railroad rates, the tariff, the use of the metric system, Russian patent law, and child

Figure 5.1 Electricity exhibition in St. Petersburg, sponsored by RTO. (*Vsemirnaia Illiustratsiia,* no. 591 [1880]: 368; courtesy of the Library of Congress.)

and female factory labor. Thorough studies of the problem at hand typically accompanied the many reports *(dokladnye zapiski)* and petitions *(khodataistva),* usually framed in a way to emphasize the advantage to the government if a particular policy were implemented. The very fact that the recommendations of the society were taken seriously and discussed by officialdom demonstrates the organization's importance. Thus, according to N. G. Filippov, the society was "an interdepartmental forum for the discussion of important industrial problems and scholarly work and for the lively exchange of opinions and heated debate."[13]

Although RTO's home base in St. Petersburg was the largest and most influential, its branch chapters extended the society's reach all over the empire. Admittedly, establishing a branch chapter involved a considerable degree of red tape—preliminary approval of the local governor, mediation by the board to the Ministry of Internal Affairs, approval by the Ministry of Finance of bylaws that governed the local chapter; but by the end of the nineteenth century forty branches were scattered across the Russian empire. The local branches had considerable autonomy to open libraries with technical periodical literature, to maintain laboratories to test materials and machines, and to provide technical consultations.[14] Although government officials and the technical intelligentsia dominated the main branch in St. Petersburg, the Moscow chapter of RTO included some of the empire's most prominent merchants and philanthropists: G. A. Krestovnikov, Timofei Savvich Morozov, V. A. Bakhrushin, several Abrikosovs, V. P. and N. A. Alekseev, and Varvara Morozova. Morozova, one of the few women in Russian science societies, occupied a particularly prominent role in educational philanthropy as well as in liberal political circles. Born into the Khludov family in 1850, Morozova, the "classical progressive Moscow philanthropist," in P. A. Buryshkin's words, was one of the founders of the Prechistenka evening courses for workers, a municipal vocational school, and the first public library in Moscow. She also chaired the Morozov Women's Club, gave fifty thousand rubles to the Shaniavsky Public University, and was a leader in an association that tried to distribute handicrafts commercially, an effort then considered a major impetus to improved design by the creation of a market for high-quality products.[15]

At its founding, RTO had four divisions—Industrial Chemistry and Metallurgy; Mechanical Engineering and Machine Building; Construction, Mining, and Architecture; and Armaments, Artillery, and Naval Technology. To reflect the development of new technologies—photography, electricity, the petroleum industry, and aviation, for example—more divisions were added later. A rather sprawling decentralized organizational structure that delegated considerable authority to divisions and to local chapters multiplied the opportunities for outreach projects and, Andreev believed, "gave every member the right to influence the society's plans."[16]

RTO and Technical Education and Vocational Training

Training a skilled industrial labor force and diffusing industrial technology throughout the population posed a challenge to governments, employers, and technical specialists all over Europe. The dominant forms of technical education throughout the nineteenth century were on-the-job training and an important variation, craft apprenticeship, a transmission of skills from father to son or from master to apprentice. Both forms were controlled by workers and required no separation of the workplace from education. By the middle of the nineteenth century, these forms of traditional technical education were increasingly perceived as problematical, especially in larger enterprises. On-the-job training and apprenticeship were too diffuse, unregulated, and out of the control of employers. As machines replaced human labor and as artisanal work was deskilled, craft apprenticeship declined. Machinery made on-the-job training expensive, and the increasing application of science to industry meant that skills could not be mastered by apprenticeship and narrow on-the-job-training alone. From the point of view of industry, the state, and the technical intelligentsia, traditional practices of on-the-job training and apprenticeship were not capable of quickly producing enough cadres with new skills and in the sectors of the economy where they were most needed. Governments, facing industrial competition and imperatives to economic growth, perceived that a skilled labor force was in the national interest. In an era of intense economic competition, industrial training could not be left to the vicissitudes of apprenticeship and craft training. Finally, workplace and workmate socialization perpetuated allegedly harmful practices and rituals that were removed from the gaze of state and civil society.[17]

Vocational education by means of schooling promised a solution to several problems. It promised a more efficient way to transmit knowledge of science and the arts, knowledge that was regarded as the basis of industry. By separating the workplace from education, vocational education offered the employer an opportunity to gain more control of the organization of work, thereby hastening the breakup of the artisanal form of production in favor of the industrial. Experts situated in the institutions of state and civil society could determine where workers were needed and what skills they needed. Institutionalized vocational training would pull children out of the labor force and into schools; in return for the opportunity cost, the employer would get better-trained workers. The intervention of representatives of the state and civil society into the lives of the lower classes meant the substitution of traditional, personal (usually masculine) authority of families and workmates by the impersonal authority of experts and the market. Perhaps most important, it meant the replacement of workplace socialization by schooling and the concomitant promise of labor discipline, occupational advancement, and the integration of young workers into modern industrial economy and urban life.[18]

In Russia, the high number of illiterate and unskilled workers contributed to the low productivity of labor and threatened to perpetuate economic backwardness. Yet adult education and technical training were a glaring gap in the education for the urban population. On-the-job training and various systems of apprenticeship were still the most common means to train the industrial labor force. Their proponents claimed that skills were best learned on the job, not in the schools. In the latter decades of the nineteenth century, government and society debated ways to put more order and accountability into apprenticeship and on-the-job training. In the highly skilled metalworking trades, basic literacy was a prerequisite for the best apprenticeship programs. But workplace training was workplace socialization, and this included practices, especially alcohol abuse, that made civil society concerned for the moral upbringingof Russia's workers.[19]

Russia was a latecomer in the development of technical education. Prior to the founding of RTO, neither the state nor the industrialists made a concerted effort to further technical education. Russia's few technical schools catered to the ministries that ran or supervised them. But, as we saw in the previous chapter, the same spirit that encouraged public discussion about the display of science and industry also facilitated discussion about the education of the laboring population for industry. Indeed, in the early 1860s, recalled Peter Kropotkin, "all Russia wanted technical education." Still, the many schemes for technical education in and out of government, including the short-lived Sunday school movement, lacked an institutional focus, direction, and guidance.[20]

Although education, broadly conceived, was an important part of the mission of the Russian Technical Society as a whole, the main thrust of its efforts was concentrated in a specialized division, the Permanent Commission on Technical and Vocational Education. The idea of a division to study technical education grew immediately after RTO's bylaws were approved and the original divisions contemplated the poor state of Russian technical education. Discussions of public lectures as a way to disseminate technical knowledge among workers led to discussions of ways to maximize the benefit of these lectures. In 1867 the director of a workshop along the St. Petersburg–Warsaw railway line proposed that RTO establish a school for his workers and their children. At an RTO board meeting in 1867, Mikhail Nikolaevich Gersevanov, a civil engineer and later director of the Engineering Institute of the Ministry of Transport, first raised the idea of a division of technical education to develop the curriculum for the new school. In April 1868, in a report on artisan education and on his observations of foreign technical education, Andreev endorsed the idea of a committee to focus on technical education. The board presented a proposal to create the Permanent Commission on Technical and Vocational Education (hereafter, the Education Commission) to a general meeting, which approved the commission on 15 May 1868.[21]

The Education Commission's bylaws conferred certain rights and responsibilities. The general meeting of the "parent" Technical Society elected a chair of the new commission and appointed the first members, known for their expertise in education and for their familiarity with technical processes. The chair of the commission was supposed to be an experienced educator with administrative experience who was capable of managing all the schools in his jurisdiction. Subsequent officers were elected by the members themselves and subject to approval by the curator of the school district, an official of the Ministry of Education. At the same time, according to the bylaws, membership on the Education Commission was neither limited in number nor subject to approval by the authorities. To support its projects, the commission received an annual budget from the Technical Society and annual subsidies from the Ministry of Finance; in addition, it had the right to solicit donations from private sources, largely from industrialists.[22]

Two of the Education Commission's leaders for many years were E. N. Andreev and A. G. Nebolsin. Andreev typified the government official sympathetic to private initiative. While working in the Ministry of Finance, he was one of the liberal economists clustered in the Russian Geographical Society during the era of the Great Reforms; he also chaired the Commission on Agricultural Education of the Free Economic Society. He was one of the charter members of RTO, served as its first secretary, and was particularly active in curriculum development. According to a study of Russian engineers, he was the "guiding spirit" of RTO during its early years and mentored younger activists in the causes of industrial growth, worker education, and labor legislation.[23]

For a free trader like Andreev, there were other ways besides a protective tariff for government to support industry; among these was a government-society partnership to develop technical education. In several reports and in addresses at meetings of RTO, Andreev made a two-pronged case for technical education, a case that was based on the efficacy of schooling and the importance of general education. His trip to Europe showed Andreev that other countries, especially Germany, regarded technical education as the key to economic development. To be sure, Andreev conceded, if master artisans and owners took responsibility for education, then apprenticeship and on-the-job training would be superior methods to impart practical experience and mechanical skills. Alas, Andreev claimed, the master artisans could not be entrusted to perform this function. In any event, they were disappearing in the machine age. Schooling, in contrast, removed the education obligation from the master artisans. More important, schooling could provide the scientific basis that would give the pupil the means to find work and adapt to new technologies. In partnership with the government, RTO could demonstrate to factory owners the efficacy of schooling and thereby help Russia compete with Europe. Last but not least, schooling not only provided a foundation for further education but also had a broader impact; in somewhat inelegant Russian, Andreev argued, "[It] can and must teach the workers morals [*moralizirovat' rabochikh*]." But technical education alone was insufficient to prepare a modern labor force: "Technique [*tekhnika*] is secondary; one can learn technique from a book or at the factory. But where can one learn to read and learn—to learn?"[24] Andreev's answer was that literacy and general education provided the essential preparation for technical training. As Balzer points out, Andreev, like several other activists in RTO, was influenced by Nikolai Ivanovich Pirogov's plea for a broad education that would be based on "individual circumstances, aptitudes and inclinations, rather than the government's social policy." Andreev observed the importance attached to general education in Europe; after the World's Fair of 1862, the French, for example, concluded that their lag behind British industry was not due to a want of technical education but to a deficiency in "general education for workers, without which technical education is not productive." General education, Andreev claimed, would inculcate a respect for the individual and would prevent premature decisions regarding the educational fate of a child (see figure 5.2).[25]

Son of an economist in the Ministry of Finance and a protégé of Andreev, A. G. Nebolsin was another one of the "locomotives" of RTO. Combining government and private service, Nebolsin further exemplifies the crossover between official and unofficial realms (see figure 5.3). He worked in the Central Statistical Committee of the Ministry of Internal Affairs as well as in the ministries of Finance and of Education. In 1861 he taught at one of the Sunday schools that briefly dotted St. Petersburg. He joined the Education Commission in 1872 and headed it for thirty years, recruiting activists

Figure 5.2 E. N. Andreev, economist and one of the founders of RTO; a promoter of technical education. (*Niva,* no. 32 [1889]: 812; courtesy of the Library of Congress.)

in the movement for worker education. One of the most active members of the Technical Society, he also used congresses, exhibitions, and the press to popularize science and technical education. Although he was considered a radical in the 1860s, he maintained a close personal relationship with Grand Duke Konstantin Konstantinovich, later the honorary patron of the society's technical schools. Nebolsin was also founder and editor of the journal *Engineering and Business Education (Tekhnicheskoe i kommercheskoe obrazovanie)* from 1892 to 1916 and helped prepare the Russian section at the Paris World Expositions of 1867, 1878, and 1900. A feature on vocational and technical education in a weekly magazine noted, "In recent years, it appears that there has not been a single activity, or a single initiative [in vocational education] without Nebolsin's authoritative participation or consultation." Later, according to Alexandra Kollontai,

Figure 5.3 A. G. Nebolsin, educator and longtime head of the Education Commission of RTO. (Courtesy of the State Museum of the History of St. Petersburg.)

Nebolsin was close to the Bolsheviks and "was a great help in [their] underground work." Not for nothing was Nebolsin listed in the files of the political police as "especially unreliable."[26]

One of the most important missions of RTO, like the missions of the science societies that preceded it, was the creation and dissemination of useful knowledge in order to publicize certain issues within its competence. The Education Commission, accordingly, saw its primary mission as one of gathering information, acquainting the public with the state of Russian technical education, and studying "the conditions for its proper organization," that is to say, schooling alongside or in place of apprenticeship and on-the-job training.[27] Three examples of the Education Commission's information gathering and dissemination functions will illustrate the range of its activities and competence: it studied child labor, it became a resource center for technical education pedagogy, and it helped frame a discussion of worker training in the context of general education. These activities involved more than just information gathering and dissemination; they also involved advocacy.

For many years the Education Commission studied child labor in a subcommittee chaired by the eminent professor and statistician Iulii Eduardovich Ianson. This study came about as a by-product of the commission's concern about attendance and performance in the vocational and technical schools it managed. On 18 May 1874 Andreev reported on the reasons for poor performance. Not unexpectedly, working children missed class or slept in class; they could not be given assignments to complete outside of class. Primary education was more difficult for adults, especially when they attended classes irregularly. Moreover, employers were allegedly using apprenticeship not to provide on-the-job training to young workers but to employ child labor to cut costs. Ianson's subcommittee proposed a restriction on child labor in order to enable a worker to acquire a primary education at a young age. Although employers stood to lose cheap labor while the children were in school, in the long run, Ianson's subcommittee contended, they would get a literate worker able to enter more highly skilled jobs, who was socialized by the discipline of schooling rather than by the workplace socialization of other workers. Although RTO was careful to restrict its investigation to the link between child labor and education rather than embark on a wide-ranging investigation of the labor question, the society became ground zero for discussion and policy formation regarding the children of workers. The discussion led to the factory legislation of 1882, an example of advocacy that produced results at the very top.[28]

The Education Commission became a resource center for technical and vocational education in myriad other ways. Publications, of course, were often the most widely used method of such outreach, and the Education Commission published its own *Proceedings,* "in order to offer its affairs to public discussion [*glasnost'*]."[29] It drafted model rules and regulations for vocational schools and classes. In addition to overseeing the teaching at vocational schools, to be discussed below, it surveyed textbooks and teaching manuals and drew up curricula and lesson plans. It ran weekly colloquiums on pedagogy and methodology, modeled after the technical colloquiums that were run by the engineering divisions of RTO, and open to teachers at all of RTO's schools. RTO appointed commissions to study specific problems (such as workers' education, women's technical education, the teaching of drawing classes, apprenticeship, and many others) and to petition the government on questions of technical education. In 1892 the Education Commission launched the Mobile Museum of Teaching Aids, which quickly became well known throughout Russia for its innovative collection. By 1902 the museum had some eighty thousand items out on loan to various schools and educational institutions. Such teaching aids were deemed critical to the success of adult education; when the students could do little or no homework, the optimal use of class time became that much more important. The Education Commission organized educational excursions, founded and maintained homes in the countryside for sickly children, ran pensions to house teachers, and raised money for insurance, burial funds, and financial aid to students. It also provided legal aid and mediation to individuals desiring to open societies, and mutual aid funds at schools. In all activities, the Education Commission solicited the opinion of outside (nonmember) experts on educational issues, thereby promoting horizontal linkages in Russian civil society.[30]

One of the most powerful ways to disseminate practical education and scientific knowledge among the population was public readings and lectures. Public lectures, accompanied by startling demonstrations and experiments that "confronted nature empirically," were highly popular among the educated public in the eighteenth century and among the semieducated in the nineteenth century. The public lecture movement helped promote a love of useful knowledge and presented the virtues of science and learning to the public.[31] In Russia, during the reform era, many associations began to sponsor public lectures to distract the working population from vice. But the local authorities and central officialdom alike were exceptionally concerned that such public events did not get out of control, and in 1876 the authorities regulated their organization. Despite the emphasis on science and useful knowledge, the government took no chances: the text of the lecture or of any excerpted readings had to be approved by the district education inspector, and the governor had to approve the speaker; no deviation from the approved text was allowed.[32] Such scrutiny on the part of autocracy certainly qualified the concepts of "open" or "public." But the cumbersome red tape and contradictory regulations, as an editorial on adult education in *Russkie vedomosti* later put it, annoyed more than suffocated the enterprising. The public lecture movement was unstoppable, and among the many societies sponsoring public lectures were the Society to Disseminate Useful Books, the Society to Organize Educational Public Amusements, the Society to Study and Disseminate Accounting, the Moscow Agricultural Society, the Free Economic Society, the Pirogov Society of Russian Physicians, the Society of Free Public Libraries, the Moscow Juridical Society, the Society for the Diffusion of Technical Knowledge, and the

Temperance Society.[33] In Kizevetter's words, the exponential increase in the number and popularity of public lectures in the 1890s constituted an "epidemic of lectures."[34]

The Russian Technical Society demonstrated its organizational skills in its program of public lectures. In 1872 RTO set up a special commission consisting of professors at St. Petersburg University and the St. Petersburg Institute of Technology to draw up principles for a program of public lectures to disseminate scientific and technical knowledge. Among the professors involved were the chemists N. N. Beketov, A. M. Butlerov, and Dmitrii I. Mendeleev. According to the principles *(osnovaniia),* the lectures were not be purely theoretical; they were to be accessible to a general audience and to show practical applications. From this point on, the "practical applications," so to speak, of the principles were in the hands of the Education Commission. Its organizational responsibilities included selecting the topics, inviting the speakers, and obtaining permission from the authorities. In addition, the commission raised money, found lecture halls (usually at the RTO facility in Solianoi gorodok in St. Petersburg or the Polytechnical Museum in Moscow), printed announcements, collected admission fees (usually fifteen kopeks), and paid the speakers an honorarium (usually fifteen rubles).[35]

In its studies of vocational and technical education and in its management of vocational schools, the Education Commission become involved in the issue of general education. To be sure, a majority of the members of RTO, as well as officials of the Ministry of Education—perhaps with memories of the short-lived Sunday school movement—regarded general education and involvement of RTO in primary schooling as outside the competence of a technical society. But as early as 1868, in his study of technical education and vocational training in Europe, Andreev concluded that the basis of European technical education was general education, a concept that meant not only literacy but also general moral and cognitive development. Furthermore, such education was best attained at an early age. However, Andreev stressed, this was not education for social mobility: "A skilled worker [*master*] must be a skilled worker and not an engineer. Owing to the inadequacy of his general development, he can become an engineer only under exceptional circumstances." The distinction between manual and mental labor was to be preserved: "We must educate people but not overeducate them." This may have made Andreev's ideas palatable to conservative officials, identified by Balzer as the "classicists," in the Ministry of Education; these officials wanted general and technical education to be on separate tracks and to limit general education subjects taught in the technical schools.[36]

But Russian officialdom did not speak with one voice, and the commission's advocacy of general education had the support of the Ministry of Finance, which was likewise concerned about the levels of education and skill in the industrial labor force, and this support gave the pronouncements of other members of RTO the imprimatur of official approval. The Ministry of Finance and RTO gathered data to prove the link between industrial performance and general education. Ivan A. Vyshnegradskii, minister of finance from 1887 to 1892 and also an honorary charter member of RTO, was an influential advocate of technical and vocational schools. If they were trained at all in industry, argued Vyshnegradskii, Russian workers received no more than narrow on-the-job training exclusively for the work to be performed at a particular plant. He contended, "The lack of general education prevents the workers in most cases from clearly understanding the operations they are required to perform and thereby diminishes the value of the work performed." Without primary education, Russian industry would continue to lag behind Europe in the technical competence of its labor force and, in a possibility that was Vyshnegradskii's bête noire, to rely on foreign technology and foreign technical personnel.[37]

The agenda of studying "the conditions for the proper organization" of technical education framed a rather open-ended study of Russian social and economic life. Nebolsin, the longtime chair of the Education Commission, took up where his predecessor Andreev left off, and became the leading proponent of general education. In his many writings and addresses on the subject, Nebolsin began with the assumption on which everyone agreed—that worker productivity was linked to technical training. But, Nebolsin argued, worker productivity was also linked to general, primary education. "Opponents of primary education," stated Nebolsin, "forget that the work of the hand is directed by the mind and that any kind of specialized or vocational education must begin after the completion of general education . . . The best way to prepare peasants and workers for vocational education is to spread literacy and general elementary education . . . The deficiencies in general primary education are the most important obstacle to the dissemination among the working class of specialized and technical knowledge."[38]

Thus, RTO joined the state, principally the Ministry of Finance, in a common cause to take job training and socialization out of the hands of other workers and employers, or at least to diminish the role of workmates and employers, and place training and socialization in the hands of professional experts and educators—to remove technical training from "plebeian" society and put it in the hands of the state and its ally, "bourgeois" civil society.

Technical Schools and Classes

At its founding, RTO was authorized to organize worker education. In 1870 the Education Commission opened its first vocational school, offering evening classes for skilled workers on the St. Petersburg–Warsaw railroad. Other schools and classes followed, first at state factories, later at private factories. RTO ran vocational schools at the most prominent machine, metalworking, and munitions factories in St. Petersburg, including the Baltic and Nevskii shipbuilding factories, the Franco-Russian Machine Plant, the Obukhovskii steel mill, the Nobel factory, the St. Petersburg Cartridge Factory, and the Siemens-Halske factory; the Putilov plant had four vocational schools. In 1874 RTO collaborated with the St. Petersburg Society of Architects to open a school to train construction foremen. In 1879 RTO opened a mechanics' school for juvenile boys in the important industrial district of Vyborg; a printers' school opened in 1884; and an electricians' school opened in 1896. RTO also ran specialized classes in sewing and pattern making, as well as classes to train stokers, boiler men, and bookstore employees. Alongside its vocational schools, RTO also ran Sunday and evening schools offering a general primary education, not just vocational training. Around the empire, the chapters of RTO also ran evening classes for workers. One of the best known of such projects were the Prechistenka courses run by the Moscow chapter, courses that grew in enrollment from three hundred in 1897 to seventeen hundred in 1912.[39] By 1912 RTO ran sixty schools, enrolling 8,461 students; altogether since the founding of the first school in 1870, some 137,087 students had attended schools of the Technical Society.[40]

RTO had broad powers to found and administer technical schools and vocational classes. The society's schools received the official stamp of approval in 1872 from minister of finance M. Kh. Reitern. In 1876 the Ministry of Finance took over supervisory responsibility for these schools, but the society continued to run them. The vocational schools were in the domain of the Ministry of Finance until 1881, after which time they were transferred to the Ministry of Education. The following year, the Ministry of Education and the State Council approved a charter of the vocational schools that standardized a great variety of existing vocational school charters and gave the Technical Society the right to found schools not only at factories but also in worker districts. Although the schools were placed under the supervision of the Ministry of Education in 1881, RTO retained considerable administrative autonomy. The Education Commission drew up the rules and regulations *(polozhenie)* for each school and was in charge of overall administration. Day-to-day management of the schools was the responsibility of RTO's education inspector; RTO also appointed inspectors of each school and ad hoc inspectors for certain subjects. It also provided one member of the council *(sovet)* of each school; the remainder of the council consisted of the school's inspector and two or more of its patrons. The school inspectors appointed teachers and were in charge of curriculum and school administration. Graduates received military service reductions, a privilege that signified that the RTO schools were on an equal plane with the rest of the public school system.[41]

RTO enjoyed its broad powers to run a network of technical schools and classes in the very sensitive area of worker education, owing to divisions within Russian officialdom, the society's support in high places, and RTO's stature as a nongovernmental organization devoted to a stronger and more prosperous Russia. Numerous studies of the imperial Russian bureaucracy have observed both the personal nature of rule and also the factions and interest groups that inhibited the formulation of consistent policy. There was no one voice in education policy, even within the ministries of Finance and Public Education. Traditionalists, concentrated in the Ministry of Internal Affairs, and bureaucratic modernizers, grouped in the Ministry of Finance, often checked each other.[42] Such a state of affairs allowed RTO to utilize patrons in high places and bureaucratic allies in support of its projects, especially in the Ministry of Finance, which was supportive of industrial schooling and of the fusion of industrial, technical and general education. The patrons of its schools were grand dukes Konstantin Nikolaevich, a champion of reform during the era of the Great Reforms, and Konstantin Konstantinovich, president of the Academy of Sciences from 1889 to 1915, the only time that a Romanov had been president. Konstantin Konstantinovich was also an honorary member of several educational institutions and learned societies, including the Russian Geographical Society, the Russian Musical Society, the Moscow Polytechnical Museum, and the Russian Archaeological Society.[43]

RTO was a favored association not only because of its imperial patronage but because of the need to enlist society in the task of industrial development. Thus in 1882, when the government had issued charters to the schools run by RTO, "the government, in return for a certain amount of desired public initiative, offered private persons a wide range of independent activity."[44] Far from resenting government intrusion, at this point in its development the Education Commission regarded the Ministry of

Finance's interests as an expression of confidence and a validation of its authority to manage the schools. RTO realized that government recognition benefited the schools materially, and accordingly RTO showed its gratitude and was careful to honor its patrons. Openings of the vocational schools were an opportunity to present toasts to the imperial family and the patrons of the school, to praise the enlightened leadership of the factory, and to emphasize the importance of learning vocational skills; important events in educated circles of the two capitals, openings were well covered in the press. As a result, despite Russia's long tradition of strict control of education, an in-house history observed, "[The society's schools] represent something unprecedented anywhere in Russia, even at the present time."[45]

Although RTO and the ministries of Finance and Education had collaborated in the establishment of technical schools for workers, the government was unwilling to surrender total authority to RTO to establish and administer such schools without approval. Permission to open schools was required from the curator of the education district, an official of the Ministry of Education, in consultation with the local authorities. All school council members, administrators, and teachers were subject to the approval of the Ministry of Finance and, after 1881, of the Ministry of Education. Nevertheless, the Education Commission could fill vacancies and the staff could conduct its duties pending ministry approval, causing minister of education Ivan Delianov to complain that the commission repeatedly thwarted the ministry's supervisory functions, an issue we will return to later in the chapter.[46] A feuilleton in the St. Petersburg *New Times (Novoe Vremia)* titled "The Society of Measures, Weights, and Numbers," the motto of RTO, poked fun of the broad powers claimed by RTO. Noting that the secretary of RTO had proposed that everything not forbidden in the bylaws was permitted, the feuilletonist mused that if the Russian Technical Society wanted to take over the carrying trades in St. Petersburg, it could do so because the bylaws did not forbid it.[47]

Running the schools required considerable organizational skills on the part of the Education Commission. It had to find classroom space, recruit teachers, develop the curriculum, review textbooks, coordinate instruction, charge tuition, and prepare school budgets. RTO officers boasted that it was more capable than the Ministry of Education of running the society's schools, a boast that an American authority on Russian technical education has endorsed. The commission's budget came from direct government subsidies, the St. Petersburg City Council, state factories, the donations of industrialists and charities, tuition, and the sale of wares made in the schools; the budget grew from 500 rubles in 1868 to 244,819 in 1912. The state or the factory owners, as appropriate, provided operating costs of the schools, and the commission dispersed the funds. Money for the schools was always short; as is true everywhere, teachers worked for low pay and often provided their services pro bono. To tap nongovernmental sources of money, the commission organized what today would be called fund-raisers—concerts and lectures, the proceeds of which went to the commission's schools.[48]

The Education Commission could take the greatest initiative in matters of personnel and pedagogy, and its members often boasted that several vocational programs were the first of their kind in Russia. Not weighed down by routine and formality, the argument ran, RTO could more easily keep up with and apply the latest pedagogy. As N. M. Korol'kov, commission member and author of a history of the commission, laconically put it, the Technical Society "had relatively more freedom of action" than did the Ministry of Education.[49] In particular, this meant that the society's vocational schools could explore alternatives to the rote method of learning—greater pupil-teacher interactivity, child-centered pedagogy, and learning-by-doing instructional methods. In multigrade schools, the commission hired separate teachers for each grade. It hired women teachers and offered coeducational instruction. Mechanical drawing, working from nature, and using colors (the so-called American method) was emphasized "in order to cultivate taste in the working population."[50] The commission used innovative instructional methods, such as slides and excursions to museums, exhibitions, and the zoological gardens. Free travel on the railroads facilitated field trips to the countryside. This pedagogy was designed to improve general education, elevate taste, and expand horizons.

From the very beginning, the Education Commission regularly received inquiries from the provinces about organizing technical schools. In St. Petersburg, for example, requests came from the Society to Promote Women's Vocational Education and the Society of Public Amusements on Vasiliev Island. Such requests included the formulation of projects and consultation with other constituencies interested in establishing their own vocational schools or societies and with chapters of RTO interested in creating their own education divisions. In 1897 discussions originating in the Moscow chapter led to the founding of the Society to Disseminate Commercial Education, whose curriculum was developed by the Education Commission and whose members reflected the commitment to practical education of the Moscow business community. In all cases, the commission mobilized private initiative in order to draw up curricula, raise money, and solve community problems. This was a clear sign, according to the commission's historian, "of public trust in the commission and of sympathy for its work," as well as a demonstration of the growing horizontal linkages in civil society.[51]

Exhibitions of school projects, individual student work, school charters, rules and regulations, curricula, instructional materials, and syllabi publicized private initiative in technical education. Exhibitions showed the product of the vocational education (pupils' work) as well as the process of learning, by displaying the instructional materials and educational infrastructure at each school (see figure 5.4). Since instructional materials were in short supply, the commission assembled a library of textbooks and teaching manuals and compiled a catalog of appropriate educational literature. Finally, it was hoped that such displays would encourage private persons to establish new schools.[52]

Despite the boasting of RTO officials and admirers, the RTO schools and classes faced no shortage of problems familiar to students of popular education everywhere. High costs, limited resources, volatile enrollment and retention figures, high turnover, and low graduation rates plagued Russia's lower vocational and technical schools.[53] The education activists in RTO sought a forum to gather information, air grievances, and solve problems. In addition to its schools and classes, policy formulation and advocacy, and its public lectures and exhibitions, RTO organized three congresses devoted to technical education and vocational training. Congresses as a key component of Russia's growing civil society will be introduced more fully in the following chapter. Suffice it to say here, beginning in the 1860s, the government authorized local, regional, and national meetings coalescing around a variety of special interests. One such special interest was the critically important matter of technical education.

RTO and the Congress of Activists in Technical and Vocational Education

The idea of holding a congress on technical education in Russia came about in 1886 at the first international congress on technical and vocational education in Bordeaux. The congress had heard reports on Russian technical education from the Russian delegate P. A. Miasoedov, an official in the Ministry of Finance and member of RTO. The congress delegates were so impressed with Russia's "considerable progress" that they proposed holding the next international congress in St. Petersburg. Although there were a few demurs among the delegates, the congress passed a resolution to hold its next congress in 1888 in St. Petersburg.[54] At a meeting of RTO on 7 May 1887, Miasoedov suggested a government-sponsored technical congress, arguing that congresses were an effective way to spread information about technical education: "The exchange of ideas and contacts

Figure 5.4 Displays of manual training classes at the Third Congress on Technical and Vocational Education, organized by RTO. (*Niva*, no. 3 [1904]: 57; courtesy of the Library of Congress.)

provides information that is not in the printed handbooks and which cannot be obtained in any of the schools." Moreover, Miasoedov claimed, the country that hosts an international congress benefits the most.[55] This opinion found expression on the pages of RTO's flagship publication, *Zapiski:* a congress on technical education could promote the shared interests of government and the technical associations, that is, promote the idea of economic progress through technical education and the dissemination of useful knowledge.[56] At that time drawing up rules and regulations for the administration of vocational schools, Count Ivan Davydovich Delianov, minister of education from 1882 to 1897, liked the idea. However, thinking that it would be difficult for the ministry to take the responsibility of organizing an international congress, Delianov, in a striking admission of the competence of a private association as well as a devolution of responsibility at a time when people involved in technical education were looking for leadership, suggested that RTO organize such a congress. Considering that Russia lacked a system of vocational schools as well as data on technical education, RTO concluded that it was premature for Russia to host an international congress. However, RTO seized the opportunity to make a counterproposal: to hold a Russian congress. Although the Ministry of Education had severely restricted teachers' congresses from the 1870s through the 1890s, the importance of technical education persuaded it to authorize a Russian national congress on vocational and technical education, to be held in St. Petersburg in December 1889.[57]

According to its bylaws, RTO could convene a congress, draft the rules and regulations *(polozhenie),* and select the executive council *(sovet)* of the congress, which in turn appointed an organizing committee. To fund the congress, RTO solicited private donations and also received a grant of three thousand rubles from the Ministry of Finance and two thousand rubles from the Ministry of Education. Attended by 1,076 administrators and teachers at technical schools; government, zemstvo, and city council employees; factory owners; and members of the Technical Society and their guests, the congress convened 16 December 1889.[58] Somewhat loose in its metaphors, the invocation at the opening of the First Congress on Technical and Vocational Education likened the educators to "eagles who [had] flocked here from all corners of" the empire: "Each one of you brings here to the altar of the Fatherland your ideas, your work, and your experience." Many of the addresses evoked patriotism and the spirit of cooperation to solve problems. In one address, professor of forestry Vasilii Tarasovich Sobichevskii claimed that participants from all walks of life were "animated by one and the same feeling—the desire to do their share to solve problems and to render their services to [their] dear motherland."[59]

The Second Congress on Technical and Vocational Education convened on 28 December 1895 in Moscow, with 1,750 delegates in attendance. The second congress had imperial patronage from Grand Duke Konstantin Konstantinovich, and the ministers of war, finance, internal affairs, justice, transport, agriculture, and education were all honorary founders of the congress; officialdom was well represented at its sessions. At the same time, the second congress was evidence of an upsurge of public activity of many different associations after the famine of 1891–1892. The agenda was notably broadened to include general education, an issue that Nebolsin and other speakers raised repeatedly in addresses. The ninth section on "general issues," taking advantage of the fact that each section could function relatively autonomously, organized its own program and sent out announcements to twenty thousand schools; government, zemstvo and municipal offices; and factory owners. Perhaps not surprisingly, section 9 was the liveliest and best attended section; forty-two papers were presented to more than five hundred delegates, almost one-third of the congress's participants.[60]

This is not the place to discuss in detail the proceedings of the congresses on technical and vocational education or the content of the many reports presented; I will leave that to students of Russian education, industrial development, and labor. Certain broader issues interest me here: the goals of the congress organizers and methods used to achieve those goals, the role the congresses played in Russian public life, and the relationship between the congress and officialdom. The congresses on technical education acted as advocates for technical literacy, in part to assert Russia's need for economic, technological, and industrial independence. By examining these aspects of the congresses, we can see how civil society worked and what role the quest to disseminate useful knowledge played in civil society.

Dissemination of useful knowledge and publicity were the stated goals of Russia's many congresses, and the congresses of technical education were no exception. They were convened to collect data, to study "the conditions for the proper organization" of technical education, and to acquaint the public with the state of Russian technical education. Of course, commissions in the ministries of Education and Finance had been discussing technical education for years, but now information gathering was set up in such a way as to authorize a rather open-ended discussion of Russian social and economic life, to solicit and shape public opinion. Although general education did not receive a great amount of attention at the first congress, the project of gathering data from educators as well as from representatives of the zemstvos and city councils "to elucidate the degree of preparation of the population for technical and vocational education" justified not only the discussion of general education but also its advocacy.[61] The creation of a section on general education at the Second Congress on Technical and Vocational Education gave the subject a legitimacy and prominence lacking at the first congress, and several speakers, repeating the arguments Andreev had made earlier, stated that general education was a prerequisite to successful technical education. "The vocational school," claimed I. A. Anopov in his study prepared for the congress, "must wherever possible develop and prepare the student to face all the unforeseen circumstances of life by making learning easier. One can specialize later . . . The system is better that does not create an educational dead end prematurely [*ne pritypliaet cheloveka prezhdevremenno*]."[62] Indeed, one might say that advocacy of an education "platform" consisting of issues framed not only by RTO but also by other technical and education societies and even by government officials was an unstated goal of the technical congresses. Not surprisingly, the results of this form of public interactivity—the soliciting and shaping of public opinion—indicated that further progress in industry and in technical education would depend on literacy and the level of general education of the working population.

The prominent zemstvo educator and inspector of Moscow city schools V. P. Vakhterov gave the opening address at the section on general education. Two years earlier, Vakhterov had given a well-publicized talk at a meeting of the Moscow Literacy Committee on behalf of universal education. According to Vakhterov, "hundreds of factory owners, engineers, landowners, and persons who [had] studied labor productivity" had testified that "illiterate workers were the most important reason for the low productivity of labor, threatening to perpetuate Russia's economic backwardness." Because workers with good technical education contributed more to the national wealth, factory owners and engineers, according to Vakhterov, favored general education in order to disseminate technical knowledge. In a thinly veiled reference to Russian dependence on foreign science and technology, Vakhterov asserted that inadequate technical education could leave nations behind "in painful dependence on other nations."[63]

The ninth section drew up plans for model schools based on data collected from 147 officials of elementary schools; the data were published in the *Proceedings (Trudy)* of the congress. A quarter of a century after RTO established its first vocational school, the congress used the approval of the authorities to discuss technical education and to air criticisms of the existing framework of technical schools, thereby pushing the boundaries of public criticism of government policy. The section passed resolutions critical of government education policy, addressing in particular the absence of local control of the schools and the absence of universal primary education. Although a Russian authority on the zemstvo liberal movement claims that there were no significant political discussion at the first two technical congresses, in fact the ninth section of the second congress drafted petitions for a greater public role in worker education, for a limitation of child labor, and for greater regulation of artisan enterprise and the relations between master artisans and apprentices.[64]

Like many congresses that mobilized constituents on behalf of a cause or causes in the late-imperial period, the congresses of technical and vocational education played an important role in public life. Although the testimony of congress organizers and officers is understandably self-serving, their self-fashioning does point to certain narratives about their public role. In the first narrative, the private initiative of RTO overcame great odds, in particular public apathy, to pursue its goals. Writing after the first congress, Nebolsin opined, "Despite the inertia and Russian distrust of a private undertaking, despite the unfamiliarity and even indifference to the discussion of issues in the public interest, the Technical Society succeeded in recruiting many people to give papers and to donate money to the congress."[65] People who allegedly had hitherto been apathetic now participated in public life, and the virtue of public participation was a second narrative of the congress organizers and admirers. Addressing fellow delegates, the president of the second congress, V. M. Golitsyn, expressed gratitude to RTO for taking the initiative in convening the congress: "The [Technical] Society in so doing has correctly understood the true needs [of society] and the present conditions."[66] The Education Commission and the organizing committees of the congresses even encouraged public input into the program. Before the first congress, not only did the commission solicit data on the state of technical education in Russia, the avowed rationale for holding the congress. In October 1887, it also asked school administrators, teachers, and industrialists to indicate which questions would be most desirable to discuss at the congress. Similarly, the organizing committee solicited the participation of other societies, such as the Free Economic Society, as well as schools in the planning process. The rules and regulations afforded considerable publicity: the general sessions were open to the public; with the consent of the chair, persons having particular expertise could be invited to meetings of the sections.[67]

Organizers believed that the congresses would energize, facilitate, and coordinate a multitude of private and public efforts to improve technical education and to promote independent activity, and the energy of people working in concert to accomplish mutual objectives was a third narrative fashioned by the congress organizers and admirers. "[The] unity of people working in one area," Golitsyn wrote, "the spirited exchange of views between two persons independently working on the same project, is without a doubt the most essential condition of any project having a general interest." Golitsyn went on to note, "The papers and discussions of the congress have aroused public interest; this interest is not ephemeral, brought about by the momentary distraction of a fashionable novelty, but a serious and thoughtful interest." Golitsyn made special note of the discussions that took place outside the meeting rooms: "This is one of the most important services of congresses: they are the living link between science and society . . . We often see that public opinion is attracted to seductive but groundless theories, beautiful but sterile apparitions. All of this disappears without leaving a trace. But to summon an all-encompassing interest and the thoughtful attention that can focus on a sequence of tasks requires a truly serious project that is met with sympathy and resonance in the general consciousness."[68] In other words, to recall the opinion frequently expressed by the leaders of OLEAE, not only is public science good for national betterment and progress; it also is good for science. Even those involved in technical education but not able to attend the congress could share in this energy and "serious and thoughtful" interest by perusing the published records. The congress published the papers and a stenographic text of the discussions; individual papers were published separately in several education journals, such as *Russkaia shkola, Pedagogicheskii sbornik, Zapiski Imperatorskogo Russkogo tekhnicheskogo obshchestva,* and *Prakticheskaia zhizn'*.[69]

In proposing such congresses, education activists within RTO, such as Andreev and Nebolsin, were figuring out what society needed and supplying that need—that is, taking initiative, initiative sanctioned and even encouraged in government circles, to mobilize public participation. Such efforts on the part of the Technical Society and of the congress organizers are a sign of an important aspect of civil society: society talking to itself. In a country whose polity was built on and favored vertical linkages and discouraged such interactivity, the congress as a whole (its discussions and publications) and in particular the solicitation of public input were a sign of the development of interactivity and horizontal linkages among different elements of society. Of course, vertical linkages could not be ignored, and the relationship between the congress and officialdom was complex. The Russian government encouraged the congress, approved the program, and recognized the common interest in furthering education and promoting industry. At the same time, congress organizers envisioned that, like their counterparts in the public spheres of Europe, they were fulfilling an important function of associations and their projects: to hold government accountable and, if necessary, to play an adversarial role.

According to its rules and regulations, the congresses on technical and vocational education were authorized to draft resolutions derived from the "theses" of individual papers or from the discussion in sections. The congress thereby facilitated the framing of many issues for public discussion. The sections crafted these recommendations in the form of resolutions that were then voted on. Resolutions that passed formed the basis for formal petitions *(khodataistva)* to the pertinent government agency, and it was the responsibility of the congress executive council to pass these petitions on to the Technical Society to present to officialdom. Like many zemstvo petitions, many, indeed most, congress petitions were ignored or held up in red tape because they allegedly exceeded the boundaries of the congresses' competence, a fact of considerable irritation to the congress participants. Although it might be tempting to conclude that petitions were attempts of civil society to wrest more power from officialdom, the specialists at the congresses were just as likely to petition for more rather than less government supervision of a very decentralized and haphazard "system" of technical education. Congresses petitioned for uniformity and standardization in the curriculum, in instruction, and in management of a great variety of technical and vocational schools, many of which were out of government hands.[70] However, for my purposes, the end result of the petitions is less significant than the process involved. The petitioning process provides an example of the congress mediating between society and the authorities, of private persons taking the initiative in policy recommendations in government-approved venues. As B. B. Veselovskii states regarding zemstvo petitions, the petitions played an important agitational role and articulated political opposition.[71] Even when the congress petitioned for more government intervention and regulation, it asserted the right of civil society to participate in the process and to hold government accountable.

The second congress is an excellent case in point. The ninth section on general questions was a "congress within a congress" and fired off some fifty petitions on a wide variety of issues. The ninth section passed several resolutions that aimed to revitalize the Sunday schools for workers—to open more Sunday schools and to broaden their curriculum, to allow more books at their libraries, and to make more space available in regular schools for Sunday schools. According to Ia. V. Abramov, the chronicler of the Sunday school movement, the ninth section, attended predominantly by "Sunday people" *(voskresniki)*, became a de facto congress on Sunday schools and "clarified many matters to the participants, as well as united and energized them."[72] Other resolutions aimed to expand opportunities for extramural learning—to remove restrictions faced by local educators in organizing public lectures, to allow public lectures in the native languages on the borderlands, and to do away with the restrictions placed on the books that public libraries could acquire. Although the second congress decided that Russia was not ready for compulsory universal education until the schools were under local control, it did pass resolutions expressing the desirability of universal education in the long run and advocating the fullest cooperation of the authorities in founding local schools. "The illiteracy of workers is the chief hindrance to the dissemination of technical knowledge and the main reason for unsatisfactory work," one resolution read. The resolutions of the ninth section requested RTO to petition government for more local control and grassroots initiative in educational matters and, at the same time, for more government spending.[73]

Needless to say, the lively discussions at the sessions of the ninth section made the government nervous. Since the authorities were unwilling to surrender total authority to RTO to establish and administer vocational schools without approval, the ninth section drafted petitions for a greater public role in worker education. "All these issues prompted heated debate," noted an internal government memorandum, "which often acquired an agitated tone and which occasionally inclined to the discussion of government measures, although these discussions did not transgress the boundaries of the permissible."[74] However, another aspect of the sessions of the ninth section troubled the authorities: the large numbers of the general public in attendance: "The open admission to the public has also caused much dissatisfaction. At some papers there were so many people that there was hardly room for members of the congress. In the presence of a large public, the discussions often took on an undesirable character, furthered by the desire of the speakers to stimulate applause. In most cases, the public applauded not the essence of the matter but very loudly at unsubstantiated phrases." Accordingly, in the rules and regulations for the third congress, attendance at panels where papers were discussed was limited to official members of the congress; the public was allowed only at the opening ceremonies and at other sessions where no discussion was planned.[75]

The government was fully aware that the congress created and promoted horizontal linkages and the capacity of society to talk to itself; to a certain degree, the Ministry of Finance and even the Ministry of Education had encouraged private initiative and a government-society partnership. Although they could not prevent such communication, conservatives concentrated in the Ministry of Internal Affairs and the Department of Police tried to regulate and confine it. In the following chapter, we will examine the politicized

Third Congress on Technical and Vocational Education. In the conclusion of the current chapter, it will be necessary to face the issue of government scrutiny of the matter of technical education and of the public projects of a society to which, because of its respected role in an area deemed by the government to be critical, it had granted privileged status.

Government Scrutiny

Everywhere states both nurtured and suppressed educational advocacy, especially on the European continent. States and established churches with a monopoly in education were suspicious of unsupervised private efforts to spread learning, especially to the mass of the population. Particularly worrisome were the efforts to reach workers. The French experience, in particular, is instructive. Since the projects of popular education were synonymous with republicanism and anticlericalism, during the Restoration and Second Empire, the French police scrutinized private efforts to provide technical education. "It would be imprudent," stated Victor Duruy, minister of education from 1863 to 1869, "to permit too much independence to an organization that united such a large number of workers and that can exercise the greatest influence over them." Accordingly, the Ministry of the Interior subjected the Association Polytechnique to "unrelenting scrutiny." In 1872 the minister of the interior announced that there would be "no more authorization for public meetings issued to organizations" and that each request for permission to hold a public lecture had to be "investigated and judged individually." Political lectures were forbidden, and prefects had to "make sure that lectures would be confined to the topics for which the lecture was approved." The police reported on "troubling lectures" and were instructed to "watch out for orators."[76]

This occasionally edgy relationship between state and society, especially on the European continent, shows that although governments by and large endorsed private efforts to disseminate useful knowledge among the upper registers of the social hierarchy, they viewed unmediated contact with the laboring population as potentially subversive. Russia followed the European pattern. At stake was the control over popular education. The previous three chapters have shown that on the whole officialdom and science societies perceived that they were working toward shared goals, and the monarchy encouraged the founding of and gave patronage to many societies. Accordingly, although the government claimed the right to authorize and supervise the activities of private associations, in general the authorities left associations free to carry out their various projects. The Free Economic

Society, the Russian Geographical Society, and the Society of Friends of Natural History, Anthropology, and Ethnography combined a service to science with a service to the betterment of Russia through the dissemination of useful knowledge. Like the learned societies it had sanctioned, the Russian government also wanted to disseminate science and useful knowledge beyond the metropolitan scientific elite. The government, too, wanted to promote modern industry, which required educated subjects and trained personnel.

While the government sanctioned societies to promote industry, the Russian authorities, like their French counterparts, were wary of public initiative in such a sensitive area as industrial education. As minister of education Shishkov admonished, "To teach the whole nation to read and write would do more harm than good."[77] In his study of the Ministry of Internal Affairs, Dan Orlovsky puts this frame of mind well: "Society, in its uncivilized and selfish condition, could not be trusted to participate in politics."[78] As the previous section showed, an alliance of state and society tried to wrest control of vocational training from the control of workers themselves. At the same time, RTO and other technical and education societies were asserting their authority and expertise in an attempt to wrest control of popular education from the state. Unlike the dissemination of agricultural techniques among landed proprietors, the cataloging of knowledge about the empire and its peoples, and the display of science and technology, technical education and vocational training among Russia's laboring population became a far more controversial issue. We have already seen that wary of unsupervised activity as the government was entering uncharted ground in legislating the Great Reforms, the Committee of Ministers warned the Free Economic Society and the Russian Geographical Society that discussion of national policy and expression of opinion about government measures could not be allowed. The sections of the 1872 Polytechnical Exposition and of the Polytechnical Museum most carefully scrutinized were those pertaining to worker education and popular amusements. Earlier in this chapter we have seen government restrictions, resembling those of continental regimes, on public lectures. The government wanted to disseminate learning but at the same time to prevent the authority of natural knowledge from upsetting traditional authorities and the values of the old order and to prevent any unauthorized contact between the educated and the mass of the population. In the view of the first chief of the Third Section, "The state should not rush ahead with education too fast. Otherwise, the people will become as knowledgeable as the monarchs and seek to curtail their power."[79] In the early 1860s, recalled Peter Kropotkin, "the ministry of education was engaged in a continuous passionate struggle against all private persons and all institutions . . . which endeavored to open teachers' seminaries or technical schools, or even simple primary schools. Technical education—in a country which was so much in want of engineers, educated agriculturalists, and geologists—was treated as equivalent to revolution."[80] The hyperbole notwithstanding, Kropotkin clearly identifies the scrutiny the tsarist government gave to private initiative in education, even in science and technical education.

Contemporaries and historians alike are in agreement that there was a sharp upsurge in public action in the 1890s in the wake of the famine of 1891–1892. According to the historian Kizevetter, "beginning in 1891 the public revival [*ozhivlenie*] took the critical form of political awakening, nourished by the ever-clearer realization that government and society were on sharply divergent paths."[81] In his history of the Russian Revolution, Orlando Figes expresses well the prevailing interpretation when he claims that when the government belatedly summoned voluntary associations to assist in famine relief, "it opened the door to a powerful new wave of public activity and debate which the government could not control and which quickly turned from the philanthropic to the political . . . The institutions of society were becoming more independent and organized, while the tsarist state was steadily becoming weaker and less able to control them. The famine crisis was the crucial turning point in this process, the moment when Russian society became politically aware of itself and its powers, of its duties to 'the people,' and of the potential it had to govern itself."[82]

The relationship between officialdom and RTO, especially its Education Commission, fit this pattern. The Russian government encouraged the commission and recognized the society's and government's common interest in furthering education and promoting industry. The Ministry of Finance by and large gave RTO a green light to promote industry and technology "at the top," so to speak—at the level of the firm and in the development of a particular technology. Finance ministers from Reitern to Witte endorsed the involvement of RTO in worker education. And not without reason Golitsyn crowed at an address before dignitaries and government officials, "There is hardly any area of public life in which public consciousness and the efforts of society, on the one hand, and government activity on the other are so closely tied together as in the area of public education."[83] However, promoting technical education and vocational training "at the bottom," while endorsed and encouraged, required careful scrutiny, especially by the Ministry of Education, the Ministry of Internal Affairs, and the Department of Police. These branches of government not only feared losing control of the classroom but also suspected the ulterior motives of the teachers and administrators. Because of these fears, the Ministry of Education and the government's security apparatus closely scrutinized RTO's leadership in technical education as well as the activities of other technical societies.

Beginning in the late 1890s, various government departments with supervisory authority over RTO and its public projects, as well as the prefects of Moscow and St. Petersburg and the *okhrana* (secret police), tried to restrict the activities of RTO. In several reports and memoranda, Russia's security apparatus pinpointed several flaws in the Education Commission and in the appointment of teachers and administrators at its technical and vocational schools. Not surprisingly, RTO had a different view of the situation. RTO complained that teachers were denied permission to teach in the technical schools and that proposals to alter the vocational curriculum were turned down by the Ministry of Education. The society repeatedly sought the removal of restrictions that slowed down or blocked the opening of new schools: "The current permission system is a harmful brake in the development of educational initiative . . . and should be replaced by a notification system [*iavochnaia sistema*] whereby the opening of an educational institution should be considered completed if its announcement does not produce within a specified time a reason for its closure."[84]

In the eyes of the police, the Education Commission had too much autonomy and too little supervision in its members and its meetings. The membership was filled with politically "unreliable" public activists *(obshchestvennye deiateli)* and few government officials. It had taken "an extremely undesirable direction in the area of worker education." As a result: "The Education Commission is a nursery of antigovernment ideas, the favorite stage for the illegal activities of unreliable persons with ill-intentioned and hostile thoughts who, having penetrated the teaching and administrative staff of the vocational schools, have freely and legally begun to educate workers in antigovernment and antireligious principles."[85] A feuilletonist in *Novoe Vremia* expressed an opinion increasingly common in government circles, that the new teachers, accountants, artisans, photographers, and aviators were "semiengineers, who have brought the smell of commerce [*torgovyi dukh*] to the society."[86] The autonomy of the branches raised the specter of national networking run by the Moscow chapter, which allegedly wanted to run schools in other provinces, thus exposing even more workers to the "unreliables." One member of RTO complained, "When it approved the bylaws 40 years ago, the government did not have in mind the revolutionary movement, or the pressure of one group within the organization to influence the rest, or the members of one chapter traveling to attend a meeting of another chapter. The bylaws that grant so much autonomy to individual chapters need to be rethought, if for no other reason than to bring peace and tranquility to the empire's transport and communications."[87]

In the view of the authorities, meetings of the Education Commission not only contained antigovernment content but were too open. According to article 27 of RTO's bylaws, guests could attend meetings by invitation from a member; article 50 allowed students to receive free passes to meetings. Students and guests were supposed to sign a register, but the society's officers had not been vigilant about enforcing even these rather liberal regulations. The political police complained that workers and students freely attended "undesirable" lectures and received antigovernment propaganda under the guise of the Education Commission's "lawful meetings." The commission went so far, according to one report, to "use public meetings to proclaim the urgent need of a constitutional form of government in Russia."[88]

More troubling to the authorities than the membership and meetings of RTO's Education Commission were the vocational education teachers; they, after all, had direct, repeated, and government-sanctioned contact with the workers. The political police claimed that technical and vocational schools, in Europe as well as in Russia, had been "targeted" by revolutionary groups because of their concentration of factory workers. Such projects allegedly had "nothing to do with technical education and everything to do with spreading liberalism and socialism among the populace."[89] The political police were careful not to lay blame directly on RTO itself. According to the authorities, the teaching staff at the evening schools and vocational courses and the lecturers hired by RTO and other technical societies included "unreliable" elements. Using legal means, "they [had] freely begun to educate workers in antigovernment and antireligious principles." The government, the authorities insisted, must ensure that institutions created to educate the population be "protected from the fashions of the time [*ograzhdeny ot prekhodiashchikh veianii vremeni*]" and that technical and vocational education be conducted in a "spirit favorable to the government."[90]

Indeed, in the 1890s RTO hired many teachers who were well known for their antigovernment activities—Nadezhda Krupskaia, Alexandra Kollontai, Elena Stasova, Anatolii Lunacharskii, A. M. Kalmykova, and V. M. Bonch-Burevich. Krupskaia taught at the Smolensk school in St. Petersburg from 1891 to 1896; during this time, Lenin often visited her at the school. No wonder that I. L. Goremykin, minister of internal affairs from 1895 to 1899, regarded these schools as producing "worker-Marxists, instilled with an antigovernment manner of thinking." Police suspicions were corroborated by Elena Stasova, one of the activists involved in the Mobile Museum of Teaching Aids, founded by RTO in 1892: "The history of the Mobile Museum is important as a cultural initiative of the intelligentsia at the turn of the century. It also shows that we in the underground [*my, pod-pol'shchiki*] knew how to use any legal opportunity for our party goals."[91]

Why were the security organs unable to stop all this antigovernment activity by "unreliable" persons? How was it that illegal political activity could continue under the cloak of a legal organization? An autocratic government is not without constraints, and many historians have documented the personalized rule of the Russian autocrat, the fragmented and divided bureaucracy, and the absence of government policy (or, rather, the plethora of ad hoc policies).[92] In the case of a very prominent association such as RTO, officialdom faced two special constraints: the patronage of RTO by powerful persons, and the society's bylaws. In the late 1890s many of the central ministries studied the question of changing an association's bylaws in the context of attempts to standardize a dizzying variety of bylaws into a few types of "model charters." At the turn of the twentieth century, the ministries of Internal Affairs and Education, along with the Department of Police, discussed a menu of options to curtail the undesirable activity of RTO's Education Commission, up to and including closing RTO and its vocational schools. But these constraints hampered government effort to make RTO more pliable and to steer it in a more approved direction.

The high esteem accorded RTO in civil society and government alike made dealing with it a delicate matter. As one police report acknowledged, the alleged sympathy of the society's members to antigovernment activity, for example, "prevent[ed] the authorities from stopping such activity." More important was patronage in high places. Having imperial patronage and prominent members, RTO "occupied an exceptional position." Because it "would cause all sorts of complaints," closing RTO would be "extremely complicated." The patronage of the vocational schools complicated the supervisory tasks of the Ministry of Education: refusing permission to open a school "might be construed by His Most August Patron as opposition to the society from the education authorities." Moreover, officialdom acknowledged that the vocational schools helped achieve important state goals and that since their closure would slow the dissemination of practical knowledge, it would be in the government's interest to keep them open.[93]

The bylaws of RTO also constrained administrative action against the society. Many in officialdom favored some sort of change in the bylaws to alter or limit membership in RTO and especially on the Education Commission, to restrict and more closely supervise the outreach activities of RTO, to make it more subordinate to the Ministry of Education, and to more clearly delineate the responsibilities of the officials of the central ministry and the school administrators.[94] However, the practice of vetting the officers of the Education Commission posed difficulties for the authorities: "A disapproval is inevitably accompanied by complaints and appeals and has to be supported by documentation of a criminal or political character." However, because the bylaws allowed all divisions of RTO to be made up of persons selected by the members themselves, to alter or limit membership on the Education Commission would be a "serious violation of bylaws . . . approved by the emperor." It would be more expedient, concluded a memorandum of the Ministry of Education, to supervise the Education Commission by strictly monitoring its activities in the schools and its selection of teachers "than by restricting the initiative of its members in the field of disseminating technical and vocational education."[95]

However, a closer vetting of vocational school teachers also presented problems. Even if teachers and administrators at the technical schools were subject to approval by the Ministry of Education, members of RTO who participated in the day-to-day affairs of the schools were "selected only by the officers of the society and were not approved by any governmental authority."[96] Moreover, article 20 of the charter of the society's technical and vocational schools permitted the chair of the Education Commission to place teachers and administrators in schools on a temporary basis while their approval was pending. According to the Moscow *okhrana,* the chair of the Education Commission abused this right:

> This procedure is one of the most disappointing features of the schools of the Technical Society. This problem puts the security organs in a very amoral position: in their efforts to guard workers from antigovernment propaganda and to prevent politically unreliable persons from teaching, they are completely defenseless to stem the flow of undesirable teachers into the classroom . . . This leads to an odd situation. The chair [of the Education Commission] appoints an unreliable individual to be a teacher and then begins the paper work for approval. But before the paperwork is even started and during the approval process, this individual, in the capacity of teacher, has complete freedom of contact with workers for illegal ends. But suppose that the Department of Police advises that the appointment of this teacher is undesirable. Then the problem is no longer about appointing an undesirable person but about firing a teacher. This is much more complicated and puts the government in an awkward position.[97]

The authorities faced much the same problem when it came to opening new schools or starting new classes. Should permission be denied, there was a continual stream of petitions and complaints. "Such complaints," the *okhrana* noted, "not only generate an excess of correspondence and explanations, but also do not always result in an outcome favorable to the education authorities." In addition, numerous government reports noted that the bylaws conferred broad powers to RTO and to its subsidiary institutions to organize meetings and symposia *without appropriate government supervision.*[98] Reports of the political police repeatedly complained that the parent RTO and its Moscow chapter used their "right" to disseminate vocational education and to open vocational schools as justification for their increased and, in the eyes of the police, suspicious activity. For example, the libraries at some schools contained "undesirable" books that were loaned to workers "without authorization." All this, complained the *okhrana,* made it more difficult for the government to keep tabs on antigovernment activity. Thus the Ministry of Internal Affairs admitted that, "lacking any provision in the law for the government to change or amend the bylaws of a private association without the consent of its members," all efforts to change the bylaws of the Russian Technical Society had "gone nowhere."[99]

As Peter Kropotkin recalled, at midcentury "all Russia wanted to study . . . In the public consciousness the school [was] a temple of science."[100] The needs of a modern economy, the increasing division of labor, and the specialization of the workforce required a greater investment in adult and technical training, and the state, zemstvos, city councils, and associations all responded to this need. Spreading education and technical training was widely regarded as an investment in the empire's future. Although Russia's backwardness in this area was a source of embarrassment in and out of government, the process by which that backwardness could be overcome was held in high hope by the public, a public created and mobilized, in part, by the intervention of associations. The vocational class created a skilled labor force and promoted a love of useful knowledge; the public lecture opened the worlds of science and learning; and the congress brought specialists together to frame issues and to hone arguments. As Nebolsin put it in a self-congratulatory way, "There is not a single question concerning technical education that has not been discussed by the Technical Society."[101] Although its membership may have been too diverse for it to have been a professional organization, RTO facilitated communication and networking among a wide spectrum of government officials, engineers, and industrialists dedicated to Russian industrial development and created an extensive unofficial infrastructure of technical and vocational education.

Such education was the linchpin in the development of a more skilled and disciplined industrial labor force. In the latter decades of the nineteenth century, the Ministry of Finance and RTO led the debate on ways to improve technical education and on-the-job training. Vocational education by means of schooling meant that experts situated in the institutions of state and civil society, rather than working-class families, could make technical education and vocational training decisions. Thus the Russian Technical Society's educational mission was part of the efforts of civil society to colonize the traditional workplace and family practices of the urban labor force. Institutionalized vocational training would pull children out of the labor force and into schools and thereby replace workplace socialization and its incumbent practices, especially alcohol abuse, with the socialization of schooling and its concomitant promise of individuality, choice, upward mobility, and the integration of young workers into modern industrial economy and urban life.

The Russian Technical Society's pursuit of applied science, its promotion of industry and industrial education, and its expertise had the endorsement of Russian officialdom. The government and science societies perceived that they were working toward shared goals, and the monarchy encouraged the founding of and gave patronage to many societies. During the era of the Great Reforms, the Russian state sanctioned and even encouraged private associations to provide technical training. As did the learned societies it had sanctioned, the Russian government also wanted to disseminate science and useful knowledge beyond the metropolitan scientific elite. It, too, wanted to promote modern industry, which required educated subjects and trained personnel. Thus, just as in earlier generations the possession of natural knowledge allowed scientists to enter the public sphere, so too in the latter nineteenth century the possession of technical expertise provided a way for the technical intelligentsia to enter the public sphere.

Although the government claimed the right to authorize and supervise the activities of private associations, by and large the authorities left associations free to carry out their various projects. In a system greased by personal patronage, RTO and its projects had protectors in high places, and patronage helps to explain the survival, even the flourishing, of RTO's education projects, as well as those of other technical societies. Well-patronized private efforts in technical education and vocational training were evidence of a state-society partnership in the mutual pursuit of national betterment. Members of RTO believed that private efforts could complement the work of the government.

Just as members of the imperial family, notables, and government officials patronized the Russian Technical Society, RTO patronized and sometimes sheltered divisions whose primary focus was not industry and technology but education. By negotiating the terrain of scientific activity, the "parent" society acted as a patron to the activities of the divisions and chapters of RTO, which had considerable autonomy and eventually operated almost as independent associations. But patronage of science, industry, and industrial education shifted from the imperial patronage of grand dukes, notables, and government officials to a civic patronage on the part of public figures *(obshchestvennye deiateli)*. Accordingly, although the tsarist government sanctioned the specialized public activities of private associations, the scope of RTO's projects as well as its claims to a voice in public policy raised the specter of a vast archipelago of unauthorized and unscrutinized public initiative in education. Moreover, the government feared that RTO would not confine itself "to the sphere of *technical* knowledge but [would] spread to *all* fields of human knowledge," that "a technical society [would] turn into a political, or an encyclopedic, one."[102]

At stake was control over popular education. Although the government had sanctioned societies to promote industry, Russian authorities resembled those in continental Europe in being cautious about public initiative in the sensitive area of industrial education. Technical education and vocational training of the laboring population became far more controversial than gathering data about the empire or displaying science and technology. The government wanted to disseminate learning without overturning traditional authorities and values and to prevent unauthorized mingling of educated people and the mass of the population. Serving working youth and adults outside the state-run education system, RTO schools played an important role in consciousness-raising. As Heather Hogan argues, "industry's need for literate workers . . . contributed not only to the workers' search for vocational education, but to a thirst for knowledge more generally; in turn, workers began to acquire the intellectual tools with which to perceive and to criticize the world around them."[103]

At the same time that an alliance of state and society tried to wrest control of vocational training from the control of workers themselves, RTO and other technical and education societies were asserting their authority and expertise in an attempt to wrest control of popular education from the state. But beginning in the 1890s, the partnership between the government and one of Russia's most prestigious and privileged associations was strained, as RTO broadened the scope of its activities and more and more claimed a voice in public policy and, as its Education Commission claimed, a voice in perhaps the most sensitive public policy area of all, popular education. The great service of RTO was to facilitate and coordinate education programs and to become a font of information about public education. Thus RTO was a vehicle by which a private organization could enter the public arena and claim a role in public policy. The efforts of RTO and of many other associations were an attempt to transform education from an object of government tutelage to a trust for the public.

CHAPTER SIX

Advocacy in the Public Sphere

Scientific Congresses

In his study of the critical role of networking in intellectual creativity, Randall Collins states, "Although lectures, discussions, conferences, and other real-time gatherings would seem superfluous in the world of texts, it is exactly these face-to-face structures which are most constant across the entire history of intellectual life."[1] Meetings of societies in general and congresses in particular are an example of such "face-to-face structures." If the nineteenth century was the "age of associations," it was also the age of congresses. Despite their importance to the development of the public sphere of civil society, congresses remain understudied. This is especially true of tsarist Russia, not known for its associational impulse or its public assemblies, and, with a few exceptions, Russian historians have not recognized the importance of Russian congresses.[2] Yet, in the last half century of imperial rule, more than one thousand congresses debated all manner of intellectual and policy matters. In the previous two chapters, we have seen how private associations furthered the dissemination of useful knowledge and the development of the nation's scientific potential via popularization and display (in the case of OLEAE) and via technical education and training for modern industry (in the case of RTO). As we have also seen, these forms of public science can show us the workings of the public sphere of civil society and the relationship between the state and private initiative in a continental regime with a long authoritarian tradition. Russia's scientific and technical intelligentsia sought new forms of communication, dissemination of knowledge, and popularization of science, as well as venues that extended beyond the reach of the local science society, venues that might give the intelligentsia a voice in public policy. One of these new forms of communication was the congress.

Just as a study of the more than ten thousand associations active in nineteenth-century Russia is beyond the scope of this book, so too is a study of more than one thousand congresses convened in the last half century of imperial Russia. This chapter will start by examining two sets of scientific congresses—the congresses of naturalists and the "Pirogov" congresses of physicians. Beginning in 1867, the Congress of Naturalists (renamed, in 1876, the Congress of Naturalists and Physicians) established the pattern of Russia's national meetings of the scientific intelligentsia. I have selected these conferences also for their longevity and for their broad scientific interests. Their meetings spawned and nurtured more scientific societies and congresses, such as the Pirogov Society of Russian Physicians. On the agenda of the Pirogov congresses were not only scientific arguments but also public health, education, and other social policies that reached the mass of the population, and, not surprisingly, by the beginning of the twentieth century these congresses came under government scrutiny. This chapter will close with the highly politicized 1904 Pirogov and technical education congresses. Although these congresses can provide a gold mine of information for students of Russian science, medicine, technology, and education, I am primarily interested in them as a manifestation of the relationship between the state and the public sphere in an age of increasing private initiative and activism.[3] The goal of all of these congresses was to advance Russia's scientific and technical infrastructure through the dissemination of useful knowledge, the popularization of science and technology, and the advocacy of a variety of policy initiatives. By the late nineteenth century, an increasingly active public sphere of debate that included advocacy and representation was no longer in doubt in tsarist Russia.

Congresses allow us to enrich our understanding of not only the workings of civil society but also its normative features. In Europe congresses were quintessential components of a Habermasian public sphere: venues for people to come together to deliberate matters of common concern. By providing a new form of communication to present the results of scholarly work and to exchange views, scientific congresses contributed to the development of science and the dissemination of useful knowledge. Often organized by an association or a group of associations, often with the cooperation of governments, congresses were particularly important in the development of the professions. Procedures schooled participants in the languages and practices of representative institutions, and the participants represented themselves, or their "constituents," before an assembly of their peers. Congresses also represented certain causes or projects before the larger arena of public opinion and before governments. Thus by mobilizing new special interest constituencies and in publicizing a variety of causes, congresses became a new form of public representation, especially in polities lacking national assemblies or for groups not otherwise represented.

Congresses of German scientists provide an excellent illustration of the features described above, and the organizers of Russia's first congresses self-consciously used German scientific congresses as a model. Beginning in 1822, a series of congresses of German scientists took place in university centers. Organized by naturalists interested in furthering the empirical study of nature, the congresses were patriotic gatherings that promoted German science by bringing together scientists scattered in many towns and often living in different political units. According to one of the driving forces of the congresses, Alexander von Humboldt, their purpose was "the personal rapprochement of men who work in the same field of knowledge; . . . [and] the formation of friendly relations which impart light to scholarship, grace to life, and tolerance and gentleness to manners."[4] However, the will of the congress organizers alone was insufficient to convene a congress: to meet, the German congresses required the permission of the local or state authorities, who insisted (and the scientists concurred) that politics not intrude into the discussions. Because of the danger of the intrusion of politics in a polity lacking a national representative assembly, congress organizers avoided "incidents likely to arouse the hostility of the authorities." Even ostensibly apolitical meetings came under the watchful eye of the authorities, who feared, rightly, that such "learned assemblies" would be drawn into politics. As physician and liberal opposition leader Rudolf Virchow wrote in 1848, "medicine is a social science, and politics is nothing more than medicine writ large."[5] Theodore Hamerow has noted that the Prussian government, suspicious of its subjects' political activities, brought politics into ostensibly nonpolitical gatherings: "Meetings of historians, naturalists, jurists, physicians, teachers, singers, etc., began to perform a quasi-political function . . . A congress of civic activists was more than just a congress of certain specialists; it was the pre-parliament which leads to the real parliament."[6] The political police of imperial Germany had the power to conduct surveillance of such meetings and to shut down those that deviated from their ostensible agendas. Despite the constraints imposed by nervous authorities or, rather, because of them, the congresses became a vital forum for the pursuit of public science and the discussion of a variety of issues of national concern.[7]

The Congresses of Naturalists

The first Russian scientific congresses were a product and a paradox of the era of the Great Reforms. Because the tsar's officials did not speak with one voice, the government's policy toward the sanctioning of congresses, like its policies in many areas, was inconsistent. The government promised *glasnost'*, but at the same time the sweeping changes of the Great Reforms heightened fear of things getting out of hand. In the same year as the emancipation of the serfs, the Committee of Ministers refused to allow local agricultural congresses requested by several governors and the Free Economic Society; Alexander II considered this decision "justified, for one must be even more careful these days." However, the introduction of the zemstvos provided a structure for regular agricultural congresses, and more than four hundred local congresses took place after 1864. Scientists fared better. As we have seen throughout this book, the Russian state regarded science and the diffusion of scientific and technical knowledge with high esteem; moreover, the state perceived the attempts of scientists to convene congresses and conventions as less political than the attempts of other groups and as interesting to only a small number of people.[8]

Although we are accustomed to think of the Russian state as the initiator of grand projects, the idea of periodic scientific congresses came from Karl Fedorovich Kessler, a professor of zoology and dean of the physics and mathematics faculty and later rector at the University of Kiev. A founder of the university's zoological museum and a member of twenty-nine learned societies, including the Free Economic Society, Kessler was an advocate of public science, that is, science free from bureaucratic tutelage. In his scientific work Kessler posited the primacy of mutual assistance over the struggle for existence in evolution. In 1856 in a memorandum to A. S. Norov, minister of education from 1854 to 1858—under whose watch university restrictions in many areas were lessened after the death of Nicholas I—Kessler proposed a different form of mutual assistance: periodic congresses of scientists and physicians. To justify expanded private initiative in Russia, Kessler argued that in many European countries periodic congresses contributed to the advancement of science: "Congresses stimulate competition among [scientists], enliven their work, ease the solution of complicated problems, and allow them to collaborate in their scholarly work." Such congresses, Kessler continued, were arguably more important in Russia than in Europe due to greater isolation of individual scientists and for this reason merited government support. Four years after submitting his memorandum, Kessler went to his hometown of Königsberg to attend the German Congress of Naturalists and Physicians, a meeting that only reinforced his conviction that such a forum was badly needed in Russia.[9]

The Ministry of Education circulated Kessler's proposal to the curators of each education district. Response demonstrated that the idea of scientific congresses had support in midlevel officialdom. The spirit of open discussion and criticism during the era of the Great Reforms, coupled with a zeal to correct incompetence, corruption, and administrative abuses after the Crimean War, meant that many government departments were open to reforming ideas, thus giving an opening for nongovernmental organizations. The curator of the Kharkov district was enthusiastic, and the trustee of the Moscow district noted that Kessler's proposal could be expanded to create congresses of historians, archaeologists, and engineers, who were just as isolated as scientists.[10] Perhaps the greatest advocate of the idea was the curator of the Odessa and Kiev education districts, N. I. Pirogov. Professor at the prestigious Medical-Surgical Academy, Pirogov joined the St. Petersburg Society for Visiting the Poor in 1846 and was the first director of the Society of Sisters of Mercy of the Exaltation of the Cross, founded during the Crimean War by Grand Duchess Elena Pavlovna. Author of "Questions of Life," an article in the journal *Morskoi Sbornik,* (1856), which advocated education for citizenship, Pirogov was a spokesman for the diffusion of applied knowledge and for universal primary education. As curator of the Odessa and Kiev education districts from 1856 to 1861, Pirogov was a "passionate supporter" of the Sunday school movement; in Nancy Frieden's words he also "supported the advancement of women, opposed restrictions on Jews, tried to limit the use of corporal punishment in schools, and sought to lighten bureaucratic controls on the average citizen."[11] Writing to his ministry superiors on 30 July 1858, Pirogov endorsed Kessler's arguments regarding the German model, the isolation of Russia's scientists, and the importance of government patronage. Pirogov went even further in his advocacy. The German congresses were held, he argued, "because of the conviction that the written word did not fully supplant the spoken word, that books and journals do not generate the same competition and spiritedness [*odushevlenie*] as speech."[12]

At the same time, other scientists as well as teachers became interested in the idea of periodic congresses; the press and several associations, including the Kiev Society of Physicians, the Moscow Physics and Medical Society, and the Moscow Society of Naturalists, took up the cause. One such scientist was the physician S. A. Smirnov, one of the founders of the Society of Russian Physicians in Moscow in 1859 and publisher of *Moskovskaia meditsinskaia gazeta,* a mouthpiece for his views on public medicine and physicians' associations. In 1860 Smirnov commented that events such as the German congresses were as yet "a dream in Russia." In a dream apparently shared by many proponents of such meetings, "the physician at one end of Russia would greet a physician at the other end, converse, express his needs and aspirations and thereby find encouragement, sympathy, and new strength." By enhancing the development of Russian science and the dissemination of useful knowledge, such a congress would be patriotic. Finally, Smirnov took the unusual step of inviting other scientists and doctors to respond: "Only a common voice can decide whether the time is ripe for such a union or whether it will remain an unrealizable dream."[13]

Well-timed in an era of officially encouraged *glasnost'*, Smirnov's appeal to public opinion prompted support and cultivated horizontal linkages in the press and among learned societies. Letters from the provinces to the editors of the medical press claimed that such congresses would benefit public health and "double or triple the scholarly activity of our scientists."[14] In the early 1860s the Ministry of Education received repeated proposals from individual scientists, physicians, and learned societies to permit periodic national congresses. For example, in 1862 Khristian Iakovlevich Giubbenet—renowned surgeon, along with Pirogov, at Sevastopol, professor of surgery at Kiev University, and president of the Kiev Society of Physicians from 1860 to 1869—submitted a proposal to A. V. Golovnin, who had been appointed minister of education the year before. In addition to the almost formulaic arguments regarding the German model and the isolation of Russian scientists, Giubbenet framed his proposal around the need for association *(tovarishchestvo)*. Moreover, not only did Giubbenet make the customary connection between science, associations, and progress; he also validated an incipient professionalization:

> Science and the spirit of association are the necessary conditions for the flourishing of any learned corporation . . . Although many feel the need for the spirit of association as a moral and ennobling principle, they consider it unfeasible. Nevertheless, this spirit of association, especially for the good of humanity and of the medical estate [*vrachebnoe soslovie*], given the social status of physicians, is essential.[15]

Pirogov's persistent advocacy and petitioning *(khodataistvo)* before his superiors resulted in the ministry's approval to hold a local congress of gymnasia science teachers of the Kiev education district in 1861. In intent, if not in scope, the general outlines of the congress adhered to those proposed by Kessler. The goals were to improve science teaching in the schools and to energize the scientific activities of the members, highlighted by Kessler in his opening address. The forty-four delegates expressed the hope that the Kiev congress would be the first of a series of annual congresses. One year later a second local congress was held in Kiev. Just to make sure everything proceeded smoothly, representatives of officialdom, including the future minister of finance, Nikolai Khristianovich Bunge, were at almost all the sessions. Nevertheless, these two congresses were the "first breach of Russian science in the armor of the censorship and formalism in the area of independent [*svobodnoe*] research."[16] Finally, in 1867, the Committee of Ministers authorized national congresses of naturalists to be held periodically in university towns and to be organized by university science societies.

The views of A. V. Golovnin and Count D. A. Tolstoi, ministers of education in the reform era, provide a glimpse of contradictory government policies as well as the opportunities for state-society cooperation. Initially, Golovnin, a supporter of scientific societies and a former secretary of the Russian Geographical Society, refused to permit periodic national congresses. Following the closing of the Sunday schools, the temporary chill in the application of private initiative, the student disorders, and the mysterious fires in St. Petersburg, the proposals could not have come at a worse time. In 1862 Golovnin was involved in the delicate drafting of new censorship and university statutes, and according to Bruce Lincoln, he thought that "Russians were not yet ready for those broader civic liberties enjoyed by the citizens of Europe." Like François Guizot in the west European political environment, Golovnin feared their abuse for political purposes.[17] Yet the tsarist government was not monolithic. The Medical Council of the Ministry of Internal Affairs was also interested in the advancement of Russian medicine; moreover, a new university statute sanctioned a greater scope of public science. Golovnin acknowledged that personal communication among scientists would be beneficial for the development of a native science infrastructure and the diffusion of useful knowledge in Russia. "A congress would be the most effective way to stimulate interest in science and a desire to do research," he wrote, "all the more that we have few scientific and medical journals and few scientists."[18] Tolstoi, an opponent of teaching science in the gymnasia, recognized that the exchange of views at such meetings furthered scientific innovation: "[For scientists] who need practical experience and knowledge of the kind brought by museums, laboratories, and observatories, which are usually in the large centers, . . . the best way to spread knowledge these days is by congresses, where scientists can cooperate and see new equipment and techniques." Tolstoi continued with an endorsement of further public activity: "Congresses of scientists promote the creation of learned societies and generally further all forms of scientific enterprise whose execution requires the unified efforts of many participants." Acknowledging the existence of a public and publicity, Tolstoi observed that such meetings would validate the efforts of scientists in the eyes of the public. Finally, the official history of the Ministry of Education provides an additional perspective on Tolstoi's motives. The naturalists merited ministry support, Tolstoi believed, because they directed their scientific work "to the study of Russia and for the benefit of Russia."[19]

Although it finally permitted the congresses and indeed recognized their value, the Ministry of Education, like its French counterpart during the Second Empire, did not relinquish its tutelary role. The ministry regarded itself as the ultimate patron of learning, a claim not hard to make, given the weak development of private patronage. It resisted requests to permit a national professional association along the lines of the British Association of Science. It likewise refused to permit creation of a permanent body to organize the science congresses or even to authorize regularly scheduled congresses. Officialdom feared that permanent or national bodies would institutionalize the enterprise and make it vulnerable to politics. Although the ministry endorsed the idea of periodic congresses, each one was organized by a different university science society in conjunction with the curators of the relevant education district. As in France under the Second Empire, the rules and regulations of each congress, as well as the program, required prior approval.[20]

In his 1866 report, Tolstoi suggested an additional reason for the government's newfound enthusiasm for the public activity of scientists: the right to decide what body of knowledge and methodology might be called a "science." Tolstoi observed, "A strictly scientific congress can help eradicate the pernicious ideas of materialism, or so-called nihilism, which have their main source in an insufficient, superficial, and even false understanding of science."[21] A few years later Tolstoi elaborated and gave his version of government concerns, in a banquet address to the second congress in Moscow in 1869. He admitted that initially the ministry had been "prejudiced against the idea" of endorsing national congresses. The natural sciences had become "confused with the abuses of science and with the most false and dismal theories, articulated only by those who misunderstood the nature of science." At stake was whether science would continue to serve the Russian state or be summoned to the service of the state's enemies. "Science is sober and cautious," Tolstoi continued, trying to distinguish "true" from "false" science. "Before it takes a step forward, it thinks about the steps it has already taken. That is why its pace is steady and its conclusions well grounded. Mistakes are the result of ignorance or, worse, incomplete knowledge and misunderstanding of the scientific enterprise." However, Tolstoi went on, the first congress gratified the ministry, its patron. By recommending the creation of a national society of chemists and of several university science societies, a goal the Ministry of Education approved, the congress inspired young people to pursue science. Moreover, in keeping with the spirit of science societies such as RGO and OLEAE, the congress was patriotic. The congress demonstrated that many scientific fields had taken root in Russia and that Russian scientists would "not forever blindly imitate foreigners." Most important for national pride, Russia would be able to show off to the Europeans "the fruits of Russian thought and genius."[22]

The first congress of Russian naturalists was held in St. Petersburg in December 1867 (see figure 6.1). The second followed two years later in Moscow; the congresses continued, usually two to three years apart, until the outbreak of World War I. By the 1901 congress in St. Petersburg, five thousand had attended the meetings.[23] Most important in the context of

Figure 6.1 First Congress of Russian Naturalists, St. Petersburg, 1867—a group of participants of the chemistry section, including Dmitrii Mendeleev (top row, second from right) and the composer Alexander Borodin (top row, fifth from left). (Courtesy of the State Museum of the History of St. Petersburg.)

my work is the meaning of these congresses, especially the early ones, for their participants and their role in opening and enriching the public sphere.

First, the scientific congresses were examples of self-organized private initiative. They conducted their business largely by rules and procedures of their own making, according to government-approved conditions *(polozhenie)*. Borrowed from contemporary German practice, these rules and procedures were organized by the new university societies of naturalists that sprang up around the empire and bear striking resemblance to practices of meetings of professional associations today. Prior to the congress, the organizing committee issued invitations to attend (similar to today's calls for papers); attempts were also made to reach independent scholars. The organizing committee requested discounted fares from the railroads and discounted rates at local hotels. Local arrangements included opportunities to visit learned societies, museums, laboratories, and the like; Kiev congresses, for example, usually included a river cruise. The organizing committee also appointed subcommittees and task forces as the need arose, as well as gathered data and prepared a budget. The Ministry of Education subsidized the costs of the congresses, including the costs of participants to attend; it also provided a subvention to publish the congress proceedings *(Trudy)*. The meetings were divided into general and specialized sections. Time limits were imposed on papers, and prizes were given for the best papers.[24]

Second, like the association, the museum, and the public lecture, congresses were an important component of efforts to popularize science and diffuse practical knowledge. Not unexpectedly, for the Russians the model was Europe. Recent studies in the history of science have demonstrated that the popularization and dissemination of natural knowledge, sometimes called the "performance of science" for utility and entertainment, was an integral component in the development of the scientific enterprise from the seventeenth through the nineteenth centuries.[25] The work of European scientists, before allegedly hidden in their offices or lifeless on the pages of their monographs, had "now come alive in human speech," the catalyst for the dissemination of scientific learning. This was especially important for a vast country such as Russia with few and widely dispersed centers of scientific learning. Such public events gave publicity to the work of scientists, and the congresses were reported extensively in the scientific and medical press. Moreover, scientists in new and increasingly specialized fields requested more sections as a way to publicize their work; the congresses and the medical societies, for example, helped define the new fields of public health and medical statistics. Although an analysis of other congresses will treat this issue more fully, the scientific congresses, like the science societies we have been discussing, had an educational agenda—to disseminate in Russia an interest in science.[26] But to a scientist-educator such as G. E. Shchurovskii, president of OLEAE and active in an age of populism, education was more than a desirable goal: naturalists had a "duty to the Russian people and to Russian society—to popularize science."[27]

Third, the congresses stressed interdependence and mutuality. In addresses before the first and second congresses, Shchurovskii opined that congresses could correct the deficiency of communication among scientists and help train the younger generation for independent scholarly work: "Congresses are a moral force, bringing scientists in contact with each other and with society and the mass of the population."[28] Like professional conferences today, the real-time interchange among scientists was considered more important than the papers themselves, most of which would be published in more complete form later. Cooperation and working together to achieve common goals advanced the scientific enterprise as they enhanced the public sphere. In one day, ran the common refrain, scientists would meet with each other more than during an entire year; the isolated zoologist in the provinces would not see as many zoologists in a lifetime. Moreover, echoing the descriptions of the museum public or the audience at public lectures, many accounts of the congresses noted the diversity and heterogeneity of the participants and the attendant liveliness of the meetings. The metaphor of enterprise and exchange that bound members of civil society was also used in the report of a commission of the Moscow City Council, which supported funding for the second congress:

> If it were necessary to address the utility of learned congresses, one could explain it by the following analogy. They have the same significance for the development of science as do trade fairs for the development of the nation's commerce. The difference is that goods and capital are exchanged at the trade fairs while information, observations and discoveries are exchanged at the congresses. But in both, persons working far apart, often unknown to each other, but nevertheless bound by common interests and needs, by mutual agreement come together in a small space and for a few days borrow from each other's precious stocks of information and counsel, which each one, acting singly, could not gather no matter how much time and effort he expended.[29]

Fourth, bringing scientists together from the far corners of Russia was patriotic and would help promote Russian science and a sense of national pride. Repeating an argument prioritizing the study of Russian geography and natural history made at the founding of RGO and OLEAE, Kessler argued that owing to its size, Russia should be the focus of study by Russian scientists. Congresses could demonstrate that studying Russia's natural wealth was feasible and necessary: "Russian scientists have their own national, or more precisely, their local, special goals—the study of our vast motherland. Only by studying Russia can we speak of a national, Russian, science." As Kessler put it in a classic statement of the scientific worldview and a justification for its dissemination, "nature is our native land [*rodina*], and an acquaintance with nature and its laws can remove prejudices and superstitions."[30] Shchurovskii said at the second congress, "By serving humanity in the abstract or the cosmopolitan idea, we will never be able to achieve what our national honor and political position in Europe require of us; we will never have our own unique, Russian science."[31]

But the importance of Russia as an object of study went beyond its importance as an understudied unit of the natural world. Congresses could demonstrate that Russian science was "worthy of a place next to European science," that Russians were not "lazy and indolent but were capable of pursuing serious scientific work." In the same dynamic that was taking place in other institutions, such as RGO and the Academy of Sciences, by domesticating a form of learning commonly regarded as a province of Europeans (and of Germans in particular), Russian scientists could proclaim their "independence" from foreign science. The congress was the beginning of "a new learned era on Russian soil," and scientific congresses were a sign of "the maturity of the Russian mind," of an independent and "self-reliant" Russian reason.[32] In short, Russia could demonstrate through its scientific congresses that it was part of the civilized world. As Kessler put it in his address at the opening ceremony of the first congress in 1867, "all civilized countries" recognized the importance of cooperative enterprises such as societies and congresses in bringing "progress and civilization"; hence their multiplication "in every civilized country."[33]

Throughout Europe congresses cultivated the capacity of citizenship and the art of representation, and their proponents in Russia looked to Europe to establish the precedent. To be sure, popular vote did not put scientists in this position; they were self-appointed. Nevertheless, when they presented papers and introduced and voted on resolutions, scientists represented themselves and their work in public before their peers. Such action was the action of the free citizen, not the government functionary. According to one Russian observer, "Science in the West long ago left its medieval cloister, when it was regarded as a luxury. Science has received the rights of citizenship, and its numerous representatives have received complete freedom to seek the means to prosper and to disseminate scientific knowledge."[34]

Because, as Kessler proclaimed in an address before the first Kiev congress, science in Russia still had not attained "full civil rights," the congresses of scientists—"those Olympic games of the new civilization"—could be the way to win that citizenship.[35] Such representation was necessary, Russian scientists argued, for the moral support of the scientists, the stimulation of scientific activity, and the diffusion of useful knowledge. Scientists also represented themselves and the scientific enterprise before the public and collectively represented themselves and the public to the Russian government. Sessions sometimes passed resolutions formulating collective policy statements; this behavior increased over the years from congress to congress, evidence of greater public confidence. Speakers occasionally attached requests that the officers of the congress petition *(khodataistvovat')* the government, usually the Ministry of Education, on behalf of certain policy initiatives. Even though, as commonly lamented, most petitions were ignored, when the congress petitioned the government, it advocated on behalf of certain interests, causes, or policies. Despite the attempts of officialdom and even congress organizers (like their German counterparts) to keep out issues that, in the words of the curator of the Moscow education district, "could divide the scientists and give the congress a polemical character," the congresses provided a forum for the discussion of a wide variety of social and professional matters. They mediated between the larger public and the government, and by doing so, they represented the public, that is, it articulated the interests of different constituencies within the public.[36]

The scientific congresses in their first two decades had their critics. Amid all the self-praise and flattery, there were concerns in the press that the public, even the scientific public, knew little about congresses or, worse, were indifferent. Dissonance within the scientific community was geminating as well. A. V. Pogozhev was troubled by the crowded meetings at the sixth and seventh congresses (see figure 6.2), where a lack of decorum—an "element of personal attack"—was occasionally permitted in the debates although it was "inappropriate in such an honorable setting as a congress of scientists." The "elite of Russian science" was allegedly upset by the applause, hissing, and whistling at the speakers; such demonstrative behavior was "unpleasant at such stern scientific gatherings."[37]

At the same time, perhaps inadvertently, Pogozhev alluded to the greatest legacy of the early scientific congresses. "A tremendous effort," Pogozhev noted in his preface in 1887, went into simply getting permission to gather together a few dozen scientists for the congress in the late 1850s. Public life in Russia was *"still fragile,"* Pogozhev remembered, and at every step there were official barriers to the creation of scientific circles and societies: "*Today we cannot imagine* how much moral distress and deceived expectations awaited the best representatives of the rather small circle of Russian scientists in the early 1860s."[38] If the "fragility" and "official barriers" of the 1850s and early 1860s were "unimaginable" by the late 1880s, it was surely in large part due to the establishment (and even official acceptance) of a public forum that gave the scientists self-esteem, fostered pride in Russian achievements, and left behind a culture of individual and collective representation before both peers and power.

The Pirogov Congresses of Russian Physicians

One important legacy of the German congresses of naturalists was to bring together physicians. Before the founding of Europe's first medical societies, physicians employed at medical and surgical academies who wanted to associate joined naturalist societies. The Swedish Physicians' Society was founded in Stockholm in 1807 to disseminate medical knowledge. In 1822 the German Society of Scientists and Physicians was founded in Leipzig; as we have seen at the beginning of this chapter, its congresses emphasized the common ties of scientists and physicians in a politically divided Germany. Yet conservative German governments restricted and regulated the meetings. As Charles McClelland argues, "early nineteenth-century professional organizations were met with hostility from the state . . . Free citizens' associations, even ostensibly professional ones, were widely regarded as subversive to public order and authority."[39] Although German governments continued to suppress national associations for decades after 1848, many local medical societies sprang up in the 1860s. Finally, in 1873 deputies to the Congress of Natural Scientists and Physicians founded the German Medical Association as a society of professional advocacy.[40]

Three separate movements among Russian physicians came together in the early 1880s to create the Pirogov congresses—a spin-off from the congresses of naturalists, the congresses of zemstvo physicians, and the existence of a new generation of medical societies. The idea of a congress of physicians first originated in the 1860s in the context of the congresses of naturalists. Although specialists in theoretical medical disciplines, mainly university and academy professors, attended the congresses of naturalists, clinical specialists and practicing physicians had no such gathering. A. V. Pogozhev, himself a zemstvo physician, claimed that, treated as second-class participants by the university scientists, physicians became more and more indifferent to the joint congresses. Similarly, the medical press—*Meditsinskoe obozrenie, Vrach*—expressed dissatisfaction with the congresses. Nevertheless, according to D. N. Zhbankov, the increasing number of participants at these congresses was evidence of "the striving of Russian

Figure 6.2 Sixth Congress of Russian Naturalists, St. Petersburg, 1879, at the great hall of the Academy of Sciences (*Vsemirnaia Illiustratsiia*, no. 575 [1880]: 61; courtesy of the Library of Congress.)

naturalists and physicians for community and of all Russian society for every manifestation of public activity." Indeed, for the first time, a majority of participants at the seventh congress in 1883 were physicians, and the subsection on zemstvo medicine and public health was the best attended.[41]

The second movement came from the congresses of zemstvo physicians, 383 of which were held between 1871 and 1917. These took place in the larger context of other provincial congresses of zemstvo professionals, such as teachers, statisticians, and agronomists. Mostly general practitioners, the zemstvo physicians were inclined to work in the public arena. Although numerous, the zemstvo congresses were localized, and it was difficult for physicians in one province to have contact with physicians in another. Indeed, the authorities liked it this way: some governors forbade physicians from other provinces to attend their zemstvo congress. Nevertheless, social and political issues, such as universal education and corporal punishment, came up. Zemstvo doctors complained about government interference in medical affairs, but at the same time many petitions generated by the zemstvo congresses were ignored. *Moskovskie vedomosti* opined, "In the zemstvos there is the idea of some kind of doctors' republic which is self-governed by its own congresses and rules."[42]

The third movement came from the medical societies. Russia's first medical association was the Society for the Emulation of Medical and Physical Sciences at Moscow University, a society founded in 1805, at the same time as the founding of OIDR and MOIP. The society's goals were to disseminate useful knowledge of the physical and medical sciences in Russia; "to stimulate, nurture, and strengthen a love" among the members "and among all other friends of learning"; and "to enrich the physical and medical societies through discoveries, experiments, and observations."[43] The era of the Great Reforms stimulated new medical societies, and from 1859 to 1868 twenty-five societies of physicians were founded. Most of the reasons for this surge of medical associations during the reform era have been well presented in the secondary literature and may be summarized briefly. An overriding ethic of service to state and society and a recognition of the importance of the state as a vehicle for modernization guided physicians' actions. The era marked the birth of a professional consciousness among practicing physicians, a consciousness marked by a frustration with government regulation of the medical profession, a faith in education and in the natural sciences, and a distaste for the bureaucratic constraints of government service and for the vicissitudes of private practice. The existence of quacks, a perceived mistrust of physicians among the general public, and a dependence either on the state or on private patients' money created the need for combined effort among physicians to escape this "humiliating position and to mediate between physicians and society."[44] At a time of expansion of the numbers of physicians, there was a concomitant increase in the number of practicing physicians in provincial towns. Because the few existing learned medical societies, mainly in the largest cities and at the universities, did not provide the kind of scientific collegiality combined with social utility needed by the new generation of practicing physicians, a new kind of medical society began to appear that reflected an awakened public awareness and a desire for independent action aimed at the public welfare. S. Iaroshevksii reported, "At first a few [physicians] timidly, cautiously gathered for private conversations, to exchange opinions, to explore new interests . . . Thus were born the first societies of physicians. From such gatherings [*beseda*] over a cup of tea arose small medical centers that spread all over our fatherland. Now there are no more or less sizable cities without a society of physicians."[45]

Typical of the age was the Society of Russian Physicians in Moscow, founded in 1859 by Fedor Ivanovich Inozemtsev, a well-known surgeon and professor at Moscow University, and S. A. Smirnov, a practicing physician, to engage in scientific and charitable activities. Inozemtsev and Smirnov first raised the idea of congresses for physicians in *Moskovskaia meditsinskaia gazeta,* a newspaper Inozemtsev and Smirnov published and edited from 1858 to 1862. They also argued that the success of medical science in Russia would depend on a "moral improvement" among physicians, which they took to mean greater independence of outside factors and "friendly collaboration rather than an isolated existence."[46] The new medical associations displayed the new professional concerns of public medicine—local studies, statistical collections, studies of public health, and sanitary conditions and epidemics. To address the disastrous conditions of public health, especially in the countryside, required outreach programs that touched the mass of the population directly. Medical societies supported free clinics, maternity shelters, feldsher schools, and bacteriological laboratories; they also organized public lectures and distributed popular brochures about diseases and preventive medicine. The result was the elevation of the values of public (sometimes also termed "community" or "zemstvo") medicine, free medical care, and public service.[47]

One factor that has been less noted in the literature regarding the spread of new medical societies in the reform era was the need to assert Russian patriotism and national pride, a sentiment we have already seen strikingly manifest in the founding of OLEAE and in the scientific congresses of the 1860s. Unlike earlier generations, when many Russian physicians were of foreign origin, by the mid nineteenth century the majority of physicians were native born. According to its bylaws, the Moscow Society of Russian

Physicians was founded to promote independent work among native physicians and to facilitate scientific, practical, and corporate intercourse among native physicians. Unlike those of many older learned medical societies, all its publications were in Russian. One of the practical means to implement the society's goals was to give training to young pharmacists "exclusively Russian in origin and nationality" to staff the society's clinic and to compete with the private Moscow pharmacies, which were "entirely in the hands of foreigners, chiefly Germans, inaccessible to Russians." The animating spirit here was an attempt to Russianize a predominantly foreign science; as Radulevich cleverly put it, "the Russian surname ending in *ov* hardly had been a recommendation for [a physician's] knowledge; one would no more have been treated by such a physician than one would have had a dress sewn by a Russian dressmaker [*modistka*]."[48]

The 1880s and 1890s witnessed a new surge in the foundation of medical societies. Best known for its advocacy of community medicine was the Pirogov Society of Russian Physicians. Inspired by the occasion of Pirogov's birthday celebration in 1881, a group of thirty-two of St. Petersburg physicians drafted the bylaws for a Moscow–St. Petersburg Medical Society, which was approved by the Ministry of Internal Affairs in 1883. As the zemstvo physician Pogozhev put it, the society "thus acquired citizenship."[49] In the number and public nature of its projects, its commissions, and its publications, as well as in its role as an umbrella national organization to network widely scattered physicians and to coordinate local projects, the Pirogov Society became one of the most prominent of Russia's associations by the end of the nineteenth century. Because previous chapters have already discussed the membership, internal organization, mission, and a sampling of projects of selected Russian associations, a similar exploration of the Pirogov Society would be repetitive. Moreover, Nancy Frieden and Peter Krug have documented the activities of the Pirogov Society.[50] Therefore, it will be more fruitful at this point in the book to focus our attention on the society's raison d'être, its flagship project and most public activity: its national congresses. More than most science societies, the Pirogov Society existed for its national meetings. Indeed, the congresses contributed greatly to the respect and authority that the public accorded to the Pirogov Society. Focusing on the congresses can highlight important dimensions of the state-society relationship.

Just as the idea of a national association of physicians received voice and energy at Pirogov's fiftieth birthday party in 1881, so too did the idea of periodic congresses of physicians. In proposing a toast to the project, the obstetrician and gynecologist Kronid Fedorovich Slavianskii proclaimed—using, like the founders of RGO, the metaphor of birth—"I drink to this all the more that I am fully confident that the birth of this child will be easy and no doubt without forceps." Even more than its parent society, the Pirogov congresses expressed "public autonomy and the quest of society for communion and self-definition" based on "collegiality, mutual respect, and common scientific and corporate interests" and "long repressed by the old bureaucratic-serf regime and stymied by all kinds of obstacles." The prominent physician, activist, and chronicler of zemstvo medicine Dmitrii Nikolaevich Zhbankov believed that the medical profession was in a better position than most other professions to convene congresses: the authorities thought that medical knowledge was very narrow and would not "arouse passions." Indeed, the Ministry of Internal Affairs approved the rules and regulations *(polozhenie)* expeditiously, and the First Congress of Russian Physicians in Honor of N. I. Pirogov was held in St. Petersburg in 1885; a total of 573 attended.[51]

This and subsequent congresses (prior to 1917 there were seventeen congresses and thirteen more specialized conferences, or *soveshchaniia*) were subsidized by the government and often by the local city councils, in a merger of state, civic, and private interests. Originally, the bylaws made a distinction between active members (physicians who did scholarly research) and participants; only the former had the right of voice and vote at the congresses. Revised bylaws in 1888, however, eliminated this distinction. After another revision in 1892, those in many ancillary branches of medicine, such as veterinarians and pharmacists, could attend, give reports, and take part in discussions; the general meetings *(obshchie sobraniia)* were public. Such "democratization" increased the likelihood of a discussion of a plethora of topics and the expression of the interests of multiple constituencies.[52] Out-of-town participants received discounted railway tickets and hotel rooms. Local excursions and entertainment were usually part of the program; the seventh congress in Odessa included an excursion to the Crimea, and the eighth in Moscow in 1902 included a tour of the city council building and tickets to the theater, two quintessential sites of the public sphere. Already by the third congress in 1889, attended by 1,648 delegates, there were complaints in the medical press about the large number of people and papers, prompting Dmitrii Zhbankov to suggest the panel format of twenty-minute papers followed by discussion. The periodic conventions were linked by a board *(pravlenie)* elected by the participants at each congress, a board that was responsible for carrying out the decisions of the congress as well as organizing the next meeting.[53]

The Pirogov congresses were a public forum for the dissemination of information and advocacy on a variety of professional and medical issues. As everywhere, physicians in the early stages of professionalization needed to assert their professional identity and self-worth in relation to quacks, charlatans, and those with lesser medical training, such as feldshers; for this, physicians needed the assistance of associations and of government. Simply convening the Pirogov congresses enabled physicians, in S. Iaroshevskii's words, to "crown the munificent [*grandioznoe*] edifice of [their] corporation, an edifice erected with a firm foundation and firm walls but still lacking interior finishing." That the physicians gathered "not only from the great university centers, but also from the most remote places and distant regions," presented to G. M. Gertsenshtein, a professor of medical statistics at the Medical-Surgical Academy and authority on syphilis in Russia, "a most remarkable and gratifying fact." From the beginning, the Pirogov congresses included a section on professional concerns, one of the most important being the negative attitude among the Russian public toward physicians. One of the tasks of the Pirogov congresses was to replace that attitude with a more positive recognition of the physicians' value to society as the guardians of public health or, as one physician put it, a recognition that it is "the doctors who are first to go into the fire when there is some national disaster, that it is the doctors who are the first casualties in epidemics." Such ideas were hardly new, but they were a sensation because they were brought up for public discussion *(glasnoe obsuzhdenie)* for the first time.[54]

In the words of a Kiev physician, the congresses were "a tribunal for deciding common problems," first and foremost of which was the sorry state of public health.[55] The first step was information gathering, and the "Pirogovtsy" took advantage of the forum to call attention to the need to gather, process, and disseminate information, one of the most important functions of the science societies and their projects. At the first congress, the statistician and economist Iu. E. Ianson proposed several petitions concerning the need for more statistical information and the registration of births and deaths. At the second congress, physician, zemstvo activist, and secretary of the Moscow Provincial Zemstvo Sanitary Commission E. A. Osipov proposed petitioning the Ministry of Internal Affairs to transfer the responsibility of gathering and compiling population statistics to the zemstvos and city councils. At the third congress, the Commission to Improve Sanitary Conditions in Russia proposed a petition to the ministry to conduct a national one-day census.[56]

The need to disseminate knowledge about hygiene, what was to become a major outreach program of the Pirogov Society of Russian Physicians, was first raised at the third congress, which recommended that the Board of the Pirogov Society appoint a commission for public hygiene education. The Pirogov congresses and the Pirogov Society's Commission for Public Hygiene Education jointly acted as advocates for further expansion of public health awareness: more local control, the inclusion of physicians on district school boards, the collection and dissemination of hygiene statistics, the teaching of hygiene in the schools, publication of brochures and flyers on medicine, and the acquisition of reading material and visual aids for public lectures and libraries. Based on the report of the commission, the fifth congress in St. Petersburg in 1893, which was attended by 1,176 delegates, petitioned the Ministry of Internal Affairs for the right to raise money for the purpose of disseminating information about hygiene in memory of the physicians who died in the typhus and cholera epidemics in 1891–1892. The congress also petitioned the ministry for permission for zemstvo doctors to organize public lectures and symposia on hygiene and to expand the list of books approved for public readings on medicine and hygiene. At the seventh congress, Nikolai Vasil'evich Sklifosovskii, professor of surgery, director of the Clinical Institute of Grand Duchess Elena Pavlovna, and one of the founders of the Pirogov congresses, described worsening school hygiene. At this congress, a commission on school hygiene drafted two petitions to teach hygiene in the technical schools and, more importantly, to include physicians on district and parish school boards. Subcommittees of this commission worked to build a collection of visual aids pertaining to hygiene, to publish brochures and flyers on medicine, to create a speakers' bureau, and to collect data on hygiene. Pirogov activists also employed the latest technologies of visual display to raise public awareness. Samples from the Russian National Hygiene Exhibition were on display at the fifth congress. The eighth congress featured an exhibition of visual aids to illustrate public lectures, using slides, magic lanterns, tables, atlases, and instruments for experiments that could be conducted in a public auditorium.[57]

At the second congress Zhbankov proposed petitioning the government to open women's medical schools and to allow the Pirogov Society to collect money for this purpose, and, in one instance when a petition produced results, in 1893 the State Council approved the charter of the St. Petersburg Women's Medical Institute. Twenty women physicians attended the sixth Pirogov congress in Kazan' and organized their own dinner. Following a report by Zhbankov, the eighth congress approved a resolution to petition the government to admit women into universities. The idea had such great public support that "even *Moskovskie vedomosti* failed to find the slightest dissenting opinion."[58]

The practitioners of general or public medicine (in the main, the zemstvo doctors) used the congresses for their professional goals and asserted the centrality of community medicine versus medical specialists on the one hand and the government on the other in public health issues. Although the first two congresses were dominated by academic medicine, beginning at the third congress in 1889, the zemstvo physicians inserted more and more into the program issues of public health as well as general questions. The selection of Fedor Fedorovich Erisman as honorary chair of the third congress was symbolic. After having come to Russia in 1869, the Swiss-born Erisman became Russia's best-known sanitary physician, compiling statistical studies of factory labor and public health for the Moscow zemstvo beginning in 1879. In 1882 he became a professor of hygiene at Moscow University; he remained a prominent activist in Moscow zemstvo medicine. His activism caught the attention of the political police, who labeled him "an extreme revolutionary and member of the International"; in Zurich, he was allegedly in contact with "dubious persons of . . . emigration."[59] A longtime spokesman for the autonomy of public health physicians, the head of the Moscow Province Public Health Council, and a colleague of Erisman's at the Moscow zemstvo, E. A. Osipov expressed the support for local control and community medicine championed by many zemstvo physicians, as well as the wariness of the central authorities: "The experience of Russian life has undoubtedly demonstrated with full clarity that the goals of local public administration can be achieved only under autonomous conditions, when work is not hindered by unwarranted regulations and incessant government scrutiny." Thus the advocacy at the Pirogov congresses was less for the "corporation" as a whole than for certain constituents within it.[60]

The virtue of association was underscored at all the congresses. The Pirogovtsy were aware that the congresses were a form of representation. Moreover, they claimed, somewhat pretentiously, that until Russian physicians had a European-type professional association that would "defend the material interest of the members and regulate relations between the public and the physicians," the Pirogov congresses would speak on behalf of Russian physicians and represent physicians before the government.[61] For example, the fifth congress claimed the right to examine the medical literature on hygiene and to decide whether to disseminate a work to the public. In order to solidify its claims to representation as well as to solicit public opinion in the support of policy, the sixth congress resolved to send drafts of its recommendations to medical societies, zemstvos, and city councils for debate.[62] By being the venue of such representation, as well as by articulating incessantly the importance of national community and collegiality among Russian physicians, the Pirogov congresses were a crucial means of self-definition and self-validation on the part of physicians, especially of the zemstvo physicians. As a result of these and other efforts, the opinions and pronouncements of the Pirogov congresses appeared ubiquitous. V. I. Radulevich wrote, "No sooner does one read about a famine in some far-off part of Russia than an association tends to it. No sooner does smallpox appear in Russia than they talk about vaccination in the medical societies . . . There is no part of Russia where an association has not gone into action to suppress an epidemic in words and in deeds."[63]

It must be readily acknowledged that the Pirogov Society and congresses were not the only model of professional organization and public action among doctors. Not all members even of the Pirogov Society, let alone other medical professionals, approved of the congresses' taking political positions and of the resulting politicization of science. As John Hutchinson shows, G. E. Rein and the St. Petersburg Physicians' Mutual Aid Society, founded by delegates to the 1889 Pirogov congress, represented an alternative model of organization that emphasized working in concert with the state rather than in opposition to it.[64]

Nonetheless, the 1890s ushered in a new age of increasing public assertiveness and opposition to the existing political order, an assertiveness embodied in the Pirogov congresses. The government was fully aware that the congress created and promoted horizontal linkages and the capacity of society to talk to itself, and although the government could not prevent such communication, it tried to regulate and confine it.

The Pirogov Congresses and Officialdom

The emphasis on community, professional identity, and representation at the Pirogov congresses emboldened physicians not only to petition the government but also to criticize officialdom for its policies and procedures. Despite N. M. Pirumova's claim that there were no significant political discussions at the Pirogov congresses before 1900, as early as the third congress in 1889 the correspondent for the newspaper the *Physician (Vrach)*, noted, "[There was] the appearance of emotional debates. In certain sections the freedom of debate even became undesirably sharp."[65] At the seventh congress, for example, a physician and professor of hygiene at Kharkov University, Irinarkh Polikhronievich Skvortsov, complained that Russia's medical statutes had not kept pace with new institutions, such as the zemstvo, and reform was needed. And the paper "Medical Assistance to the Peasantry" by the zemstvo physician and publicist Veniamin Osipovich Portugalov got much attention for its critique of the Russian socioeconomic system and of the exploitation of capital—allegedly the most important factors in mortality.[66]

Famine relief was a particularly striking example of the efforts of the Pirogov congresses on behalf of public health and, often, against officialdom.

The seventh congress, in April 1899, coincided with another famine and epidemics along the Volga River, following the poor harvest of 1898; the congress assembled in Kazan', one of the famine-stricken areas. After speaking about the tragic situation of the famine victims, Dmitrii Zhbankov proposed that the congress request the government to undertake an immediate investigation of the famine, to publicize the causes of Russia's chronic famines, and to take drastic measures to relieve famine victims and eliminate the causes of famine. The congress took the initiative and created its own Committee for Medical and Food Relief. In addition, the committee drew up a questionnaire to solicit information for a medical-sanitary description of famine localities; made contact with the zemstvos and zemstvo doctors to carry out relief; collected data on famine, disease, and local conditions; and raised money. In its petition to the Ministry of Internal Affairs, whose domain included public health and medicine, the congress expressed dissatisfaction with the current methods of famine relief, proposing instead more public control: "Broader and more active participation of the most competent public institutions and medical organizations [is necessary] in this matter, because energetic activity of such institutions, subject to public supervision and free from various formal obstacles, will enjoy [public] trust and will be the surest guarantee of success."[67] The committee, aware that the district zemstvos did not have the means to act quickly, organized medical-food detachments to distribute aid to the neediest localities. Indeed, the governor of Kazan' expressed no objections to the presence of the famine relief committee, as long as its activity was monitored "to ensure that the food detachments did not contain elements who could exploit their contacts with the peasants for illegal purposes."[68]

But the governor's qualifier about the "elements" of the food detachments was precisely what made the security agencies suspicious. The Department of Police reported, "The persons who run the food canteens are not always selected with the greatest caution and they spread false ideas among the population about the obligation of the government to provide relief."[69] In 1902 the eighth Pirogov congress again petitioned the Ministry of Internal Affairs for permission to send medical and food detachments to the neediest localities, as well as for permission to raise money. In the conclusion of his report to Grand Duke Sergei Aleksandrovich, who was the Moscow governor, the Moscow chief of police, Major General Dmitrii Fedorovich Trepov, stated that requests to allow collections of donations for famine relief should be rejected: "The direct contact with the people of such a politically dubious part of the intelligentsia is superfluous as far as aid is concerned. Since the government has already provided assistance, it can only be harmful, for persons in this category will try to fraternize with the populace, not so much to offer them material assistance as to bring them propaganda and antigovernment agitation."[70]

The issue of famine relief put the ability of government and society to cooperate to a serious test, and the papers and actions of the Pirogov congresses increasingly challenged state authority and became an irritant to officialdom. Another contentious issue was corporal punishment of peasants. Many physicians felt that because they were required to be present at executions and to undertake physical examinations of those punished, physicians were complicitous in harsh punishments meted out by the authorities. In a paper on public health and school hygiene at the sixth congress in 1894, Zhbankov claimed that because it hindered the moral and cultural development of the countryside, corporal punishment of the peasants should be abolished. At the request of the sixth congress, Zhbankov and Valenin Ivanovich Iakovenko collected materials on which to base a petition, one that coincided with similar petitions from the Free Economic Society and from the Ninth Congress of Naturalists and Physicians. The materials were published in 1899 as *Corporal Punishment in Russia (Telesnoe nakazanie v Rossii)*; the proceeds of the sale of this publication went to famine relief. Government ministers and their allies in the conservative press, such as *Moskovskie vedomosti,* ignored the petitions, maintaining that they constituted "interference on the part of public organizations and learned societies in legislative issues." Nevertheless, corporal punishment of peasants was finally abolished in 1904.[71]

We may view the increasingly critical public sphere from the point of view of officialdom at the eighth Pirogov congress, held in Moscow from 3 to 10 January 1902, "the beginning of the Pirogov Society's revolutionary activity" that foreshadowed the highly politicized ninth congress. From this point on, the parent Pirogov Society became "extremely oppositionist by presenting itself as a focal point of the politically imbalanced elements of the intelligentsia."[72] According to police reports, from its first assembly the congress expressed its "opposition to the current political system." After the opening remarks by the chair of the board of the Pirogov Society, instead of the customary Russian national anthem, "it was thought more appropriate to play a lullaby on the organ."[73] Following this, the chair did the ritual reading, common at jubilee meetings of associations, of congratulatory telegrams from patrons and friends. Two of the telegrams came from "heroes" of the public health physicians. Congratulations came from Rudolf Virchow, a prominent physician and pathologist, who was also a leading advocate of public health reform and a liberal representative in the Prussian parliament and an opponent of Bismarck. Virchow was prominent in the movement for medical professionalization in Germany and claimed that "physicians were the natural representatives of the poor and much of the social question lies within their jurisdiction." A second telegram came from Erisman, who had returned to his native Switzerland when he was removed by the authorities from his teaching post after student disturbances at Moscow University in 1896. The police report stated, "The reading of congratulatory telegrams gave the members of the congress an excuse for provocative demonstrations. They were silent after the telegram from Grand Prince Sergei Aleksandrovich, they hissed at the telegram from the Moscow governor, but there was deafening applause at the telegrams from Rudolf Virchow, and especially the one from Erisman."[74] Subsequent sessions featured passionate papers on criticism of government policies, on higher education for women, on restrictions of Jews in higher education, and on corporal punishment. Officials of the Ministry of Internal Affairs and the Department of Police concurred that the program of future Pirogov congresses needed to be reviewed carefully, and the Pirogov Society was warned that matters not within the competence of physicians were not to be brought up. The right-wing newspaper the *Citizen (Grazhdanin)* chimed in: "The Pirogovtsy have arrogated to themselves the right to deliberate on matters that don't concern them."[75] To the consternation of the authorities, an assembly of physicians was turning into a political demonstration.

This was only the beginning of a struggle between society and the state over the use of the public sphere. The government was fully aware that the congress created and promoted communication and the capacity of society to talk to itself. Indeed, officialdom encouraged congresses of the scientific and technical intelligentsia for that very reason. However, communication not only strengthened horizontal linkages among different groups; it also bypassed the vertical lines of communication between society and government. Although it could not prevent such communication, officialdom tried to regulate and confine it. The tension between civil society and the state in this matter may be seen best if we turn to two politicized congresses on the eve of the Revolution of 1905.

The State, the Public, and the 1904 Congresses

At the end of the nineteenth century the Russian government faced a dilemma. As it had nurtured science since the eighteenth century, officialdom recognized that the state needed scientific expertise generated in civil society. Private initiative helped the government to achieve its goals of bringing prosperity and prestige to the empire. At the same time, the bearers of this expertise were becoming more and more independent of the state. They regarded themselves as servants of the nation, of "the people." At the turn of the twentieth century, congresses of the scientific and technical intelligentsia already exhibited mounting criticism of state policy and administration in many areas as well as frustration with continuing impediments to private and public initiative. The surge of antigovernment expression in the public sphere culminated in two scientific congresses in 1904—the Third Congress of Technical and Vocational Education and the Ninth Pirogov Congress of Russian Physicians—that nearly coincided with the secret congress of the Union of Liberation. A letter intercepted by the police put it this way: "In Piter, these two congresses [technical education and Pirogov] are an inexhaustible topic for everyone."[76] The final section of this chapter will examine these two politically charged congresses as a public forum for the expression not only of antigovernment views but also of a vision of greater autonomy of civil society.

The Third Congress on Vocational and Technical Education

Over three thousand delegates convened at St. Petersburg University for the Third Congress on Vocational and Technical Education. As usual, a large contingent of honored guests was present at the opening ceremony, demonstrating the collaboration of all walks of Russian life—officers of the Russian Technical Society rubbed shoulders with N. S. Vannovskii and S. I. Veshniakov of the State Council; the minister of agriculture and state properties, A. S. Ermolov; the deputy minister of education, S. M. Luk'ianov; vice president of the Imperial Academy of the Arts, I. I. Tolstoi; the mayor of St. Petersburg, I. I. Lelianov; the rector of St. Petersburg University, A. M. Zhdanov; and other government officials, academics, educators, and engineers—a fact emphasized by N. P. Petrov, president of the Technical Society from 1895 to 1905 and member of the State Council.[77] But, noted *Osvobozhdenie,* the newspaper of the liberal emigration, the gathering was very diverse, "from top-quality bureaucrats to public school teachers from way out in the provinces, . . . a well-formed army of educators for the inspiring principle of 'Down with autocracy.'" Even "top-quality bureaucrats" were not immune to the public mood, and the opening address by V. I. Kovalevskii, former assistant minister of finance and future president of RTO, hinted that "further progress in vocational education depended on a change in the existing political system."[78]

Soon after the congress opened, there was "an unusual hustle and bustle" as "members crowded the corridors and auditoriums, delivered papers, conducted discussions, and debated resolutions."[79] The congress rules *(polozhenie)*, published in advance in the general press, stated rather broad criteria for membership at the congress, criteria that included not only teachers and administrators of vocational and technical schools but also "outsiders" from various technical societies and the zemstvos. Although the general public was permitted only at ceremonial meetings at which discussion was not scheduled, the chairs of sessions had the right to invite or permit nonmembers to attend and even to have voice. As a result, panels overflowed and outsiders mingled with congress members and were able to participate in discussions and even in voting.[80]

Controversial topics came up in various sections. Reflecting the advocacy of local control, an issue that animated many of the delegates, the first section passed a resolution stating that secondary schools needed more autonomy and the freedom to select their own personnel; the third section passed a resolution calling for the government to eliminate the obstacles to Jews in all educational institutions. But most "stormy" was the section on workers' education. At the session of 29 December, the chair, Karl K. Mazing, announced that all sessions would be open to the public and that everyone had the right to participate in discussions, a decision that allegedly opened the door to "all the agitators" of the congress.[81] Delivered in front of education administrators, papers criticized the Ministry of Education for thwarting the outreach efforts of RTO and other technical societies. Despite the efforts of the congress officers to keep the discussion on topic, the section discussed all manner of subjects—public school teachers, the expansion of powers of the zemstvos and city councils, universal education, zemstvo taxes, government insurance, workers' hours, adult education, Sunday schools, temperance, leisure time—all of which would work better, the argument ran, with the granting of civil liberties.[82] Nikolai Veniamovich Kasatkin appealed to the intelligentsia "to wrest [from the Ministry of Education] the right to educate the ignorant masses." Another speaker, P. I. Kozhenevskii, stated that "the time was ripe to settle accounts with the government and destroy the bureaucratic wall that separated the people from the intelligentsia." Kozhenevskii continued, "Only the principle of public life and the full rights of citizenship can lead the Russian people to happiness."[83] Given the floor, a delegate from the Social-Democratic Party, German Nikolaevich Vasil'ev, expressed his surprise at "the servile language" of the congress officers, who discussed "minor questions of technical education at a time when all of Russia wants to overthrow autocracy." At this point, Mazing rang a bell to interrupt the speaker, but Vasil'ev continued: "You boast that you work hard and have organized some 130 panels—well, the Committee of Ministers has a mass of meetings, but nothing ever comes of them." Laughter from the audience momentarily stopped Vasil'ev before he continued: "Enough of these meek speeches, let's speak plainly what we all want, let's boldly cry 'Down with autocracy!'" After another ring from the chair, Vasil'ev concluded his remarks and was met with a furious round of applause. When Mazing warned future speakers to refrain from bringing up subjects not pertaining to the topic of the section, there was hissing and whistles. Finally, a paper on public libraries ended by stating that a library system could be properly organized "only under a constitutional order, when the government would be made up of representatives freely elected by the people."[84] As a result of these outbursts, the chief of police informed Mazing that the next two scheduled sessions would be cancelled. The officers of the congress found it impossible to keep order. At the same time, they feared that the closing of the section would merely result in the agitators flocking to other sections; indeed, the police noted that work at other sections was occasionally interrupted by "invasions of flying detachments" from the workers' education section.[85]

On 4 January an incident led to the closing of the congress one day early. At a banquet in honor of the teacher-delegates the night before, which was hosted by St. Petersburg schoolteachers, the band in the banquet hall had drowned out an address, ironically on freedom of speech, by the leader of the teachers' movement and an activist in the teachers' congresses, N. V. Chekhov, to the irritation of many delegates. The next day, shortly after the chair of the workers' education section had managed to cut off a discussion of labor unions, an artisan by the name of Stepanov, accused in the foreign and underground press of being involved in the pogrom in Kishinev the previous year, rose to speak. Before he had managed to begin his report, one of the participants grabbed him and yelled, "Murderer! Tsarist executioner!" and pushed him out of the meeting room. Most of the four hundred participants in the section jumped out of their seats, yelling, "Murderer!" and pursued Stepanov through the corridors of the university. The altercation was short lived: someone shouted that the Cossacks were coming and, as the crowd was running back into the meeting room, a student of the organizing committee saved Stepanov from "the enraged crowd of Jews" and locked him in an office. After persuading a few lingering members of the crowd to leave Stepanov alone, the secretary of the congress, the journalist and educator A. N. Al'medingen, led him out of the building, past a row "mainly of Jews" shouting, "Stepanov was at the pogrom! He has blood on his hands!" After order was restored, the incident prompted a discussion of the pogrom, causing the chair to close the session. Some three hundred remained in the hall and discussed the problem of granting political rights to workers. The debates continued in the evening session, and to stop them, the chair had to turn out the lights. That night the St. Petersburg prefect shut down the rest of the congress.[86]

The report of the Department of Police (see figure 6.3) assessed the shortcomings of the third congress. First, the absence of any qualification requirement to attend the congress allowed too many "outsiders" allegedly without competence in the areas of vocational and technical education to take part in the proceedings. Second, the rules of the congress were violated frequently, papers were not carefully examined in advance, and too many chairs of sessions were not well prepared or were incapable of conducting a meeting. Finally, the programs of the individual sections were too broadly defined, providing an opportunity to discuss extraneous matters. Because there were insufficient measures to guarantee "a peaceful and orderly conduct of business," any "objective discussion" was impossible. One commentator noted, "You can't discuss complex and serious matters before a crowd . . . Those speakers who didn't talk about serious matters but spoke in loud, empty phrases . . . were rewarded by noisy applause." As a result, "from the very first meeting, the most well-attended section turned into a noisy mob that interfered with the business of other sections and provoked the most extreme measure—shutting down the congress." Tsar Nicholas II penned on the police report, "This is appalling! They don't know how to behave at a serious meeting."[87]

In their assessment of the events, the congress organizers distanced themselves from the "outside agitators" and stressed the harmony among the congress participants. Thus, at the "splendid" opening in the evening of 26 December, royal patrons were "greeted warmly," as was a proposal to express gratitude to the emperor and to pay homage to the patrons of technical education and vocational training. Beyond this, the congress organizers justified both the content of the papers and discussions as well as the procedures followed at the sessions. Regarding the papers, the congress organizers acknowledged that there was more interest in general questions than there had been at the second congress. They claimed that they had carefully examined all paper proposals, especially those of the section on worker education. Although the organizers insisted that while the resolutions, such as that for a smaller zemstvo unit, were outside the parameters of a congress on vocational and technical education, narrowly defined, these resolutions were connected to the spread of education among the peasants, the improvement of workers' lives, and public initiative. While it was true, the organizing committee acknowledged, that such resolutions

Figure 6.3 Employees of the Department of Police, 1892. (Courtesy of the Central State Archive of Documentary Films, Photographs, and Sound Recordings, St. Petersburg.)

may have detracted from the businesslike conduct of the congress, in and of themselves they were not illegal and did not justify the extreme measure taken by the authorities. As to the alleged lapses in procedures, the organizers claimed that all speakers were official members of the congress and only members voted on resolutions. While the organizers regarded the presence of outsiders as undesirable and inadmissible, it was practically impossible to check attendance carefully. Because none of the chairs of sessions had reported anything untoward before 4 January, the organizers regarded the closing incident as external to the congress, and it did not interrupt the work of the sections.[88]

"The congress was a big public success," crowed the liberal *Russkaia mysl'*. "The thousands of people who gathered in St. Petersburg left enriched in their knowledge, experience, and refreshed in an atmosphere of genuine communion. All of them will go home with a rekindled faith in the force of knowledge, in the fruits of their effort, and in the coming victory of reason and light over darkness and ignorance."[89] *Osvobozhdenie,* the liberal oppositionist paper published abroad, gloated "Now in Russia not one meeting of educated people can go by without a discussion of the need to change the existing, unbearable order." Like more and more meetings of this period, the congress demonstrated to its participants that they were not alone: "All over Russia there is the same pulse of public dissatisfaction . . . Everywhere the dismantling of the political order has proceeded quite far such that activists scattered all over the country are not isolated but are soldiers in a single army in the struggle against autocracy."[90] But not all delegates went home immediately. Perhaps the most immediate consequence of the closing of this contentious congress was that a goodly number of participants and public confounded the attempts of the authorities to suppress public discussion and went cross-town to the sessions of the ninth Pirogov Congress.

The Ninth Pirogov Congress of Russian Physicians

Over two thousand delegates gathered at the Ninth Pirogov Congress of Russian Physicians, held in St. Petersburg 4–11 January 1904 (see figures 6.4 and 6.5). The attendance figures do not include an undetermined number who came from the congress on technical and vocational education. Subsidized by three government ministries (Finance, Internal Affairs, and Education), the Pirogov congress had many sections, including sections on public medicine, factory medicine, and professional issues, all planned and coordinated by an organizing committee chaired by S. M. Luk'ianov, deputy minister of education. Among the congress officers were some of

Figure 6.4 Ninth Pirogov Congress of Russina Physicians, St. Petersburg, 1904—a reception for congress participants sponsored by the city council. (Courtesy of the State Museum of the History of St. Petersburg.)

Figure 6.5 A session of the 1913 Pirogov Congress of Russina Physicians in St. Petersburg, showing a meeting hall full and the presiding officers. (Courtesy of the Central State Archive of Documentary Films, Photographs, and Sound Recordings, St. Petersburg.)

the best-known members of the Pirogov Society—G. N. Gabrichevskii, current president and head of the Pirogov Society's Malaria Commission; D. N. Zhbankov, the zemstvo activist; P. I. Kurkin, a Moscow zemstvo medical statistician; G. E. Rein, professor at the Imperial Military-Medical Academy; V. D. Shervinskii, professor at Moscow University; and K. I. Shidlovskii, member of the society's executive board and member of the "Liberation" political movement. The general meetings were scheduled for the auditorium of the Military-Medical Academy; when this proved to be overcrowded, meetings were moved to the hall of the city council. An information bulletin was distributed daily, and the proceedings were covered in the press. Printed outlines of papers contained "theses," customarily proposals for resolutions to be voted on by the congress delegates. Three exhibits accompanied the congress, and the organizers arranged tours of St. Petersburg. At the opening ceremony, "the huge assembly hall appeared to be a sea of heads," in which the "heads" numbered approximately six thousand.[91]

In his opening address, V. I. Razumovskii, professor at the University of Kazan', observed that all the topics scheduled for discussion at the congress had special significance in light of the "reassessment of values" occurring in all areas of life, at a time when science "no longer dispassionately analyzes facts but has entered the service of humanity."[92] In many ways the 1904 congress was the culmination of two generations of scientists who had served humanity with the reforming zeal of missionaries. But at the ninth Pirogov congress, science not only was in the service of humanity, progress, or even of the medical profession but was in large part in the service of opposition to the regime. In the "spirit of public meetings," speakers linked various aspects of public health and community medicine to social, economic, and political reform. And they abandoned the practice of composing deferential petitions to the government in favor of making direct policy recommendations.[93]

In the section on public medicine, the criminologist Dmitrii A. Dril' argued that cooperation between government, local authorities, and private initiative was the only way to solve the urgent problem of poverty. Several speakers connected tuberculosis to overcrowded conditions in the Pale of Settlement and concluded that Jews must have freedom of movement. Similarly, in discussions of alcoholism, participants emphasized the need to eradicate the conditions breeding the disease and criticized the state liquor monopoly. A paper at the section on factory medicine raised the issue of corporal punishment and called upon all physicians to scorn those doctors who were summoned to be present at corporal punishments and who "thereby sanctioned this odious practice." Papers on childhood diseases, school doctors, and school hygiene led to a discussion of a variety of education issues. The zemstvo physician Dr. D. Ia. Dorf proposed transferring the administration of the schools from the Ministry of Education and the church to local school boards, whose revamped membership would include teachers, physicians, and zemstvo representatives. In one day the congress passed resolutions that called for supporting the eight-hour day, introducing the zemstvos into nonzemstvo provinces, abolishing corporal punishment and the death penalty, placing schools under local control, and ending discrimination against the Jews. And, to tweak the authorities, the congress sent greetings to Leo Tolstoy, just as the congress on technical education had done, and expressed sympathy to the educator Genrikh Fal'bork, who had been arrested at the conclusion of the technical congress.[94]

The discussions of papers and the ensuing resolutions did not stop at socioeconomic reform; they went for the jugular of politics. Papers linked improvements in zemstvo medicine to a broader franchise in the zemstvos and city councils, to national political representation, to the establishment of the rule of law in the countryside, and to the creation of local all-estate zemstvos. Papers on school hygiene—in which, according to one police report, "it was hard to find anything on school hygiene"—emphasized the importance of the dissemination of information and the abolition of censorship in order to improve public health. "In order to free these animating forces from the clutches of administrative arbitrariness," a resolution demanded greater freedom of association *(iavochym poriadkom)* and "the use of the courts rather than of administrative measures to handle infractions of the laws." An effective fight against the scourges to public health in Russia, such as tuberculosis, "could only be waged with the guarantee of individual freedom and the freedoms of speech, press, and assembly." The pattern was clear: improvement in *x* could come about only by the creation of *y*, where *x* was any one of a number of public health problems facing the country and *y* was fundamental change in Russia's political institutions.[95]

A feuilleton in the *St. Petersburg News* parodied the way political solutions were presented for medical problems. Describing an ostensibly typical scene after an orator had talked about a rare illness, the paper reported, "[An] orator raises his voice and comes to a completely unexpected conclusion: 'Ladies and gentlemen, it is impossible to fight this serious and rare disease as long as we don't have a different legal system and we don't have local zemstvos!' There is thunderous applause! Afterward, fighting other illnesses appeared to be surprisingly simple. If the speakers are to be believed, freedom of conscience would be quite good for tuberculosis! There is no better treatment for sciatica than the freedom to form labor unions! Abolition of the passport system will wipe out long bouts of constipation! And curbing administrative arbitrariness will really alleviate skin infection!"[96]

Needless to say, the authorities kept a very watchful eye on the congress. The content of papers, discussions, and resolutions was incendiary to a government that jealously guarded its political monopoly. Indeed, a scientific congress could "easily turn into an organ of public propaganda for the constitutional appetites of the liberals."[97] In addition, the authorities were angry at two other important aspects of the congress—the violation of procedures and the behavior of the audience. Despite the request of the city prefect that a list of papers and speakers be submitted in advance, the organizing committee did not do this until 17 November, only six weeks before the opening of the congress. Revised lists continued to be submitted well after the deadline, and acceptance of papers did not close until the congress had already convened. Thus, according to a lengthy report of the Department of Police, there was little time to check the list of speakers, let alone inspect the content of papers. As a result, it was impossible to forestall discussion of topics allegedly not connected to the goals of the Pirogov Society.[98]

The consequences were predictable. Despite the efforts of the congress officers, many deviations from the program were permitted in both papers and discussions. Moreover, although admission to the sessions was supposed to be by pass only, which was meant to limit attendance to registered members, outsiders were able to get in to the meetings. A large number of tickets were distributed for the first general session, making it impossible to keep the crowd out of the meeting halls. In crowded rooms, it was impossible for the chairs of the section meetings to distinguish members from nonmembers. According to a report of the St. Petersburg *okhrana,* the public devised clever ways to get into the meeting halls. The passes of those who had been admitted were collected and handed out or sold to the crowds waiting at the door. Tickets were allegedly tossed out the windows to those waiting below, where the passes allegedly "wound up in the hands of the Jews who were assiduously following the discussions."[99] The admission of a large number of outsiders included crossovers from the Congress on Technical and Vocational Education. (Some outsiders were prevented from sneaking in: the *okhrana* admitted that it was not able to get a report at one of the sessions on public medicine because its secret agent did not have a pass and could not get in.) Thus "the influx of nonphysicians, primarily at the nontheoretical sections, was indeed significant and, thanks to the ease of admission, it began to lose its character as a congress of Russian physicians and gradually turned into an assembly not only of Russian physicians but also of pharmacists, veterinarians, and other disciplines related to medicine."[100]

Who were these "outsiders," and why did they bother authorities? The authorities saw an audience that differed vastly from that to which they were accustomed at staid meetings of scientists, even at earlier Pirogov congresses. At the session on school hygiene, there were many women, especially *kursistki* (students of the higher schools), only a small number of whom were medical students. At many sessions, there were allegedly many Jews (the archetypal outsider in the eyes of many Russian officials), and "many participants observed that there had never been so many Jews at a Pirogov congress." The Jews were allegedly an "organized party with prepared speeches, resolutions, selected speakers and a crowd of supporters . . . They turned the congress into an instrument of protests, not always connected to the papers, such as connecting tuberculosis to the Pale of Settlement."[101] The apparent solidarity, organization, and discipline also among the zemstvo physicians helped elect as deputy chair of the congress

M. I. Petrunkevich, a prominent zemstvo physician, member of the Union of Liberation, and brother of I. I. Petrunkevich, the famous zemstvo activist. Equally disturbing to the authorities, the audience too seemed organized: the crowds that gathered at the Military-Medical Academy and the city council, "apparently after a signal from the meeting hall, expressed their approval at the congress's resolutions with loud cheers and with similar exclamations greeted the most popular participants."[102] The physicians Ia. Iu. Kats, D. Ia. Dorf, Zhbankov, and A. I. Shingarev and zemstvo veterinarian Rodionov and others were "orators," who, according to the police, played to and mingled with the audience. To save time at some sessions, several papers were read consecutively before opening the meeting to discussion; but sometimes the restless audience would interrupt these readings by shouting, "Enough! It's time to start the debates!" Some "strident" speeches were greeted with "prolonged, noisy" applause and cries of "Bravo!" It seemed that too many in the audience had come not for the papers but only for the debates. One commentator remarked, "They preferred to discuss resolutions rather than malaria!" With its "agitated mood," its "emotional debates," its "demonstrable opposition to the existing system," and its "shouts, hisses, and whistles," the audience was allegedly little more than "an antigovernment mob."[103]

The congress came to a tumultuous end on 11 January. On the eve of the closing session, some delegates and members of the general public gathered on Mikhailov Square to express sympathy with the "cause" of the congress. The *okhrana* reported that over two thousand attended the closing session at the Assembly of the Nobility. Everyone expected that a reading of the final redaction of the congress's resolutions would further galvanize the public. However, after the ritual reading of the final report of the congress, the chair of the congress, S. M. Luk'ianov, announced that due to circumstances beyond his control, the resolutions would not be read, and he adjourned the congress. This announcement was met with a chorus of shouts, whistles, and hisses. One zemstvo man shouted, "How can they laugh at us . . . Whoever heard of treating a scientific society this way!" Most of the public headed for the doors, but students, *kursistki,* and some of the doctors remained in the hall, protesting the insolence of the authorities and demanding that the resolutions be read; amid the hubbub some tried to give speeches. At this point, a police officer signaled the military band on stage to play "God Save the Tsar," further infuriating the audience. "Thus healthy and bold thoughts were drowned out by Plehve's brass," a medical student from Tomsk wrote in a letter intercepted by the police.[104] Issues of *Osvobozhdenie* as well as Social-Democratic leaflets circulated among the crowd, and shouts of "Down with autocracy!" could be heard. A few of the more irate audience tried to stop the military band from playing by breaking up the chairs and throwing them at the band. A part of the crowd went to a smaller hall, where Rodionov read a resolution demanding individual freedom, freedom of speech and assembly, and the removal of censorship, adding that because these were unattainable under the existing system, it was necessary to muster forces for a struggle against the government using any means possible. After loud applause, the crowd sang the revolutionary song "We Renounce the Old World" ("Otrechim-sia ot starogo mira") and the "Marseillaise." At this point a police detachment entered, dispersed the crowd, made several arrests, and confiscated all materials of the congress.[105]

To their participants and supporters, the Pirogov congresses served a grateful society. Thus the overworked community physician, as portrayed in one article about the Pirogov congresses, is working with all sorts of obstacles and sinking in the swamp of daily routine, and, behold! The Pirogov congresses offer a helping hand. This exhausted doctor comes to the congress and is refreshed and exhilarated, hears lively speech, and realizes that others live just as bad, if not worse, and, of course, immediately proclaims, "Long live public life [*obshchestvennost'*], long live the Pirogov Society!"[106] Moreover, the gathering of physicians from around the empire was said to have a democratizing influence. Many different types of physicians could "come together" and break down barriers. This view remained powerful despite increasing evidence that by representing interests, congresses divided society and the medical profession just as much as congresses united them. Finally, participants saw themselves as engaged in a battle with the government on behalf of the downtrodden, for which they "won the respect of society and the press."[107] In the words of Dr. Smirnov, the Pirogov congresses were "the beginning of the public initiative of a mature, self-conscious intelligentsia to fight the government for the political, economic, and social well-being of the Russian people. The [ninth] Pirogov congress has been fixed in our minds as the most outstanding and enlightened event in Russian life; but history will record it on its tablets as the first congress in the battle for political freedom." A letter intercepted by the police put it more succinctly: "The doctors were audacious. They called things by their proper names."[108]

No previous congress had received as much press coverage. Although one observer conceded that the general public knew the Pirogov congresses mainly from laconic newspaper notices, Zhbankov claimed, "All the resolutions and protests were carried all over the country."[109] The organ of the Pirogov Society of Russian Physicians, its *Zhurnal,* carried excerpts of press coverage, asserting, "The voice of public opinion has, at last, begun to take shape even in Russia." *Vrachebnyi vestnik,* employing an oft-repeated metaphor, wrote that the Pirogov congresses brought the "fresh stream [*zhivaia struia*] to the Russian stagnant torpor [*vialaia olmoovshchina*], accustomed to idleness and concerned only about its belly." In this, congresses also "took the pulse of Russian life."[110] The major newspapers had reports almost every day. *Novosti* wrote that the congress, "a major public institution," was justified in not limiting itself to narrow, specialized medical questions and needed a broad program covering everything pertaining to public health. *Sankt-Peterburgskie vedomosti* reported that sections of the congress demanded instituting freedom of speech, press, and assembly; ending discrimination against the Jews; and instituting genuine local self-government.[111] *Russkie vedomosti* wrote that the physicians at the Pirogov congresses were not technicians but influential public figures, "tribunes of medicine." *Iuzhnye zapiski* wrote that Pirogov congresses had become "the best guide for our organs of self-government, and even the government listens to them . . . The congresses unite science, physicians, and society in public service, all the more valuable in Russia, where public initiative is very weak. Even if its petitions are ignored, the fact that such an expert institution can frame the issues has great significance."[112]

Like officialdom, the conservative press was irritated by the outspoken behavior of the Pirogov congresses. According to the zemstvo deputy A. A. Stakhovich, the "generals" in private practice, removed from the zemstvo and municipal doctors, accused the congress organizers of being unprepared dilettantes distracted by general issues not related to medicine: "Some think that the congress was so discredited that it is unlikely that the next [Pirogov congress] would be permitted."[113] The organ of the Imperial Military-Medical Academy, whose opinions we can presume reflected those of the government medical establishment, noted that the resolutions were dominated by the section of public medicine,

> that is, by those participants farthest removed from pure medicine . . . Persons not having any relationship to the congress played a significant role in the public health section . . . The "crowd" consisted of representatives of extremely emotional nationalities and their noisy gestures of approval or disapproval not only of speakers and resolutions but also of the selection of chairs of sessions and, consequently, of the agenda. There was no room for legitimate participants, and questions were decided not by vote but by voice. It is not surprising that resolutions went beyond the competence of the congress, displayed inappropriate political posturing [*politikikanstvo*], and attached unwarranted importance to the interests of the Hebrew tribe . . . The noise of the streets reached the meeting rooms of the scientific sections, interfering with their peaceful work. A scientific congress should not have to take place amid

> shouts from the streets, and if the Pirogov congress cannot guarantee order, the scientific sections should separate and organize their own congresses.[114]

Finally, according to the newspaper *Grazhdanin,* the Pirogov congresses were "not medical meetings at all but something completely new, unauthorized, and not anticipated by law—a constituent assembly."[115]

PUBLIC "INTERACTION RITUALS," or "ceremonial gatherings," according to Randall Collins, "gather the intellectual community, focus the members' attention on a common object uniquely their own, and build up distinctive emotions around those objects."[116] Nineteenth-century European congresses were such "interaction rituals." Congresses, like their parent societies, embodied and served positive knowledge and science. Congresses were a moment of accounting, of self-examination, of summing up, of disseminating and popularizing the progress made in a given field of knowledge during a unit of time. Congresses "harnessed intellectual expertise to political activism, lent influence to classes and occupational groups excluded from government, and satisfied the political aspirations of the professoriate."[117] They complemented the printed word, of course, although in their "distinctive emotions" the participants of congresses expressed a preference for the spoken word. As forums that solicited and shaped public opinion, congresses were a new form of citizenship and representation. The annual congresses of the British Social Science Association were called an "outdoor parliament" by the *Times* in 1862: "a peripatetic Parliament in which every man is his own representative, in which women are already franchised, in which small minorities may find a voice for their crotchets, and in which unappreciated philosophers of both sexes may meet together to talk over the welfare of the world."[118]

The Russian scientific and technical congresses were patriotic endeavors for the study of the participants' vast *(neob'iataia)* motherland, to use the formulaic phrase. Only by studying Russia could scientists speak of a native, Russian science. Patriotic service to the nation was a sentiment shared by participants and officialdom. Thus, despite the sharper tone at the turn of the century, congresses were by and large occasions of state-society cooperation, collaboration, and mutuality. The leaders of RTO and of the Pirogov Society were figuring out what society needed and supplying that need—that is, taking initiative, initiative sanctioned and even encouraged in government circles. The government found it useful to allow, even encourage, large meetings of the scientific and technical intelligentsia in order to exchange ideas and practices and to further the development of a scientific and technical infrastructure. Because of this usefulness and because of the patronage in high places of RTO, the government gave the congresses on technical education more latitude than it gave teachers' congresses. Even the Department of Police concluded that while the Pirogov congresses were less significant for science—"scientific congresses don't make discoveries and scientific questions don't require votes"—much valuable clinical and empirical experience was exchanged.[119]

The national scientific and technical congresses regularly brought together the scientific and technical intelligentsia from all over the empire, giving them not only "an opportunity for mutual acquaintance" but one that took place "on Russian soil."[120] In a fragmented society whose polity was built on vertical linkages, congresses promoted and strengthened horizontal linkages; congresses were a vital means by which society communicated with itself. Such communication was especially important in the provinces. In a telling commentary on the development of metropolitan civil society, Zhbankov claimed that congresses were often little noticed in the capitals, "where there [were] so many meetings and distractions." In contrast, they were much more significant in provincial towns, where "the general public, and especially students, regularly attended sessions, followed the debates and resolutions, and discussed the congress on the streets and at home."[121]

Congresses were conducted in the language of representation. As many students of late-imperial Russia, especially students of the professions, have noted, associations and their meetings and congresses were all the more important in public life, given the absence of a nationwide representative institution and the illegality of political parties and unions.[122] The delegates elected congress officers, and resolutions were openly debated and decided by majority vote. Delegates advocated certain causes or projects before the larger arena of public opinion and before a government unaccustomed to receiving policy recommendations that did not come from officialdom or high personages. The patriotic exercise of expertise allowed the scientific and technical congresses greater latitude to play the role of advocate. In turn this allowed the congresses to mediate on behalf of society to the authorities and to hold government accountable for policy decisions. In submitting petitions or making policy recommendations to the government, congress participants were, of course, acting in their own interests, no doubt rather more than they cared to admit. But they were also acting on behalf of other constituencies, that is, claiming to represent them.

The congresses of naturalists are an example of meetings that by and large stayed aloof from politics; the scientists regarded themselves as engaging in patriotic service to the state and to science. In contrast, delegates to the Pirogov and technical education congresses, committed to social and professional issues, more and more saw themselves as serving "the people" and, as a result, were drawn into politics. In a country where everyone was denied the vote, activists saw congresses as an excellent stage for fashioning the tsar's subjects into citizens. Such activity, it was hoped by participants of congresses and their admirers, would be the kind of organized public activity that could encourage greater local autonomy and initiative. The more-politicized congresses provided an opportunity for disenfranchised subjects to demand political rights. By seeking to represent society, they acquired the "rights of citizenship."[123] Indeed, the historian Kizevetter, writing of three national congresses in 1896 that passed resolutions to abolish capital punishment and to institute universal primary education, stated, "One sensed that the period of public suppression [*obshchestvennaia podavlennost'*] [had] expired, [and] mouths opened, society began speaking, and attempts to stifle the rising public [*nachavshiisia obshchestvennyi pod"em*] could only open the floodgates." A congress participant reporting in *Osvobozhdenie* put it this way: "The major achievement in recent years is that people have stopped being afraid to speak."[124] Congresses emboldened the autocrat's subjects as they sought to emancipate Russian public life from government tutelage.

Conclusion

An Unstable Partnership

BEGINNING IN THE LATTER PART of the eighteenth century, Russian associations began a slow and halting growth. Many were ephemeral, but a few prominent learned societies survived periodic crackdowns under Catherine II, Alexander I, and Nicholas I. The era of the Great Reforms ushered in a time of rapid growth, and by century's end Russia possessed the institutional core of civil society—a network of associations in St. Petersburg, Moscow, and other major cities. But the development of civil society in Russia presents a paradox. On the one hand, associations and their works were all over the empire, acting with ever-greater assertiveness and a louder voice. On the other hand, imperial Russia collapsed in 1917, and civil society did not generate a lasting liberal democratic regime. What, then, was the meaning of associations in an autocratic country? What was their relationship to the state? What was the nature of the civil society they helped shape? How can we explain the paradox of associational ubiquitousness and the failure of civil society to generate the kind of political regime under which associations could flourish? As British sociologist Keith Tester suggests, the most important question is not whether civil society has existed or exists among a particular people, whether it is strong or weak, or which institutions it possesses or lacks, important as these questions are, but why people operate as if it had meaning.[1] Associations tell the story of how special interest groups of men entered the public arena, subjected their projects to the scrutiny of government and public alike, and staked their claim to represent the nation. They tell the story of how highly contested efforts to assist the state in bringing progress to nation and empire led to the gradual but incomplete emancipation of society from a personalized autocracy and arbitrary officialdom.

Much in the Russian experience of association resembles that of Europe and North America. Although the meaning of associations has varied from country to country, and although associations had contradictory impulses, numerous studies of associations and public life, especially on the European continent, have discovered common patterns. A sign of the prior appearance of a degree of individualism in society, associations enhanced a sensibility of freely established individual identities, autonomy, and choice. At the same time, to combat the isolation experienced by individuals breaking away from traditional ascribed identities, associations provided new group solidarities, and venues where sociability merged with education, improvement, and philanthropy. Science and other learned societies gathered information about the realm and promoted the diffusion of useful knowledge; as science promised the power to understand and improve the natural world, it also was regarded as holding the key to understanding and improving human institutions. Recent studies in the history of science have demonstrated that by asserting the role of science in public life, the "performance of science" for utility and entertainment was critical in the development of the scientific enterprise from the seventeenth through the nineteenth centuries. In mobilizing national resources and carrying out their projects, science societies provided the opportunity to experience the natural world directly and thereby disseminated the two pillars of the scientific method—observation and experiment. Such popularization validated the pursuit of science to its practitioners, to the state (the chief patron of science societies, especially on the Continent), and to the educated public. Public science was argued to be good for science. In advancing the goals of utility and improvement, and in mobilizing a public eager to participate in a culture of learning, the leaders of many associations claimed to be working for the common good.

Like their European counterparts, Russian monarchs sanctioned and encouraged associated private initiative in the pursuit of natural knowledge, for the prestige of the monarchy and the prosperity of the realm. Natural knowledge promised useful knowledge, and from the beginning science had a public agenda. Because societies such as the Free Economic Society promised the production and dissemination of useful knowledge, as well as the augmentation of Russia's scientific potential, they were a critical helpmate to state and monarch in the pursuit of two pillars of the Enlightenment: improvement and utility. Societies such as the Russian Geographical

Society and the Russian Technical Society framed the study of Russia's human and natural resources for the purposes of economic growth and prosperity. As patrons of science, they mobilized private resources that otherwise were scattered over a vast empire. Associations gathered, cataloged, and processed information, thereby reducing access costs to useful knowledge. Findings were shared before peers and disseminated to government officials and to the educated public. As entrepreneurs of science, societies such as OLEAE and RTO carried out myriad projects, and by the end of the nineteenth century, their publications, expeditions, public lectures, classes, collections, prize competitions, laboratories, exhibitions, museums, commissions, meetings, and congresses were too numerous to count.

Making associations the centers for the production and dissemination of vast amounts of empirical information took considerable initiative, planning, coordination, and organization. As their jubilee addresses and editions tirelessly pointed out, associations enabled the many to accomplish what the few could not. Indeed, science societies took a position alongside the Academy of Sciences and the universities as the only institutions, other than the state itself, that had the capacity to mobilize human resources for the cause of progress and thereby to enhance what historians of science and technology call the "scientific potential" of the nation. The drawing in of corresponding members and other observers from across the land created communities of practical knowledge, communities that extended beyond the scientists of St. Petersburg and Moscow, and thereby helped to create the infrastructure to popularize science and to raise the level of scientific literacy. Moreover, Russia's associations were able to promote and pursue the same goals as did their counterparts in Europe and North America. Voluntary associations presented typical nineteenth-century themes, language, projects, and hierarchies of value. The popularization of science and other outreach activity aspired to make better citizens. Associations promoted values commonly regarded as deficient in autocratic Russia: opportunity, individual initiative, autonomy, self-reliance, self-improvement, a spirit of enterprise, organizational skills, industriousness, rationality, the ability to control one's destiny, and a belief in science and progress. All of this is civil society in action.

Although Russia's learned societies served an abstract "science," from the beginning service to state and monarch was their primary impulse. As in Europe, such service resulted in a certain degree of dependence of societies upon patronage at high levels. Monarchs and state officials validated the scientific enterprise, and the scientists knew that their work was valued, that their pursuits were socially useful. Paradoxically, government patronage created among the members of Russia's science societies a sense of self-confidence and self-worth, a sense of pride and collective accomplishment, and an ethos of public service. The critical collective identity of the learned societies, as Randall Collins notes of intellectual communities in general, was less the content of their discussions but "the consciousness of the group's continuity itself as an activity of discourse."[2] To be sure, such communities were sanctioned and patronized by the government; many members, especially of the St. Petersburg societies, were government officials. Nevertheless, these scientific communities were not of the government. Thus, to their members and proponents, associations had the "support," "sympathy" *(sochustvie),* "cooperation," "collaboration" *(sodeistvie),* and "animation" *(ozhivlenie)* not only of the scientific community but also of educated society at large.

To enhance prestige and prosperity in service to monarch and state was a Russian subject's patriotic duty, and this exercise of patriotism accounts for the great degree of nourishment of scientific societies on the part of various government departments. As was common on the European continent, especially in the German and Scandinavian states, many members of the learned societies had a dual identity as scientists and naturalists on the one hand and as civil servants on the other. In both capacities, members of Russia's science societies relentlessly pursued the study of Russia, of the enormous and boundless *(neob"iataia)* Russia, to use the formulaic adjective. By directing the pursuit of practical knowledge to the pursuit of knowledge about Russia, by directing scientific inquiry to the needs of Russia, science societies could "speak in the vernacular." Moreover, such patriotic pursuits had two important by-products—the independence of Russian science and learning from European science, and the enhancement of the reputation of Russian science and scientists, especially important during the era of the Great Reforms. Projects of public science such as Moscow's Polytechnical Exposition and Museum enhanced cultural life and cultivated civic pride; they also displayed the scientists' mastery, stewardship of learning, and civic mindedness.

Although associated science and patriotic public service were intertwined in a double helix, important changes occurred, especially in their relationship to the state. Three moments may be singled out: post-1812, post-1855, and post-1891. All three moments followed major national mobilizations, even traumas: the victory over Napoleon, the defeat in the Crimean War, and the famine of 1891–1892. Although the first two differ in that the first followed a military victory while the second followed a defeat, both moments were characterized by a strong sense of public duty to assist the government in moments of national peril. The rhetoric of patriotic service pervaded the addresses of leaders of the Moscow Agricultural

Society and, later, of the Russian Geographical Society and of the myriad societies that sprang up after 1855, the best example of which was OLEAE. However, there were important shifts between the first two periods. After the defeat of Napoleon, patriotic sentiment was largely confined to noble and official Russia, and the science societies, consisting of a relatively small coterie of scientists, government officials, and landowners, directed their service to the monarch and the fatherland. Later, in keeping with the opening of public life during the era of the Great Reforms, the concept of public duty was expressed more broadly, and service to the "people" entered the discourse. Patronage of the monarch and state was replaced by a more decentralized "civic" patronage, as evidenced in the Moscow Polytechnical Museum and the many educational projects of the Russian Technical Society. The mission of associations became more self-consciously one of education and the popularization of science and learning. After the Crimean defeat and the first decade of the new reign of Alexander II, the interests of state and society converged harmoniously. During the reform era it was widely recognized in officialdom that the dissemination of knowledge and a modern scientific infrastructure were key components of modern power. At the same time, loyalty to the government and a willingness to work with the government hung on for a very long time among the scientific and technical intelligentsia. But by the 1890s the idea that public science served the monarch had for all practical purposes disappeared, and service to the state had faded from view. Those societies, such as RTO and the Pirogov Society, that were engaged in social and economic issues incorporated among their members a very vocal contingent that served almost exclusively the "people."

Studies of eighteenth- and nineteenth-century Europe demonstrate that voluntary associations were both a cause and a consequence of the development of civil society. Associations signified the potential for the self-organization of society, especially important in authoritarian regimes, which made it difficult for their subjects to act freely in concert. The "art of association" included the skills to speak in public, compile reports, administer institutions, and publicize projects. The formal bylaws, the conduct of meetings, and the election of officers exposed members to constitutional structures and parliamentary procedures. The exercise of private initiative and the participation in public life were important steps in the gradual emancipation of subjects from authoritarian states and the development of civil society. At the same time, however, most European associations and the learned societies in particular wished to share with the state the task of bringing prosperity to the realm. Members of associations, especially in continental Europe, acknowledged the state's role as enlightened legislator of the nation. There was no desire on the part of most associations to be independent of the state or to oppose sovereign authority. The freedom of action of associations was more likely to grow in scope as long as they stayed within confined boundaries and did not encroach on territory considered the exclusive prerogative of the state. The partnership between private associations and government departments suited both: monarchs and state officials sanctioned private initiative, and associations assisted the state to achieve common goals. Members of science societies were content to check politics at the door. Over time, however, associations, even many learned societies, could not escape controversial issues. States that sanctioned private initiative, therefore, insisted on their prerogative to scrutinize and regulate the public action of associations.

From the end of the eighteenth to the end of the nineteenth centuries, the Russian state did much to create civil society by sanctioning and patronizing private associations. For more than a century, government departments found it quite useful to have the learned societies apply knowledge, in a dispassionate way, to social and economic problems; to collect and analyze data; and even to make policy recommendations, of course only when asked to do so. For this reason, the government was willing to concede to associations considerable latitude for the autonomous management of their own affairs. As in Europe, government subsidies, royal patronage, and the presence of government and court officials and even members of the imperial family on the governing boards fostered the crossover between official and unofficial realms. Just as "polite science" fit well into the "gentlemanly order" in Great Britain, applied science fit well into the bureaucratic order in Russia. To many members, associations presented an opportunity for a pragmatic, advantageous reciprocal relationship with the imperial government. For this reason many associations assiduously cultivated an ethos of earnest service and usefulness in order to gain prestige and patronage for their projects. This was especially the case of learned societies such as the Free Economic Society, the Russian Geographical Society, and the Society of Friends of Natural History, Anthropology, and Ethnography. These and societies like them combined a service to science with a patriotic service to the cause of the betterment of Russia through the dissemination of useful knowledge.

Because Russia's learned societies assiduously cultivated their patriotic role in the dissemination of useful knowledge, by and large a relationship of cooperation and mutuality developed between Russian associations and the central government ministries. To be sure, the partnership was unequal: the state maintained its prerogative to approve the charter and bylaws of societies and to scrutinize their activities; and there were periodic crackdowns on private initiative in the reigns of Catherine II, Alexander I, and Nicholas I, and even after the Great Reforms. But like the learned societies they sanctioned, government departments also disseminated science and useful knowledge, promoted industry, and sought literate subjects and trained personnel. After all, recognition of Russia's backwardness and deficiencies in many areas of administration motivated the Great Reforms in the first place. Following the Crimean War, during the early years of the reign of Alexander II, the government sought to improve state administration and to enlist public commitment to projects of national renewal through the use of state-sanctioned "publicity" and "public discussion" *(glasnost')*. Numerous Russian delegations visited scientific and educational institutions in Europe, and ministries such as the Ministry of Finance sanctioned and even encouraged private associations such as OLEAE and RTO to provide technical training and found schools, to study productive resources, and to organize public lectures and exhibitions. All of these public projects gained the support of a newly vigorous Russian press. We have seen private initiative in the reform era in the discussion of economic policy under the auspices of the Russian Geographical Society and in the efforts of OLEAE to popularize science. The interests of state and society initially were shared interests, and state and society were willing to collaborate in a mutually advantageous partnership.

Government approved charters accorded certain privileges to associations: the ability to choose new members, to elect officers, to create divisions and branches, to schedule meetings, to establish decision-making mechanisms, and to set their own mission and goals. This meant that these communities of scientists had an autonomous inner life and were not merely creations or extensions of the state. In their internal affairs (and in Russian law), they were private associations *(chastnye obshchestva)* possessing their own will *(vol'noe)*. Legal recognition, as well as a system of rules and bureaucratic practices, gave a certain tutelary protection to associations. To their members and to the educated public, associations demonstrated the value and possibilities of private initiative. Created by individual initiative, associations mobilized others and thereby created spaces of independent action in which individual and collective initiative became self-perpetuating. In a country with a strong state tradition and fragmentary social structure, associations fostered the creation of institutions, habits, and mores that were already more widespread and ran more deeply in Europe. Myriad projects took concerted, focused energy to carry out and demonstrated the organizational talents and the suppleness wanting in the cumbersome Russian bureaucracy. To be sure, as in continental Europe, these spaces were not independent of the regulation of the authorities; and more even than on the European continent, officialdom circumscribed the exercise of initiative in Russian associations. But unlike its twentieth-century successor, autocracy did not systematically intrude into private life. Organized public initiative under autocracy had to begin somewhere, and within the unavoidable constraints of autocratic power, Russian associations were by and large self-defined, self-organized, and self-managed communities offering a free, that is, not coercive, associational life.

The exercise of associated initiative meant also cooperation to achieve common goals. In forging new bonds and affinities with other scientists, physicians, amateurs, educators, and government officials, members of associations cultivated an independent sociability. Public occasions and ceremonies enriched and commemorated individual and group lives and broke down a sense of isolation, long the bane of a vast and autocratically governed empire. Thus associations became the vehicle by which society learned about itself and communicated with itself. Information gathering, the publication of survey data, the funding of projects, and, myriad corresponding members' observations of the natural and human worlds were a major contribution to the fund of knowledge about the Russian empire. By emphasizing change and progress, associations fostered a public aware of its place in a changing world, of its place in history. Public meetings and congresses brought speakers and audiences in contact with each other and, by being reported in the societies' publications as well as in the press, with the broader educated society, both metropolitan and provincial, thereby creating horizontal linkages that bypassed Russian officialdom. In a country whose polity was built on vertical linkages that discouraged such communication, associations mobilized a public, framed issues, and promoted the sense of public duty and civic pride that had been missing from Russian national life.

But the dilemma of government policy regarding associations consisted in the fact that the government wanted to disseminate learning while at the same time confining and controlling it, lest the authority of natural knowledge and technical expertise challenge traditional authorities and the values of the old order. Although officials in the Ministry of Finance believed that private initiative would help the state to educate its subjects, officialdom in general and the Third Section and the Ministry of Internal Affairs in particular were suspicious of any unauthorized contact between the educated and the mass of the population. Unlike the dissemination of agricultural techniques among landed proprietors, the cataloging of knowledge about the empire and its peoples, and the display of science and technology—all of which had the approval of officialdom—the broad dissemination of knowledge became a far more controversial issue. Education and technical training became a wedge issue between activist associations and an increasingly suspicious officialdom. Educators and liberals (many of whom emerged from the hopeful years at the beginning of the era of the Great Reforms and later from the nonrevolutionary populist movement and who were active in the Pirogov Society and in the education division of RTO and of many other associations) wanted to go further in the dissemination of popular education than the government was willing to permit.

Members of associations populated a civil society that had been created earlier by the tsarist state for its own purposes. Associations were autonomous centers of scientific expertise and authority where politically powerless subjects could acquire the capacity of public voice and assert their right to participate in and influence public affairs. The charters and bylaws of science societies, the "founding documents," as they were repeatedly called, were microconstitutions that defined a legal relationship with authority, articulated collective goals, conferred certain privileges, and set rules for self-administration and self-management of affairs, allowing their members a degree of maneuverability in public not afforded the population as a whole. The legal status of associations such as the Russian Technical Society often gave official sanction to a variety of public projects and to the pursuit of interests in the public realm. By means of display, performance, and publicity, special interest constituencies of scientists entered the public arena and subjected themselves and their projects to the scrutiny of the government and the public, thereby becoming "public somebodies," to borrow the felicitous term of Leonore Davidoff and Catherine Hall.[3] The societies' publications, experiments, lectures, and meetings became forums to define and frame science, to raise consciousness, and to form values and opinions in public. By giving voice to social problems, by framing and creating public opinion, associations became the training ground for civic engagement in public affairs. Because authoritarian regimes everywhere closed the channels of representative politics, associations were that much more important in the project to arouse civic consciousness.[4] Such public enterprises cultivated the capacity of individual and collective representation before both peers and power. Scientists, scholars, and activists represented themselves and their projects in public before their peers, at forums often called "parliaments of science." In striving to act for the betterment of the realm and the nation, scientists collectively also claimed to represent the nation, through publicity, policy initiatives, and petitions to the Russian government. By thereby contesting the historic claim of the monarchy and officialdom to represent the nation, associations mediated interests between officialdom and an aspiring political nation.

To thus represent the nation in the review and formulation of state policy jeopardized the precarious partnership between officialdom and associations. Officialdom regarded the review and formulation of national policy to be within the arena of politics, territory beyond the scope and competence of private associations. But while cooperation and mutuality prevailed up to and including the era of the Great Reforms, the increasing civic activism of associations such as the Russian Technical Society and the Pirogov Society of Russian Physicians demonstrated a desire on the part of members and leaders to expand the scope of their authorized activities, thereby challenging the tutelage of the authorities. Gradually, more and more associations became assertive in their conduct, an assertiveness often concentrated in autonomous divisions concerned with education and public enemies. Although many societies, such as RGO, avoided politically sensitive projects in the latter nineteenth century, the initiative and self-organization of associations were conducive to the spirit of opposition. Their own claims to greater freedom of action became a core component of the struggle for the greater freedom of civil society. By the end of the nineteenth century, many, though by no means all, associations wanted the government to sanction a broader scope of activity and greater autonomy. Continued government tutelage only created more resentment and fostered an adversarial relationship. Moreover, since the government was no longer capable of guiding national betterment (as it still was after the Crimean defeat), public duty was more and more in the spirit of opposition.

Although historians have rightly identified certain major national crises—the famine of 1891, events leading up to the Revolution of 1905, for example—as galvanizing public action in a spirit of opposition to the government, this unprecedented public assertiveness came from somewhere. Thanks to the development of Russian associations, the spirit of participation in public life and its organizational framework and network were already in place. Overcoming the fear of the authorities, private Russians had come together voluntarily and formed a public. Despite the attempts of officialdom to keep out certain divisive topics, public meetings, often called "parliaments" in the press, provided a national forum. By convening a public "forum" on vital national questions, associations such as the Technical Society and the Pirogov Society of Russian Physicians gained in esteem, authority, and trust among the educated population, gains that came at the government's expense. Thus associations demonstrated what public life could be, even under autocracy, and why this public life was threatening to the authorities. They created and assiduously cultivated the microspaces of initiative and autonomy where the capacity of citizenship could appear.

Although civil associations, along with the press, were among the strongest components of Russian civil society, by themselves they could not create a strong and enduring civil society. The balance between associational autonomy and state control was never guaranteed in rights and, as a result, was perpetually negotiated. A rapidly growing network of associations could not entirely compensate for the absence of a tradition of strong property rights, rule of law, local powers and privileges, and intermediary constituted political bodies (organs of local self-rule, municipal corporations, some sort of assembly of the estates, and, later, political parties) that might have protected civil society from arbitrary state power, as ineffectual as such power often was in the last decades of the imperial regime. Until very late in its life, the tsarist regime could still have worked in partnership with members of civil society. But autocracy equated privately organized activity in the public realm with ideas of constitutions and limited government and was unwilling to sanction a political space to an increasingly assertive public. The authorities thereby drove more and more ordinary citizens into confrontations that in the end only weakened the state. If the greatest hindrance to the development of a strong and vibrant civil society is a state that is too strong, a tyranny, then no less threatening to such a development is a state that is too weak.

If the capacity of citizenship could sprout on the inhospitable ground of autocratic rule, could the Russian experience—and, in particular, its experience in association—teach us about the relationship between civil society and the state? It goes without saying that civil society and the capacity of citizenship did not fall out of the sky; they had to be articulated and experienced in public arenas. Many different forms of civil society can exist under a variety of regimes, only one of which is liberal democracy; and associations, by themselves, cannot create a liberal regime. To a great degree in partnership with autocracy, actors in Russia's growing civil society had to act as if civil society was institutionally secured in rights. In a country such as Russia, where arbitrary autocratic-bureaucratic authority prevailed, the emergence of civil society was not a consequence of the inviolability of person and domicile, property rights, and the rule of law, as often theorized in the Western tradition, but was concurrent with their development. The members and leaders of Russian associations had to act as if they enjoyed the rights of assembly and association in order to claim those rights—to act, in Daniel Gordon's words, as "citizens without sovereignty." In the absence of civil rights and local political powers, associations became not a consequence of the development of civil society but a leading element in its emergence. Voluntary associations helped create a space where social identities were formed, rights were asserted and defended, and claims were mediated. Under tutelary autocratic authority such voluntary processes were or easily became attempts to establish a new political community. As elsewhere in continental Europe, associations were the institutional framework for the emancipation of society from the state.[5] But the success of such emancipation, of course, was contingent upon a degree of willingness on the part of the state to "manumit" society and to tolerate the development of political associations and a political public sphere to mediate this process. Russia's failure to develop viable democratic institutions was not a failure of civil society but of autocratic intransigence. Although it sanctioned civil associations, for too long the state was unwilling to tolerate the existence of a political public sphere that could have allowed the full development of the process that associations began.

List of Abbreviations

Arkhiv RAN — *Arkhiv Rossiiskoi akademiia nauk (Archive of the Russian Academy of Sciences), Moscow*

Arkhiv RGO — *Arkhiv Russkogo geograficheskogo obshchestva* St. Petersburg *(Archive of the Russian Geographical Society)*

BME — *Bol'shaia meditsinskaia entsiklopediia. 2nd ed. 36 vols. Moscow, 1956–1965.*

BSDET — *Bibliograficheskii slovar' deiatelei estestvoznaniia i tekhniki. 2 vols. Moscow, 1958–1959.*

d. — *delo (folder)*

DOD — *Departament obshchikh del (Department of General Affairs of the Ministry of Internal Affairs)*

DP — *Departament politsii (Department of Police)*

d/p — *deloproizvodstvo (secretariat; of the Department of Police)*

eks. — *ekspeditsiia (expedition, office; of the Third Section)*

ES — *Entsiklopedicheskii slovar'. 86 vols. St. Petersburg, 1890–1907.*

ES Biografii — *Entsiklopedicheskii slovar' Brokgauza i Efrona: Biografii. Moscow, 1991–.*

f. — *fond (record group)*

GARF — *Gosudarstvennyi arkhiv Rossiiskoi federatsii (State Archive of the Russian Federation), Moscow*

Izvestiia OLEAE — *Izvestiia Obshchestva liubitelei estestvoznaniia, antropologii i etnografii. Moscow, 1864–1917.*

l. — *list (page; plural ll.—listy)*

MERSH — *Modern Encyclopedia of Russian and Soviet History. 60 vols. Gulf Breeze, Fla., 1976–.*

MNP	*Ministerstvo narodnogo prosveshcheniia (Ministry of Education)*
MOSX	*Moskovskoe obshchestvo sel'skogo khoziaistva*
MOO	*Moskovskoe okhrannoe otdelenie (Moscow Security Bureau)*
MVD	*Ministerstvo vnutrennikh del (Ministry of Internal Affairs)*
ob.	*reverse side*
OLEAE	*Obshchestvo liubitelei estestvoznaniia, antropologii i etnografii (Society of Friends of Natural History, Anthropology, and Ethnography)*
OO	*Osobyi otdel (Special Department of the Department of Police)*
op.	*opis' (inventory)*
OR RGB	*Otdel rukopisei, Rossiiskaia gosudarstvennaia biblioteka (Manuscript Division of the Russian State Library), Moscow*
PSZ	*Polnoe sobranie zakonov Rossiiskoi imperii (Complete Collection of Laws of the Russian Empire). St. Petersburg, 1830–1917.*
RBS	*Russkoe biograficheskii slovar' (Russian Biographical Dictionary). 25 vols. Moscow, 1896–1918.*
RGIA	*Rossiiskii gosudarstvennyi istoricheskii arkhiv (Russian State Historical Archive), St. Petersburg*
RGO	*Russkoe geograficheskoe obshchestvo (Russian Geographical Society)*
RTO	*Russkoe tekhnicheskoe obshchestvo (Russian Technical Society)*
Shilov	*D. N. Shilov, comp., Gosudarstvennye deiateli Rossiiskoi imperii: Glavy vysshikh i tsentral'nykh uchrezhdenii, 1802–1917: Bibliograficheskii spravochnik. St. Petersburg, 2001.*
Trudy VEO	*Trudy Vol'nogo ekonomicheskogo obshchestva. St. Petersburg, 1766–1917.*
TsIAM	*Tsentral'nyi istoricheskii arkhiv Moskvy (Central Historical Archive of Moscow)*
VEO	*Vol'noe ekonomicheskoe obshchestvo (Free Economic Society)*
Zapiski RTO	*Zapiski Imperatorskogo Russkogo tekhnicheskogo obshchestva i svod privilegii. St. Petersburg, 1867–1917.*

Notes

Introduction

1. Eugene M. Kayden, *The Cooperative Movement in Russia during the War: Consumers' Cooperation* (New Haven, Conn., 1929), 4.
2. Marc Raeff, *Understanding Imperial Russia: State and Society in the Old Regime,* trans. Arthur Goldhammer (New York, 1984), cited passage, 170. The argument here is taken from, among others, Martin Malia, *The Soviet Tragedy: A History of Socialism in Russia, 1917–1991* (New York, 1994); Richard Pipes, *Russia under the Old Regime* (New York, 1974); Geoffrey Hosking, *Russia: People and Empire, 1552–1917* (Cambridge, Mass., 1997), 181–182; Martin Malia, *Russia under Western Eyes: From the Bronze Horseman to the Lenin Mausoleum* (Cambridge, Mass., 1999), 143. On rights, see W. E. Butler, "Civil Rights in Russia: Legal Standards in Gestation," and Raymond Pearson, "Privileges, Rights, and Russification," both in Olga Crisp and Linda Edmondson, eds., *Civil Rights in Imperial Russia* (Oxford, 1989), 1–12 and 85–102, respectively. On Russia's fragmented social structure, see Gregory Freeze, "The Soslovie (Estate) Paradigm and Russian Social History," *American Historical Review* 91 (1986): 11–36; Alfred J. Rieber, "The Sedimentary Society," in Edith W. Clowes, Samuel Kassow, and James West, eds., *Between Tsar and People: Educated Society and the Quest for Public Identity in Late-Imperial Russia* (Princeton, N.J., 1991), 343–366; and Elise Kimerling Wirtschafter, *Structures of Society: Imperial Russia's People of Various Ranks* (DeKalb, Ill., 1994), and *Social Identity in Imperial Russia* (DeKalb, Ill., 1997).

3. The metaphor of the "double helix" belongs to Dena Goodman and applies to ancien régime France. See Dena Goodman, *The Republic of Letters: A Cultural History of the French Enlightenment* (Ithaca, N.Y., 1994), 2.
4. Quintin Hoare and Geoffrey Nowell Smith, eds. and trans., *Selections from the Prison Notebooks of Antonio Gramsci* (New York, 1971), 238. That is, civil society is primitive, nascent, as well as jellylike, shapeless, and amorphous. See also Norberto Bobbio, "Gramsci and the Concept of Civil Society," in John Keane, ed., *Civil Society and the State: New European Perspectives* (London, 1988), 73–100.
5. Raeff, *Understanding Imperial Russia,* 129.
6. Jacob Walkin, *The Rise of Democracy in Pre-revolutionary Russia: Political and Social Institutions under the Last Three Czars* (New York, 1962), 183–184.
7. Cited passages from Terence Emmons, "The Zemstvo in Historical Perspective," in Terence Emmons and Wayne S. Vucinich, eds., *The Zemstvo in Russia: An Experiment in Local Self-Government* (Cambridge, 1982), 433; Orlando Figes, *A People's Tragedy: A History of the Russian Revolution* (New York, 1996), 162. See also W. Bruce Lincoln, *The Great Reforms: Autocracy, Bureaucracy, and the Politics of Change in Imperial Russia* (DeKalb, Ill., 1990), xvi; S. Frederick Starr, "Civil Society and the Impediments to Reform," in William G. Miller, ed., *Toward a More Civil Society? The USSR under Mikhail Sergeevich Gorbachev* (New York, 1989), 307; Daniel Brower, *The Russian City between Tradition and Modernity, 1850–1900* (Berkeley, Calif., 1990), 40; Terence Emmons, *The Formation of Political Parties and the First National Elections in Russia* (Cambridge, Mass., 1983), 1–5. Laura Engelstein, "The Dream of Civil Society in Tsarist Russia: Law, State, and Religion," in Nancy Bormeo and Philip Nord, eds., *Civil Society Before Democracy: Lessons from Nineteenth-century Europe* (Lanham, Md., 2000), 23–41.
8. Abraham Ascher, *P. A. Stolypin: The Search for Stability in Late Imperial Russia* (Stanford, Calif., 2001), 77; Abraham Ascher, *The Revolution of 1905: Russia in Disarray* (Stanford, Calif., 1988), 341. See also Victoria Bonnell, *Roots of Rebellion: Workers' Politics and Organizations in St. Petersburg and Moscow, 1900–1914* (Berkeley, Calif., 1983), 102–103, 149–151; Mark Steinberg, *Moral Communities: The Culture of Class Relations in the Russian Printing Industry, 1867–1907* (Berkeley, Calif., 1992); Mark Steinberg, "Vanguard Workers and the Morality of Class," in Lewis H. Siegelbaum and Ronald Grigor Suny, eds., *Making Workers Soviet: Power, Class and Identity* (Ithaca, N.Y., 1994), 66–84, especially 76–77; Heather Hogan, "Class Formation in the St. Petersburg Metalworking Industry: From the 'Days of Freedom' to the Lena Goldfields Massacre," in Siegelbaum and Suny, *Making Workers Soviet,* 85–112.
9. Ronald Grigor Suny, *The Soviet Experiment: Russia, the USSR, and the Successor States* (New York, 1998), 15 (emphasis added). An authority on artisans has claimed, "Tsarist Russia, with its highly centralized autocratic system, had an *exceedingly weak tradition of voluntary association* . . . Mass-based political parties, trade unions, cooperatives, and *other voluntary*

associations did not appear until the 1905 Revolution and for a dozen years they led a precarious existence." Victoria Bonnell, "Voluntary Associations in Gorbachev's Reform Program," in Alexander Dallin and Gail W. Lapidus, eds., *The Soviet System in Crisis: A Reader of Western and Soviet Views* (Boulder, Colo., 1991), 151–160; quotation, 151 (emphasis added).

10. Theodore Von Laue, *Why Lenin? Why Stalin? Why Gorbachev? The Rise and Fall of the Soviet System,* 3rd ed. (New York, 1993), 17–18. The words are Von Laue's, but the view is widely shared. See also Walkin, *Rise of Democracy,* 183–184; Hosking, *Russia,* 181–182; Malia, *Russia under Western Eyes,* 143.
11. Yuri Afanasyev, "Russia's Vicious Circle," *New York Times,* 28 February 1994. Admittedly, this is an "op-ed" piece, not a scholarly work. However, the wide dissemination of such generalizations makes it all the more important to subject them to scholarly scrutiny. Not all historians in Russia are as stark as Afanasyev in their assessment of the state-civil society relationship. See note 16 below.
12. Geoff Eley, "Nations, Publics and Political Cultures: Placing Habermas in the Nineteenth Century" in Craig Calhoun, ed., *Habermas and the Public Sphere* (Cambridge, Mass., 1992), 325 (emphasis added). Such a view contains considerable irony. Along with David Blackbourn, Eley spearheaded a paradigm shift in the conceptualization of nineteenth-century Germany that challenged Germany's alleged *Sonderweg* and failed civil society. See David Blackbourn and Geoff Eley, *Peculiarities of German History: Bourgeois Society and Politics in Nineteenth-century Germany* (Oxford, 1984.) But regarding Russia, Eley lapses into the same conventional view he refuted so effectively for Germany.
13. The felicitous quoted phrase is Butler's, from his "Civil Rights in Russia: Legal Standards in Gestation," 9.
14. Here I borrow my approach from Bruce Lincoln, who two decades ago found the origins of the Great Reforms in the quiet, long-term action of enlightened bureaucrats rather than in dramatic short-term events—the failure of the Russian military in the Crimean War and serf revolt. W. Bruce Lincoln, *In the Vanguard of Reform: Russia's Enlightened Bureaucrats, 1825–1861* (DeKalb, Ill., 1982), xi–xiv.
15. For recognition of the need for more work on Russian civil society, see Raeff, *Understanding Imperial Russia,* 176.
16. In their introduction to a recent collection, Jane Burbank and David Ransel also note that "historians [have] emphasized Russia's failures" and call for "an escape from the established frame of imperial decline," for a de-emphasis on the "state-society dichotomy, and for "more open-ended historical investigation." Jane Burbank and David L. Ransel, eds., *Imperial Russia: New Histories for the Empire* (Bloomington, Ind., 1998), xv–xvi. Scholars in Russia have begun to examine the development of civil society, liberalism, and associations. See A. D. Stepanskii, *Istoriia obshchestvennykh organizatsii dorevoliutsionnoi Rossii* (Moscow, 1977); Stepanskii, "Materialy legal'nykh obshchestvennykh organizatsii tsarskoi Rossii," in *Arkheograficheskii ezhegodnik 1978* (Moscow, 1979), 69–80; Stepanskii, *Samoderzhavie i obshch-*

estvennye ogranizatsii Rossii na rubezhe XIX–XX vv. (Moscow, 1980); Stepanskii, *Obshchestvennye organizatsii v Rossii na rubezhe XIX–XX vv.* (Moscow, 1982); B. N. Mironov, *Sotsial'naia istoriia Rossii perioda imperii (XVIII–nachalo XX v.): Genezis lichnosti, demokraticheskoi sem'i, grazhdanskogo obshchestva i pravovogo gosudarstva* (St. Petersburg, 1999), especially vol. 2: 110, 261–63, 290–91; A. N. Medushevskii, "Formirovanie grazhdanskogo obshchestva: reformy i kontrareformy v Rossii," in *Reformy i reformatory v istorii Rossii: Sbornik statei* (Moscow, 1996), 69–78; V. V. Vitiuk, *Stanovlenie idei grazhdanskogo obshchestva i ee istoricheskaia evoliutsiia* (Moscow, 1996); V. V. Shelokhaev, "Russkii liberalism kak istoriograficheskaia i istoriosofskaia problema," *Voprosy istorii,* no. 4 (1998): 26–41; Shelokhaev, *Liberal'naia model' pereustroistva Rossii* (Moscow, 1996); I. S. Rozental', *Moskva na pereput'e: Vlast' i obshchestvo v 1905–1914* (Moscow, 2004); A. S. Tumanova, *Samoderzhavie i obshchestvennye organizatsii v Rossii* (Tambov, 2002); V. Ia. Grosul, *Russkoe obshchestvo XVIII–XIX vekov: Traditsii i novatsii* (Moscow, 2003); V. M. Shevyrin, *Vlast' i obshchestvennye organizatsii v Rossii, 1914–1917* (Moscow, 2003); G. N. Ul'ianova, *Blagotvoritel'nost' v Rossiiskoi imperii XIX–nachalo XX veka* (Moscow, 2005).

17. The phrase is taken from the apt title of an exploration of civil society. See Clowes, Kassow, and West, eds., *Between Tsar and People.* See also Crisp and Edmondson, eds., *Civil Rights*, vi–vii; Douglas Smith, *Working the Rough Stone: Freemasonry and Society in Eighteenth-century Russia* (DeKalb, Ill., 1999), 86; Adele Lindenmeyr, *Poverty Is Not a Vice: Charity, Society, and the State in Imperial Russia* (Princeton, N.J., 1996), 111, 231; David Wartenweiler, *Civil Society and Academic Debate in Russia, 1905–1914* (Oxford, 1999); Manfred Hagen, *Die Entfaltung politischer Öffentlichkeit in Russland, 1906–1914* (Wiesbaden, 1982); Guido Hausmann, ed., *Gesellschaft als lokale Veranstaltung: Selbstverwaltung, Assoziierung und Geselligkeit in den Städten des ausgehenden Zarebreiches* (Göttingen, 2002); Christine Ruane, *Gender, Class and the Professionalization of Russian City Teachers, 1860–1914* (Pittsburgh, 1994); Gary Marker, *Publishing, Printing, and the Origins of Intellectual Life in Russia, 1700–1800* (Princeton, N.J., 1985); Louise McReynolds, *The News Under Russia's Old Regime: The Development of a Mass-Circulation Press* (Princeton, N.J., 1991), 3–4; Jeffrey Brooks, *When Russia Learned to Read: Literacy and Popular Literature, 1861–1917* (Princeton, N.J., 1985), xxi; Joan Neuberger, *Hooliganism: Crime, Culture, and Power in St. Petersburg, 1900–1914* (Berkeley, Calif., 1993), 111; Louise McReynolds, *Russia at Play: Leisure Activities at the End of the Tsarist Era* (Ithaca, N.Y., 2003); Murray Frame, *School for Citizens: Theater and Civil Society in Imperial Russia* (New Haven, Conn., 2006).

18. Roger Scruton, *A Dictionary of Political Thought* (New York, 1982), 28–29, 33–34. A study of Hamburg, Germany, defines the voluntary association *(verein)* as "an assemblage of persons having a constitution . . . [,] being in existence independent of a change of membership . . . [,] jointly pursuing

one or several goals with a set of bylaws, not having a profit motive, and being at least partly autonomous." Herbert Freudenthal, *Vereine in Hamburg: Ein Beitrag zur Geschichte und Volkskunde der Geselligkeit* (Hamburg, 1968), 11–12. Most definitions emphasize that membership is "driven by choice rather than necessity" and that associations are self-governing communities "united for a specific purpose or purposes and held together by recognized or sanctioned modes of procedure and behavior," the major purpose of which is not "related to the business of making a living." David Sills, "Voluntary Associations: Social Aspects," *International Encyclopedia of the Social Sciences* 16 (New York, 1968), 362–379; Morris Ginsberg, "Association," *Encyclopedia of the Social Sciences* (New York, 1937), 2: 284–286; Stuart Blumin, *The Emergence of the Middle Class: Social Experience in the American City, 1760–1900* (New York, 1989), 193; James E. McClelland III, *Science Reorganized: Scientific Societies in the Eighteenth Century* (New York, 1985), 13; Peter Clark, *British Clubs and Societies, 1580–1800: The Origins of an Associational World* (Oxford, 2000), 16; W. B. Munro, "Civic Organizations," *Encyclopedia of the Social Sciences,* 3: 498; Mark E. Warren, *Democracy and Association* (Princeton, N.J., 2001), 8, 10, 30, 34, 59, 61, 70, 77–78, 81.

19. Maurice Agulhon, "L'histoire sociale et les associations," *Revue de l'économie sociale* 14 (1988): 35–44, especially 36; Agulhon, "Vers une histoire des associations," *Esprit* 6 (1978): 13–18; Agulhon, *Le Cercle dans la France bourgeoise, 1810–1848: Étude d'une mutation de sociabilité* (Paris, 1977), 19–61. See also McClelland, *Science Reorganized,* xxiii, 1–2.
20. Dana Villa asserts the importance of political associations, the constituted intermediary powers of local self-rule, in "Tocqueville and Civil Society," in Cheryl B. Welch, ed., *The Cambridge Companion to Tocqueville* (Cambridge, 2006), 216–244. I am grateful to my colleague Paul Rahe for bringing this work to my attention.
21. Jan Golinski, *Science as Public Culture: Chemistry and Enlightenment in Britain, 1760–1820* (Cambridge, 1992); Geoffrey V. Sutton, *Science for a Polite Society: Gender, Culture and the Demonstration of Enlightenment* (Boulder, Colo., 1995); Colin A. Russell, *Science and Social Change in Britain and Europe, 1700–1900* (New York, 1983); Henry Lowood, *Patriotism, Profit and the Promotion of Science in the German Enlightenment: The Economic and Scientific Societies, 1760–1815* (New York, 1991), 4–5; Jan C. C. Rupp, "The New Science and the Public Sphere in the Premodern Era," *Science in Context* 8, no. 3 (1995): 487–507, especially 487, 491, 496.
22. Ian F. McNeely, "The Intelligence Gazette *(Intelligenzblatt)* as a Road Map to Civil Society," in Frank Trentmann, ed., *Paradoxes of Civil Society: New Perspectives on Modern German and British History* (New York, 2000), 151; Michael John, "Associational Life and the Development of Liberalism in Hanover, 1848–66," in Konrad H. Jarusch, and Larry Eugene Jones, ed., *In Search of a Liberal Germany* (New York, 1990), 161–186, especially 161–162; Katherine Auspitz, *The Radical Bourgeoisie: The Ligue de l'enseignement and the Origins of the Third Republic, 1866–1885* (Cambridge,

1982), 75; Stefan-Ludwig Hoffmann, "Democracy and Associations in the Long Nineteenth Century: Toward a Transnational Perspective," *Journal of Modern History* 75, no. 2 (June, 2003): 269–299, especially 276; Thomas McCarthy, "Practical Discourse: On the Relation of Morality to Politics," in Craig Calhoun, ed., *Habermas and the Public Sphere* (Cambridge, Mass., 1992), 51–72, especially 63; McClelland, *Science Reorganized,* 1, 24–25.

23. John Gray, "Totalitarianism, Reform and Civil Society," in Ellen Frankel Paul, ed., *Totalitarianism at the Crossroads* (New Brunswick, N.J., 1990): 97–142; quotation, 100. Consider the definition of Reinhard Bendix: civil society is "the institutions in which the individual can pursue common interests without detailed direction or interference from government." Reinhard Bendix, *Kings or People: Power and the Mandate to Rule* (Berkeley, Calif., 1978): 523.

24. Jean L. Cohen and Andrew Arato, *Civil Society and Political Theory* (Cambridge, Mass., 1992); John Keane, ed., *Civil Society and the State;* Salvador Giner, "The Withering Away of Civil Society?" *Praxis International* 5 (October 1985): 247–267; *Hegel's Philosophy of Right,* trans. T. M. Knox (London, 1967). To understand Hegel, I have relied on Manfred Riedel, *Between Tradition and Revolution: The Hegelian Transformation of Political Philosophy*, trans. Walter Wright (Cambridge, 1984), and Z. Pelczynski, *The State and Civil Society in Hegel* (Cambridge, 1984). See also Victor M. Perez-Diaz, *The Return of Civil Society: The Emergence of Democratic Spain* (Cambridge, Mass., 1995), 95–97; Adam B. Seligman, *The Idea of Civil Society* (Princeton, N.J., 1992), 50. The "mapping" metaphor of "terrain" and "irregular topography" comes from Philip Nord, *The Republican Moment: Struggles for Democracy in Nineteenth-century France* (Cambridge, 1995), xiv. In a conference devoted to his work, Jürgen Habermas himself acknowledged the difficulty in defining civil society: "The now current meaning of the term 'civil society' . . . no longer includes a sphere of an economy regulated via labor, capital, and commodity markets and thus differs from the modern translation, common since Hegel and Marx, of *'societas civilis'* as 'bourgeois society' *('bürgerliche Gesellschaft').* Unfortunately, a search for clear definitions in the relevant publications is in vain." Jürgen Habermas, "Further Reflections on the Public Sphere," in Craig Calhoun, ed., *Habermas and the Public Sphere* (Cambridge, Mass., 1992), 453–454.

25. On these strands of thought, see John Keane's contribution "Despotism and Democracy" to his edited collection, *Civil Society and the State,* 35–71; Isabel V. Hull, *Sexuality, State, and Civil Society in Germany, 1700–1815* (Ithaca, N.Y., 1996), quotation, 164.

26. Hoare and Smith, *Selections from the Prison Notebooks,* 12–13, 235. See also Alvin W. Gouldner, *The Two Marxisms: Contradictions and Anomalies in the Development of Theory* (New York, 1980), 346–347, 355–361; Jean Cohen, *Class and Civil Society: The Limits of Marxian Critical Theory* (Amherst, Mass., 1982), 23–52; Keane, *Civil Society and the State,* 23; Norberto Bobbio, "Gramsci and the Concept of Civil Society," in C. Moufee, ed., *Gramsci and Marxist Theory* (London, 1979), xxx.

27. Bronislaw Geremek, "Civil Society and the Present Age," *The Idea of Civil Society* (Research Triangle Park, N.C., 1992), 11–18; Zbigniew Rau, "Some Thoughts on Civil Society in Eastern Europe and the Lockean Contractarian Approach," *Political Studies* 35 (1987): 573–592; Rau, ed., *The Emergence of Civil Society in Eastern Europe and the Soviet Union* (Boulder, Colo., 1991); David Reidy Jr. "Eastern Europe, Civil Society, and the Real Revolution," *Praxis International* 12, no. 2 (July 1992): 168–180; Bronislaw Geremek, "Civil Society Then and Now," *Journal of Democracy* 3 (April 1992): 3–12; Jeffrey C. Isaac, "Civil Society and the Spirit of Revolt," *Dissent* (Summer 1993): 356–361. The "discovery" of civil society as a category of analysis has also reached China. See the articles by Heath B. Chamberlain, Philip C. C. Huang, Mary Backus Rankin, William T. Rowe, Richard Madsen, and Frederick Wakeman Jr. in a special issue of *Modern China* (19, no. 2 [April 1993]), devoted to the public sphere, as well as Martin Whyte, "Urban China: A Civil Society in the Making?" in Arthur L. Rosenbaum, ed., *State and Society in China: Consequences of Reform* (Boulder, Colo., 1992), 77–78, 82. Two historians who emphasize process over product are Frank Trentmann (see *Paradoxes of Civil Society*) and Philip Nord (see *Republican Moment*).
28. Jürgen Habermas, *The Structural Transformation of the Public Sphere: An Inquiry into a Category of Bourgeois Society,* trans. Thomas Burger (Cambridge, Mass., 1989), 23, 27, 83. Habermas responds to critics in "Further Reflections" and incorporates associations into a revised theory of civil society in *Between Facts and Norms: Contributions to a Discourse Theory of Law and Democracy,* trans. William Rehg (Cambridge, Mass., 1996), 355.
29. Keane, *Civil Society and the State,* 65.
30. Hull, *Sexuality, State, and Civil Society,* especially 199–228; Margaret Jacob, *Living the Enlightenment: Freemasonry and Politics in Eighteenth-century Europe* (New York, 1991), 145.
31. Edward Shils, "The Virtue of Civil Society," *Government and Opposition* 26, no. 1 (Winter 1991): 3–20, especially 10; Keane, *Civil Society and the State,* 55–61.
32. Ivan Karp, Christine Mullen Kreamer, and Steven D. Levine, eds., *Museums and Communities: The Politics of Public Culture* (Washington, D.C., 1992), 4–5.
33. A good introduction to the professions is Harley D. Balzer, ed., *Russia's Missing Middle Class: The Professions in Russian History* (Armonk, N.Y., 1996). See also Nancy Frieden, *Russian Physicians in an Era of Reform and Revolution, 1856–1905* (Princeton, N.J., 1981); Clowes, Kassow, and West, *Between Tsar and People;* Scott J. Seregny, *Russian Teachers and Peasant Revolution: The Politics of Education in 1905* (Bloomington, Ind., 1989); Seregny, "Zemstvos, Peasants and Citizenship: The Russian Adult Education Movement and World War I," *Slavic Review* 59, no. 2 (Summer 2000): 290–315; Ruane, *Gender, Class and Professionalization;* John F. Hutchinson, *Politics and Public Health in Revolutionary Russia, 1890–1918* (Baltimore, 1990); Laura Engelstein, *The Keys to Happiness: Sex and the*

Search for Modernity in Fin-de-Siècle Russia (Ithaca, N.Y., 1992); William Wagner, *Marriage, Property and Law in Late Imperial Russia* (Oxford, 1994); and William C. Fuller Jr., *Civil-Military Conflict in Imperial Russia, 1881–1914* (Princeton, N.J., 1985). Among many works on the zemstvos, see Terence Emmons and Wayne S. Vucinich, eds., *The Zemstvo in Russia;* V. F. Abramov, *Rossiiskoe zemstvo: ekonomiki, finansy i kul'tura* (Moscow, 1996).

34. This study is not an attempt to "find" the missing bourgeoisie, a commonplace concept in the historiography, let alone to assert its importance. The explanatory power of such an approach is, in any event, considerably weakened when European historians have challenged the existence of a bourgeoisie as an economic and political class. See, especially, Blackbourn and Eley, *Peculiarities;* R. Holt, "Social History and Bourgeois Culture in Nineteenth-century France," *Comparative Studies in Society and History* 27 (October 1985): 713–726; Ralf Dahrendorf, *Society and Democracy in Germany* (Garden City, N.Y., 1967); Keith Michael Baker, "Defining the Public Sphere in Eighteenth-century France: Variations on a Theme by Habermas," in Craig Calhoun, ed., *Habermas,* 181–211; Carol E. Harrison, *The Bourgeois Citizen in Nineteenth-century France: Gender, Sociability and the Uses of Emulation* (Oxford, 1999); and, most boldly and most recently, Sarah Maza, *The Myth of the French Bourgeoisie: An Essay on the Social Imaginary, 1750–1850* (Cambridge, 2003).

35. On professionalization, see Gerald L. Geison, ed., *Professions and the French State, 1700–1900* (Philadelphia, 1984); Konrad H. Jarausch, *The Unfree Professions: German Lawyers, Teachers and Engineers, 1900–1950* (Oxford, 1990).

36. Marion W. Gray, *Productive Men, Reproductive Women: The Agrarian Household and the Emergence of Separate Spheres during the German Enlightenment* (New York, 2000), 131. See also Hull, *Sexuality, State and Civil Society,* 210–215. In Britain, Clark notes the "male dominated associational world" (*British Clubs,* 3, 203), as do Leonore Davidoff and Catherine Hall, in *Family Fortunes: Men and Women of the English Middle Class, 1780–1850* (Chicago, 1987), 292, 427; Carol Harrison does the same for France (*Bourgeois Citizen,* 12, 21).

37. For a discussion of the pertinent criteria in the European literature, see Clark, *British Clubs,* 16; McClelland, *Science Reorganized,* xiii; Christiane Eisenberg, "Working-Class and Middle-Class Associations: An Anglo-German Comparison, 1820–1870," in Jürgen Kocka and Allen Mitchell, eds., *Bourgeois Society in Nineteenth-century Europe* (Oxford, 1993), 153–154; Jan Golinski, *Making Natural Knowledge: Constructivism and the History of Science* (Cambridge, 1998), 65–66; Mary Terrall, "Metaphysics, Mathematics and the Gendering of Science in Eighteenth-century France," in William Clark, Jan Golinski, and Simon Schaffer, eds., *The Sciences in Enlightened Europe* (Chicago, 1999), 247–269; Paula Findlen, *Possessing Nature: Museums, Collecting, and Scientific Culture in Early Modern Italy* (Berkeley, Calif., 1994); Warren, *Democracy and Association,* 57–58; Freudenthal, *Vereine,* 12–13.

38. In Russia and elsewhere, the most public activities of associations are the best documented; the many informal internal communications among members are much less well preserved. In addition, the leaders of associations tended not to leave behind reflections of their work or the work of their associations. To compound the problem of sources, unlike the centralized state apparatus, whose methodical records have been assiduously catalogued by Soviet-era archivists, the records of decentralized voluntary associations have never had a high priority. Yet the bulletins and minutes of meetings, scientific papers, transactions of conferences and congresses, catalogs of exhibitions, and annual reports are in ample supply. See A. D. Stepanskii, "Materialy legal'nykh obshchestvennykh organizatsii tsarskoi Rossii," *Arkheograficheskii ezhegodnik za 1978,* especially 73.
39. Patrick L. Alston, *Education and the State in Tsarist Russia* (Stanford, Calif., 1969), 243. See also Reginald Zelnik, *Labor and Society in Tsarist Russia: The Factory Workers of St. Petersburg, 1855–1870* (Stanford, Calif., 1971), 292–297.
40. Quoted in Allen Sinel, *The Classroom and the Chancellery: State Educational Reform in Russia under Count Dmitry Tolstoi* (Cambridge, Mass., 1973), 1.
41. E. I. Lamanskii, quoted in Zelnik, *Labor and Society,* 84.
42. N. M. Pirumova, *Zemskoe liberal'noe dvizhenie: Sotsial'nye korni i evoliutsiia do nachala XX veka* (Moscow, 1977); Pirumova, *Zemskaia intelligentsia i ee rol' v obshchestvennoi bor'be* (Moscow, 1986).
43. Caspar Ferenczi, "Freedom of the Press under the Old Regime, 1905–1914," in Crisp and Edmondson, *Civil Rights,* 191–214. See also McReynolds, *News,* 21–24.
44. Simone Chambers and Will Kymlicka, eds., *Alternative Conceptions of Civil Society* (Princeton, N.J., 2002), 1; Clark, *British Clubs,* viii.
45. On the counterreforms, see P. A. Zaionchkovskii, *Rossiiskoe samoderzhavie v kontse XIX stoletiia* (Moscow, 1970).

1. European Societies and the State

1. Victor M. Perez-Diaz, *The Return of Civil Society: The Emergence of Democratic Spain* (Cambridge, Mass., 1995), 91–92.
2. Philip Nord, *The Republican Moment: Struggles for Democracy in Nineteenth-century France* (Cambridge, 1995), xiv, 6–7.
3. Daniel Gordon, *Citizens without Sovereignty: Equality and Sociability in French Thought, 1670–1789* (Princeton, N.J., 1994), 3.
4. Quoted in Margaret C. Jacob, "The Moral Landscape of the Public Sphere: A European Perspective," *Eighteenth-century Studies* 28, no. 1 (Autumn 1994): 95–113; quotation, 102.
5. Quoted in Robert J. Goldstein, *Political Repression in Nineteenth-century Europe* (London, 1983), 48.
6. D. B. Robertson, "Hobbes's Theory of Association in the Seventeenth-century Milieu," in D. B. Robertson, ed., *Voluntary Associations: A Study of*

Groups in Free Societies (Richmond, Va., 1966), 109–112; Otto Gierke, *Natural Law and the Theory of Society, 1500–1800,* trans. Ernest Barker (Boston, 1957), lx.

7. Alf Lüdtke, *Police and State in Prussia,* trans. Pete Burgess (Cambridge, 1989), xv. Civil society has been regarded as largely a creation of the state. See David A. Bell, "The 'Public Sphere,' the State, and the World of Law in Eighteenth-century France," *French Historical Studies* 17 (Fall 1992): 934, 955.
8. Dena Goodman, *The Republic of Letters: A Cultural History of the French Enlightenment* (Ithaca, N.Y., 1994), 250; Carol E. Harrison, *The Bourgeois Citizen in Nineteenth-century France: Gender, Sociability and the Uses of Emulation* (Oxford, 1999), 24; Jean-Pierre Chaline, *Sociabilité et Érudition: Les sociétés savants en France, XIXe–XXe siècles* (Paris, 1995), 35, 69, 72–73; James Van Horn Melton, *The Rise of the Public in Enlightenment Europe* (Cambridge, 2001), 136.
9. P. H. J. H. Gosden, *Self-Help: Voluntary Associations in the Nineteenth Century* (London, 1973), 30–31.
10. Gordon, *Citizens without Sovereignty,* 3. See also Marvin Becker, *The Emergence of Civil Society in the Eighteenth Century: A Privileged Moment in the History of England, Scotland and France* (Bloomington, Ind., 1994), 45.
11. Cited passage in Carol Harrison, *Bourgeois Citizen,* 24. Voluntary associations in the United States, Britain, and Germany have received much attention from historians. They have been less studied in the historiography of the preeminent statist power of modern Europe, France. Exceptions are Maurice Agulhon, "Vers une histoire des associations," *Esprit* 6 (1978): 13–18, especially 14; Margaret C. Jacob, *Living the Enlightenment: Freemasonry and Politics in Eighteenth-century Europe* (New York, 1991), 27, 29; Melton, *Rise of the Public,* 64–67; David A. Bell, *Lawyers and Citizens: The Making of a Political Elite in Old Regime France* (Oxford, 1994), 12.
12. Quoted by Alexis de Tocqueville in *The Ancien Régime and the French Revolution,* trans. Stuart Gilbert (London, 1966), 131
13. Tocqueville, *Ancien Régime,* 80, 94, 159. See also Tocqueville, *Democracy in America,* ed. Phillips Bradley (New York, 1945), 2: 109.
14. Raymond Huard, "Political Associations in Nineteenth-century France: Legislation and Practice," in Nancy Bormeo and Philip Nord, eds., *Civil Society before Democracy: Lessons from Nineteenth-century Europe* (Lanham, Md., 2000), 139. See also Eugene N. Anderson and Pauline R. Anderson, *Political Institutions and Social Change in Continental Europe in the Nineteenth Century* (Berkeley, Calif., 1967), 276–277.
15. Jürgen Habermas, *Between Facts and Norms: Contributions to a Discourse Theory of Law and Democracy,* trans. William Rehg (Cambridge, Mass., 1996), 360.
16. Cited passages from Roger Chartier, *The Cultural Origins of the French Revolution,* trans. Lydia G. Cochrane (Durham, N.C., 1991), 30. Chartier's inspiration is Jürgen Habermas, *The Structural Transformation of the Public Sphere: An Inquiry into a Category of Bourgeois Society,* trans. Thomas

Burger (Cambridge, Mass., 1989). See also Larry Diamond, "Rethinking Civil Society: Toward Democratic Consolidation," *Journal of Democracy* (July 1994): 4–17, especially 5; David Gordon, "Philosophy, Sociology and Gender in Enlightenment Conceptions of Public Opinion," *French Historical Studies* 17 (1992): 902; Michael Warner, *The Letters of the Republic: Publication and the Public Sphere in Eighteenth-century America* (Cambridge, Mass., 1990), xiii, 61; and Goodman, *Republic of Letters*, 2, 5, 34.

17. Keith Michael Baker, *Inventing the French Revolution: Essays on French Political Culture in the Eighteenth Century* (New York, 1990), 114.
18. Much of this discourse was derived from John Locke. See *The Second Treatise of Government*, C. B. Macpherson, ed. (Indianapolis, Ind., 1980), chap. 7, paras. 90–94. See also John Keane, ed., *Civil Society and the State: New European Perspectives* (London, 1988), 35–72; and Dwayne Woods, "Civil Society in Africa and Europe: Limiting State Power through a Public Sphere," *African Studies Review* 33, no. 2 (February 1992): 79.
19. The Le Chapelier Law of 1791 banned occupational associations, and by a decree of 8 August 1793 the Convention abolished the national academy and other learned societies, confiscated their assets, and subjected their libraries, botanical gardens, and museums to surveillance; four years later all clubs were dissolved. By the constitution of 1795, all associations violating public order were prohibited; the state claimed the right to shut down any organization that became political, entered into combination or correspondence with other associations, or held public meetings. See Chaline, *Sociabilité*, 31–32; Agulhon, "Vers une histoire ," 14–15; Maurice Agulhon, "L'histoire sociale et les associations," *Revue de l'économie sociale* 14 (1988): 35–44, especially 38; Harrison, *Bourgeois Citizen*, 22–24, 37.
20. Quoted in E. N. Anderson and P. R. Anderson, *Political Institutions*, 275.
21. Tocqueville, *Ancien Régime*, 88.
22. David Thompson, *France: Empire and Republic, 1850–1940: Historical Documents* (New York, 1968), 164. See also Chaline, *Sociabilité*, 72; Harrison, *Bourgeois Citizen*, 22–24, 26–27; Huard, "Political Associations," 137–138. Why twenty members? Agulhon speculates that a group numbering fewer than twenty appeared to have been formed on the basis of familiarity of its members, a "natural" process. A group of more than twenty, conversely, appeared unnatural and premeditated and thus smacked of politics. Agulhon, "L'histoire sociale," 38.
23. Agulhon, "L'histoire sociale," 38; Katherine Auspitz, *The Radical Bourgeoisie: The Ligue de l'enseignement and the Origins of the Third Republic, 1866–1885* (Cambridge, 1982), 5; Dorinda Outram, *Georges Cuvier: Vocation, Science and Authority in Post-Revolutionary France* (Manchester, 1984), 119.
24. Agulhon, "L'histoire sociale," 38; Chaline, *Sociabilité*, 72–73, Harrison, *Bourgeois Citizen*, 29.
25. Harrison, *Bourgeois Citizen*, quotation 3; Nord, *Republican Moment*, 11.
26. Unions were legalized in 1884 and mutual aid societies in 1898. The prefect was obliged to send a list of registered associations to the Ministry of Internal Affairs every year. Associations were obliged to notify the authorities within

three months about changes to their bylaws and administrative structure. Gifts to associations were illegal. See Agulhon, "L'histoire sociale," 40; Thompson, *France,* 167; *The Progress of Continental Law in the Nineteenth Century, by Various Authors* (Boston, 1918), quotation 97; A. R. H. Baker, "Sound and Fury: The Significance of Musical Societies in Loir-et-Cher during the Nineteenth Century," *Journal of Historical Geography* 12, no. 3 (July 1986): 249–267, especially 251; E. N. Anderson and P. R. Anderson, *Political Institutions,* 280; Steven M. Beaudoin, "'Without Belonging to Public Service': Charities, the State and Civil Society in Third Republic France, 1870–1914," *Journal of Social History* 31, no. 3 (Spring 1998): 671–699. Russian jurists followed these developments. A. I. Elistratov, *Ocherk gosudarstvennogo prava: Konstitutsionnoe pravo,* 2nd ed. (Moscow, 1905); *Materialy po peresmotru ustanovlennykh dlia okhrany gosudartsvennogo poriadka iskliuchitel'nykh zakonopolozhenii* (St. Petersburg, 1905), 9: 45–48.

27. Tocqueville, *Democracy in America,* 2: 321–322.
28. Ibid., 2: 109.
29. Ibid., 2: 114.
30. Tocqueville, *Ancien Régime,* 91.
31. Tocqueville, *Democracy in America,* 1: 340, 2: 123. This view was picked up by much postwar social science. Arnold Rose believed that voluntary associations were rare in France. See "Voluntary Associations in France," in Arnold Rose, *Theory and Method in the Social Sciences* (Minneapolis, 1954). Orvoell Gallagher claimed that "the French government historically repressed associations as representing possible subversive or revolutionary forces." Orvoell R. Gallagher, "Voluntary Associations in France," *Social Forces* 36 (December 1957): 153–160.
32. Tocqueville, *Democracy in America,* 2: 125.
33. Tocqueville, *Ancien Régime,* 132. See also Gordon, *Citizens without Sovereignty,* 29; E. N. Anderson and P. R. Anderson, *Political Institutions,* 277.
34. Agulhon, "L'histoire sociale," 38; Harrison, *Bourgeois Citizen,* 33; Huard, "Political Associations," 135. The need to balance the proscriptive centralizing tradition in France against the existence of many "intermediary bodies," that is, to distinguish between "representation and reality," is also the argument of Pierre Rosanvallon, *The Demands of Liberty: Civil Society in France since the Revolution,* trans. Arthur Goldhammer (Cambridge, Mass., 2007), 2–4, 186–187. This book appeared too late for me to integrate it into my own understanding of French political culture. For bringing it to my attention, I am grateful to my colleague Paul Rahe, whose own book will also shortly appear: *Soft Despotism, Democracy's Drift: Montesquieu, Rousseau, Tocqueville, and the Modern Prospect* (New Haven, 2009).
35. Harrison, *Bourgeois Citizen,* quotation, 48; Beaudoin, "'Without Belonging to Public Service,'" 673, 684, 689.
36. Agulhon, "Vers une histoire," 13; Agulhon, "L'histoire sociale," 37, 40–41; Harrison, *Bourgeois Citizen,* 34–35. A law of 10 June 1868 permitted public meetings (Auspitz, *Radical Bourgeoisie,* 6). Ninety percent of the associations formed between 1860 and 1914 in the provincial town of Roanne were founded after 1880, and fifty percent were founded after 1900 (Stefan

Ludwig Hoffmann, "Democracy and Associations in the Long Nineteenth Century: Toward a Transnational Perspective," *Journal of Modern History* 75, no. 2 [June 2003]: 269–299, especially 289). At the same time, this rapid growth is relative to earlier numbers in France; compared to Britain, a far smaller proportion of the population belonged to voluntary associations (Jose Harris, *Private Lives, Public Spirit: A Social History of Britain, 1870–1914* [Oxford, 1993], 220, citing a French study of the 1870s).

37. Daniel McMillan, "Energy, Willpower, and Harmony: On the Problematic Relationship between State and Civil Society in Nineteenth-century Germany," in Frank Trentmann, ed., *Paradoxes of Civil Society: New Perspectives on Modern German and British History* (New York, 2000), 177, 184, 188. See also Eckhart Hellmuth, ed., *The Transformation of Political Culture: England and Germany in the Late Eighteenth Century* (Oxford, 1990), 35; Georg G. Iggers, "The Political Theory of Voluntary Associations in Early Nineteenth-century German Liberal Thought," in D. B. Robertson, ed., *Voluntary Associations: A Study of Groups in Free Societies: Essays in Honor of James Luther Adams* (Richmond, Va., 1966), 141–158, especially 156; Isabel Hull, *Sexuality, State, and Civil Society in Germany, 1700–1815* (Ithaca, N.Y., 1996), 208. There is an extensive literature on German associations. See Thomas Nipperdey, "Verein als soziale Struktur in Deutschland im späten 18. und frühen 19. Jahrhundert," in Thomas Nipperdey, *Gesellschaft, Kultur, Theorie* (Göttingen, 1976), 174–205; Richard van Dülmen, *The Society of the Enlightenment: The Rise of the Middle Class and Enlightenment Culture in Germany,* trans. Anthony Williams (New York, 1992); Michael John, "Associational Life and the Development of Liberalism in Hanover, 1848–1866," in Konrad H. Jarusch and Larry Eugene Jones, eds., *In Search of a Liberal Germany* (New York, 1990), 161–186.
38. Goldstein, *Political Repression,* 47.
39. Quoted in Thomas Nipperdey, *Germany from Napoleon to Bismarck, 1800–1866,* trans. Daniel Noland (Princeton, N.J., 1996), 236. See also Alfons Hueber, "Das Vereinsrecht im Deutschland des 19. Jahrhunderts," in Otto Dann, ed., *Vereinswesen und bürgerliche Gesellschaft in Deutschland* (Munich, 1984), 115–132.
40. Nipperdey, *Germany,* 355. Samples of early German constitutions may be found in Edwin H. Zeydel, ed., *Constitutions of the German Empire and German States* (Wilmington, Del., 1974), 77, 197, 227, 347, 370, 432.
41. Eleanor L. Turk, "German Liberals and the Genesis of the German Association Law of 1908," in Konrad H. Jarusch and Larry Eugene Jones, eds., *In Search of a Liberal Germany* (New York, 1990), 237–260, especially 237–239. If a nonpolitical association did not discuss public issues, it could be established merely by notifying the local authorities. Closed meetings did not require prior permission. In contrast, a political association was obliged to register with the authorities; to submit bylaws, membership lists, and the agendas of meetings; to allow the local police to attend meetings and otherwise scrutinize its activities; and to exclude from membership women, minors, and students. E. N. Anderson and P. R. Anderson, *Political Institutions,* 278.

42. Part of the system of internal administration, the political police, according to Alex Hall, "extended the official arm of government into the homes and lives of nearly every citizen in the country." This included the practice of "requiring each person to register locally at the nearest police station and to complete essential formalities before moving to a different area." Such facts of German life, according to Hall, "seriously put in question the validity of the *Rechtsstaat* principle." Quoting the newspaper *Der Stukkateur* in 1907, Hall notes, "In Germany there exists not the rule of law, but the power of the police." Alex Hall, *Scandal, Sensation, and Social Democracy: The SPD Press and Wilhelmine Germany, 1890–1914* (Cambridge, 1977), 2, 89–93. See also Goldstein, *Political Repression,* 49; Marven Krug, "Reports of a Cop: Civil Liberties and Associational Life in Leipzig during the Second Empire," in James Retallack, ed., *Saxony in German History: Culture, Society and Politics, 1830–1933* (Ann Arbor, Mich., 2000), 217–286, especially 272, 276.
43. Robert Nemes, "Associations and Civil Society in Reform-Era Hungary," *Austrian History Yearbook* 32 (2001): 25–45; quotation, 31. Sweden had a similar law on assemblies in 1864. See E. N. Anderson and P. R. Anderson, *Political Institutions,* 280. See also "Obshchestva," *ES* 21: 607–628, especially 609.
44. New associations still had to provide the authorities with their bylaws and the names of officers, and all organizations had to give the authorities twenty-four hours' notice of meetings to discuss public affairs. All public meetings were to be conducted in German unless given exemption by the authorities. Police surveillance continued at public meetings, but the convener, not the police, would be responsible for closing the assembly for infractions of the rules. Heuber, "Das Vereinsrecht," quotation, 131; Turk, "German Liberals," 256; A. Hall, *Scandal,* 63; Krug, "Reports of a Cop," 277, 283; Nipperdey, *Germany,* 235–236.
45. E. N. Anderson and P. R. Anderson, *Political Institutions,* 281.
46. David Blackbourn, *The Long Nineteenth Century: A History of Germany, 1780–1918* (New York, 1998), 125. See also Theodore S. Hamerow, *The Social Foundations of German Unification, 1858–1871: Ideas and Institutions* (Princeton, N.J., 1969), 339–358.
47. Dülman, *The Society of the Enlightenment,* 99, 119, 126.
48. Hueber, "Das Vereinsrecht," 123.
49. Hull, *Sexuality, State, and Civil Society,* quotation, 221. See also Nipperdey, "Verein," 201; McNeely, "Intelligence Gazette," 151; John, "Associational Life," 161–186; Nipperdey, *Germany,* 235–236; Klaus Tenfelde, "Civil Society and the Middle Classes in Nineteenth-century Germany," in Bermeo and Nord, eds., *Civil Society before Democracy,* 93. A local study of Leipzig concluded that the majority of voluntary associations were "untouched by police interference" (quoted in Krug, "Reports of a Cop," 272).
50. Jacob, *Living the Enlightenment,* 47, 85, 161, 179.
51. Ibid., 15, 32, 180, 183–184, 216. Jacob is, in part, attempting to refute the idea of the undemocratic consequences of Enlightenment societies posited by August Cochin and Reinhart Koselleck. See Cochin cited in François Furet,

Interpreting the French Revolution, trans. Elborg Forster (New York, 1981), 28–29, 52–54, 164–204, and Reinhart Koselleck, *Critique and Crisis: The Enlightenment and the Pathogenesis of Modern Society* (Cambridge, Mass., 1988). The emancipatory impulse of associations is also discussed in Van Dülmen, *Society of the Enlightenment,* 130, 137; Vernon Lidtke, *The Alternative Culture: Socialist Labor in Imperial Germany* (New York, 1985), 16–17; Mary P. Ryan, "Civil Society as Democratic Practice: North American Cities during the Nineteenth Century," *Journal of Interdisciplinary History* 29, no. 4 (Spring 1999): 559–584, especially 571–572; Anne Frior Scott, *Natural Allies: Women's Associations in American History* (Urbana, Ill., 1992), 2–3, 120; Theda Skocpol, Marshall Ganz, and Ziad Munson, "A Nation of Organizers: The Institutional Origins of Civic Voluntarism in the United States," *American Political Science Review* 94, no. 3 (September, 2000): 527–546; and Jocelyn Elise Crowley and Theda Skocpol, "The Rush to Organize: Explaining Association Formation in the United States, 1860s–1920s," *American Journal of Political Science* 45, no. 4 (October, 2001): 813–829.

52. Cited phrase from Hull, *Sexuality, State, and Civil Society,* 207. See also Nipperdey, "Verein," 195–204; McNeely, "Intelligence Gazette," 151; John, "Associational Life," 161–162; Hoffmann, "Democracy and Associations," 281–283, 295.

53. John Gascoigne, *Joseph Banks and the English Enlightenment: Useful Knowledge and Polite Culture* (Cambridge, 1994), 31–32; Joel Mokyr, *The Gifts of Athena: Historical Origins of the Knowledge Economy* (Princeton, N.J., 2002), 1–4, 28–29; Larry R. Stewart, *The Rise of Public Science: Rhetoric, Technology and Natural Philosophy in Newtonian Britain, 1660–1750* (Cambridge, 1992), xxii, xxv; Mary Terrall, *The Man Who Flattened the Earth: Maupertuis and the Sciences in the Enlightenment* (Chicago, 2002), 365; Jacques Roger, "The Living World," in G. S. Rousseau and Roy Porter, eds., *The Ferment of Knowledge: Studies in the History of Eighteenth-century Science* (Cambridge, 1980), 255–283, especially 278; E. C. Spary, *Utopia's Garden: French Natural History from the Old Regime to the Revolution* (Chicago, 2000), 4.

54. Quoted passage from Terrall, *Man Who Flattened the Earth,* 13. My understanding of Enlightenment science has also been informed by G. S. Rousseau and Roy Porter, eds., *The Ferment of Knowledge;* Stewart, *Rise of Public Science;* Thomas Broman, "The Habermasian Public Sphere and 'Science in the Enlightenment,'" *History of Science* 36 (1998): 123–149; E. C. Spary, "The 'Nature' of the Enlightenment," in William Clark, Jan Golinski, and Simon Schaffer, eds., *The Sciences in Enlightened Europe* (Chicago, 1999), 272–304; Margaret C. Jacob, *Scientific Culture and the Making of the Industrial West* (New York, 1997), 9, 107–108, 127; and J. L. Heilbron, "Natural Philosophy and Science," in Alan Charles Kors, ed., *The Encyclopedia of the Enlightenment* (Oxford, 2003), 3: 134–142.

55. James E. McClelland III, *Science Reorganized: Scientific Societies in the Eighteenth Century* (New York, 1985), 1–3, 13; Terrall, *Man Who Flattened the Earth,* 28–29; Robert Fox and George Weisz, eds., *The Organization of*

Science and Technology in France, 1808–1914 (Cambridge, 1980), 281; Van Dülmen, *Society of the Enlightenment,* 127; William H. Brock, *Science for All: Studies in the History of Victorian Science and Education* (Aldershot, UK, 1996), 173–174, 188–190; Gascoigne, *Joseph Banks,* 2, 7, 34; Jan Golinski, *Making Natural Knowledge: Constructivism and the History of Science* (Cambridge, 1998), 61; David Blackbourn and Geoff Eley, *The Peculiarities of German History: Bourgeois Society and Politics in Nineteenth-century Germany* (New York, 1984), 148–149; and David Blackbourn, ed., *The German Bourgeoisie: Essays on the Social History of the German Middle Class from the Late Eighteenth to the Early Twentieth Century* (London, 1991), 1–12; Robert Fox, "Learning, Politics and Polite Culture in Provincial France: The Societies Savantes in the Nineteenth Century," *Historical Reflections/Reflexions Historiques* 7, no. 2–3 (1980): 554.

56. Mokyr, *Gifts of Athena,* cited passages 43, 56, 72, 102. See also A. E. Musson and Eric Robinson, *Science and Technology in the Industrial Revolution* (Toronto, 1969), 58–59, 101; Amanda Anderson, *The Powers of Distance: Cosmopolitanism and the Cultivation of Detachment* (Princeton, N.J., 2001), 4–6; McClelland, *Science Reorganized,* xxi, 193, 199, 298; Van Dülmen, *Society of the Enlightenment,* 1–2, 66–67; Arnold Thackray, "Natural Knowledge in Cultural Context: The Manchester Model," *The American Historical Review* 79 no. 3 (June 1974): 672–709; Harrison, *Bourgeois Citizen,* 86, 120; R. J. Morris, "Clubs, Societies and Associations," in F. M. L. Thompson, ed., *Cambridge Social History of Britain, 1750–1950* (Cambridge, 1990) 3: 395–443; and Peter Clark, *British Clubs and Societies, 1580–1800: The Origins of an Associational World* (Oxford, 2000): 271.

57. Cited passage in Paul Farber, *Finding Order in Nature: The Naturalist Tradition from Linneaus to E. O. Wilson* (Baltimore, 2000), 30; Van Dülmen, *Society of the Enlightenment,* 137.

58. Mokyr, *Gifts of Athena,* quotations, 56, 102; Jan Golinski, *Science as Public Culture: Chemistry and the Enlightenment in Britain, 1710–1820* (London, 1992), 58; Golinski, *Making Natural Knowledge,* 103, 109; Richard Yeo, *Defining Science: William Whewell, Natural Knowledge and Public Debate in Early Victorian Britain* (Cambridge, 1993), 36–38; Thackray, "Natural Knowledge," 693; Simon Schaffer, "Natural Philosophy and Public Spectacle in the Eighteenth Century," *History of Science* 21 (1983): 1–43; Stewart, *Rise of Public Science.*

59. Melton, *Rise of the Public,* 100, 197, 206. See also Musson and Robinson, *Science and Technology,* 58, 89, 126; Fox, "Learning, Politics and Polite Culture," 554; Lynn Merill, *The Romance of Victorian Natural History* (Oxford, 1989), 32, 47; Philippa Levine, *The Amateur and the Professional: Antiquarians, Historians and Archaeologists in Victorian England, 1838–1886* (Cambridge, 1986), 52; Susan A. Crane, *Collecting and Historical Consciousness in Early Nineteenth-century Germany* (Ithaca, N.Y., 2000), 91; Lissa Roberts, "Going Dutch: Situating Science in the Dutch Enlightenment,"

in Clark, Golinski, and Schaffer, eds. *The Sciences* 350–388, especially 364; Agulhon, "Vers une histoire," 16–17.

60. Jacob, *Scientific Culture,* 116.

61. Lorraine Daston, "Afterword: The Ethos of Enlightenment," in Clark, Golinski, and Schaffer, eds., *The Sciences,* 500. See also Goodman, *Republic of Letters,* 27; Baker, "Sound and Fury," 250; Roberts, "Going Dutch," 351. Tocqueville believed that "when an opinion is represented by a society, it necessarily assumes a more exact and explicit form. It numbers its partisans and engages them in its cause; they, on the other hand, become acquainted with one another and their zeal is increased by their numbers . . . Opinions are maintained with a warmth and energy that written language can never attain." *Democracy in America,* 1: 199.

62. "Public Somebodies" from Leonore Davidoff and Catherine Hall, *Family Fortunes: Men and Women of the English Middle Class, 1780–1850* (Chicago, 1987), 445. See also Harrison, *Bourgeois Citizen,* 66–69; Terrall, *Man Who Flattened the Earth,* 5, 361; Spary, *Utopia's Garden,* 221, 227, 236; Schaffer, "Natural Philosophy," 1–2; Stewart, *Rise of Public Science,* xxii–xxv, 101–104, 260; Broman, "The Habermasian Public Sphere and Science," especially 128, 137; Steven Shapin, "The Audience for Science in Eighteenth-century Edinburgh," *History of Science* 12 (1974): 95–121, especially 95, 99–100; Paul Wood, "Science, Universities and Public Space in Eighteenth-century Scotland," *History of Universities* 14 (1994): 99–135, especially 100, 108, 121.

63. Tony Bennett, "The Exhibitionary Complex," in Nicholas B. Dirks, Geoff Eley, and Sherry B. Ortner, eds., *Culture/Power/History: A Reader in Contemporary Social Theory* (Princeton, N.J., 1994), 123–154; quotation, 137. See also Gascoigne, *Joseph Banks,* 7; Outram, *Georges Cuvier,* 94, 109–110; R. J. Morris, ed., *Class, Power, and Social Structure in British Nineteenth-century Towns* (Leicester, 1986), 14; Alan Kidd and K. W. Roberts, eds., *City, Class and Culture: Studies of Social Policy and Cultural Production in Victorian Manchester* (Manchester, 1985), 2, 10, 15; Harrison, *Bourgeois Citizen,* 134, 136; Spary, *Utopia's Garden,* 8–9, 99, 191.

64. Van Dülmen, *Society of the Enlightenment,* quotation 1; Lawrence Goldman, "The Social Science Association, 1857–1886: A Context for Mid-Victorian Liberalism," *English Historical Review* 101, no. 398 (June 1986): 95–134, especially 96; Michael Harrison, "Art and Philanthropy: T. C. Horsfall and the Manchester Art Museum," in Kidd and Roberts, eds., *City, Class and Culture,* 120–147, especially 120; Kathleen D. McCarthy, *Noblesse Oblige: Charity and Cultural Philanthropy in Chicago, 1849–1929* (Chicago, 1982), ix; Carol E. Harrison, *Bourgeois Citizen,* 51, 56, 58, 63, 64, 69, 86; Blackbourn and Eley, *Peculiarities,* 188; Christine Eisenberg, "Working-class and Middle-class Associations: An Anglo-German Comparison, 1820–1870," in Jürgen Kocka and Allen Mitchell, eds., *Bourgeois Society in Nineteenth-century Europe* (Oxford, 1993), 151–178, especially 162; Peter Clark, *British Clubs,* 12.

65. The challenge comes from historians of culture. See Carol E. Harrison, *Bourgeois Citizen,* and Sarah Maza, *The Myth of the French Bourgeoisie: An Essay on the Social Imaginary, 1750–1850* (Cambridge, Mass., 2003). Many historians of class, however, claim that the pursuit of science prepared the bourgeoisie for more than mere participation in public life; science was an important means by which the bourgeoisie became the "hegemonic" class. See also R. J. Morris, "Voluntary Societies and British Urban Elites, 1780–1850: An Analysis," *Historical Journal* 26 (March 1983): 95–118; Davidoff and Hall, *Family Fortunes.*
66. Jürgen Kocka, "'Bürgertum' and Professions in the Nineteenth Century: Two Alternative Approaches," in M. Burrage and R. Torstendahl, eds., *Professions and the Theory in History: Rethinking the Study of Professions* (London, 1990): 62–74, quotation 65. See also Blackbourn, *German Bourgeoisie,* 9; Peter Paret, *Art as History: Episodes in the Cultural and Political History of Nineteenth-century Germany* (Princeton, N.J., 1988), 14–15; Fox and Weisz, *Organization,* 254; McClelland, *Science Reorganized,* xxiv; Van Dülmen, *Society of the Enlightenment,* 133; Chaline, *Sociabilité,* 137; Thackray, "Natural Knowledge," 690; Bernard Lightman, *Victorian Science in Context* (Chicago, 1997), 179, 313; Mary Ryan, *Cradle of the Middle Class: The Family in Oneida County, New York, 1790–1865* (Cambridge, 1981), 106, 129; R. J. Morris, "Middle Class Culture, 1700–1914," in D. Fraser, ed., *A History of Modern Leeds* (Manchester, 1980), 200.
67. George W. Stocking Jr., *Victorian Anthropology* (New York, 1987), quotation 186. See also Blackbourn and Eley, *Peculiarities,* 148–149; Michael E. Rose, "Culture, Philanthropy and the Manchester Middle Classes," in Kidd and Roberts, eds., *City, Class and Culture,* 106; Blackbourn, *German Bourgeoisie,* 11–12; Michael Harrison, "Art and Philanthropy," 120.
68. Geoff Eley, "Rethinking the Political: Social History and Political Culture in Eighteenth- and Nineteenth-century Britain," *Archiv für Sozialgeschichte* 21 (1981): 431; Craig Calhoun, ed., *Habermas and the Public Sphere* (Cambridge, Mass., 1992), 7–9; Chartier, *Cultural Origins,* 17, 21, 27, 30; Nipperdey, *Germany,* 235; Goodman, *Republic of Letters,* 2, 5; Trentmann, *Paradoxes,* 3.
69. Gordon, *Citizens without Sovereignty*, 38.
70. Quoted in Margaret C. Jacob, *The Cultural Meaning of the Scientific Revolution* (Philadelphia, 1988), 203.
71. Levine, *Amateur,* 52; Janet R. Horne, *A Social Laboratory for Modern France: The Musée Social and the Rise of the Welfare State* (Durham, N.C., 2002), 106, 291; Lissa Roberts, "Going Dutch," 382–384; James C. Scott, *Seeing Like a State: How Certain Schemes to Improve the Human Condition Have Failed* (New Haven, Conn., 1998). On science, industry, and education, see Charles R. Day, *Education for an Industrial World: The Écoles d'Arts et Métiers and the Rise of French Industrial Engineering* (Cambridge, Mass., 1987); Daniel R. Hedrick, *When Information Came of Age: Technologies of Knowledge in the Age of Reason and Revolution, 1750–1850* (Oxford, 2000).

72. I borrow the phrase "learned assemblies" from McClelland, *Science Reorganized,* 10; Hamerow, *The Social Foundations of German Unification,* quotations, 339, 356, 358. See also Nipperdey, *Germany,* 440.
73. Klaus Tenfelde, "Civil Society and the Middle Classes," 87, 93.
74. Horne, *Social Laboratory,* 105.
75. Sarah A. Curtis, *Educating the Faithful: Religion, Schooling and Society in Nineteenth-century France* (DeKalb, Ill., 2000), 147. I am grateful to Christine Haynes for calling this book to my attention.
76. Quoted in Chaline, *Sociabilité,* 205. See also Frederick Artz, *The Development of Technical Education in France, 1500–1850* (Cambridge, Mass., 1966), 188; Fox and Weisz, *Organization,* 241, 263; and Day, *Education for the Industrial World,* 2.
77. Cited passages in Auspitz, *Radical Bourgeoisie,* 61, 66, 70–71. On anticlericalism, see also Sanford Elwitt, *The Third Republic Defended: Bourgeois Reform in France, 1880–1914* (Baton Rouge, 1986), 235; on Duruy, see Sandra Horvath-Peterson, *Victor Duruy and French Education: Liberal Reform in the Second Empire* (Baton Rouge, 1984), 113.
78. Crane, *Collecting and Historical Consciousness,* 90–91; Peter Clark, *British Clubs,* 434, 488.
79. Clark, *British Clubs,* 434.
80. The basic rights governing the public sphere are spelled out in Habermas, *Structural Transformation,* 83. In addition to civil liberties, these include personal freedom, inviolability of domicile, equality before the law, property rights, and the right of petition. Habermas acknowledges that a *robust* civil society "can develop only in the context of a liberal political culture and the corresponding patterns of socialization" (*Between Facts and Norms,* 371; emphasis added). Habermas's critics also argue that even in the "strong public sphere" polities of North America and western Europe, access to the public sphere is not uniform for all groups. For example, see the essays by Nancy Fraser and Geoff Eley in Calhoun, ed., *Habermas and the Public Sphere.*
81. Michael Sonenscher, "The Enlightenment and Revolution," *Journal of Modern History* 70 (June, 1998): 371–383, quotation 378; Hull, *Sexuality, State and Civil Society,* quotation, 207.
82. Cited passages from Jacob, *Living the Enlightenment,* 219; Jacob, *Scientific Culture,* 9, 107–108, 127; and Joyce Appleby, Lynn Hunt and Margaret C. Jacob, *Telling the Truth about History* (New York, 1994), 27, 29. See also Thackray, "Natural Knowledge," 686.
83. Margaret C. Jacob, "Science Studies after Social Construction: The Turn toward the Comparative and the Global," in Victoria E. Bonnell and Lynn Hunt, eds., *Beyond the Cultural Turn: New Directions in the Study of Society and Culture* (Berkeley, Calif., 1999), 95–120, especially 101, 105, 113. See also Frank M. Turner, "Public Science in Britain, 1880–1919," in Frank M. Turner, *Contesting Cultural Authority: Essays in Victorian Intellectual Life* (Cambridge, 1993), 211; Lightman, ed., *Victorian Science in Context,* 5; Ian Inkster and Jack Morrell, *Metropolis and Province: Science in British Culture, 1780–1850* (London, 1983), 18, 39, 158.

84. Jacob, *Living the Enlightenment,* quotation 33; Ulrich M. Hof, "German Associations and Politics in the Second Half of the Eighteenth Century," in Eckhart Hellmuth, ed., *The Transformation of Political Culture: England and Germany in the Late Eighteenth Century* (Oxford, 1990), 210–211.
85. Gordon, "Philosophy, Sociology and Gender in Enlightenment Conceptions of Public Opinion," 902; Gordon, *Citizens without Sovereignty,* 38.

2. The Application of Science

1. Marc Raeff, *The Origins of the Russian Intelligentsia: The Eighteenth-century Nobility* (New York, 1966), 155–157; Raeff, *Understanding Imperial Russia: State and Society in the Old Regime,* trans. Arthur Goldhammer (New York, 1984), 199, 229, 234–235, 245.
2. Johann Ignaz von Felbiger, "On the Responsibilities of Man and Citizen," cited in J. L. Black, *Citizens for the Fatherland: Education, Educators and Pedagogical Ideals in Eighteenth-century Russia* (Boulder, Colo., 1979), 243–244. Felbiger was an Augustinian abbot in Prussian Silesia. His teaching methods were adopted in Austria in 1774. *The Duties of Man and Citizen (O dolzhnostiakh cheloveka i grazhdanina)* became a textbook in schools founded by Catherine; between 1783 and 1796, forty-three thousand copies were published in six printings. See also Isabel de Madariaga, *Russia in the Age of Catherine the Great* (New Haven, Conn., 1981) 495–497; Gary Marker, *Publishing, Printing, and the Origins of Intellectual Life in Russia, 1700–1800* (Princeton, N.J., 1985), 193; S. A. Kozlov, *Agrarnye traditsii i novatsii v dorevoliutsionnoi Rossii: Tsentral'nye nechernozemnye gubernii* (Moscow, 2002), 327–329.
3. Madariaga, *Russia in the Age,* 89. See also Robert E. Jones, *Provincial Development in Russia: Catherine II and Jakob Sievers* (New Brunswick, N.J., 1984), 10–12.
4. K. A. Papmehl, *Freedom of Expression in Eighteenth-century Russia* (The Hague, 1971), 54–55, 72. The local instructions from the deputies to the commission were silent on the principles of freedom of expression, let alone on those of any other civil liberty.
5. Marker, *Publishing,* 67, 85, 122; Papmehl, *Freedom of Expression,* 8, 16, 27, 38, 92, 121. The Academy of Sciences, founded in 1724, along with Moscow University, founded in 1755, enjoyed an important privilege: they acted as their own censors. See also Charles A. Ruud, *Fighting Words: Imperial Censorship and the Russian Press, 1804–1906* (Toronto, 1982), 17, 29.
6. Madariaga, *Russia in the Age,* 537, 540. See also Marker, *Publishing,* 103–134.
7. Felbiger, "On the Responsibilities," 235.
8. Richard van Dülmen, *The Society of the Enlightenment: The Rise of the Middle Class and Enlightenment Culture in Germany,* trans. Anthony Williams (New York, 1992), 20, 24.

9. Raeff, *Understanding Imperial Russia,* 110, 141; Black, *Citizens for the Fatherland,* 122; Papmehl, *Freedom of Expression,* 79.
10. Douglas Smith, *Working the Rough Stone: Freemasonry and Society in Eighteenth-century Russia* (DeKalb, Ill., 1999), quotation 15. See also Raeff, *Origins of the Russian Intelligentsia,* 161–166; Madariaga, *Russia in the Age,* 521–531.
11. The Free Russian Association at Moscow University (1771–1783) studied and perfected the Russian language; its members included Catherine's friend Princess Ekaterina Dashkova, the German-born historian Gerhard Frederick Miller, the writer and publisher N. I. Novikov, the historian Prince M. M. Shcherbatov, and the writers A. P. Sumarokov, D. I. Fonvizin, and G. P. Derzhavin. The Free Society of Friends of Literature, Science, and the Arts, founded in St. Petersburg in 1801 and in existence until 1825, also promoted learning and correct exposition. It published compositions such as "On Monarchy," "On the Separation of Powers of the Political Body," "On Love of the Fatherland," "On Pride," as well as a composition on *The Spirit of the Laws.* See Raeff, *Understanding Imperial Russia,* 134–137; I. P. Kulakova, "Universitetskoe prostranstvo (Moskva i Moskovskii universitet v XVIII v.)," *Na rubezhe vekov* 3 (1997): 55–68; Irina I. Komarova, comp., *Putevoditel' po nauchnym obshchestvam Rossii* (New York, 2000), 62; RGIA, f. 733 [Ministry of Education], op. 18, d. 43, l. 5 ["Doklad o deiatel'nosti Vol'nogo obshchestva slovesnosti, nauk i khudozhestv"]; Smith, *Working the Rough Stone,* 16, 24, 78–86; Alexander M. Martin, *Romantics, Reformers, Reactionaries: Russian Conservative Thought and Politics in the Reign of Alexander I* (DeKalb, Ill., 1997), 10–11, 20.
12. Adele Lindenmeyr, *Poverty Is Not a Vice: Charity, Society, and the State in Imperial Russia* (Princeton, N.J., 1996), 99–115; quotations, 101, 111.
13. M. Aronson calls the salons and circles a "birzha literaturnogo potrebleniia." See M. Aronson and S. Reiser, *Literaturnye kruzhki i salony* (Leningrad, 1929), 21. See also Raeff, *Understanding Imperial Russia,* 133–139; A. N. Pypin, *Obshchestvennoe dvizhenie v Rossii pri Aleksandre I,* 2nd ed. (St. Petersburg, 1885), 363, 384, 438, 450, 459; Raeff, *Origins of the Russian Intelligentsia,* 159–165; Papmehl, *Freedom of Expression,* 80–82.
14. Cited passages in Cynthia H. Whittaker, *The Origins of Modern Russian Education: An Intellectual Biography of Count Sergei Uvarov, 1786–1855* (DeKalb, Ill., 1984), 100; and Alexander Vucinich, *Science in Russian Culture: A History to 1860* (Stanford, 1963): 295. Gotthelf Fischer von Waldheim, a zoology professor who came to Moscow University from Germany in 1804, was one of the founders of the Moscow Society of Naturalists in 1805. (L. I. Kursanov and V. A. Deinega, "Moskovskoe obshchestvo ispytatelei prirody," *Uchenye zapiski Moskovskogo gosudarstvennogo universiteta, Iubileinaia seriia 14: Biologiia* (Moscow, 1940), 353–362, especially 353; RGIA, f. 733, op. 18, d. 6, l. 25 ["Ob uchrezhdenii Moskovskgo obshchestva ispytatelei prirody"].) See also W. Bruce Lincoln, *Petr Petrovich Semonov-Tian-Shanski: The Life of a Russian Geographer* (Newtonville, Ma., 1980): 11.

15. David Wartenweiler, *Civil Society and Academic Debate in Russia, 1905–1914* (Oxford, 1999), 13.
16. Jean-Pierre Chaline, *Sociabilité et Érudition: Les sociétés savants en France, XIXe–XXe siècles* (Paris, 1995), 40.
17. Nikolai Anufriev, "Pravitel'stvennaia reglamentatsiia obrazovaniia chastnykh obshchestv v Rossii," in A. I. Elistratov, ed., *Voprosy administrativnogo prava* (Moscow, 1916), 15–44, especially 17. See also Raeff, *Understanding Imperial Russia,* 141.
18. *PSZ,* 21 (1782), no. 15379. In revised form, the Ustav blagochiniia became the "Ustav o preduprezhdenii i presechenii prestuplenii" in vol. 14 of the Code of Laws. See also Anufriev, "Pravitel'stvennaia reglamentatsiia," 17–18; I. E. Andreevskii, *Politseiskoe pravo* (St. Petersburg, 1874), 1: 234–235; V. F. Deriuzhinskii, *Politseiskoe pravo* (St. Petersburg, 1903), 86; A. I. Elistratov, *Ocherki administrativnogo prava* (Moscow, 1922), 154; Ts. A. Iampol'skaia and A. M. Shchiglik, *Voprosy teorii i istorii obshchestvennykh organizatsii* (Moscow, 1971), 180; and A. D. Stepanskii, *Samoderzhavie i obshchestvennye organizatsii Rossii na rubezhe XIX–XX vv.* (Moscow, 1980), 4–5. A discussion of other articles of the Police Code may be found in John P. LeDonne, *Ruling Russia: Politics and Administration in the Age of Absolutism, 1762–1796* (Princeton, N.J., 1984), 96–97, 109–110, 113–114.
19. Novikov's Friendly Learned Society, organized in 1782, was shut down four years later amid the government crackdown against his publishing and educational ventures. The Society of Friends of Russian Learning, organized in 1789 by Ivan Ivanovich Melissino, the curator of Moscow University and founder of the newspaper *Moskovskie vedomosti,* published to spread learning and science and to combat Freemasonry, was closed after two meetings, a casualty of government fear of the revolution breaking out in France. The Free Society of Friends of Russian Literature, founded in 1816, two years later named itself the Learned Republic (*Uchenaia respublika,* evoking the European "republic of letters") and was led by an elected president, the officer and writer F. N. Glinka. Among its members were well-known writers and future Decembrists: A. A. and N. A. Bestuzhev, A. S. Griboedov, A. A. Del'vig, V. K. Kiukhel'beker, and K. F. Ryleev. See A. V. Svetlov, "Obshchestvo liubitelei Rossiiskoi uchenosti pri Moskovskom universitete," *Istoricheskii arkhiv* (Leningrad, 1950), 5: 300–323; V. Bazanov, *Uchenaia respublika* (Moscow, 1964), 139–142, 159; Komarova, *Putevoditel',* 61, 84, 335; Papmehl, *Freedom of Expression,* 137.
20. Raeff, *Understanding Imperial Russia,* 142.
21. RGIA, f. 733, op. 91, d. 108, l. 1; Anufriev, "Pravitel'stvennaia reglamentatsiia," 17, 20; Andreevskii, *Politseiskoe pravo,* 228–229; "Shishkov, A.S.," *RBS,* 23: 316–320. This action against the learned societies anticipated the better-known "iron" censorship regulations drafted by Shishkov in 1826. On the crackdown at the universities in the latter part of the reign of Alexander I, see Vucinich, *Science in Russian Culture,* 1: 233–238, 259–260; James T. Flynn, *The University Reform of Tsar Alexander I, 1802–1835* (Washington,

D.C., 1988), 84–112, 161–171; and Whittaker, *Origins of Modern Russian Education,* 74–76.

22. Raeff, *Understanding Imperial Russia,* 142; Martin, *Romantics, Reformers, Reactionaries,* 113–120, 199.
23. Henry Lowood, *Patriotism, Profit and the Promotion of Science in the German Enlightenment: The Economic and Scientific Societies, 1760–1815* (New York, 1991), 132.
24. Kenneth Hudson, *Patriotism with Profit: British Agricultural Societies in the Eighteenth and Nineteenth Centuries* (London, 1972), xi, 3, 15; Jan Golinski, *Science as Public Culture: Chemistry and Enlightenment in Britain, 1760–1820* (Cambridge, 1992), 56; Steven Shapin, "The Audience for Science in Eighteenth-century Edinburgh," *History of Science* 12 (1974): 95–121; Sir E. John Russell, *A History of Agricultural Science in Great Britain, 1620–1954* (London, 1966), 55–65, 110–136.
25. Charles Coulston Gillispie, *Science and Polity in France at the End of the Old Regime* (Princeton, N.J., 1980), quotation 369; C. B. A. Behrens, *Society, Government and the Enlightenment: The Experiences of Eighteenth-century France and Prussia* (New York, 1985), 139.
26. Marion W. Gray, *Productive Men, Reproductive Women: The Agrarian Household and the Emergence of Separate Spheres during the German Enlightenment* (New York, 2000), 175–180; quotations, 175. See also Lowood, *Patriotism,* 9, 54, 56, 95.
27. Edgar Melton, "Enlightened Seigniorialism and Its Dilemmas in Serf Russia, 1750–1830," *Journal of Modern History* 62 (December 1990): 675–708, quotations 679, 707; and Paul Dukes, *Catherine the Great and the Russian Nobility: A Study Based on the Materials of the Legislative Commission of 1767* (Cambridge, 1967), 216. See also Steven L. Hoch, *Serfdom and Social Control in Russia: Petrovskoe, a Village in Tambov* (Chicago, 1986), 8–9, 187; David Ransel, *The Politics of Catherinian Russia: The Panin Party* (New Haven, Conn., 1975), 281; Michael Confino, *Domaines et séigneurs en Russie vers la fin du XVIIIe siècle: Étude de structures agraires et de mentalités économiques* (Paris, 1963), 19–25; S. V. Pakhman, *O znachenii i postepennom uchrezhdenii sel'skikh obshchestv v Rossii* (Kazan', 1855), 13. The Russian historian Sergei A. Kozlov has broken ranks with most of his Soviet predecessors, who either ignored the improving landlords or minimized their significance, and claims that the Russian nobility did not become alienated from estate management. See Kozlov, *Agrarnye traditsii,* 8, 35, 160, 342.
28. Robert E. Jones, *The Emancipation of the Russian Nobility* (Princeton, N.J., 1973), 137. In addition to the celebrated Nakaz, Catherine encouraged a scheme, or what might be called the "Baltic model," for the gradual emancipation of the serfs by leasing estates whenever they changed hands, in order to restrict the landlord's rights over peasant labor. The importance of a "Baltic connection" will be noted later in this chapter. See Madariaga, *Russia in the Age,* 61–64, 133, 142.

29. On Lomonosov's contribution, see V. V. Oreshkin, *Vol'noe ekonomicheskoe obshchestvo v Rossii, 1765–1915: Istoriko-ekonomicheskii ocherk* (Moscow, 1963), 14–17.
30. Sievers's letter, along with other documents pertaining to the founding of the agricultural society, were printed in the first volume of *Trudy Imperatorskogo Vol'nogo ekonomicheskogo obshchestva* (1765) and reprinted in *Ustavy Imperatorskogo Vol'nogo ekonomicheskogo obshchestva i Vysochaishie reskripty, emu dannye, 1765–1898* (St. Petersburg, 1899), 4 (hereafter *Ustavy IVEO*). On Sievers, see Jones, *Provincial Development,* 44–56. See also *RBS,* 18: 407–412; A. I. Khodnev, *Istoriia Imperatorskogo Vol'nogo ekonomicheskogo obshchestva s 1765 do 1865 goda* (St. Petersburg, 1865), 1–2; Roger P. Bartlett, "J. J. Sievers and the Russian Peasantry under Catherine II," *Jahrbücher für Geschichte Österuropas* 32, no. 1 (1984), 16–33; Madariaga, *Russia in the Age,* 133, 142. A. P. Berdyshev counters the claims of Soviet historian S. M. Novikov that Catherine was not too pleased with the idea of a private association but did not want to forbid it because of the presumed effect that decision would have on European public opinion. In Berdyshev's view, Catherine herself first had the idea of an association. See A. P. Berdyshev, *Andrei Timofeevich Bolotov: Vydaiushchiisia deiatel' nauk i kul'tury, 1738–1833* (Moscow, 1988), 14; James Arthur Prescott, "The Russian Free Economic Society: Foundation Years," *Agricultural History* 5, no. 3 (July 1977): 503–512.
31. "Vsepoddanneishee predstavlenie Gosudaryne Imperatritse Ekaterine II pri koem podnesseny plan i pervonachal'nyi ustav Obshchestva," in *Ustavy IVEO,* 4; Pakhman, *O znachenii,* 30. On the importance of personal patronage network in autocratic politics, see Ransel, *Politics,* 1.
32. *Ustavy IVEO,* 11–18; Khodnev, *Istoriia,* 1–8; Papmehl, *Freedom of Expression,* 44. Taubert was a pioneer in the compilation of Russian population statistics. See *RBS,* 20: 366–372. Masons also used the beehive as a symbol of industriousness. See Margaret C. Jacob, *Living the Enlightenment: Freemasonry and Politics in Eighteenth-century Europe* (New York, 1991), 167. On beekeeping as an attractive branch of agriculture in the eighteenth century, see Lowood, *Patriotism,* 172.
33. Joel Mokyr, *The Gifts of Athena: Historical Origins of the Knowledge Economy* (Princeton, N.J., 2002), 43, 288.
34. Pakhman, *O znachenii,* quotations, 11. By 1850 its endowment was a half million rubles, the most of any Russian voluntary association.
35. Quoted in Khodnev, *Istoriia,* 11. The bylaws were published in the complete collection of Russian laws, *PSZ,* 27 (1765), no. 12502; *PSZ,* 2nd ser., 34 (1859), no. 34192; *PSZ,* 47 (1872), no. 51195; in many separate editions, such as *Ustavy IVEO,* 18–24; and in the first volume of the society's *Trudy*. The following discussion in the text is based on nineteenth-century charters. I have used the collection *Ustavy IVEO* and *Proekty Ustava Imperatorskogo Vol'nogo Ekonomicheskogo Obshchestva* (St. Petersburg, 1913), which compare the 1872 bylaws and two drafts of revised bylaws, as well as *K istorii Vol'nogo Ekonomicheskogo Obshchestva* (St. Petersburg, 1907), doc. no. 180.

36. Cited passage in *Ustavy IVEO*, 4. See also Khodnev, *Istoriia*, 618; Pakhman, *O znachenii*, 30. The election was a two-step process: preliminary balloting was followed by a runoff of the top three candidates. In later years these features of the charter were frequently noted in the liberal press. See, for example, a series of reports in the "Iz obshchestvennoi khroniki" sections of *Vestnik Evropy*, in no. 5 (1896): 434–436; no. 6 (1896): 861–863; no. 6 (1897): 875–876; and no. 10: 846–848.
37. *Ustavy IVEO*, 18–24.
38. Hudson, *Patriotism with Profit*, quotations, 398; Arnold Thackray, "Natural Knowledge in Cultural Context: The Manchester Model," *American Historical Review* 79, no. 3 (June 1974): 672–709, especially 683; Peter Clark, *British Clubs and Societies, 1580–1800: The Origins of an Associational World* (Oxford, 2000), 271.
39. Cited passages in Chaline, *Sociabilité*, 70–71, 137; Golinski, *Science as Public Culture*, 14; Frederick Artz, *The Development of Technical Education in France, 1500–1850* (Cambridge, Mass., 1966), 79.
40. Cited passages in Clark, *British Clubs*, 438; Hudson, *Patriotism with Profit*, 18, 46, 101; Philippa Levine, *The Amateur and the Professional: Antiquarians, Historians and Archaeologists in Victorian England, 1838–1886* (Cambridge, 1986), 51, 64. See also Michael J. Cullen, *The Statistical Movement in Early Victorian Britain: The Foundations of Empirical Social Research* (New York, 1975), 89, 115–116.
41. Cited passages in Chaline, *Sociabilité*, 30–31, 69, 165; Gillispie, *Science and Polity in France*, 370. See also Robert Fox, *The Culture of Science in France, 1700–1900* (Brookfield, Vt., 1992), 2, 11.
42. Lowood, *Patriotism*, 140.
43. Cited passage in Khodnev, *Istoriia*, 641. See also *RBS*, 22: 318–324; *RBS*, 13: 466–467; *RBS*, 11: 68–70; *RBS*, 10: 185; *RBS*, 8: 741; *RBS*, 6: 119–130; *RBS*, 21: 18; A. P. Berdyshev, *150 let sluzheniia Otechestvu: Iz istorii Vol'nogo ekonomicheskogo obshchestva* (Moscow, 1992–1993), 1: 13, 18–19; *Tri veka Sankt-Peterburga: Entsiklopediia* (St. Petersburg, 2001), 1: 17–18. On the "Baltic Enlightenment," see Lisbet Koerner, "Daedalus Hyperboreus: Baltic Natural History and Mineralogy in the Enlightenment," in William Clark, Jan Golinski, and Simon Schaffer, eds., *The Sciences in Enlightened Europe* (Chicago, 1999), 389–414, quotation, 405. In the early years, minutes were kept in German; papers and published articles were also often written in German and translated into Russian. Khodnev (*Istoriia*, 3) suggests that Lehmann, along with Taubert and Nartov, may have composed the plan for the organization of the society. For more on Lehmann, see Nathan Marc Brooks, "The Formation of a Community of Chemists in Russia: 1700–1870" (Ph.D. diss., Columbia University, 1989), 70–78. On the Masons, see A. I. Serkov, *Russkoe masonstvo, 1731–2000: Entsiklopedicheskii slovar'* (Moscow, 2001), 200, 575, 611, 744, 875.
44. *Ustavy IVEO*, 46. As early as 1766 one of the society's charter members, T. I. Klingstedt, described the achievements of English scientific farming in the *Transactions*. Arthur Young and the chemist Iu. Liebich (Justus von Liebig)

were two of the most famous honorary members. Women were admitted as full members in 1824 on the basis of owning property. Kozlov, *Agrarnye traditsii,* 214–215; Berdyshev, *150 let,* 1: 28–29, 43; Joan Klobe Pratt, "The Russian Free Economic Society, 1765–1915" (Ph.D. diss., University of Missouri, 1983), 24–25. On membership categories in French societies, see Chaline, *Sociabilité,* 76–81.

45. Cited in Khodnev, *Istoriia,* 630. See also Berdyshev, *150 let,* 1: 30.
46. In the first issue of *Trudy,* quoted in A. N. Neustroev, *Bibliograficheskoe opisanie pervykh LIV chastei Trudov Imperatorskogo Vol'nogo ekonomicheskogo obshchestva* (St. Petersburg, 1874), 107.
47. Reports suggest that the great magnates had a poor attendance record at meetings. At the same time, headquartered in distant St. Petersburg, the organization seemed remote to the rank-and-file provincial nobility. Alexander Herzen's uncle provides one example of such sociability. Up to age seventy-five, he "was present at all the great balls and dinners, took part in every ceremonial assembly and annual function, whether it was of an agricultural or medical or fire insurance society or of the Society of Natural Philosophy . . . and, on the top of it all, perhaps because of it, preserved to old age some degree of human feeling and a certain warmth of heart" (*My Past and Thoughts: The Memoir of Alexander Herzen,* abridged by Dwight MacDonald [New York, 1974], 18).
48. Jurij [Iurii] Lotman, "The Decembrist in Everyday Life," in Jurij M. Lotman and B. A. Uspenskij, *The Semiotics of Russian Culture,* ed. Ann Shukman (Ann Arbor, Mich, 1984), 71–124; quotation, 101.
49. Prince Peter Oldenburgskii, a prominent educator and administrator, especially in the area of women's education, was president from 1841 to 1859; Grand Prince Nikolai Konstantinovich was honorary president in 1862; and Grand Duchess Elena Pavlovna, a catalyst in gathering reforming bureaucrats, became an honorary member in 1860. Senior government officials—including E. P. Kovalevskii (minister of education and Free Economic Society president from 1861 to 1865), A. M. Kniazhevich (minister of finance, 1858–1862 and, in his youth, a founder in 1822 of *Biblioteka dlia Chteniia,* a magazine of translated fiction), and A. A. Zelenoi (minister of state properties)—continued to play important roles. *RBS,* 9: 5–10; 12: 251–257; E. D. Kuskova, "Rol' Imperatorskogo Vol'nogo ekonomicheskogo obshchestva v obshchestvennoi zhizni za poslednie 25 let," *Vestnik sel'skogo khoziaistva,* no. 51–52 (1915): 14; *BSDET,* 1: 53.
50. RGIA, f. 560 [Ministry of Finance], op. 22, d. 232, l. 84 ["Po voprosu o peresmotre ustava VEO"].
51. Kozlov, *Agrarnye traditsii,* 215. See also Khodnev, *Istoriia,* 14–15, 37, 87–94.
52. A. T. Bolotov, *Zhizn' i prikliucheniia, 1738–1795* (Moscow, 1931) 2: 318; quoted in Dukes, *Catherine the Great,* 99–100. Several of Bolotov's treatises on agriculture were published in the society's *Trudy* and won gold and silver medals. Bolotov was also a member of the Leipzig Economic Society.

Bolotov's *Ekonomicheskii magazin* was a "compendium of sundry economic news, experiments, discoveries, applications, manuals, notes, and advice." That is to say, it pursued the same agenda as the Free Economic Society. Cited passage in *RBS,* 3:183. See also *Liudi russkoi nauki: Biologiia, meditsina, sel'skoe khoziaistvo* (Moscow, 1963): 681–690.

53. *PSZ,* 2nd ser., 20 (1845), no. 18864; Khodnev, *Istoriia,* 360–363; A. D. Stepanskii, "Materialy legal'nykh obshchestvennykh organizatsii tsarskoi Rossii," *Arkheograficheskii ezhegodnik za 1978 g.* (Moscow, 1979), 69–80; V. Ia. Grosul, *Russkoe obshchestvo XVIII–XIX vekov: Traditsii i novatsii* (Moscow, 2003), 252. After 1866 Russia's agricultural societies were placed in the domain of the Ministry of State Properties. Kozlov, *Agraryne traditsii,* 169; *Pakhman, O znachenii,* 51; B. V. Tikhonov, "Obzor *Zapisok mestnykh sel'skokhoziaistvennykh obshchestv 30–50kh godov XIX v.,*" *Problemy istochnikovedeniia* (Moscow, 1961), 92–162, especially 98, 118. In 1845 the Free Economic Society absorbed the separate Forestry Society, founded in St. Petersburg in 1832.

54. Cited passage in Stepan Maslov, comp., *Istoricheskoe obozrenie deistvii i trudov Imperatorskogo Moskovskogo obshchestva sel'skogo khoziaistva* (Moscow, 1850), 2. See also Khodnev, *Istoriia,* 361.

55. Cited passage in Pakhman, *O znachenii,* 44. See also "O uchrezhdennom v Moskve Obshchestva sel'skogo khoziaistva," *PSZ,* 36 (1819), no. 27623. The judgment of Golitsyn is Alexander Herzen's (*My Past and Thoughts,* 97). Golitsyn, a Mason, was also a member of the Moscow Society of Naturalists and an honorary member of the Society of Russian History and Antiquities and founder of many Moscow charitable institutions. On Golitsyn, see *RBS,* 5A: 164–167; Serkov, *Russkoe masonstvo,* 253; "Vospominaniia o kniaze D. V. Golitsyne," *Niva,* no. 13 (1894): 1–2; Reginald Zelnik, *Labor and Society in Tsarist Russia: The Factory Workers of St. Petersburg, 1855–1870* (Stanford, Calif., 1971), 31–32. Maslov, *Istoricheskoe obozrenie,* appendix, 139. Prince Gagarin, another Mason, was also a member of the Moscow Society of Naturalists and on the board of women's educational institutions in Moscow. See *RBS,* 4: 92–93; Serkov, *Russkoe masonstvo,* 214.

56. Kozlov, *Agrarnye traditsii,* 52. On the crackdown within the universities in the latter part of the reign of Alexander I, see note 21 above.

57. Kozlov, *Agrarnye traditsii,* quotation, 346; also 149, 256–257, 269, 344; A. P. Perepelkin, comp., *Istoricheskaia zapiska o tridtsatiletnei deiatel'nosti Imperatorskogo Moskovskogo obshchestva sel'skogo khoziaistva* (Moscow, 1890), 45–50; Maslov, *Istoricheskoe obozrenie,* 1–8, 25; L. G. Golovanova, *Moskovskoe obshchestvo sel'skogo khoziaistva, 1818–1861: Ocherki iz istorii russkoi obshchestvenno-agronomicheskoi mysli i sel'skogo khoziaistva v I-oi polovine XIX v.,* Avtoreferat kandidatskoi dissertatsii (Moscow, 1953), 7; S. A. Kozlov, "175 let Moskovskomu obshchestvu sel'skogo khoziaistva: Traditsii i novatsii," in *Nauchnye trudy Mezhduvedomstvennogo soiuza ekonomistov i Vol'nogo ekonomicheskogo obshchestva Rossii* (St. Peters-

burg, 1996), 3: 232–240; Berdyshev, *Andrei Timofeevich Bolotov,* 242; N. S. Trusova and O. A. Bliumfel'd, "Iz istorii vozniknoveniia i nachal'noi deiatel'nosti Moskovskogo obshchestva sel'skogo khoziaistva, 1820–1830 gg.," Akademiia nauk SSSR, *Materialy po istorii sel'skogo khoziaistva i krest'ianstva SSSR* (Moscow, 1959), 3: 280–324, especially 281; *RBS,* 3: 486–488; *RBS,* 10: 447–448; *RBS,* 11: 95; *RBS,* 13: 92–97; *RBS,* 17: 436–439; *RBS,* 18: 146–147; *RBS,* 22: 376–381; Whittaker, *Origins of Modern Russian Education,* 101.

58. Maslov, *Istoricheskoe obozrenie,* 12–13 and appendix, 6; Perepelkin, *Istoricheskaia zapiska,* 20. The bylaws were originally published in *Zemledel'cheskii zhurnal,* no. 1 (1821).
59. "Otnoshenie G. Ministra vnutrennikh del O. Kozodavleva k Prezidentu Obshchestva Kniaziu D. V. Golitsynu," quoted in Maslov, *Istoricheskoe obozrenie,* 3–4; appendix, 15–16; Pakhman, *O znachenii,* 47.
60. Cited passage in Maslov, *Istoricheskoe obozrenie,* appendix, 22. In addition to dues, members were obliged to contribute to occasional collections as needed *(po proizvolu).* From 29 charter members in 1818, the society grew to 150 active and honorary members, including 16 foreigners, in 1821 and to 244 active members (of whom 129 resided in Moscow and 115 in the provinces), 38 honorary members, 9 corresponding members, and 41 foreigners in 1823. Provincial governors and marshals of the nobility became active members, elected in absentia *(zaochnoe izbranie).* See also Kozlov, *Agrarnye traditsii,* 345, 353–354.
61. Maslov, *Istoricheskoe obozrenie,* 3.
62. Ibid., 14, 123 129, 131; appendix, 132, 137.
63. Quoted in Kozlov, *Agrarnye traditsii,* 367. On Preobrazhenskii, see *BSDET,* 2: 148. The "motor" metaphor recalls the French societies' "locomotives."
64. Cited in Perepelkin, *Istoricheskaia zapiska,* 22, and also quoted in Kozlov, *Agrarnye traditsii,* 345.
65. Mokyr, *Gifts of Athena,* 56. Of the Royal Society, it was observed that "much of [members'] time was taken up with local affairs, but there were also discussions of new methods and ideas which helped to break down resistance to innovation always to be found in the countryside" (Russell, *History of Agricultural Science,* 55).
66. Chaline, *Sociabilité,* quotations, 162, 167, 184. See also Shapin, "Audience for Science," 101–102.
67. Thackray, "Natural Knowledge," 683; P. Clark, *British Clubs,* 271; Hudson, *Patriotism with Profit,* 5–7, 10, 13, 31, 33; Artz, *Development of Technical Education,* 79–81; Marvin Becker, *The Emergence of Civil Society in the Eighteenth Century: A Privileged Moment in the History of England, Scotland and France* (Bloomington, Ind., 1994), 5; Gray, *Productive Men,* 131; Lowood, *Patriotism,* 103.
68. Chaline, *Sociabilité,* 162–163. Mokyr considered the Royal Society of the Arts, founded in London in 1754, to be the "classic example of an access-cost reducing institution," for it awarded prizes for the "best inventors

and for the best agricultural innovations and useful knowledge" (*Gifts of Athena,* 44–45).

69. P. Clark, *British Clubs,* 437–440.
70. Arthur Young quoted in Behrens, *Society, Government and the Enlightenment,* 139. See also Chaline, *Sociabilité,* 167; Lowood, *Patriotism,* 132–140, 163, 169; Gillispie, *Science and Polity in France,* 369, 387.
71. Quoted in Neustroev, *Bibliograficheskoe opisanie,* 527. The overall activities of the society may be culled from many different accounts: Khodnev, *Istoriia;* A. N. Beketov, *Istoricheskii ocherk dvadtsatipiatiletnei deiatel'nosti Imperatorskogo Vol'nogo Ekonomicheskogo Obshchestva s 1865 do 1890g.* (St. Petersburg, 1890); N. G. Kuliabko-Koretskii, "Kratkii istoricheskii ocherk deiatel'nosti I. V. E. Obshchestva so vremeni ego osnovaniia, preimushchestvenno v dele sobiraniia i razrabotki statisticheskikh svedenii o Rossii i rasprostraneniia znanii v naselenii," *Trudy VEO,* no. 3 (1897): 395–412; Oreshkin, *Vol'noe ekonomicheskoe obshchestvo;* and Pratt, "Russian Free Economic Society."
72. Khodnev, *Istoriia,* 95, 130–148. For more than a half a century, the *Transactions* were Russia's only agricultural journal, except for Bolotov's short-lived *Sel'skii zhitel'* (1778–1779) and his *Ekonomicheskii magazin,* which N. I. Novikov published as a supplement to *Moskovskie vedomosti* from 1780 to 1789. The *Transactions* were also published in German as *Mitteilungen der Freien Oekonomischen Gesellschaft.* Later, the *Transactions* also published materials of agricultural societies that did not have their own publications. See also Berdyshev, *150 let,* 1: 80, 85, 118; Tikhonov, Obzor *Zapisok,* 139; Kozlov, *Agrarnye traditsii,* 266, 291, 324; Pratt, "Russian Free Economic Society," 46; Confino, *Domaines,* 233.
73. Although 1,200 copies of the *Transactions* were printed in 1765 and 2,400 in 1766, sales soon dropped off; in a vast empire, distribution outside St. Petersburg was a perennial problem. From 1821 to 1841, the *Transactions* were published irregularly, and only 600 copies were printed when regular publication resumed. However, by 1850 an advertising campaign got 6,000 new subscribers. From the 1760s to 1850, typically 1,000 copies of scientific treatises were published, a number that would seem to exceed that of the corresponding French agricultural societies. Khodnev, *Istoriia,* 97–98, 103–105, 141–148.
74. Khodnev, *Istoriia,* 97–98; Berdyshev, *150 let,* 1: 46–51. In 1778 a Kursk merchant donated three hundred rubles so that the society could acquire foreign seeds. In 1844 the society opened a seed station that ordered seeds from regular suppliers.
75. The charter was silent about government censorship. See V. I. Semevskii, *Krest'ianskii vopros v Rossii v XVIII i pervoi polovine XIX veka* (St. Petersburg, 1888), 1: 410; Papmehl, *Freedom of Expression,* 44, 67.
76. Khodnev, *Istoriia,* 367. Discussion of the essay competitions can be found in Semevskii, *Krest'ianskii vopros,* 1: xi, 309–339; Confino, *Domaines,* 202–203, 232–234, 237–251; Jones, *Emancipation,* 137–138; p. 183, n. 77;

A. I. Khodnev, *Krakdii obzor stoletnei deiatel'nosti Imperatorskogo Vol'nogo ekonomicheskogo obshchestva s 1765 do 1856 goda* (St. Petersburg, 1865); V. V. Oreshkin, "Trudy Vol'nogo ekonomicheskogo obshchestva: Zarozhdenie kapitalizma," in *Nauchnye trudy Mezhdunarodnogo soiuza ekonomistov i Vol'nogo ekonomicheskogo obshchestva Rossii* vol. 2 (St. Petersburg, 1995): 150–167; and Roger Bartlett, "'I.E.' and the Free Economic Society's Essay Competition of 1766 on Peasant Property," British Study Group on Eighteenth-century Russia, *Newsletter,* no. 8 (1980): 58–67.

77. The opinion is that of V. I. Semevskii, the nineteenth-century authority on the peasant question and member of the society. The essays were published during the first few years of the publication of the *Trudy*. The most complete analysis of the essays is in Semevskii, *Krest'ianskii vopros,* 1: 45–94; quotation, 57). An anonymous essay attributed to Voltaire argued that while peasant freedom and landownership were desirable, this was a matter that had to be left up to the landlords. An anonymous essay (possibly written by Aleksandr Radishchev) connected property rights to the origins of Lockean civil society and to the individual's desire to be a useful member of society. Grigorii Korob'in, deputy of the nobility from the Kozlov district, went so far as to argue that peasants should receive property rights. Other essays included an eloquent Lockean defense of property rights by the French physiocrat Graslin. An essay recommending peasant landownership by the Russian Aleksei Ia. Polenov was not published until ninety-seven years later. See also Khodnev, *Istoriia,* 23–35; Oreshkin, *Vol'noe ekonomicheskoe obshchestvo,* 73–77; Dukes, *Catherine the Great,* 93–94.

78. *Trudy VEO* 8 (1768): 1–59; Khodnev, *Istoriia,* 40–41; Confino, *Domaines,* 237; Popov, "Dvorianskii liberalizm," 141–143; Pratt, "Russian Free Economic Society," 32–36; Madariaga, *Russia in the Age,* 136.

79. Quoted in Semevskii, *Krest'ianskii vopros,* 1: 414, 417; also quoted in N. Popov, "Dvorianskii liberalizm pervoi chetverti XIX v.: Agrarno-krest'ianskii vopros v Vol'nom ekonomicheskom obshchestve," *Voprosy grazhdanskoi istorii* (Leningrad, 1935), 1: 154.

80. Khodnev, *Istoriia,* 235, 413–414, 449–450, 454. Khodnev also claims that there was considerable discussion of free versus serf labor. See also Oreshkin, "Trudy," 161–166.

81. Quoted in Kozlov, *Agrarnye traditsii,* 261.

82. Cited passages from Khodnev, *Istoriia,* 26–30, and Semevskii, *Krest'ianskii vopros,* xi, where later essay competitions are also discussed in 1: 309–339. See also Khodnev, *Istoriia,* 403–404, 447–448; Oreshkin, *Vol'noe ekonomicheskoe obshchestvo,* 59–63; Confino, *Domaines,* 202–203, 232–234, 237–251; Berdyshev, *150 let* 1: 56, 59. (What was good for scientific objectivity may become a liability for the historian: many unsigned manuscripts.)

83. Quoted in Papmehl, *Freedom of Expression,* 52.

84. *Ustavy IVEO,* 61; Khodnev, *Istoriia,* 7–12, 37–38, 76; Lowood, *Patriotism,* 122; Confino, *Domaines,* 38; Pratt, "Russian Free Economic Society," 36–44; Berdyshev, *150 let,* 1: 116.

85. Cited passage in Pakhman, *O znachenii*, 41; Khodnev, *Istoriia*, 413–414; E. I. Indova, "Voprosy zemledeliia v *Trudakh Vol'nogo ekonomicheskogo obshchestva* vo vtoroi polovine XVIII veka," in *Ezhegodnik po agrarnoi istorii vostochnoi Evropy 1970 g.* (Riga, 1977), 122–123.
86. A. T. Bolotov, *Zhizn' i prikliucheniia*, 2: 318; quoted in Dukes, *Catherine the Great*, 99–100. See also Confino, *Domaines*, 38; Pratt, "Russian Free Economic Society," 36–44; *Khodnev, Kratkii obzor*, 7–12.
87. Berdyshev, *Bolotov*, 116; Kozlov, *Agrarnye traditsii*, 15, 139, 262.
88. Pakhman, *O znachenii*, 4–5, 33. The original charter was amended in 1770 and 1815, and a new charter, approved by Alexander I in 1824, broadened the scope of the society's activities. See *Ustavy IVEO*, 25–37 (the 1770 charter), 38–40 (the 1815 amendments), and 41–58 (the 1824 charter). See also Khodnev, *Istoriia*, 618.
89. Khodnev, *Istoriia*, 30–35; B. B. Veselovskii, *Istoriia zemstva za sorok let* (St. Petersburg, 1909), 405; Joan Kolbe Pratt, "The Free Economic Society and the Battle against Smallpox: A 'Public Sphere' in Action," *Russian Review* 61, no. 4 (October, 2002): 560–578; Pratt, "Russian Free Economic Society," 77–79; the "bridge" metaphor from Mokyr, 35.
90. Khodnev, *Istoriia*, 258; Pratt, "Russian Free Economic Society," 24, 68–74; Walter Pintner, *Russian Economic Policy under Nicholas I* (Ithaca, N.Y., 1967), 115–116; *RBS*, 19: 477–480.
91. Khodnev, *Istoriia*, 278–296, 468, 471, 476; Kozlov, *Agrarnye traditsii*, 149, 169; Berdyshev, *150 let*, 1: 66–67, 116; Shilov, 483–489. On N. S. Mordvinov's contributions to political economy, see Susan P. McCaffray, "Capital, Industriousness, and Private Banks in the Economic Imagination of a Nineteenth-century Statesman," in Susan P. McCaffray and Michael Melancon, eds., *Russia in the European Context 1789–1914: A Member of the Family* (New York, 2005), 33–48. On his contributions to provincial libraries, see Susan J. Smith-Peter, "Provincial Public Libraries and the Law in Nicholas I's Russia," *Library History* 21 (July 2005): 103–119.
92. Khodnev, *Istoriia*, 491–494, 499, 503; Berdyshev, *150 let*, 1: 69–72.
93. Khodnev, *Istoriia*, 290–296; Berdyshev, *150 let*, 1: 10, 73–77, 117. The society's efforts at collection and display are given extensive treatment in I. P. Ivanitskii, "Sel'skokhoziaistvennye muzei v krepostnoi Rossii, 1765–1861 gg.," in *Ocherki istorii muzeinogo dela v Rossii* (Moscow, 1960), no. 2: 3–65.
94. Moskovskii Muzei prikladnykh znanii, *Zasedaniia Komiteta muzeia za 1877–82* (*Izvestiia OLEAE* 36 no. 3 [Moscow, 1883]: 29); Khodnev, *Istoriia*, 231, 291–293, 478–484. Among the items in the society's collection was gold from California in 1848. Each province had a local committee, chaired by the governor, to collect items for display. A total of 3,516 articles were exhibited. On agricultural exhibitions in Germany, see Lowood, *Patriotism*, 261, 269, 275.
95. Mikhailo Puzanov, "O sel'skokhoziastvennykh vystavakh v Rossii, kak o mogushchestvennom rychage obshchenarodnogo preuspeianiia," *Trudy* VEO 3, no. 4 (1864): 243–275, especially 243, 274–275. See also N. Zarubin,

"Neskol'ko slov o sel'skokhoziaistvennoi vystavke, ustroiennoi Vol'nym Ekonomicheskim Obshchestvom, po sluchaiu ego stoletnego iubileia," *Trudy VEO* 4 (1865): 326–336, 397–410, 460–473. The society often issued travel grants to members traveling to foreign exhibitions. For example, V. I. Mochul'skii reported on the New York World's Fair in 1853, and Khodnev reported on the Great Exhibition in London in 1862 and on the South Kensington Museum (Khodnev, *Istoriia,* 92). The organizers of British agricultural exhibitions and shows believed that such methods of popularization were the only way to reach the illiterate and conservative farmers. Yet it was not until the advent of the railway network that this became possible beyond a single locality (Hudson, *Patriotism with Profit,* 48, 55).

96. Khodnev, *Istoriia,* 263, 278–280; Berdyshev, *150 let,* 1: 69.
97. Pakhman, *O znachenii,* 3–4.
98. Cited in Maslov, *Istoricheskoe obozrenie,* 34; appendix, 134, and in Kozlov, *Agrarnye traditsii,* 51. The number of subscriptions grew from four hundred in its first year to eight hundred in 1823. There were frequent title changes. From 1841 to 1850 it was the *Journal of Agriculture and Sheep Breeding* [*Zhurnal sel'skogo khoziaistva i ovtsevodstva*], and from 1851 to 1859 it was again the *Journal of Agriculture* [*Zhurnal sel'skogo khoziaistva*]. For the next three years it was simply *Agriculture* [*Sel'skoe khoziaistvo*], and then from 1862 to 1869 it became the *Journal of the Moscow Agricultural Society* [*Zhurnal Moskovskogo obshchestva sel'skogo khoziaistva*]. For the next seven years it was *Russian Agriculture* [*Russkoe sel'skoe khoziaistvo*]. Finally, in 1877 it became the *Transactions of the Moscow Agricultural Society* [*Trudy Moskovskogo obshchestva sel'skogo khoziaistva*], a title that it retained until 1917. It also published as supplements the *Notes of the Silk Farming Committee* [*Zapiski komiteta shelkovodstva*], the *Notes of the Forestry Committee* [*Zapiski komiteta lesovodstva*], and the *Notes of the Committee of Sugar Beet Farming* [*Zapiski komiteta sakharovarov*] from 1834 to 1840. See Berdyshev, *150 let,* 1: 81; Tikhonov, "Obzor *Zapisok,*" 96. Kozlov discusses censorship (*Agrarnye traditsii,* 51–53, 176, 354).
99. Chaianov quoted in Kozlov, *Agrarnye traditsii,* 235. For more on Maslov, see *RBS,* 10A: 114–117; Serkov, *Russkoe masonstvo,* 527–528.
100. S. A. Maslov, "Donesenie o poezdke nepremennogo sekretaria obshchestva na VI s"ezd germanskikh khoziaev," *Zhurnal sel'skogo khoziaistva i ovtsevodstva,* no. 9 (1842): 217; Maslov, *Istoricheskoe obozrenie,* 54, 96–98; appendix, 122; Perepelkin, *Istoricheskaia zapiska,* 126; Kozlov, *Agrarnye traditsii,* 17, 201, 209, 270, 472, 508. In his introduction to the Russian translation of Thaer, N. S. Mordvinov, perhaps a century ahead of his time, posed the question, "How should we regard agriculture in Russia?" Mordvinov continued, "In my view, as a factory that produces grain instead of cloth and other articles. Consequently, agriculture is subject to the same laws as those that govern other forms of industry." Tikhonov, "Obzor *Zapisok,*" 92. On Thaer, see *BSDET,* 2:286.
101. Quoted in Maslov, *Istoricheskoe obozrenie,* appendix, 123, 134. See also Neustroev, *Bibliograficheskoe opisanie,* 104–105; Berdyshev, *150 let,* 1: 118.

102. Ben Eklof, *Russian Peasant Schools: Officialdom, Village Culture, and Popular Pedagogy, 1861–1914* (Berkeley, Calif., 1986), 19–37.
103. [S. A. Maslov], *O vsenarodnom rasprostranenii gramotnosti v Rossii na religiozno-nravstvennom osnovanii* (Moscow, 1848), 1: 1–13. (Maslov's tract was published in one volume in 1845, in two volumes in 1845–1846, and in four volumes in 1848–1849). On Prokopovich, see *RBS,* 15: 35–37.
104. [Maslov], *O vsenarodnom rasprostranenii gramotnosti* 1:19. The testimonials and endorsements are scattered throughout the volumes. Maslov wrote, "The education appropriate to every class of the working population is that which is allied with industriousness and with the rules taught by religion, the observance of which make them a habit." In addition to his tireless work on behalf of the Moscow Agricultural Society, Maslov found time to be a member of foreign agricultural societies in Baden, Vienna, Sweden, Hungary, Saxony, Lyon, and Holland. On Maslov, see *RBS,* 10A: 114–117. On "family values" under Nicholas I, see Richard S. Wortman, *Scenarios of Power: Myth and Ceremony in Russian Monarchy* (Princeton, N.J., 1995), 1: 334–342.
105. Maslov, *Istoricheskoe obozrenie,* 29–31; appendix, 30, 76; *RBS,* 13: 92–97; Kozlov, *Agrarnye traditsii,* 150; *Liudi russkoi nauki: Biologiia, meditsina, sel'skoe khoziaistvo,* 691–697; V. V. Kondrat'ev, "Dokumenty o deiatel'nosti Moskovskogo obshchestva sel'skogo khoziaistva v 1861–94 gg.," *Sovetskie arkhivy,* no. 1 (1982): 48–51. Over the years, more and more pupils came from the lower urban clerical and commercial classes. During the years 1822–1859, 1,200 pupils attended the school; during the years 1827 to 1860, 730 completed the course of study (Golovanova, *Moskovskoe obshchestva sel'skogo khoziaistva,* 12–13; Trusova and Bliumfel'd, "Iz istorii vozniknoveniia," 289–291, 305–311).
106. Khodnev, *Istoriia,* 260, 656; Kozlov, *Agrarnye traditsii,* 151–152; Berdyshev, *150 let,* 1: 109; *RBS* 19: 477–480. In 1837 the Free Economic Society placed a bust of Stroganova in its meeting room; she was one of only two women to be so honored, the other being Catherine the Great. Pratt notes that graduates of the agricultural school did not become estate administrators as intended by the society, but instead became civil servants, although it must be pointed out that Russia's schools were notorious for graduates who did not return to their milieu of origin upon graduation.
107. Maslov, *Istoricheskoe obozrenie,* 123; Berdyshev, *150 let,* 1: 111–112.
108. Cited passage in [Maslov], *O vsenarodnom rasprostranenii gramotnosti,* 1: 85. See also S. S. Lashkarev, "O pol'ze vvedeniia gramotnosti mezhdu pomeshchich'imi krest'ianami," in [Maslov], *O vsenarodnom rasprostranenii gramotnosti,* 3: 234–243.
109. Maslov, *Istoricheskoe obozrenie,* 132–133.
110. [Maslov], *O vsenarodnom rasprostranenii gramotnosti,* quotations 4:87. Maslov, *Istoricheskoe obozrenie,* 105, 128, 183, 262. Although Maslov did not cite specific titles, it is quite likely that one he had in mind was Konstantin Grum, *Rukovodstvo k vospitaniiu, obrazovaniiu i sokhraneniiu zdorov'ia detei,* which had just been published in St. Petersburg. See also Susan Smith-Peter, "Books behind the Altar: Religion, Village Libraries, and the Moscow

Agricultural Society," *Russian History/Histoire Russe* 31, no. 3 (Fall 2004): 213–233.

111. James Van Horn Melton, *The Rise of the Public in Enlightenment Europe* (Cambridge, 2001), 98.
112. Moskovskoe obshchestvo sel'skogo khoziaistvo, *Kratkii obzor piatidesiatiletnei deiatel'nosti, 1820–1870* (Moscow, 1871), 53. On Parfenii, see *RBS,* 3: 330.
113. [Maslov], *O vsenarodnom rasprostranenii gramotnosti,* quotation 1: 36; also 1: 38, 60, 194; 4: 11, 27.
114. Berdyshev, *150 let,* 1: 93, 96.
115. Maslov, *Istoricheskoe obozrenie,* 9, 20, 30–31, 51, 65–67, 76–78; quotation, appendix, 127–129. See also Kozlov, *Agrarnye traditsii,* 348; Golovanova, *Moskovskoe obshchestvo sel'skogo khoziaistva,* 14; Trusova and Bliumfel'd, "Iz istorii vozniknoveniia," 311–323; *Liudi russkoi nauki: Biologiia, meditsina, sel'skoe khoziaistvo,* 691–697.
116. Maslov, *Istoricheskoe obozrenie,* 13, 44, 65–67, 80; appendix, 58, 143; Trusova and Bliumfel'd, "Iz istorii vozniknoveniia," 297–305; Kozlov, *Agrarnye traditsii,* 348. In 1833 a division of the Moscow Agricultural Society became the Horticultural Society.
117. Quoted in Maslov, *Istoricheskoe obozrenie,* appendix, 124, 131–132, 135, 137. President S. I. Gagarin used the same words in an address to the society in February 1845.
118. Confino, for example, claims that the society was never able to expand and diversify its activities beyond publication (*Domaines,* 28–34, 176–177). Few provincial landlords read the society's *Transactions,* and many copies were unsold each year. It is worthy of noting, however, that the Society for the Translation of Foreign Books, established at Catherine's initiative in 1768, was left with unsold books; it ceased to exist after the establishment of the Russian Academy in 1783. Russian copies of Diderot's *Encyclopedia* were also left unsold. The problem went beyond the scope of the Free Economic Society or any other learned society (Jones, *Emancipation,* 25–26). Regarding serfdom, Hoch observes, "If agricultural improvement were given any consideration at all, it was clearly secondary to labor management" (Hoch, *Serfdom and Social Control,* 8–9, 187). Even had they considered improvement desirable, most estate owners lacked the capital necessary to invest in improvements or declined to use capital for such purposes.
119. D. V. Golitsyn quoted in Maslov, *Istoricheskoe obozrenie,* appendix, 112. See also E. Melton, "Enlightened Seignorialism," 707; Kozlov, *Agrarnye traditsii,* 169, 381, 385; Pintner, *Russian Economic Policy,* 115–116. Almost a century after the founding of the Free Economic Society, A. Zabelin wrote in the *Agriculture Journal,* "Our whole society, including the landowners, is so unaccustomed to independence and shows such apathy toward public affairs that in every public matter, even those that directly concern their own class [*soslovnye*] interests, all lean on the government" (quoted in Kozlov, *Agrarnye traditsii,* 302).
120. Pratt, "Russian Free Economic Society," 196.

121. In an account of his travels around Tver', Vladimir, Iaroslavl', and Nizhnii Novgorod provinces in 1842, the improving landlord, writer, and traveler D. P. Shelekov wrote, "Here there is the bustle of labor and industry; the people here are homogeneous, intelligent, God-fearing, active, energetic, and enterprising . . . The whole region is imbued with the elements of citizenship which, however, are still in the state of a seed or an embryo" (quoted in Kozlov, *Agrarnye traditsii,* 11; see also 162, 342, 351, 389).
122. Kozlov, "175 let," 239; Kozlov, *Agrarnye traditsii,* 13–14. Golovanova credits the society with undermining the principles of *barshchina* farming: "It concentrated all progressive agronomy and agricultural practice and unified and guided the activity of the innovating landowners" (*Moskovskoe obshchestvo sel'skogo khoziaistva,* 7).
123. Lotman, "Decembrist," 144.
124. Mokyr, *Gifts of Athena,* 102. Mokyr identifies several methods of science particularly important in this context: regular observation, careful classification, "meticulously compiled agricultural data," and "the diffusion and cataloguing of techniques leading eventually to the adoption of the best practice techniques" (5, 35, 37.)
125. Berdyshev, *150 let,* 1: 10. See also Oreshkin, "Trudy," 150–167.
126. Quoted in Margaret Jacob, *Scientific Culture and the Making of the Industrial West* (New York, 1997), 179.
127. Khodnev, *Istoriia,* 11, 36–37. However, during the second half of the nineteenth century, the sense of pride in "a boundless fatherland" was tempered by a sense that Russia in fact did not have everything.
128. Khodnev, *Istoriia,* 36–37. According to the charter, members had the right to publish their work in foreign languages, so that foreigners, too, could become better acquainted with Russia. (Khodnev, *Istoriia,* 130.)
129. For more on the Moscow Agricultural Society and the study of national identity, see Kozlov, *Agrarnye traditsii,* 303.
130. Anufriev, "Pravitel'stvennaia reglementatsiia," 18; Kozlov, *Agrarnye traditsii,* 260, 303, 331.
131. Mokyr, *Gifts of Athena,* 37.
132. Raeff, *Understanding Imperial Russia,* 99.
133. Maslov, *Istoricheskoe obozrenie,* appendix, 112.

3. The Quest for National Identity

1. Cited passages from Peter Paret, *Art as History: Episodes in Culture and Politics of Nineteenth-century Germany* (Princeton, N.J., 1988), 51; Susan A. Crane, *Collecting and Historical Consciousness in Early Nineteenth-century Germany* (Ithaca, N.Y., 2000), 6; and Roy Porter, "The Terraqueous Globe," in G. S. Rousseau and Roy Porter, eds., *The Ferment of Knowledge: Studies in the Historiography of Eighteenth-century Science* (Cambridge, 1980), 285–324; quotation, 323. I have also been informed by Philippa Levine, *The Amateur and the Professional: Antiquarians, Historians and Archaeologists in Victorian England, 1838–1886* (Cambridge, 1986), 40;

James Clifford, "Objects and Selves—An Afterword," in George W. Stocking Jr., ed., *Objects and Others: Essays on Museums and Material Culture* (Madison, Wisc., 1985), 3: 237; Colin A. Russell, *Science and Social Change in Britain and Europe, 1700–1900* (New York, 1983), 81; George W. Stocking, *Victorian Anthropology* (New York, 1987), 47, 53–55, 71, 243; James Clifford, *The Predicament of Culture: Twentieth-century Ethnography, Literature and Art* (Cambridge, 1988), 215–251; Bruce G. Trigger, *A History of Archaeological Thought* (Cambridge, 1989), 162–163; Celia Applegate, "Localism and the German Bourgeoisie: the 'Heimat' Movement in the Rhenish Palatinate before 1914," in David Blackbourn and Richard Evans, eds., *The German Bourgeoisie: Essays on the Social History of the German Middle Class from the Late Eighteenth Century to the Early Twentieth Century* (New York, 1992), 224–254; and H. Glenn Penny and Matti Bunzl, eds., *Worldly Provincialism: German Anthropology in the Age of Empire* (Ann Arbor, Mich., 2003), 1–2.

2. Cited passages in John Gascoigne, *Joseph Banks and the English Enlightenment: Useful Knowledge and Polite Culture* (Cambridge, 1994), 9, 110; and Joan Evans, *A History of the Society of Antiquaries* (Oxford, 1956), vi. See also E. C. Spary, *Utopia's Garden: French Natural History from the Old Regime to the Revolution* (Chicago, 2000), 22; Steven Conn, *Museums and American Intellectual Life, 1876–1926* (Chicago, 1998), 34, 96–97; Trigger, *History,* 15, 85.
3. Levine, *Amateur and Professional,* 69; Mill cited in Peter J. Bowler, *The Invention of Progress: The Victorians and the Past* (Oxford, 1989), 2. This is also the argument of C. Dellheim, *The Face of the Past: Preservations of the Medieval Inheritance in Victorian England* (Cambridge, 1982), 13, 45–49, 54–58, 64–65, 71. See also Benedict Anderson, *Imagined Communities: Reflections on the Origins and Spread of Nationalism,* rev. ed. (London, 1991), 292.
4. Lynn L. Merrill, *The Romance of Victorian Natural History* (New York, 1989), 47. See also Robert Fox, "Learning, Politics and Polite Culture in Provincial France: The Sociétés Savantes in the Nineteenth Century," *Historical Reflections/Réflexions Historiques* 7, no. 2–3 (1980): 554; Levine, *Amateur and Professional,* 52; Crane, *Collecting,* 91; J. N. Hays, "The London Lecturing Empire, 1800–1850," in Ian Inskter and Jack Morrell, eds., *Metropolis and Province: Science in British Culture, 1780–1850* (London, 1983), 91–119, especially 93; Marston Bates, *The Nature of Natural History* (Princeton, N.J., 1950; repr., 1990), 254; Daniel J. Sherman, *Worthy Monuments: Art Museums and the Politics of Culture in Nineteenth-century France* (Cambridge, Mass., 1989), 241; Stocking, *Victorian Anthropology,* 62–63, 266–268; Dellheim, *Face of the Past,* 45–49; Catherine A. Lutz and Jane L. Collins, *Reading the National Geographic* (Chicago, 1993), 20; Sally Gregory Kohlstedt, *The Formation of the American Scientific Community: The American Association for the Advancement of Science, 1848–1860* (Urbana, Ill., 1976), 7, 26, 29, 35, 42.

5. E. C. Spary, "The 'Nature' of the Enlightenment," in William Clark, Jan Golinski, and Simon Schaffer, eds., *The Sciences in Enlightened Europe* (Chicago, 1999), 272–304; quotation, 294. The notion of science as "performance," often "manly performance," is pervasive in the literature. See, for example, Carol E. Harrison, *The Bourgeois Citizen in Nineteenth-century France: Gender, Sociability and the Uses of Emulation* (Oxford, 1999), 68; Jan Golinski, *Making Natural Knowledge: Constructivism and the History of Science* (Cambridge, 1998), 66; and Simon Schaffer, "Natural Philosophy and Public Spectacle in the Eighteenth Century," *History of Science* 21 (1983), 1. On collecting as gendered practice, see Leora Auslander, "The Gendering of Consumer Practices in Nineteenth-century France," in Victoria De Grazia and Ellen Furlough, eds., *The Sex of Things: Gender and Consumption in Historical Perspective* (Berkeley, Calif., 1996), 85–87. I am grateful to Chris Ruane for pointing out this source.
6. Joel Mokyr, *The Gifts of Athena: Historical Origins of the Knowledge Economy* (Princeton, N.J., 2002), 5, 30; Henry Lowood, *Patriotism, Profit and the Promotion of Science in the German Enlightenment: The Economic and Scientific Societies, 1760–1815* (New York, 1991), 223, 229; Crane, *Collecting,* 15, 43, 63–64; Curtis Hinsley, *Savages and Scientists: The Smithsonian Institution and the Development of American Anthropology, 1846–1910* (Washington, D.C., 1981), 20, 39; Kohlstedt, *Formation,* 59.
7. Levine, *Amateur and Professional,* 40; Jean-Pierre Chaline, *Sociabilité et Érudition: Les sociétés savants en France, XIXe–XXe siècles* (Paris, 1995), 10, 175–176; Brent Edwin Maner, "The Search for a Buried Nation: Prehistorical Archaeology in Central Europe, 1750 to 1945" (Ph.D. diss., University of Illinois, 2001), 89–91, 181, 199.
8. Spary, "'Nature' of the Enlightenment," quotation 289; Porter, "Terraqueous Globe," 301–302; Merrill, *Romance,* 54–56; Trigger, *History,* 27, 45, 49, 61, 66.
9. Crane, *Collecting,* 43. In addition, the Carlsbad decrees censored publications. Prince Metternich revealed the thin ice on which German associations skated: "The awakening of the historical spirit might seem very desirable; but Austria, committed to the established order, must ask, to what end is history to be used? In a time which turns everything to poison, history offers weapons against the established order as well as for it" (quoted in Crane, *Collecting,* 91). See also Maner, "Search for a Buried Nation," 9, 89–91.
10. Hans Rogger sees evidence of this "discovery of the folk" in the eighteenth century. However, the interest on the part of individual explorers, geographers, naturalists, writers, and editors did not receive sustained institutional expression. See Hans Rogger, *National Consciousness in Eighteenth-century Russia* (Cambridge, Mass., 1960), especially chap. 4.
11. *RBS,* 8: 391–394; *RBS,* 17: 493–521; D. N. Shilov, 639–643; *ES Biografiia,* 3: 493–494; 5: 24–25; *Slavianovedenie v dorevoliutsionnoi Rossii: Bibliograficheskii slovar'* (Moscow, 1979), 295; V. P. Kozlov, "Rumiantsevskii kruzhok," *Voprosy istorii,* no. 7 (1981): 178–183; V. P. Kozlov, "Kruzhok li-

ubitelei otechestvennoi istorii," *Voprosy istorii,* no. 6 (1987): 184–190; A. N. Pypin, "Zametka (Shchukinskii muzei v Moskve)," *Vestnik Evropy,* no. 11 (November 1896): 435–438; A. N. Pypin, *Ocherki literatury i obshchestvennosti pri Aleksandre I* (Petrograd, 1917), 424; A. A. Kochubinskii, *Admiral Shishkov i kantsler Rumiantsev: Nachal'nye gody russkogo slavianovediia* (Odessa, 1887–1888), 303.

12. M. G. Khalanskii and D. I. Bagaleia, eds., *Istoriko-filologicheskii fakul'tet Khar'kovskogo universiteta za pervye 100 let ego sushchestvovaniia, 1805–1905* (Khar'kov, 1908), 312–319; quotation, 315.
13. *RBS,* 8: 616–619; Pypin, *Ocherki literatury,* 447–448; *MERSH,* 16: 104–105; N. G. Sukhova, "Petr Ivanovich Keppen kak geograf," *Izvestiia Russkogo geograficheskogo obshchestva,* no. 5 (1993): 1–11; *Slavianovedenie v dorevoliutsionnoi Rossii,* 182–183. See also V. Bazanov, *Uchenaia respublika* (Moscow, 1964), 139–142; V. P. Kozlov, *Kolumby Rossiiskikh drevnostei,* 2nd ed. (Moscow, 1985), 25; E. M. Murzaev, "Istoki," *Izvestiia Rossiiskoi akademii nauk: Seriia Geograficheskaia,* no. 5 (1994): 123–138, especially 129–130.
14. The charter is in *PSZ,* 31 (1810–1811), 24492. On the society's activities, see O. Bodianskii, "Zapiska ob Imperatorskom Obshchestve istorii i drevnostei Rossiiskikh pri Moskovskom universitete," *Chteniia v Imperatorskom Obshchestve istorii i drevnostei Rossiiskikh,* no. 3 (July–September, 1877): 1–3; I. E. Zabelin, "Istoricheskii ocherk deiatel'nosti Obshchestva istorii i drevnostei Rossiiskikh c 1804 po 1884 gody," *Spisok uchenykh trudov, issledovanii i materialov, napechatannykh v povremennykh izdaniiakh Imperatorskogo Obshchestva istorii i drevnostei Rossiiskikh za 1815–1888 gg.* (Moscow, 1889), v–ix; I. A. Demidov and V. V. Ishutin, "Obshchestvo istorii i drevnostei rossiiskikh pri Moskovskom universitete," *Istoriia i istoriki: Istoriograficheskii ezhegodnik,* 1975 (Moscow, 1978), 256; V. Ger'e, "Novoe obshchestvo istorii pri Moskovskom universitete," *Vestnik Evropy* 4 (1895): 433–446; and Kozlov, *Kolumby.* 37. OIDR predated by fifteen years the major German society of antiquities, the Gesellschaft für ältere deutsche Geschichtskunde in Frankfurt (Crane, *Collecting,* 83).
15. Beketov quoted in the address of V. O. Kliuchevskii on the occasion of the society's centenary celebration in 1904, in "Stoletnyi iubilei obshchestva istorii i drevnostei rossiiskikh," *Istoricheskii vestnik* (July, 1904): 326–330; quotations, 328. See also Kochubinskii, *Admiral Shishkov* 39.
16. Pavel Stroev, "O sredstvakh udobneishikh k otrytiiu pamiatnikov Otechestvennoi Istorii i ob uspeshneishem sposobe obrabotyvat' onye," *Trudy i Letopisi Obshchestva istorii i drevnostei Rossiiskikh* 4, book 1 (1823): 277–301; citations, 279, 281, 283–284. At Rumiantsev's suggestion, in 1815 Stroev became the overseer of the Commission to Print Government Charters and Contracts (Kozlov, *Kolumby,* 21, 48.) See also *RBS,* 19: 532–536; *Slavianovedenie v dorevoliutsionnoi Rossii,* 324–325.
17. Stroev, "O sredstvakh," 285–288. Stroev's address is discussed in all the society's histories. See, for example, I. E. Zabelin, "Istoricheskii ocherk," 12–15; P. E. Pavlov, "Stoletie pervogo russkogo istoricheskogo obshchestva,"

Istoricheskii vestnik (March, 1904): 1045–1054; Demidov and Ishutin, "Obshchestvo," 256; *RBS*, 3: 161–166. Shortly before Stroev's address, B. Bikhman and F. P. Adelung, members of Keppen's "circle," proposed creating a single national museum of Russian antiquities, "a temple of Russian history" (Kozlov, *Kolumby*, 48–49). On this, see also Kevin Tyner Thomas, "Collecting the Fatherland: Early Nineteenth-century Proposals for a Russian National Museum," in Jane Burbank and David L. Ransel, eds., *Imperial Russia: New Histories for the Empire* (Bloomington, Ind., 1998), 91–107.

18. W. Bruce Lincoln, *In the Vanguard of Reform: Russia's Enlightened Bureaucrats, 1825–1861* (DeKalb, Ill., 1982), 91–101; Lincoln, *Petr Petrovich Semenov Tian-Shanskii: The Life of a Russian Geographer* (Newtonville, Mass., 1980), 11–15; V. M. Shtein, "Rol' Vsesoiuznogo Geograficheskogo obshchestva v razvitii obshchestvennoi mysli," *Izvestiia Vsesoiuznogo Geograficheskogo obshchestva*, no. 1–2 (1945): 7–8; N. N. Stepanov, "Russkoe geograficheskoe obshchestvo i etnografiia, 1845–1861," *Sovetskaia geografiia*, no. 4 (1946): 187–189. Stepanov establishes noble lineage for the favorable Soviet opinion of the society in a positive review of the society's publications in 1855 by Nikolai Chernyshevskii.
19. *RBS*, 10: 466–470; A. I. Alekseev, *Fedor Petrovich Litke* (Moscow, 1970), 183, 199; "Litke, Fedor Petrovich," *MERSH*, 20: 84–86; Lincoln, *In the Vanguard of Reform*, 92–93; Lincoln, *Petr Petrovich Semenov Tian-Shanskii*, 12.
20. Quoted passages from B. E. Raikov, *Russkie biologi-evoliutsionisty do Darvina: Materialy k istorii evoliutsionnykh idei v Rossii* (Moscow, 1951–1959), 2: 67; and B. E. Raikov, *Karl Ber: Ego zhizn' i trudy* (Moscow, 1961), 53, 56. See also "Karl Maksimovich Ber, 1792–1876," *Liudi russkoi nauki: Biologiia, meditsina, sel'skoe khoziaistvo* (Moscow, 1963), 56–72.
21. P. P. Semenov, *Istoriia poluvekovoi deiatel'nosti Imperatorskogo Russkogo geograficheskogo obshchestva, 1845–1895* (St. Petersburg, 1896), 1: xxii.
22. *RBS*, 7: 128–130; 11: 19–34; *BSDET*, 1: 128–129; A. G. Isachenko, ed., *Russkoe Geograficheskoe Obshchestvo: 150 let* (Moscow, 1995), 10; Cynthia H. Whittaker, *The Origins of Modern Russian Education: An Intellectual Biography of Count Sergei Uvarov*, 1786–1855 (DeKalb, Ill., 1984), 185.
23. F. P. Vrangel' (1796–1870), an explorer of the Artic, was chief administrator of Russian Alaska from 1829 to 1835. Struve (1793–1864), grandfather of Peter Struve, founded Pulkovo Observatory in 1839. Dal' finished medical school at the University of Dorpat (Tartu) and also studied at the Naval Academy. Arsen'ev (1789–1865) taught geography and statistics at St. Petersburg University. Although he was expelled from the university for his liberal views, he was elected to the Academy of Sciences in 1836. On Struve, see *Liudi russkoi nauki: Ocherki o vydaiushchikhsia deiateliakh estestvoznaniia i tekhniki* (Moscow, 1961), 94–103; on Vronchenko, see *ES Biografii*, 3: 507–508; on Vrangel', see *BSDET*, 1: 189; on Chikhachev, see *RBS*, 22:

418–420; on Rikord, who was a member of several other learned societies, including VEO, see *RBS,* 16: 201–205, and A. I. Serkov, *Russkoe masonstvo, 1731–2000: Entsiklopedicheskii slovar'* (Moscow, 2001), 699; on Kruzenstern, see *RBS,* 9: 455–460; on Arsen'ev, see E. M. Murzaev, "K 150-letiiu Russkogo geograficheskogo obshchestva," *Izvestiia Rossiiskoi akademii nauk: Seriia geograficheskaia,* no. 5 (1994): 123–138, especially 130–132; on Semenov, see *Liudi russkoi nauki: Geologiia, geografiia* (Moscow, 1962), 460–468. Rikord and Arsen'ev were Masons (Serkov, *Russkoe masonstvo,* 70, 699). On the British society, see *Journal of the Royal Geographical Society of London* 1 (1832): vi–xii. Litke and Kruzenstern were honorary members. For sketches of the most prominent early members, see also Ian Cameron, *To the Farthest Ends of the Earth: 150 Years of World Exploration by the Royal Geographical Society* (New York, 1980), 17–18.

24. Quoted in Semenov, *Istoriia,* 1: 1. See also F. R. Osten-Saken, *Dvadtsatipiatiletie Imperatorskogo Russkogo geograficheskogo obshchestva* (St. Petersburg, 1872), 1–4; Alekseev, *Fedor Petrovich Litke,* 189–193; T. A. Lukina, "K istorii osnovaniia Russkogo geograficheskogo obshchestva: Po materialam neopublikovannoi perepiski Karla Bera," *Izvestiia Vsesoiuznogo geograficheskogo obshchestva,* no. 6 (1965): 508–510; N. G. Sukhova, "Eshche raz o predystorii Russkogo geograficheskogo obshchestva: K 145-letiiu so dnia osnovaniia," *Izvestiia Vsesoiuznogo geograficheskogo obshchestva* 122, no. 5 (1990): 403–404; N. G. Sukhova, "Karl Ber i geograficheskaia nauka v Rossii," *Izvestiia Russkogo geograficheskogo obshchestva* 125, no. 2 (1993): 27–35; Murzaev, "Istoki," 123–138. On Middendorf, see also *BSDET,* 2: 34–35; on Dal', see *RBS,* 6: 42–48.

25. Alekseev, *Fedor Petrovich Litke,* 198–199; L. G. Berg, *Vsesoiuznoe geograficheskoe obshchestvo za sto let* (Moscow, 1946), 32. Thirty years earlier Vice Admiral Shishkov, president of the Academy of Sciences, had objected to the creation of a Society for the Emulation of Education and Charity (Obshchestvo sorevnitelei prosveshcheniia i blagotvoreniia) on the grounds that its projected mission would duplicate that of the academy. See RGIA, f. 733 [Ministry of Education], op. 18, d. 37, ll. 27–30 ["Uchrezhdenie Vol'nogo obshchestva liubitelei Rossiiskoi slovesnosti"]. See also Murzaev, "Istoki," 125. Making geography a science was also one of the objectives of the Royal Geographical Society (Cameron, *To the Farthest Ends of the Earth,* 200).

26. Semenov, *Istoriia,* 1: xxi. Litke's speech may be found in appendix 1, pt. 3: 1317–1319.

27. Osten-Saken, *Dvadtsatipiatiletie,* 3; Berg, *Vsesoiuznoe geograficheskoe obshchestvo,* 34. See also B. A. Val'skaia, "Petrashevtsy v Russkom geograficheskom obshchestve," *Ocherki istorii russkoi etnografii, fol'kloristiki i antropologii,* no. 7 (Leningrad, 1977): 57.

28. Cited passages from Lukina, "K istorii osnovaniia," 511, and Sukhova, "Eshche raz," 405. At the same time, Baer regarded too large a number of charter members as unwieldy. "But I have one request," he wrote to Litke in 1844. "We don't need many people at the beginning. Then nothing will

happen. I think that five is enough, six at the most" (quoted in Murzaev, "Istoki," 124).

29. Quotations in Lukina, "K istorii osnovaniia," 512, 515. On the government subsidy, see RGIA, f. 1341 [Senate], op. 59, d. 921, l. 1 ob. ["Uchrezhdenie RGO"].
30. Cited passages in Lukina, 512, 513. Litke's first wife, Iuliia Uil'iamovna (née Braun), also from a Baltic German family, gave birth prematurely to a stillborn child in the summer of 1843, just after Litke's return from a naval expedition in the Gulf of Bothnia; weakened by the ordeal, she did not survive the year's end (Alekseev, *Fedor Petrovich Litke,* 183).
31. Quoted in Alekseev, *Fedor Petrovich Litke,* 203.
32. Carol E. Harrison, *The Bourgeois Citizen in Nineteenth-century France: Gender, Sociability and the Uses of Emulation* (Oxford, 1999), 12–13. See also Leonore Davidoff and Catherine Hall, *Family Fortunes: Men and Women of the English Middle Class, 1780–1850* (Chicago, 1987), 319–320.
33. Arkiv RGO, op. 1–1845, d. 1, ll. 33–35; *PSZ,* 2nd ser., 20 (1845), no. 19259; RGIA, f. 1284 [Ministry of Internal Affairs], op. 66 (1862), d. 37 ["O politiko-ekonomicheskom komitete RGO"], ll. 62–67 ob. ["Proekt pravil o politiko-ekonomicheskom komitete RGO"]; Semenov, *Istoriia,* 1: 9, 48–50.
34. On the tension in the Academy of Sciences, see Alexander Vucinich, *Science in Russian Culture: A History to 1860* (Stanford, Calif., 1963), 295–296, 304–308, 356–360.
35. K. S. Veselovskii, "Otgoloski staroi pamiati," *Russkaia starina* 100, no. 10 (1899): 6, cited in Val'skaia, "Petrashevtsy," 55. It must be recognized that such an evaluation cut both ways. The conservative statesman Baron M. A. Korf once described the Geographical Society as an organization "composed of a majority of young men of all callings . . . who as a result of its inexpensive membership fee, gather once a week to chat and listen to the latest gossip" (quoted in Lincoln, *Petr Petrovich Semenov Tian-Shanskii,* 15).
36. *Vospominaniia general-fel'dmarshala grafa Dmitriia Alekseevicha Miliutina, 1843–1856,* ed. L. G. Zakharova (Moscow, 2000), 138.
37. Arkiv RGO, op. 1–1845, d. 1, ll. 33–35; *PSZ,* 2nd ser., 20 (1845), no. 19259; RGIA, f. 1284, op. 66 (1862), d. 37, ll. 62–67 ob.; RGIA, f. 869 [Miliutin], op. 1, d. 769, ll. 15–16 ["Dokumenty N. A. Miliutina o deiatel'nosti v RGO"], also published as "Otdel'noe mnenie D. A. i N. A. niliutinykh i V. S. Poroshina na proekte Ustava Obshchestva," in Semenov, *Istoriia,* quotation pt. 3, appendix 2: 1320. See also *Vospominaniia Miliutina,* 136; Lincoln, *Petr Petrovich Semenov Tian-Shanskii,* 12–13. At the time, Nikolai Miliutin was head of the municipal division of the Economics Department of the Ministry of Internal Affairs. For biographical information, see *RBS,* 16: 5–22 (Reitern); *RBS,* 14: 514–517 (Popov); *RBS,* 2: 270 (Arapetov); *RBS,* 5: 230–233 (Girs); *ES Biografii,* 3: 562 (Gagemeister); *RBS,* 14: 577–580 (Poroshin); *RBS,* 16: 201–205 (Rikord); and *Entskiklopedicheskii slovar' Russkogo bibliograficheskogo instituta Granat* (Moscow, 1910), 28: 651–652 (V. A. Miliutin), and 28: 657–665 (Nikolai Miliutin).

38. Arkiv RGO, op. 1–1845, d. 1, ll. 33–35; *PSZ,* 2nd ser., 20 (1845), no. 19259; RGIA, f. 1284, op. 66 (1862), d. 37, ll. 62–67 ob.; Semenov, *Istoriia,* 1: 9.
39. *Vospominaniia Miliutina,* quotation 145; Semenov, *Istoriia,* 1: quotation 11; Lincoln, *Petr Petrovich Semenov Tian-Shanskii,* 12–13.
40. Cited passages in "Doklad Soveta Russkogo Geograficheskogo Obshchestva," in Semenov, *Istoriia,* 3, appendix 3: 1322.
41. A-v-s-v [G. N. Potanin], "Russkoe geograficheskoe obshchestvo i ego poluvekovaia deiatel'nost'," *Russkoe bogatstvo* 4 (1896): 139–144; quotation, 140 (emphasis added). A-v-s-v is identified as G. N. Potanin, a writer for *Russkoe bogatstvo* by I. F. Masanov, *Slovar' psevdonimov russkikh pisatelei, uchenykh i obshchestvennykh deiatelei* 4 vols. (Moscow, 1956), 1:69.
42. Semenov, *Istoriia,* 1: 9.
43. A-v-s-v, "Russkoe geograficheskoe obshchestvo," 142. Beginning in the 1860s, provincial branches often helped those who had been ostracized for their political views, most famously, Peter Kropotkin, who participated in the RGO expedition along the Amur River in 1864, was secretary to the Division of Physical Geography, and in 1871 was offered the position of RGO secretary, which he declined. See Peter Kropotkin, *Memoirs of a Revolutionist* (Boston, 1930), 228–241. The work of the Siberian Division, in particular, has received the attention of scholars. See Mark Bassin, "The Russian Geographical Society, the 'Amur Epoch,' and the Great Siberian Expedition, 1855–1863," *Annals of the Association of American Geographers* 73, no. 2 (1983): 240–256; Bassin, *Imperial Visions: National Imagination and Geographical Expansion in the Russian Far East, 1840–1865* (Cambridge, 1999); and Claudia Weiss, "The Imperial Russian Geographical Society and Russian Siberian Politics: A Scientific Society as a Place of Encounter for Scientific and Imperial Interests in 19th-century Russia" (paper presented to the Association for the Study of Nationalities annual meeting, New York, 2003).
44. Semenov, *Istoriia,* 1: 12–13, 16; Alekseev, *Fedor Petrovich Litke,* 210.
45. GARF, f. 109, 1 ekspeditsiia (1848), d. 201, ll. 5–6 ob. ["O geograficheskom obshchestve"]. On the politics of mapmaking, see Valerie Kivelson, *Cartographies of Tsardom: The Land and Its Meanings in Seventeenth-century Russia* (Ithaca, N.Y., 2006), 5–10.
46. GARF, f. 109, 1 ekspeditsiia (1848), d. 201, quotation 3, 3ob. ll. 1–4 ["O vybore Vitse-Prezidenta v Russkom Geograficheskom Obshchestve"]; Semenov, *Istoriia,* 1: xxvi; Lincoln, *Petr Petrovich Semenov Tian-Shanskii,* 12–13. Later, Miliutin's recollection of the "election campaign" confirmed Litke's fear of election campaigning behind closed doors: "We gathered at Murav'ev's apartment on Zagorodnyi prospekt, and over tea and through thick clouds of tobacco smoke, we discussed the campaign and divided up responsibility" (*Vospominaniia Miliutina,* 169). Murzaev uses the phrase "palace coup" ("Istoki," 134–135).
47. Cited passages in Semenov, *Istoriia,* 1: 58; Alekseev, *Fedor Petrovich Litke,* 218. See also *Vospominaniia Miliutina,* 159.
48. Semenov, *Istoriia,* 1: 2.
49. Murzaev, "Istoki," 134–135.

50. Semenov, *Istoriia,* 1: 58–59; Alekseev, *Fedor Petrovich Litke,* 216–217.
51. GARF, f. 109, 1 ekspeditsiia (1848), d. 210, l. 1, 9–10 ["Vypiska iz chastnykh svedenii, poluchennykh General-Adiutantom Grafom Orlovym"], and ll. 12–12 ob. ["O pis'me General-Adiutanta Grafa Stroganova"]. On the Petrashevtsy, see Val'skaia, "Petrashevtsy." On Lamanskii, see *ES Biografii,* 6: 512.
52. Quoted in Berg, *Vsesoiuznoe geograficheskoe obshchestvo,* 26. Berg exonerates Litke. Concerning his "comeback" as second-term vice president after 1857, Berg notes that Litke's conduct in the Geographical Society was irreproachable. Litke strictly adhered to the 1849 bylaws, invited politically suspect persons to work for the society, and petitioned on behalf of Polish exiles in Siberia after 1863.
53. Lincoln, *Petr Petrovich Semenov Tian-Shanskii,* 12–13, quotation; Semenov, *Istoriia* 1: 58–59.
54. Ivan Snegirev, "O prostonarodnykh izobrazheniiakh," *Trudy Obshchestva liubiteli Rossiiskoi slovesnosti,* pt. 4 (Moscow, 1824), 119–148; Kozlov, *Kolumby,* 22. The author of books on Russian proverbs, on folk celebrations and rituals, and on woodcuts, Snegirev was the first to subject such examples of folk wisdom to scholarly analysis. See *RBS,* 19: 7–11.
55. Mark Bassin, "Inventing Siberia: Visions of the Russian East in the Early Nineteenth Century," *American Historical Review* 96, no. 3 (June, 1991): 763–794. See also Anthony Netting, "Russian Liberalism: The Years of Promise, 1842–1855" (Ph.D. diss., Columbia University, 1967), 597; M. K. Azadovskii, "Znachenie geograficheskogo obshchestva v istorii russkoi fol'kloristiki," in *Ocherki istorii russkoi etnografii, fol'kloristiki i antropologii,* no. 3 (Trudy Instituta etnografii im. N. N. Miklukho-Maklaia, vol. 91) (Moscow, 1965), 7.
56. Litke quoted in Berg, *Vsesoiuznoe geograficheskoe obshchestvo,* 33. See also Wladimir Berelowitch, "Aux origins de l'ethnographie russe: la société de géographie dans les années 1840–1850," *Cahiers du Monde russe et soviétique* 31, nos. 2–3 (1990): 265–274.
57. K. M. Baer, "Ob etnograficheskikh issledovaniiakh voobshche i v Rossii v osobennosti," *Zapiski Russkogo geograficheskogo obshchestva,* 2nd ed., nos. 1–2, (1849): 64–81; quotation, 77.
58. Ibid., 64.
59. Ibid, 65. See also N. N. Stepanov, "Russkoe geograficheskoe obshchestvo i etnografiia," 188–191.
60. Semenov, *Istoriia,* 1: 37–38. On Grigor'ev, see *ES Biografii,* 4: 366–367; Nathaniel Knight, "V. V. Grigor'ev in Orenburg, 1851–1862: Russian Orientalism in Service of Empire?" *Slavic Review* 59, no. 1 (Spring 2000): 74–100. On Savel'ev, see *RBS,* 18: 25–28. Baer's cause may have also been hurt by passages from the printed version of Baer's 1846 address that allegedly made fun of local officials in Arkhangel'sk; the censor cut them from a second printing. See Raikov, *Baer,* 61.
61. Quoted in Shtein, "Rol' Vsesoiuznogo geograficheskogo obshchestva," 17. See also M. Aronson and S. Reiser, *Literaturyne kruzhki i salony* (Leningrad, 1929), 221, 227; *MERSH,* 24: 36–39.

62. Quoted in E. M. Murzaev, "N. I. Nadezhdin kak istoriko-geograf i deiatel' geograficheskogo obshchestva," *Izvestiia Akademii nauk,* ser. Geograficheskaia, no. 4 (1992): 106–119; quotation, 110. See also B. A. Val'skaia, "Diskussiia v geograficheskom obshchestve o russkom slovare geograficheskoi terminologii Ia. V. Khanykova," in D. A. Ol'derogge, ed., *Strany i narody vostoka,* vol. 18: *Geografiia, etnografiia, istoriia. Pamiati A. V. Koroleva* (Moscow, 1976), 254; *RBS,* 11: 19–34; *Slavianovedenie v dorevoliutsionnoi Rossii,* 246–247; Stepanov, "Russkoe geograficheskoe obshchestvo i etnografiia," 192–195.
63. S. A. Kozlov, *Agrarnye traditsii i novatsii v dorevoliutsionnoi Rossii: Tsentral'nye nechernozemnye gubernii* (Moscow, 2002), quotation 256; *Vospominaniia Miliutina,* 137.
64. N. I. Nadezhdin, "Ob etnograficheskom izuchenii narodnosti russkoi," *Zapiski Russkogo geograficheskogo obshchestva,* 2nd ed., nos. 1–2 (1849): 149–194, quotation, 149. Nadezhdin's talk received extensive coverage in the in-house histories of the society: see Osten-Saken, *Dvadtsatipiatiletie,* 48; Semenov, *Istoriia,* 1: 38–39, 51.
65. Nadezhdin, "Ob etnograficheskom izuchenii," 51, 166–167. The "volcanic ash of history" metaphor comes from Semenov, *Istoriia,* 1: 51. I have taken some liberty with Semenov's metaphor. The literal Russian reads a bit differently: "as if in the ashes of the pogroms of history." Semenov, it must be noted, wrote his history in 1896. Pogroms, however, do not leave much standing. The metaphor of volcanic ash, under which an entire civilization lies preserved, seems to fit better the ideas of Litke, Baer, and Nadezhdin.
66. Osten-Saken, *Dvadtsatipiatiletie,* quotations 49; Berg, *Vsesoiuznoe geograficheskoe obshchestvo,* 146–147; Azadovskii, "Znachenie geograficheskogo obshchestva," 9–11.
67. N. Nadezhdin, "Instruktsiia etnograficheskaia," in "Svod instruktsii dlia Kamchatskoi ekspeditsii, predprinimaemoi Russkogo geograficheskogo obshchestva," cited in Azadovskii, "Znachenie geograficheskogo obshchestva," 10. See also Semenov, *Istoriia,* 1: 38–39; L. M. Saburova, "Russkoe geograficheskoe obshchestvo i etnograficheskie issledovaniia (dorevoliutsionnyi period)," *Ocherki istorii russkoi etnografii, fol'kloristiki i antropologii,* no. 7 (Trudy Instituta etnografii im. N. N. Miklukho-Maklaia, vol. 104) (Moscow, 1977): 6–7. Sending questions soliciting this kind of information among a small population was quite likely intended as a pilot project to be expanded in the future.
68. Osten-Saken, *Dvadtsatipiatiletie,* 51–52; Semenov, *Istoriia* 1: 40, 121; Azadovskii, "Znachenie geograficheskogo obshchestva," 5–7. A Soviet version of this ethnographic collection, *Russkie,* was published in 1967. On Sadovnikov, see *RBS,* 18: 44–48; on Afanas'ev, see *RBS,* 2: 375–379.
69. Cited passages in K. D. Kavelin, "Nekotorye izvlecheniia iz sobiraemykh v I.R.G. obshchestve etnograficheskikh materialov o Rossii, s zametkami o ikh mnogostoronnei zanimatel'nosti i pol'ze dlia nauki," *Geograficheskie izvestiia,* vyp. 3 (1850): 3: 323–339; quote, 323; and Semenov, *Istoriia,* 1: 121. In a report to the Society on the preliminary findings of the ethnographic

questionnaires, Konstantin Kavelin provided what might be called an in-house evaluation, an evaluation that went beyond the almost formulaic praise for the study of "fast disappearing ways of life."

70. Cited passages in Osten-Saken, *Dvadtsatipiatiletie,* 44–45, 51–52, 121; Kavelin, "Nekotorye izvlecheniia," 339; Nadezhdin, "Ob etnograficheskom izuchenii," 150. See also Kozlov, *Kolumby,* 260, 331.
71. V. Rudakov, "Piatidesiatiletie Arkheologicheskogo obshchestva," *Istoricheskii vestnik,* no. 5 (1896): 648–658, quotation, 652; "Imperatorskoe Russkoe arkheologicheskoe obshchestvo," *ES,* 3: 231–235; G. I. Vzdornov, *Istoriia otkrytiia i izucheniia russkoi srednevekovoi zhivopisi XIX veka* (Moscow, 1986), 126–128; A. M. Razgon, "Rossiiskii istoricheskii muzei: Istoriia ego osnovaniia i deiatel'nost', 1872–1917 gg.," in *Ocherki muzeinogo dela v Rossii* (Moscow, 1960), vol. 2; and Katia Dianina, "A Nation on Display: Russian Museums and Print Culture in the Age of the Great Reforms" (Ph.D. diss., Harvard University, 2002), chap. 7.
72. Lincoln, *Petr Petrovich Semenov Tian-Shanskii,* 49–51.
73. Michael Cullen, *The Statistical Movement in Early Victorian Britain: The Foundations of Empirical Social Research* (New York, 1975), quotations 126, 146; James C. Scott, *Seeing Like a State: How Certain Schemes to Improve the Human Condition Have Failed* (New Haven, Conn., 1998), 27.
74. Semenov, *Istoriia* 1: 41; *My Past and Thoughts: The Memoirs of Alexander Herzen,* trans. Constance Garnett (New York, 1974), 179.
75. Cited passage in Osten-Saken, *Dvadtsatipiatiletie,* 8. See also Lincoln, *Petr Petrovich, Semenov Tian-Shanskii,* 49–61; Semenov, *Istoriia,* 1: 41–47, 123–139.
76. Semenov, *Istoriia,* 1: xvii–xxi; N. G. Sukhova, "Petr Ivanovich Keppen kak geograf," *Izvestiia Russkogo geograficheskogo obshchestva* 125, no. 5 (1993): 1–11, especially 1, 6; *RBS* 8: 616–619. Arsen'ev authored numerous volumes of descriptive statistics of the Russian empire. See *RBS,* 2: 317–321, quotation, 318.
77. Kropotkin, *Memoirs,* 98.
78. Isachenko, *Russkoe Geograficheskoe Obshchestvo,* 148–153. Bezobrazov was secretary of the Geographical Society from 1862 to 1864. For biographical information on Bezobrazov, see *RBS,* 2: 648–650, and S. A. Vengerov, *Kritiko-biograficheskii slovar' russkikh pisatelei i uchenykh* (St. Petersburg, 1889), 1: 306–324; on Vernadskii, see *ES Biografii,* 3: 247, and *RBS,* 3Q: 600–602; on Gorlov, see *ES Biografii,* 4: 255; on Terner, see Shilov, 720–724. See also Murzaev, "Istoki," 133.
79. Quoted in Shtein, "Rol'," 16. See also V. G. Chernukha, "Politiko-ekonomicheskii komitet Russkogo geograficheskogo obshchestva (28 fevralia 1859 g.–26 noiabria 1862 g.)," *Vspomogatel'nye istoricheskie ditsipliny* (Leningrad, 1989), 20: 89–102, especially 92–93, 96–98; V. G. Chernukha, "Deiatel'nost' politiko-ekonomicheskogo komiteta Russkogo geograficheskogo obshchestva (28 fevralia 1859 g.–26 noiabria 1862 g.)," *Vspomogatel'nye istoricheskie ditsipliny* (Leningrad, 1990), 21: 74–88, especially 88.

80. RGIA, f. 1405 [Ministry of Justice], op. 539, d. 8, ll. 2–3 ob. ["Proekt Polozheniia politiko-ekonomicheskgo komiteta RGO"]; RGIA, f. 1284, op. 66 (1862), d. 37, l. 14 ["Proekit pravil Politiko-ekonomicheskgo komiteta RGO"]; RGIA, f. 91 [Free Economic Society], op. 1, d. 304, l. 1 ["Materialy ob uchrezhdenii politiko-ekonomicheskgo komiteta"]; *Zapiski Russkogo geograficheskogo obshchestva*, no. 2 (1862): 24; Chernukha, "Deiatel'nost'," 75–79. The Committee of Political Economy of the Free Economic Society also held seminars on absentee landlords, mining statutes, the availability of credit, mortgages and property appraisals, taxes, guilds, the metric system, technical schools, the labor market, private credit and private banks, and economic crises in Russia. See A. I. Khodnev, *Istoriia Imperatorskogo Vol'nogo ekonomicheskogo obshchestva s 1765 do 1865 goda* (St. Petersburg, 1865): 356–357; *Kratkie svedeniia III-go otdeleniia VEO s ianvaria po mai 1866 g.* (Moscow, 1866): 1–6.
81. *Zapiski RGO*, no. 2 (1862): 25; "Vozobnovlenie zasedanii Politicheskogo-ekonomicheskgo komiteta," *Vek*, no. 50 (1861): 1403–1404. In 1861, for example, a sample of coverage in *Vek* includes no. 13 (29 March); no. 15 (12 April); no. 20 (24 May); nos. 25–26 (5 July); no. 33 (23 August); no. 50 (20 December). A sample of the coverage in *Ukazatel' ekonomicheskii* in the first three months of 1861 alone includes no. 2: 25–26; no. 6: 72; no. 10: 116–118; no. 14: 153–155; no. 18: 209–213; and no. 20: 234. See also M. E. Uralova, "Imperatorskoe Russkoe geograficheskoe obshchestvo vo vtoroi polovine XIX v.: K istorii obshchestvennoi zhizni v Rossii," Avtoreferat kandidatskoi dissertatsii Rossiiskoi akademii nauk, Institut russkoi istorii (St. Petersburg, 1994): 18; Reginald Zelnik, *Labor and Society in Tsarist Russia: The Factory Workers of St. Petersburg, 1855–1870* (Stanford, Calif., 1971), 85–86.
82. *Ukazatel' ekonomicheskii*, no. 1 (2–14 January 1860): 10.
83. Chernukha, "Deiatel'nost'," 74, 81–83.
84. RGIA, f. 1263 [Committee of Ministers], op. 1, d. 2978 ["Zhurnal Komiteta ministrov"], ll. 253–254 ["O politiko-ekonomicheskom komitete"]; RGIA, f. 1405, op. 539, d. 8, ll. 2–2 ob.; *Zapiski RGO*, no. 2 (1862): 79–80.
85. Quoted in Chernukha, "Deiatel'nost'," 86. See also S. Frederick Starr, *Decentralization and Self-Government in Russia, 1830–1870* (Princeton, N.J., 1972), 261–262.
86. RGIA, f. 1263, op. 1, d. 2978, ll. 248–270, especially ll. 249–252, 265 ["Zhurnal Komiteta ministrov (16 October 1862)"]; RGIA, f. 1284, op. 66 (1862), d. 37, ll. 62–66, 88–89 [DOD MVD "Izlozhenie dela"], 106–112 ["Vypiska iz zhurnala Komiteta ministrov, 30 October 1862"]; RGIA f. 1297 [Ministry of Internal Affairs, Medical Department], op. 148, d. 180, l. 19 ff. ["O deiatel'nosti meditsinskikh obshchestv"]. New liberal periodicals followed such discussions closely. See "Nashi uchenye obshchestva," *Vek*, no. 42 (1861): 1217–1219; "Uchenye obshchestva," *Ukazatel' ekonomicheskii*, no. 7 (1860) and no. 46 (1860). Although this did not apply to already existing societies, into the charters of new societies was inserted a requirement

that associations needed to inform the police in advance about the day, time, place, and topics of meetings.

87. RGIA, f. 1284, op. 66 (1862), d. 37, ll. 114–117 ["RGO to Minister of Internal Affairs Valuev, 10 December 1862"]; Chernukha, "Deiatel'nost'," 87.
88. On "Baltic natural history," see Lisbet Koerner, "Daedalus Hyperboreus: Baltic Natural History and Mineralogy in the Enlightenment," in William Clark, Jan Golinski, and Simon Schaffer, eds., *The Sciences in Enlightened Europe* (Chicago, 1999), 389–422, quotations, 404, 413, 414.
89. Mokyr, *Gifts of Athena*, 37, 43, 72.
90. Osten-Saken, *Dvadtsatipiatiletie*, 44. This openness became part of the discourse about the society. Semenov's golden jubilee account of the society repeats almost word for word but does not attribute the silver jubilee assessment (*Istoriia*, 1: xxiv).
91. Merrill, *Romance*, 78, 97; Trigger, *History*, 210; David Blackbourn, *The Long Nineteenth Century: A History of Germany, 1780–1918* (New York, 1998), 275.
92. Osten-Saken, *Dvadtsatipiatiletie*, 45.
93. Semenov, *Istoriia* 1: xxii. Semenov articulated the same views in an address at the society's golden jubilee in 1896: see *Zhurnal iubileinogo sobraniia Imperatorskogo Russkogo geograficheskogo obshchestva 21-go ianvaria 1896 goda* (St. Petersburg, 1896), iii–xvi, especially v, x.
94. Cited passages in Uralova, "Imperatorskoe Russkoe geograficheskoe obshchestvo," 11–12; "Geograficheskoe obshchestvo Imperatorskoe Russkoe," *ES*, 15: 369. The Third Section report is in GARF, f. 109, 1 ekspeditsiia (1848), d. 201, l. 1.
95. A meeting of 8 January 1847. Litke Quoted in Val'skaia, "Petrashevtsy," 57; political police cited in GARF, f. 109, 1 ekspeditsiia (1848), d. 201, l. 1.
96. Quoted in Val'skaia, "Petrashevtsy," 57.

4. Patriotism and Useful Knowledge

1. I have been informed by a rich historiography of science societies and their public projects that includes: Ian Inkster and Jack Morrell, eds., *Metropolis and Province: Science in British Culture, 1780–1850* (London, 1983); Richard van Dülmen, *The Society of the Enlightenment: The Rise of the Middle Class and Enlightenment Culture in Germany*, trans. Anthony Williams (New York, 1992); James E. McClelland, *Science Reorganized: Scientific Societies in the Eighteenth Century* (New York, 1985); Arnold Thackray, "Natural Knowledge in Cultural Context: The Manchester Mode," *American Historical Review* 79 (June 1974): 672–709; Colin A. Russell, *Science and Social Change in Britain and Europe, 1700–1900* (New York, 1983); and Robert Fox, "Learning, Politics and Polite Culture in Provincial France: The Societies Savantes in the Nineteenth Century," *Historical Reflections/Reflexions Historiques* 7, no. 2–3 (1980): 554. On the "performance of science" see Jan Golinski, *Science as Public Culture: Chemistry and Enlightenment in Britain,*

1760–1820 (Cambridge, 1992); Geoffrey V. Sutton, *Science for a Polite Society: Gender, Culture and the Demonstration of Enlightenment* (Boulder, Colo., 1995); Jan C. C. Rupp, "The New Science and the Public Sphere in the Premodern Era," *Science in Context* 8, no. 3 (1995): 487–507, especially 487, 491, 496; and Carol E. Harrison, *The Bourgeois Citizen in Nineteenth-century France: Gender, Sociability and the Uses of Emulation* (Oxford, 1999).

2. Paul Farber, *Finding Order in Nature: The Naturalist Tradition from Linneaus to E.O. Wilson* (Baltimore, 2000), quotation 30. On museums and exhibitions, the extensive work includes Silvio Bedini, "The Evolution of Science Museums," *Technology and Culture* 6 (1965): 1–29; Eugene Ferguson, "Technical Museums and International Exhibitions," *Technology and Culture* 6 (1965): 30–46; Jeffrey A. Auerbach, *The Great Exhibition of 1851: A Nation on Display* (New Haven, Conn., 1999), 9–31; Steven Conn, *Museums and American Intellectual Life, 1876–1926* (Chicago,. 1998); Keith Walden, *Becoming Modern in Toronto: The Industrial Exhibition and the Shaping of a Late Victorian Culture* (Toronto, 1997); Kenneth Hudson, *A Social History of Museums: What the Visitors Thought* (London, 1975), 46; Tony Bennett, *The Birth of the Museum: History, Theory, Politics* (New York, 1995); and Bennett, "The Exhibitionary Complex," in Nicholas B. Dirks, Geoff Eley, and Sherry B. Ortner, eds., *Culture/Power/History: A Reader in Contemporary Social Theory* (Princeton, N.J., 1994): 123–154; quotation, 137.
3. Quoted in Lyndel Saunders King, *The Industrialization of Taste: Victorian England and the Art Union of London* (Ann Arbor, Mich., 1985), 125; see further discussion on 27–35, 41, 45, 49, 133–139.
4. Thackray, "Natural Knowledge," 686, 693; Auerbach, *Great Exhibition,* 10, 94, 108, 111; Paul Greenhalg, *Ephemeral Vistas: The Expositions Universelles, Great Exhibitions, and World's Fairs, 1851–1939* (Manchester, 1988), 29, 145; Kenneth Hudson, *Directory of World Museums,* 2nd ed. (New York, 1981), 41–42; Sanford Elwitt, "Social Reform and Social Order in Late Nineteenth-century France: The Musée Social and Its Friends," *French Historical Studies* 11 (April 1980): 431–451; Harrison, *Bourgeois Citizen,* 80, 81, 84.
5. Liudmilla Jordanova, "Objects of Knowledge: Historical Perspective on Museums," in Peter Vergo, *The New Museology* (London, 1989); 22–40, quotation, 32–33; Ivan Karp, Christine Mullen Kraemer, and Steven D. Lavine, eds., *Museums and Communities: The Politics of Public Culture* (Washington and London, 1992), quotation 15; Brian Wallis, "Selling Nations: International Exhibitions and Cultural Diplomacy," in Daniel J. Sherman and Irit Rogoff, eds., *Museum Culture: Histories, Discourses, Spectacles* (Minneapolis, 1994), quotation 272; and Wendy M. K. Shaw, *Possessors and Possessed: Museums, Archaeology and the Visualization of History in the Late Ottoman Empire* (Berkeley and Los Angeles, 2003), 149–50.
6. Quoted in Anthony Netting, "Russian Liberalism: The Years of Promise, 1842–1855" (Ph.D. diss., Columbia University, 1967), 657.

7. Quoted in S. V. Rozhdestvenskii, *Istoricheskii obzor deiatel'nosti Ministerstva narodnogo prosveshcheniia, 1802–1902* (St. Petersburg, 1902), 478.
8. Quoted in V. Ia. Grosul, *Russkoe obshchestvo XVIII–XIX vekov: Traditsii i novatsii* (Moscow, 2003), 272.
9. Anuchin quoted in M. S. Bastravkova and G. E. Pavlova, "Nauka: vlast' i obshchetsvo," in *Ocherki russkoi kul'tury XIX veka: Vlast' i kul'tura* (Moscow, 2000), 2: 356. See also S. A. Tokarev, *Istoriia russkoi etnografii: Dooktiabr'skii period* (Moscow, 1966), 282.
10. The ministry official is quoted in Adele Lindenmeyr, *Poverty Is Not a Vice: Charity, Society, and the State in Imperial Russia* (Princeton, N.J., 1996), 121. The 1863 university charter is "Obshchii Ustav Imperatorskikh Rossiiskikh Universitetov," in *PSZ*, 2nd ser., 38 (1863): no. 39752. See also Rozhdestvenskii, *Istoricheskii obzor*, 478.
11. Tokarev, *Istoriia russkoi etnografii*, 77; Alexander Vucinich, *Science in Russian Culture, 1861–1917* (Stanford, Calif., 1970), 77. On censorship, see Charles Ruud, *Fighting Words: Imperial Censorship and the Russian Press, 1804–1906* (Toronto, 1982), 126. "Mail-order study group" quotation from Netting, "Russian Liberalism," 84.
12. RGIA, f. 735 [Ministry of Education], op. 6, d. 181, l. 1 ["Ob uchrezhdenii periodicheskikh s"ezdov naturalistov i vrachei"].
13. RGIA, f. 744 [Ministry of Education], op. 1, d. 24, ll. 19–20 ["O vnesenii predstavleniia v Sovet ministrov o ezhegodnykh s"ezdakh"]; L. I. Kursanov and V. A. Deinega, "Moskovskoe obshchestvo ispytatelei prirody," *Uchenye zapiski Moskovskogo gosudarstvennogo universiteta, Iubileinaia seriia 14: Biologiia* (Moscow, 1940), 353–362, especially 353–354; S. Iu. Lipshits, *Moskovskoe obshchestvo ispytatelei prirody za 135 let ego sushchestvovaniia, 1805–1940: Istoricheskii ocherk* (Moscow, 1940). Solov'ev cited in V. V. Serbinenko, *Vladimir Solov'ev: Zapad, vostok i Rossiia* (Moscow, 1994), 13. On Russian evolutionists, see B. E. Raikov, *Russkie biologi-evoliutsionnisty do Darvina: Materialy k istorii evoliutsionnoi idei v Rossi* 4 vols. (Moscow, 1951–1959); B. E. Raikov, *Predshestvenniki Darvina v Rossii: Iz istorii russkogo estestvoznaniia* (Leningrad, 1956); and Daniel P. Todes, *Darwin without Malthus: The Struggle for Existence in Russian Evolutionary Thought* (Oxford, 1989).
14. Arkhiv Rossiiskoi akademii nauk [hereafter Arkhiv RAN], f. 446 [A. P. Bodganov], op. 1a, d. 59 ["Materialy po OLEAE"], quotation l. 9; *Protokoly zasedanii Obshchestva liubitelei estestvoznaniia, antropologii i etnografii* [hereafter *Protokoly zasedanii OLEAE*] published in *Izvestiia Obshchestva liubitelei estestvoznaniia, antropologii i etnografii* [hereafter *Izvestiia* OLEAE] 3, no. 1 (1866): col. 5. See also V. V. Bogdanov, "Obshchestvo liubitelei estestvoznaniia, antropologii i etnografii pri Moskovskom gosudarstvennom universitete," *Uchenye zapiski Moskovskogo gosudarstvennogo universiteta: Biologiia, Iubileinaia seriia*, no. 53 (1940): 363. For an example of a foundation story in Europe, see Jean-Pierre Chaline, *Sociabilité et Érudition: Les sociétés savants en France XIXe–XXe siècles* (Paris, 1995), 70–71.

15. On Bogdanov, see Raikov, *Russkie biologi-evoliutsionisty,* 4: 203–467.
16. For biographical information on Shchurovskii, see B. E. Raikov, *Grigorii Efimovich Shchurovskii: Uchenyi, naturalist i prosvetitel'* (Moscow, 1965), 7–8, 17, 34, 58–65, and *RBS,* 24: 159–162. See also *Protokoly zasedanii OLEAE,* in *Izvestiia OLEAE* 3, no. 2 (1886): cols. 109–110; *Iubilei G. E. Shchurovskogo* (published in *Izvestiia OLEAE* 33 [1885]); and G. Shchurovskii, "Ob obshchedostupnosti ili populiarizatsii estestvennykh nauk," *Zhurnal Ministerstva narodnogo prosveshcheniia* (January, 1868): 39–52.
17. The details of the society's founding may be found in RGIA, f. 733, op. 142, d. 92 ["Ob uchrezhdenii OLEAE"], ll. 1–10 ["Popechitel' Moskovskogo uchebnogo okruga"; "Vypiska iz zhurnala Uchenogo komiteta Ministerstva narodnogo prosveshcheniia, 11 February 1864"], and in Arkhiv RAN, f. 446, op. 1a, d. 59, ll. 11–12. The society's charter and bylaws [*ustav*] may be found in *Protokoly zasedanii OLEAE,* in *Izvestiia OLEAE* 3, no. 1 (1866), cols. 1–2. See also I. A. Kablukov, "Iz vospominanii o deiatel'nosti Obshchestva liubitelei estestvoznaniia, antropologii i etnografii," *Priroda* (December, 1913): 1463–1470; V. V. Bogdanov, *Piatidesiatiletie Imperatorskogo Obshchestva liubitelei estestvoznaniia, antropologii i etnografii, 1863–1913* (Moscow, 1914), 25; Raikov, *Grigorii Efimovich Shchurovskii,* 68–69; Raikov, *Russkie biologi-evoliutsionnisty,* 4: 321–326; P. S. Lipets and T. S. Makashina, "Rol' Obshchestva liubitelei estestvoznaniia, antropologii i etnografii v organizatsii russkoi etnograficheskoi nauki," *Ocherki istorii russkoi etnografii, fol'kloristiki i antropologii* (Moscow, 1965), 3: 40. On Davidov, see *RBS,* 6: 2–4.
18. Kablukov, "Iz vospominanii," 1464; Bogdanov, *Piatidesiatiletie,* 25; Raikov, *Grigorii Efimovich Shchurovskii,* 68–69.
19. Arkhiv RAN, f. 446, op. 1a, d. 59, ll. 11–12. See also Kursanov and Deinega, "Moskovskoe obshchestvo ispytatelei prirody," 353–362.
20. RGIA, f. 733, op. 142, d. 92, ll. 1–10, quotation l. 10. On Beketov, see *BSDET,* 1: 53.
21. The above passages are from Shchurovskii's address to the society's twenty-second meeting (23 April 1867), just before the opening of the 1867 Ethnographic Exposition. See *Protokoly zasedanii OLEAE,* in *Izvestiia OLEAE* 3, no. 2 (1886): cols. 65–66.
22. A. P. Bogdanov, *Piatidesiatiletie,* quotation 25; *Protokoly zasedanii OLEAE,* in *Izvestiia OLEAE* 3, no. 1, (1866), col. 3; Lipets and Makashina, "Rol' Obshchestva liubitelei," 39; R. S. Lipets and T. S. Makashina, "Etnograficheskaia deiatel'nost' Obshchestva liubitelei estestvoznaniia, antropologii i etnografii," *Sovetskaia etnografiia,* no. 6 (1964): 115–129, especially 117; "Iz Moskvy," *Golos* (30 July 1871): 2–3. Many in the scientific community did not share the enthusiasm of the founders of OLEAE for publishing in Russian, arguing that foreign scientists were not going to learn Russian in order to read Russian scientific papers. See M. Menzbir, "Nauchnyi obzor: Russkie estestvenno-istoricheskie obshchestva i universitety," *Russkaia mysl'* 8 (1892): 155–181, especially 175. Menzbir was an officer in the "rival" society, MOIP.

23. *Protokoly zasedanii OLEAE,* in *Izvestiia OLEAE* 3, no. 1 (1866): col. 157; V. V. Bogdanov, "Obshchestvo liubitelei estestvoznaniia," 364.
24. *Protokoly zasedanii OLEAE,* in *Izvestiia OLEAE* 3, no. 2 (1886), cols. 108–134; Bodganov, *Piatidesiatiletie OLEAE,* 25; Kablukov, "Iz vospominanii," quotation 1464.
25. Quotations in *Protokoly zasedanii OLEAE,* in *Izvestiia OLEAE* 3, no. 1, (1886), cols. 2–3, and 3, no. 2 (1886), cols. 109–110; Bodganov, *Piatidesiatiletie,* 33. See also Tokarev, *Istoriia russkoi etnografii,* 284.
26. OLEAE, *Vserossiiskaia etnograficheskaia vystavka* (Moscow, 1867), 3.
27. See Shurovskii's addresses in *Protokoly zasedanii OLEAE,* in *Izvestiia OLEAE* 3, no. 2 (1886), cols. 108–112, and in *Protokoly zasedanii* in *Izvestiia OLEAE* 9, no. 1 (1872): 13–21; A. P. Bogdanov, "Obrazovatel'nyi politekhnicheskii muzei v Moskve," in Moskovskii muzei prikladnykh znanii, *Materialy, kasaiushchiesia ustroistva muzeia, rechi, proiznesennye pri ego otkrytii i Otchet Vysochaishe uchrezhdennogo komiteta muzeia* [hereafter *Materialy*], published in three parts in *Izvestiia OLEAE,* pt. 1 (vol. 15, 1874), pt. 2 (vol. 17, 1875), and pt. 3 (vol. 22, no. 1, 1877), 1: 13–21.
28. *Protokoly zasedanii OLEAE,* in *Izvestiia OLEAE* 3, no. 1 (1866): 118; *Protokoly zasedanii etnograficheskogo otdela OLEAE,* in *Izvestiia OLEAE* 48, no. 1 (1886), 4. Funded by a gift from V. A. Daskhov, the collection would later be known as the Daskhov Ethnographic Division of the Rumiantsev Public Museum. For more on the Rumiantsev Museum, see K. I. Kestner, *Materialy dlia istoricheskogo opisaniia Rumiantsovskogo muzeia* (Moscow, 1882); Moskovskii i Rumiantsovskii muzei, *Piatidesiatiletie Rumiantsovskogo muzeia 1862–1912: Istoricheskii ocherk* (Moscow, 1913), 3–9; Katia Dianina, "Nation on Display: Russian Museums and Print Culture in the Age of the Great Reforms" (Ph.D. diss., Harvard University, 2002), chap. 7, 1–9; *MERSH,* 23: 229–230, 237–241. The decrees authorizing the transfer of the Rumiantsev Museum to Moscow may be found in *PSZ,* 2nd ser., 36 (1861): no. 37036, and *PSZ,* 2nd ser., 37 (1862): no. 38385. On the transfer from the vantage point of an insider, see V. V. Stasov, "Rumiantsovskii muzei: istoriia ego perevoda iz Peterburga v Moskvy v 1860–1861 godakh," *Russkaia starina* 1 (1883), reprinted in *Sobranie sochinenii V. V. Stasova* (St. Petersburg, 1894), 3: 1687–1712.
29. RGIA, f. 331 [Ministry of Agriculture and State Properties], op. 46, d. 70, ll. 95–97 ["Doklad ob ustroistve v 1867 g. Russkuiu etnograficheskuiu vystavku"]; Arkhiv RAN, f. 446, op. 1, d. 93 ["Materialy po OLEAE"], l. 1; TsIAM, f. 459 [Kantseliariia Popechitelia Moskovskogo uchebnogo okruga], op. 2, d. 3181, ll. 1–3; "Naimenovanie Obshchestva liubitelei estestvoznaniia, antropologii i etnografii pri Imperatorskom Moskovskom universitete," *PSZ,* 2nd ser., 42 (1867): no. 44397. The official accounts of the 1867 exposition are *Vserossiskaia etnograficheskaia vystavka, ustroennaia Imperatorskom Obshchestvom liubitelei estestvoznaniia* (Moscow, 1867) and a later compilation of material: OLEAE, *Etnograficheskaia vystavka 1867 goda* (Moscow, 1868). For more on the ethnographic exhibition, see

"Proekt Politekhnicheskoi vystavki," in *Politekhnicheskaia vystavka Imperatorskogo Obshchestva liubitelei estestvoznaniia, antropologii i etnografii* (Moscow, 1869), 5; Tokarev, *Istoriia russkoi etnografii,* 286; Lipets and Makashina, "Etnograficheskaia deiatel'nost', 119; Lipets and Makashina, "Rol' OLEAE," 43–46; and Nathaniel Knight, "The Empire on Display: Science, Nationalism and the Challenge of Human Diversity in the All-Russian Ethnographic Exposition of 1867" (paper presented at the American Association for the Advancement of Slavic Studies annual meeting, Washington, D.C., 2001).

30. In addition to the sources cited in note 2, see Charles R. Day, *Education for the Industrial World: The Écoles d'Arts et Métiers and the Rise of French Industrial Engineering* (Cambridge, Mass., 1987), 19; Paula Findlen, "The Museum: Its Classical Etymology and Renaissance Genealogy," *Journal of the History of Collections* 1 (1989): 59–78; and Paula Findlen, *Possessing Nature: Museums, Collections and Scientific Culture in Early Modern Italy* (Berkeley, Calif., 1994). To learn about world's fairs, good starting points are John E. Findling and Kimberly D. Pelle, *A Historical Dictionary of World's Fairs and Expositions, 1851–1988* (Westport, Conn., 1900), and Robert Rydell, *The Books of the Fairs: Materials about World's Fairs, 1834–1916, in the Smithsonian Institution Library* (Chicago, 1991); Greenhalg, *Ephemeral Vistas.* On the organization of the Crystal Palace exhibition, see Auerbach, *Great Exhibition,* 10–15, 20–21, 27–33. A Russian account is *Obozrenie Londonskoi Vsemirnoi vystavki po glavneishim otrasliam manufakturnoi promyshlennosti* (St. Petersburg, 1852).

31. Quoted in William H. Brock, "The Decline of Science," in William H. Brock, *Science for All: Studies in the History of Victorian Science and Education* (Aldershot, UK, 1996), 1. See also Hudson, *Social History of Museums,* 45, 58, 192; "Institutions and Associations," in *Encyclopedia of World Art* 16 vols. (New York, 1959–1968), 8: 161–162; Daniel J. Sherman, *Worthy Monuments: Art Museums and the Politics of Culture in Nineteenth-century France* (Cambridge, Mass., 1989), 212; Conn, *Museums,* 196–203.

32. Russell, *Science and Social Change,* 235–236; Auerbach, *Great Exhibition,* 125, 197–199; Jan Golinski, *Making Natural Knowledge: Constructivism and the History of Science* (Cambridge, 1998), quotation 95.

33. Cited passages in Conn, *Museums,* 5, 79; and George Stocking, *Victorian Anthropology* (New York, 1987), 186. In this vein also are Burton Benedict, ed., *The Anthropology of World's Fairs* (Berkeley, Calif., 1983); Greenhalgh, *Ephemeral Vistas;* Walden, *Becoming Modern;* Sharon MacDonald, ed., *The Politics of Display: Museums, Science, Culture* (London, 1998), 5, 9, 12; D. K. van Keuren, "Museums and Ideology: Augustus Pitt-Rivers, Anthropological Museums and Social Change in Later Victorian Britain," *Victorian Studies* 28 (August, 1984): 171–189, especially 185.

34. Werner Plum, *Les Expositions universelles au 19eme siècle, spectacles du changement socio-culturel,* Pierre Gallissaires trans. (Bonn, 1977), quotation 53; Hudson, *Social History of Museums,* 41–42; Golinski, *Making*

Natural Knowledge, 95–97; Conn, *Museums,* 123, 283; Frederick B. Artz, *The Development of Technical Education in France, 1500–1850* (Cambridge, Mass., 1966), 133, 143–145; Dorinda Outram, *Georges Cuvier: Vocation, Science and Authority in Post-Revolutionary France* (Manchester, 1984), 162–165; Farber, *Finding Order in Nature,* 25–29; Eileen Hooper-Greenhill, *Museums and the Shaping of Knowledge* (London, 1992), 170–171.

35. A. I. Khodnev, *Istoriia Imperatorskogo Vol'nogo ekonomicheskogo obshchestva s 1765 do 1865 goda* (St. Petersburg, 1865), 491–493, 499; "Doklad Komissii po ustroistvu v Moskve politekhnicheskoi vystavki," *Doklady Moskovskoi gorodskoi dumy* (25 August 1870): 3. This report and others have been compiled in a volume commissioned by OLEAE, *Materialy,* which records the genesis of the museum. See *Materialy,* 1: 1-12. Similarly, in the 1860s, the young generation of Russian chemists began to fill positions at Russian institutions of higher education and spread their views of chemistry throughout the country. See Nathan Brooks, "The Formation of a Russian Chemical Community, 1800–1917" (Ph.D. diss., Columbia University, 1982), 652–653, 671. See also *MERSH,* 2: 245–246.
36. A. M. Naumov, "Po povodu predpolagaemoi politekhnicheskoi vystavki v Moskve v 1872 g.," *Otechestvennye zapiski* 194, no. 2 (1871): 151–176, especially 161; Viktor Butovskii, "Pis'mo k izdateliam," *Moskovskie vedomosti,* no. 176 (14 August 1871): 3; Butovskii, "Zametka o muzeiakh Parizha i Londona," *Moskovskie vedomosti,* no. 186 (26 August 1871): 3–4; Butovskii, "Muzeum i shkola," *Moskovskie vedomosti,* no. 191 (3 September 1871): 3–4. See also Bogdanov, *Piatidesiatiletie,* 45–47. For background on Russia's manufacturing exhibitions, see A. I. Mikhailovskaia, "Iz istorii promyshlennykh vystavok v Rossii pervoi poloviny XIX veka," *Ocherki istorii muzeinogo dela v Rossii* (Moscow, 1961), 5: 79–154, and V. G. Petelin, "Pervaia vystavka manufakturnykh izdelii Rossii," *Voprosy istorii,* no. 3 (1981): 178–181. On Russia at the world's fairs, see David C. Fisher, "Russia and the Crystal Palace in 1851" (paper delivered at the Midwest Russian History Workshop, Madison, Wisc., April 20–21, 2001).
37. *Ukazatel' ekonomicheskii,* no. 22 (28 May 1860): 1–3. Though unsigned, the editorial was quite likely written by either Ivan Vernadskii or V. P. Bezobrazov, who were, as we have seen, economists known for their liberal views and public activities.
38. *Vek,* no. 50 (1861): 1405–1406.
39. *Protokoly zasedanii OLEAE,* in *Izvestiia OLEAE* 3, no. 2 (1886): cols. 90, 229–230; A. P. Bogdanov, "Pervyi kamen' osnovaniia Politekhnicheskoi vystavki," Arkhiv RAN, f. 446, op. 1a, d. 41a, ll. 30–30 ob. Later, the official newspaper of the exposition repeated this account. See *Vestnik Politekhnicheskoi vystavki,* no. 5 (May 5 1872): 1. I discuss the 1872 Polytechnical Exposition in "Pictures at an Exhibition: Science, Patriotism and Civil Society in Imperial Russia," *Slavic Review* 67, no. 4 (Winter 2008), 934–966.

40. Petelin, "Pervaia vystavka," 178–181; Mikhailovskaia, "Iz istorii promyshlennyich vystavok," 79–154; N. P. Melnikov, "Istoriia vystavok," *Vserossiiskaia khudozhestvennaia i promyshlennaia vystavka v Nizhnem-Novgorode v 1896 g.* (Odessa, 1896), 20.
41. *Vestnik Moskovskoi Politekhnicheskoi vystavki,* no. 48 (1872): 2; *Golos,* no. 158 (9 June 1871): 2; *Materialy,* 1: 55; *Politekhnicheskaia vystavka Imperatorskogo Obshchestva liubitelei estestvoznaniia, antropologii i etnografii* (Moscow, 1870), 5–6. Pos'et was a member of numerous associations, including OLEAE, RGO, and the Russian Technical Society. See Shilov, 539–542.
42. "Moskovskaia politekhnicheskaia vystavka s voennoi tochki zreniia," *Oruzheinyi sbornik* nos. 3, 4 (1872): quotations 1–2, 14; "Doklad Komiissii," 2. The major military journals—*Voennyi sbornik, Morskoi sbornik, Artilleriiskii zhurnal, Oruzheinyi sbornik*—and the newspaper *Russkii invalid* assiduously reported on displays of military technology in Europe and Russia. For a discussion of one of Miliutin's projects, the modernization of small arms, see Joseph Bradley, *Guns for the Tsar: American Technology and the Small Arms Industry in Nineteenth-century Russia* (DeKalb, Ill., 1990). The 1872 Polytechnical Exposition also eventually spawned a second museum, the better-known Imperial Historical Museum, in Red Square. See A. M. Razgon, "Rossiiskii istoricheskii muzei: Istoriia ego osnovaniia i deiatel'nosti, 1872–1917 gg.," in *Ocherki muzeinogo dela v Rossii,* no. 2 (Moscow, 1960), and Dianina, "A Nation on Display," chap. 7, 38–58.
43. "Uchrezhdenie Komiteta dlia ustroistva v Sankt-Peterburge obshchego muzeia prikladnykh znanii," *PSZ,* 2nd ser., 46 (1871): no. 49623; *Protokol chetvertogo zasedaniia Kommissii po obsuzhdeniiu programmy i plana Moskovskogo tsentral'nogo politekhnicheskogo muzeia* (Moscow, 1874), 1–4; N. Kh. Vessel', "Kensingtonskii muzei i sistema ego deistvii: Znachenie podobnogo muzeia u nas dlia rasprostraneniia tekhnicheskikh znanii," *Zapiski RTO,* no. 3 (1871): 127–156; N. Kh. Vessel', "Kak voznik pervyi v Rossii Muzei prikladnykh znanii v Peterburge, v Solianom gorodke: Iz moego dnevnkia," *Russkaia shkola,* no. 1 (January 1894): 9–30. An advocate of educational democratization, Vessel' was also editor of the journals *Uchitel'* and *Pedagogicheskii sbornik.* He wrote several studies of general and technical education, including *Nasha sredniaia obshcheobrazovatel'naia shkola* (St. Petersburg, 1903). See *Pedagogicheskaia entsiklopediia* (Moscow, 1964), 1: 323.
44. "Doklad Komissii," 2. Opened as a trade school for orphans in 1839, the Moscow Technical School became well known in Russia for combining theoretical knowledge with practical training. Viktor Della-Vos, the school's director from 1868 to 1880, has been credited with developing the first systematic program of workshop instruction. This program of manual training was displayed at the Centennial Exhibition in Philadelphia in 1876; seeming to offer an alternative to costly apprenticeship, it was later adopted by American educators. According to an American student of the problem, Della-Vos "demonstrated how new mechanical skills could be quickly and easily incul-

cated by reducing them to their component parts, which students then emulated with ease." For more on Della-Vos, see Politekhnicheskoe Obshchestvo sostoiashchee pri Moskovskom vysshem tekhnicheskom uchilishche, *Pamiati Viktora Karlovicha Della-Vos* (Moscow, 1891); *RBS*, 6: 192–194; W. J. Schurter, "The Development of the Russian System of Tool Construction (1763–1893) and Its Introduction into the United States' Industrial Education Programs, 1876–1893" (Ph.D. diss., University of Maryland, 1980), quotation 5; Harley David Balzer, "Educating Engineers: Economics, Politics and Technical Training in Tsarist Russia" (Ph.D. diss., University of Pennsylvania, 1980), 45–46. Both Della-Vos and Shatilov were members of multiple associations: among the memberships Della-Vos held were OLEAE, RTO, the Society for the Diffusion of Technical Knowledge, VEO, and the Moscow Agricultural Society; Shatilov was also a member of VEO, OLEAE, MOIP, the Forestry Society, and others (*RBS*, 22: 542–546).

45. "Doklad Komissii," 6.
46. *Vestnik Moskovskoi Politekhnicheskoi vystavki*, no. 73 (1872): 3; N. A. Shokhin, *Istoricheskii ocherk postroiki Muzeia prikladnykh znanii* (Moscow, 1894), 3–4.
47. Bogdanov's views are in *Protokoly zasedanii OLEAE* in *Ivestiia OLEAE* 9, no. 1 (1872): quotation 35. Della-Vos's views are quoted in "Torzhestvennoe otkrytie Politekhnicheskoi vystavki," *Izvestiia OLEAE* 10, no. 2 (1874): ix–xi; and *Protokoly zasedanii OLEAE*, in *Izvestiia OLEAE* 3, no. 2 (1886), col. 65–66. See also *Vestnik Moskovskoi politekhnicheskoi vystavki*, no. 23 (1872): 1–2, and no. 32 (1872): 1; *Golos*, no. 285 (15 October 1871): 2.
48. *Golos*, no. 45 (14 February 1871): quotation 1; *Politekhnicheskaia vystavka* (1869): 33.
49. *Protokol chetvertogo zasedaniia Kommissii*, 6; "Doklad Komissii," 2. See also V. K. Della-Vos, "Neskol'ko slov o proekte ustroistva tsentral'nykh muzeev v Rossii," in *Materialy*, 1: 21–24; *Vestnik Politekhnicheskoi vystavki*, no. 5 (1872): 1. On Popov, see *RBS*, 14: 561–565.
50. RGIA, f. 1263, op. 1 [1872], st. 475, d. 3598, ll. 14–25 ["Osobyi zhurnal Komiteta ministrov po predstavleniiu Ministra finansov ob uchrezhdenii muzeia prikladnykh znanii"]. The story is also recounted by Shchurovskii: "Rech' proiznesennaia pri otkrytii Politekhnicheskogo muzeia 30 noiabria 1872 tovarishchem pochtenogo predsedatelia muzeia G. E. Shchurovskim," in *Materialy*, 1: 53–58, especially 56–57. On Cherkasskii, see *Kniaz' Vladimir Aleksandrovich Cherkaskii: ego stat'i, ego rechi i vospominaniia o nem* (Moscow, 1879); *RBS*, 22: 198–208; S. Frederick Starr, *Decentralization and Self-Government in Russia, 1830–1870* (Princeton, N.J., 1972), 74–79; Thomas C. Owen, *Capitalism and Politics in Russia: A Social History of the Moscow Merchants, 1855–1905* (Cambridge, 1981), 75. The address to Alexander II is discussed in V. A. Nardova, *Gorodskoe samoupravlenie v Rossii v 60-kh-nachalo 90-kh godov XIX v.: Pravitel'stvennaia politika* (Leningrad, 1984), 153–162, and L. F. Pisar'kova, *Moskovskaia gorodskaia duma, 1863–1917* (Moscow, 1998), 236–238.

51. Owen, *Capitalism and Politics,* 29; Alfred J. Rieber, *Merchants and Entrepreneurs in Imperial Russia* (Chapel Hill, N.C., 1982), 137.
52. RGIA, f. 733, op. 142, d. 530, ll. 11–13 ["Ob uchrezhdenii muzeia prikladnykh znanii"]; RGIA, f. 1263, op. 1 (1872), st. 475, d. 3598, ll. 13–25. On Isakov, see *RBS,* 8: 143–144; *ES,* 25: 363. On the Museum of Applied Knowledge in St. Petersburg, see Vessel', "Kak voznik," 9–30.
53. RGIA, f. 1263, op. 1 (1872), st. 475, d. 3598, ll. 13–25; Bogdanov, *Piatidesiatiletie,* 7. Committee members included Cherkasskii's successor, the merchant-Slavophile Ivan A. Liamin, mayor of Moscow from 1871 to 1873; two members of the City Council, the merchant-Slavophile A. K. Krestovnikov and K. K. Shil'dbakh; the chair of the Moscow Stock Exchange Committee, Timofei S. Morozov; two members of the Stock Exchange Society, Nikolai A. Naidenov and Nikolai M. Borisovskii; two members of OLEAE, A. P. Bogdanov, and its vice president, Avgust Iu. Davidov; the director of the Imperial Technical School, Viktor Della-Vos; and playwright, charter member of the Society of Russian Playwrights, and official of the Moscow governor general's office, Vladimir Ivanovich Rodislavskii. See *Materialy,* 1: 50. On Rodislavskii, see *RBS,* 16: 305–307.
54. RGIA, f. 733, op. 142, d. 466a ["Ob ustroistve v Moskve Politekhnicheskoi vystavki i Politekhnicheskogo muzeia"], l. 46–47, 157–158; RGIA f. 934 [P. P. Durnovo], op. 2, d. 158, l. 1–2 [G. E. Shchurovskii to P. P. Durnovo, 19 November 1870]; *Protokoly zasedanii OLEAE* in *Izvestiia OLEAE* 3, no. 2 (1886): col. 273; "Moskovskaia politekhnicheskaia vystavka, *Moskovskie vedomosti,* no. 115 (9 May 1872): 4. See also Anne Lincoln Fitzpatrick, *The Great Russian Fair: Nizhnii Novgorod, 1840–1890* (New York, 1990), 169.
55. Bogdanov, "Doklad," in *Materialy,* 1: 7, 10.
56. Moskovskii muzei prikladnykh znanii, *Zasedaniia Komiteta muzeia prikladnykh znanii, 1876 godu* (Moscow, 1878), 24, published as a supplement to *Izvestiia OLEAE* 22, no. 2 (Moscow, 1878). (Hereafter, *Zasedaniia Komiteta muzeia.*)
57. N. V. Nikitin, "Otchet o proizvedennom po porucheniiu Imperatorskogo obshchestva liubitelei estestvoznaniia osmotra zagranichnykh muzeev," in *Materialy,* 2: 30–49, quotations, 35, 44. On Nikitin, see *Moskva: Entsiklopediia* (Moscow, 1997), 558. Russian educators and scientists were well informed about the history and purpose of the South Kensington Museum. See also Vessel', "Kensingtonskii muzei," 127–156. See also *Golos,* no. 256 (16 September 1871): 1.
58. See *Zasedaniia Komiteta muzeia,* 6, 14–15, 23–24, 33, 47, 75–78, 155; Nikitin, "Otchet," quotation, 42. See also Evgeniia Kirichenko, "K voprosu o poreformennykh vystavkakh Rossii kak vyrazhenie istoricheskogo svoeobraziia arkhitektury vtoroi poloviny XIX v.," in G. Iu. Sternin, *Khudozhestvennye protsessy v russkoi kul'ture vtoroi poloviy XIX v.* (Moscow, 1984), 83, 136, especially 119.) I am grateful to Katia Dianina for alerting me to this source.
59. *Protokoly Zasedanii OLEAE* in *Izvesttia OLEAE* 9, no. 1 (1872), quotation 33; TsIAM, f. 227 [Muzei prikladnykh znanii], op. 2, d. 6, ll. 133–133 ob.,

136–137. Among the organizations from which help was solicited were the Imperial Technical School, the Society of Russian Physicians, the Moscow Architectural Society, the Russian Society of Friends of Horticulture, the Society to Disseminate Technical Knowledge, the Society to Disseminate Useful Books, and the Imperial Philanthropic Society.

60. *Vestnik Moskovskoi Politekhnicheskoi vystavki,* no. 1 (1 May 1872): quotation 2; *Golos,* no. 147 (29 May 1871): 3.

61. "Godichnyi otchet Vysochaishe uchrezhdennogo komiteta po ustroistvu muzeia prikladnykh znanii," in *Materialy,* quotation 3: 4; *Zasedaniia Komiteta muzeia,* 145. The designs for the Crystal Palace Exhibition were displayed at the Institute of Civil Engineers in London. See Auerbach, *Great Exhibition,* 42.

62. *Materialy,* 1: 77–79, and 3: 5–10; and reports scattered in *Protokoly zasedaniia OLEAE.* On Shokhin, see *Moskva: Entsiklopediia* (Moscow, 1997), 916.

63. GARF, f. 109 [Third Section], 1 ekspeditsiia (1870), d. 32, ll. 15–15 ob.; *Protokoly zasedanii Komiteta po ustroistvu Politekhnichskoi vystavki* vol. 1 (Moscow, 1869), 8–9; OLEAE, *Protokoly zasedanii Vysochaishe uchrezhdennogo Komiteta dlia ustroistva muzeia prikladrykh znanii 1872–1875 g.* (Moscow, 1876): 20–21, 50; "Godichnyi otchet Vysochaishe uchrezhdennogo Komiteta po ustroistvu muzeia prikladnykh znanii," in *Materialy,* 2: 3; *Protokoly zasedanii OLEAE,* in *Izvestiia OLEAE* 9, no. 1 (1872): 38. See also "Iz Moskvy," *Golos,* no. 192 (13 July 1871): 2; *Golos,* no. 40 (9 June 1872): 1; *Vestnik Moskovskoi politekhnicheskoi vystavki,* no. 29: 2, no. 31:3, no. 32:3, no. 85:2. The organization committee also created a special apartment commission to help out-of-towners find accommodations.

64. "Moskovskaia Politekhnicheskaia vystavka," *Moskovskie vedomosti,* no. 116 (11 May, 1872): 4; no. 128 (23 May, 1872): 4; *Vestnik Moskovskoi Politekhnicheskoi vystavki* nos. 14, 19, 27, 28, 30, 31, 100, 112, 126.

65. V. K. Della-Vos, referring to the 1872 Polytechnical Exposition, in "Rech' o zadachakh muzeia prikladnykh znaniia, proiznesennaia pri otkrytii muzeia 30 noiabria 1872 g.," *Materialy,* 1: 58–62; quotation, 61.

66. "Torzhestvennoe otkrytie Politekhnicheskoi vystavki," *Izvestiia OLEAE* 10, no. 2 (1874): ix–xi; *Vestnik Moskovskoi Politekhnicheskoi vystavki,* nos. 22, 31, 37. In an expanded version of his banquet address, a series of public lectures on Peter the Great, Solov'ev emphasized Peter's role as teacher of the nation. See also Richard Wortman, *Scenarios of Power: Myth and Ceremony in Russian Monarchy* (Princeton, N.J., 2000), 2: 123–124.

67. Benedict, *Anthropology of World's Fairs;* Stocking, *Victorian Anthropology;* Van Keuren, "Museums and Ideology," 185.

68. "Torzhestvennoe otkrytie," quotations ix–xi; *Vestnik Moskovskoi Politekhnicheskoi vystavki,* no. 22, 31, 37.

69. *Moskovskie vedomosti,* no. 116 (11 May 1872): quotation 4, and *Vestnik Moskovskoi Politekhnicheskoi vystavki,* nos. 5, 18, 24, 38, 42, 45, 48, 58, 73, 77, 80, 83, 85–87, 120, 122, 136. On the "industrial enlightenment" see

Joel Mokyr, *The Gifts of Athena: Historical Origins of the Knowledge Economy* (Princeton, N.J., 2002) quotations 28, 35.

70. *Golos*, no. 84 (23 July 1872): 2–3.
71. *Golos*, no. 84 (23 July 1872): 2–3; *Moskovskie vedomosti*, no. 116 (11 May 1872): quotation 4. At the same time, one correspondent hinted that some visitors viewed the model home "with dishes that you never see anywhere" with some amusement (*Golos*, no. 209 [30 July 1872]: 2–3).
72. Wendy Salmond, *Arts and Crafts in Late Imperial Russia: Reviving the Kustar Art Industries, 1870–1917* (Cambridge, 1996): quotations 1–4; Evgeniia Kirichenko, "K voprosu o poreformennykh vystavkakh," quotation 121. Descriptions of the kustar section may be found in *Vestnik Politekhnicheskoi vystavki*, nos. 39, 41, 46, 54, 57, 78, 107.
73. *Golos*, no. 39 (1872): 3; *Moskovskie vedomosti*, no. 145 (11 June 1872): 2–3. On Gartman, see *RBS*, 4: 242–243; Rieber, *Merchants and Entrepreneurs*, 169–170. On Nikitin, see *Moskva: Entsiklopediia*, 558.
74. Evgeniia Kirichenko, *Russian Design and the Fine Arts, 1750–1917*, trans. Arch Tait (New York, 1991), quotations 99, 102; Kirichenko, "K voprosu o poreformennykh vystavkakh," 109, 117–121. See also V. G. Lisovskii, *"Natsional'nyi stil'" v arkhitekture Rossii* (Moscow, 2000), 135; Dianina, "Nation on Display, chap. 7. I am grateful to Katia Dianina for alerting me to Lisovskii's book.
75. "Godichnyi otchet Vysochaishe uchrezhdennogo komiteta po ustroistvu muzeia prikladnykh znanii," *Materialy*, 3: 12–13; "Dokladnaia zapiska Moskovskogo muzeia prikladnykh znanii," Arkhiv RAN, f. 446, op. 1a, d. 69, ll. 16–17 ["Materialy po Politekhnicheskomu muzeiu"]; "Otchet o deiatel'nosti Politekhnicheskogo muzeia v 1878 g.," *Protokoly zasedanii OLEAE* in *Izvestiia OLEAE* 37, no. 1 (1881): 80, 87, 92–93, 166.
76. Della-Vos, "Neskol'ko slov," *Materialy*, 1: 21; and Della-Vos, "Rech' o zadachakh," *Materialy*, quotation 1: 59; Bogdanov in *Trudy Antropologichekogo otdela OLEAE* 3 (*Izvestiia OLEAE* 27 [1878]: 4.
77. V. V. Stasov, "*Moskovskie vedomosti* i Politekhnicheskii muzei," *Sankt-Peterburgskie vedomosti*, no. 214 (1871), reprinted in *Sobranie sochinenii V. V. Stasova*, 2: cols. 259–268; quotation, cols. 262–263.
78. A. S. Vladimirskii, "Otchet kommissii po sostavleniiu kollektsii prikladnoi fiziki za istekshii god," *Materialy*, 2: 29–30; I. P. Arkhipov, "Otchet organizatsionnoi kommissii tekhnicheskogo otdela muzeia," *Materialy*, 3: 18–21. Many places in the minutes of the meetings of the museum committee indicate the reception of donations, often "in kind," to the museum from manufacturers. See also D. A. Naumov, "O sostave sel'skokhoziaistvennogo otdela v Politekhnicheskom muzee ko vremeni ego otkrytiia," and A. S. Vladimirskii, "O sostave kollektsii po prikladnoi fizike v Politekhnicheskom muzee," in *Materialy*, 1: 62–67 and 67–69, respectively.
79. Della-Vos, "Rech' o zadachakh muzeia," *Materialy*, 1: 60–61.
80. Bogdanov, "Obshcheobrazovatel'nyi politekhnicheskii muzei v Moskve," in *Materialy*, 1: 16.

81. *Vestnik Moskovskoi Politekhnicheskoi vystavki,* no. 73 (1872): 3; "Doklad Komissii," 2, 6; A. I. Chuprov, "Doklad po povodu politekhnicheskogo muzeia," *Materialy,* 1: 24–27, quotation 25. The report was originally presented to the board of the newly founded Moscow Society to Disseminate Technical Knowledge.
82. Steven Shapin, "The Audience for Science in Eighteenth-century Edinburgh," *History of Science* 12 (1974): 95–121; Larry R. Stewart, *The Rise of Public Science: Rhetoric, Technology and Natural Philosophy in Newtonian Britain, 1660–1750* (Cambridge, 1992); Simon Schaffer, "Natural Philosophy and Public Spectacle in the Eighteenth Century," *History of Science* 21 (1983): 1–43; Donald M. Scott, "The Popular Lecture and the Creation of a Public in Mid-nineteenth-century America," *Journal of American History* 66, no. 4 (March 1980): 791–809; J. N. Hays, "The London Lecturing Empire, 1800–1850," in Ian Inskter and Jack Morrell, eds., *Metropolis and Province: Science in British Culture, 1780–1850* (London, 1983), 91–119; Bernard Lightman, ed., *Victorian Science in Context* (Chicago, 1997).
83. *Otchet Sankt-Peterburgskogo Komiteta gramotnosti za 1895* (St. Petersburg, 1895), 129.
84. *Vestnik Moskovskoi Politekhnicheskoi vystavki,* no. 8 (1872): 1–2; "Godichnyi otchet Komiteta muzeia," *Materialy,* 2: 22–23, and 3: 11–12. Lectures could be illustrated using the museum's large collection of transparencies. Among the lecture series was a course of Russian history taught by Solov'ev and later published by the museum. (S. M. Solov'ev, *Kurs obshedostupnykh chtenii po russkoi istorii* [Moscow, 1874].)
85. *Protokoly zasedanii OLEAE,* in *Izvestiia OLEAE* 3, no. 1, (1866) col. 4; OLEAE, *Voskresnye ob"iasneniia kollektsii Muzeia prikladnykh znanii, 1877–1878* in *Izvestiia OLEAE* 22, no. 4 (Moscow, 1878): v.
86. From the remarks of Shchurovskii when he opened a meeting of OLEAE, 15 October 1878, in *Protokoly zasedaniia OLEAE, 1876–1880* in *Izvestiia OLEAE* 37, no. 1 (1881), quotation 87; and Della-Vos, "Rech' o zadachakh muzeia," *Materialy,* 1: quotation 62.
87. "Donesenie Soveta Imperatorskogo Obshchestva liubitelei estestvoznaniia v zasedanii 26 noiabria 1872 g.," *Materialy,* 1: 46; *Voskresnye ob"iasneniia kollektsii (1877–1878)* in *Izvestiia OLEAE* 36, no. 1, (Moscow, 1879). By 1894 OLEAE had published fourteen volumes of Sunday demonstrations in its *Izvestiia.* The tenth volume contains an index to the first ten years ("Ukazatel' Voskresnykh ob"iasnenii kollektsii Politekhnicheskogo muzeia, 1877–1887," *Izvestiia OLEAE* 53, no. 1, 1887).
88. Bogdanov's introduction to *Voskresnye ob"iasneniia kollektsii (1877–1878),* viii.
89. *Voskresnye ob"iaseniia kollektsii (1877–1878),* vii; "Otkrytie Moskovskogo muzeia prikladnykh znanii (Politekhnicheskogo) v zdanii na Lubianskoi ploshchadi, 30 maia 1877 goda," in Moskovskii muzei prikladnykh znanii, *Zasedaniia Komiteta muzeia za 1877–1882 goda* in *Izvestiia OLEAE* 36, no. 3 (Moscow, 1883), 14.

90. GARF, f. 109, 3 ekspeditsiia (1872), d. 94, ll. 102–103, 123–127; RGIA, f. 733, op. 142, d. 530, ll. 11–12, 84–93 ob. ["Ob ustroistve v Moskve Politekhnicheskoi vystavki i muzeia"]; "Pravila dlia ustroistva narodnykh chtenii v gubernskikh gorodakh," *PSZ,* 2nd ser., 51, (1876), no. 56762.
91. *Voskresnye ob"iasnennia kollektskii (1877–1878),* vi–vii. Data that might permit a determination of the composition of the museum public are not available. The historian must rely on anecdotal evidence.
92. Vagner quoted in Raikov, *Grigorii Efimovich Shchurovskii,* 70; Kablukov, "Iz vospominanii," 1464.
93. V. V. Bogdanov, "Obshchestvo liubitelei estestvoznaniia," 363.
94. Robert Wohl, *A Passion for Wings: Aviation and the Western Imagination, 1908–1918* (New Haven, Conn., 1994), 152; N. D. Duz', *Istoriia vozdukhoplavaniia i aviatsii v Rossii: Period do 1914 g.* (Moscow, 1979), 95; *Istoriia Moskvy* (Moscow, 1952–1959), 5: 397–398, 409, 428.
95. Cited in Wohl, *A Passion for Wings,* 152. On other uses of the museum at the close of the nineteenth century, see Arkhiv RAN, f. 446, op. 1, d. 93, ll. 19–21; A. P. Bogdanov, *Piatidesiatiletie,* 17–21, 31–33; V. V. Bogdanov, "Obshchestvo liubitelei estestvoznaniia," 365–367. On OLEAE and the Moscow Zoo, see A. P. Bogdanov, "Zametki o zoologicheskikh sadakh: Iz putevykh vpechatlenii po zagranichnym zoologicheskim sadam," *Izvestiia OLEAE* 25, no. 1 (1876): 1–2, 22, 32; OLEAE, *Letopis' zoologicheskikh trudov* (Moscow, 1888), 5–6.
96. Kablukov, "Iz vospominanii," 1464.
97. A. P. Bogdanov, "Zametki o zoologicheskikh sadakh," 1–40, quotations 1–2.
98. From the remarks of Shchurovskii when he opened a meeting of OLEAE, 15 October 1878, in *Protokoly zasedaniia OLEAE, 1876–1880* in *Izvestiia OLEAE* 3, no. 1 (1881), 87. See also Della-Vos, "Rech' o zadachakh muzeia," *Materialy,* 1: 61–62; Kablukov, "Iz vospominanii," 1464. On the stimulation of national pride, see N. K. Bestiuzhev-Riumin, "Sankt-Peterburg, 30 ianvaria 1873," *Golos,* no. 31 (31 January 1873), cited in Dianina, "Nation on Display," 41.
99. Stasov, "Moskovskie vedomosti i Politekhnicheskii muzei," cols. 262–263.
100. Della-Vos "Rech' o zadachakh muzeia," 61. See also *Vestnik Moskovskoi Politekhnicheskoi vystavki,* no. 31 (1872): 5.
101. A. P. Bogdanov, "Zadachi budushchego po otnosheniiu k Moskovskomu Politekhnicheskomu museiu," *Zasedaniia Komiteta muzeia za 1877–1882 goda,* 1.
102. Quote from V. V. Stasov, "Nasha etnograficheskaia vystavka i ee kritiki," *Sankt-Peterburgskie vedomosti,* nos. 179, 182 (1867), reprinted in *Sobranie sochinenii,* 3: cols. 935–948; quotation, col. 936. Not surprisingly, Della-Vos, Davidov, and Bogdanov all referred to individual initiative in various reports. See, respectively, "Torzhestvennoe otkrytie Politekhnicheskoi vystavki," *Protokoly zasedanii OLEAE, 1872–1873 (Izvestiia OLEAE* 10, no. 2, 1874): xi; 22; and *Zasedaniia Komiteta muzei, 1877–1882:* 1.

5. Government and the Public Trust

1. Cited passage in I. M. Maksin, *Ocherk razvitiia promyshlennogo obrazovaniia v Rossii* (St. Petersburg, 1909), 147. On the broader issues, see David Landes, *The Unbound Prometheus: Technological Change and Industrial Development in Western Europe from 1750 to the Present* (Cambridge, 1969), 151–152, 340–347; Michael Rose, "Culture, Philanthropy," in Alan Kidd and K. M. Roberts, eds., *City, Class and Culture: Studies of Social Policy and Cultural Production in Victorian Manchester* (Manchester, 1995), 112; Sanford Elwitt, "Social Reform and Social Order in Late Nineteenth-century France: The Musée social and Its Friends," *French Historical Studies* 11 (April 1980): 431–451; Thomas W. Laqueur, *Religion and Respectability: Sunday Schools and Working Class Culture, 1780–1850* (New Haven, Conn., 1976), 242.
2. Alfred J. Rieber, "The Rise of Engineers in Russia," *Cahiers du monde russe et soviétique* 31, no. 4 (October–December 1990): 539–568, especially 539, 563.
3. Jean-Pierre Chaline, *Sociabilité et Érudition: Les sociétés savants en France, XIXe–XXe siècles* (Paris, 1995), 169; Sanford Elwitt, *The Third Republic Defended: Bourgeois Reform in France, 1880–1914* (Baton Rouge, 1986), 241–242, 247, 252, 256–257, 285; Sandra Horvath-Peterson, *Victor Duruy and French Education: Liberal Reform in the Second Empire* (Baton Rouge, 1984), 107–109; Katherine Auspitz, *The Radical Bourgeoisie: The Ligue de l'enseignement and the Origins of the Third Republic, 1866–1885* (Cambridge, 1982), 85; Philip Nord, *The Republican Moment: Struggles for Democracy in Nineteenth-century France* (Cambridge, 1995), 106, 210–211; Carol E. Harrison, *The Bourgeois Citizen in Nineteenth-century France: Gender, Sociability and the Uses of Emulation* (Oxford, 1999), 141–143; A. E. Musson and Eric Robinson, *Science and Technology in the Industrial Revolution* (Toronto, 1969), 101. For the origins of such democratization of learning in the eighteenth century, see Dena Goodman, *The Republic of Letters: A Cultural History of the French Enlightenment* (Ithaca, N.Y., 1994), 264–269.
4. Harley David Balzer, "Educating Engineers: Economics, Politics and Technical Training in Tsarist Russia" (Ph.D. diss., University of Pennsylvania, 1980), 171. See also Balzer, "Russian Technical Society," *MERSH*, 32: 176–180.
5. *PSZ*, 2nd ser., 41 (1866), no. 43219; *Tridtsatipiatiletie E. N. Andreeva: Osoboe zasedanie Postoiannoi komissii po tekhnicheskomu obrazovaniiu* (St. Petersburg, 1886), 9–10; *Pamiati E. N. Andreeva: Torzhestvennoe zasedanie Russkogo tekhnicheskoe obshchestva 21 noiabria 1890 g.* (St. Petersburg, 1990), 29–34; N. N. Gritsenko, *Nauchno-tekhnicheskie obshchestva SSSR: Istoricheskie ocherki* (Moscow, 1968), 11; N. G. Filippov, *Nauchno-tekhnicheskie obshchestva Rossii, 1866–1917* (Moscow, 1975), 24; V. M. Kostomarev, *Iz deiatel'nosti Russkogo Tekhnicheskogo Obshchestva v oblasti mashinostroeniia* (Moscow, 1957), 12–13. For background concern-

ing industry, technology, and labor, see Reginald Zelnik, *Labor and Society in Tsarist Russia: The Factory Workers of St. Petersburg, 1855–1870* (Stanford, Calif., 1971). For biographical material on Andreev, see *RBS,* 2: 123–125; on Alekseev, see *RBS,* 2:11; on Bestuzhev-Riumin, see *Voennaia entsiklopediia* (St. Petersburg, 1911), 1: 517; on Gersevanov, see *BSDET,* 1: 231, and *Niva* 43 (1889): 1057–1058; on Okunev, see *RBS,* 12: 206–208. A plethora of engineering societies began in 1866 (Balzer, "Educating Engineers," 66–67). The biographical data on the major players in Russian associations is adequate on their service careers (for those who worked for the government at some point in their lives) but tends to be very laconic on their lives in private associations. The historian may infer that the impulses to participate in and lead societies came from a desire for sociability or from a sense of public duty, but more complete knowledge must await further study.

6. *Pamiati E. N. Andreeva,* 30.
7. *PSZ,* 2nd ser., 41 (1866), no. 43219; Russkoe tekhnicheskoe obshchestvo, *Kratikii istoricheskii ocherk Imperatorskogo Russkogo Tekhnicheskogo obshchestva s ego osnovaniia po 1 ianvaria 1893* (Moscow, 1894), 1–2; Filippov, *Nauchno-tekhnicheskie obshchestva,* 26–27; Gritsenko, *Nauchno-tekhnicheskie obshchestva,* 21–22; Kostomarev, *Iz deiatel'nosti,* 12–13.
8. Filippov, *Nauchno-tekhnicheskie obshchestva,* 31; Balzer, "Educating Engineers," 323; *ES,* 10: 347–348. On Del'vig, see *RBS,* 6: 198–201; on V. I. Kovalevskii, see *Al'manakh sovremennykh russkikh gosudarstennykh deiatelei* (St. Petersburg, 1897), 945–946, and Harley D. Balzer, "Public-Private Partnerships in Russian Education: Historical Models and Lessons," in Marsha Siefert, ed., *Extending the Borders of Russian History: Essays in Honor of Alfred J. Rieber* (Budapest, 2003), 457–479, especially 459.
9. To be elected an active member, one was required to obtain the recommendation of five current active or honorary members, to undergo the submission and review of qualifications, and to receive the vote of a two-thirds majority. *Kratkii istoricheskii ocherk,* 3; Filippov, *Nauchno-tekhnicheskie obshchestva,* 29–30.
10. Filippov, *Nauchno-tekhnicheskie obshchestva,* 34, 39–40, 127, 154; N. G. Filippov, "Dokumenty gosudarstevnnykh arkhivov po istorii nauchno-tekhnicheskikh obshchestv dorevoliutsionnoi Rossii," in *Problemy nauchno-tekhnicheskikh dokumentov i arkhivov* (Moscow, 1984), 112–132, especially 124; *Kratkii istoricheskii ocherk deiatel'nosti Imperatorskoso Russkogo tekhnicheskogo obshchestva s ego osnovaniia po 1-e ianvaria 1893 g.* (Moscow, 1894), 5, 8–12.
11. In addition, several more specialized journals were later published in St. Petersburg: *Electricity (Elektrichestvo),* the *Photographer (Fotograf), Railroad Affairs (Zheleznodorozhnoe delo),* and *Aeronautical Technology (Tekhnika vozdukhoplavaniia).*
12. Filippov, *Nauchno-tekhnicheskie obshchestva,* 34, 39–40, 127, 154; *Kratkii istoricheskii ocherk,* 5, 8–12. Electricity demonstrations were frequently covered in the popular press, with illustrations. For example, see "Elektrotekhnicheskaia vystavka v S.-Peterburge," *Vsemirnaia illiustratsiia,* no. 591

(1880): 371–374; "Elektricheskaia vystavka v Spb.," *Niva,* no. 3 (1886): 81–82; "Zal gromkoi peredachi zvukov na elektrickeskoi vystavke," *Niva,* no. 4 (1886): 114; G. O. Levit, *Istoriia energeticheskikh obshchestv SSSR* (Moscow, 1957), 21, 25. The Division of Photography was created in 1878; from then on the division was instrumental in organizing exhibitions of photography. See *A Portrait of Tsarist Russia: Unknown Photographs from the Soviet Archives* (New York, 1989), 12–15. On exhibits to popularize aviation, see Duz', *Istoriia vozdukhoplavaniia,* 48; M. M. Pomortsev, "Ocherk deiatel'nosti Vozdukhoplavatel'nogo otdela Russkogo tekhnicheskogo obshchestva," *Zapiski RTO* 4 (1900): 311–345.

13. Filippov, *Nauchno-tekhnicheskie obshchestva,* 6–7, 9, 97, 103, 120, 122–123, 201–202; quotation, 201.
14. GARF, f. 63 [Otdelenie po okhraneniiu obshchestvennoi besopasnosti i poriadka v Moskve (hereafter, MOO)] (1897), d. 616, l. 8 ob. ["Dokladnaia zapiska popechitelia Moskovskogo uchebnogo okruga"]; Filippov, *Nauchno-tekhnicheskie obshchestva,* 36; Zelnik, *Labor and Society,* 287–289.
15. P. A. Buryshkin, *Moskva kupecheskaia* (Moscow, 1991), 34, 98, 220–221; Alfred J. Rieber, *Merchants and Entrepreneurs in Imperial Russia* (Chapel Hill, N.C., 1982), 165–177, 307; Jo Ann Ruckman, *The Moscow Business Elite: A Social and Cultural Portrait of Two Generations, 1840–1905* (DeKalb, Ill., 1984), 105–106; Joseph Bradley, "Merchant Moscow after Hours: Voluntary Associations and Leisure," in James L. West and Iurii A. Petrov, eds., *Merchant Moscow: Images of Russia's Vanquished Bourgeoisie* (Princeton, N.J., 1998), 133–143. On Moscow entrepreneurs and philanthropists, see G. N. Ul'ianova, *Blagotvoritel'nost' moskovskikh predprinimatelei, 1860–1914* (Moscow, 1999).
16. *Pamiati E. N. Andreeva,* 32.
17. Landes, *Unbound Prometheus,* 151, 343; B. P. Cronin, *Technology, Industrial Conflict and the Development of Technical Education in Nineteenth-century England* (Aldershot, UK, 2001), 2–5.
18. H. S. Person, "Industrial Education," *Encyclopedia of the Social Sciences* (New York, 1937), 4: 692–697 (hereafter, *ESS*); I. L. Kandel, "Vocational Education," *ESS,* 8: 272–275; David Montgomery, *The Fall of the House of Labor: The Workplace, the State and American Labor Activism, 1865–1925* (Cambridge, 1987), 184–185; Landes, *Unbound Prometheus,* 151, 340–341; Cronin, *Technology,* 4–5, 163–167, 174–175.
19. Victoria E. Bonnell, *Roots of Rebellion: Workers' Politics and Organizations in St. Petersburg and Moscow, 1900–1914* (Berkeley, Calif., 1983), 58; Mark D. Steinberg, *Moral Communities: The Culture of Class Relations in the Russian Printing Industry, 1867–1907* (Berkeley, Calif., 1992), 54–55, 74–77; *Balzer,* "Educating Engineers," 88, 213.
20. Peter Kropotkin, *Memoirs of a Revolutionist* (Boston, 1930), 247; Maksin, *Ocherk razvitiia,* 6–9; A. G. Nebolsin, *Istoriko-statisticheskii ocherk obshchego i spetsial'nogo obrazovaniia v Rossii* (St. Petersburg, 1884), 131; I. A. Anopov, *Opyt sistematicheskogo obozreniia materialov k izucheniiu sovremennogo sostoianiia srednego i nizshego tekhnicheskogo i remeslennogo*

obrazovaniia v Rossii (St. Petersburg, 1889), i–ii. On the Sunday school in general, see Laqueur, *Religion and Respectability.* The standard history of the Sunday school in Russia is Ia. V. Abramov, *Nashi voskresnye shkoly, ikh proshloe i nastoiashchee* (St. Petersburg, 1900), especially 6, 24–41, 73–74. Abramov compares the Russian movement in the 1850s and 1860s with the French League of Education. See also Zelnik, *Labor and Society,* 174–199.

21. E. N. Andreev, *Obzor deiatel'nosti Russkogo tekhnicheskogo obshchestva po tekhnicheskomu obrazovaniiu* (St. Petersburg, 1872), 1–4.
22. B. N. Tits, *Ocherk istorii Postoiannoi komissii po tekhnicheskomu obrazovaniiu pri Imperatorskom Russkom tekhnicheskom obshchestve, 1868–1889* (St. Petersburg, 1889), 1–3, 21–22; N. M. Korol'kov, *Kratkii obzor deiatel'nosti Postoiannoi komissii po tekhnicheskomu obrazovaniiu* (St. Petersburg, 1912), 59. The Education Commission became an autonomous division of the society in 1883 but retained the name "commission."
23. Balzer, "Educating Engineers," 171–174.
24. Cited passages in E. N. Andreev, *Obzor prepodavaniia v germanskikh politekhnicheskikh shkolakh* (St. Petersburg, 1858), 1, 3, 20, 43; Andreev, *Stoit li pooshchrat' russkaia promyshlennost'?* (St. Petersburg, 1866), 6–7. His views are further developed in Andreev, "Doklad ob obrazovanii masterov," *Zapiski RTO* 4 (1868): 167–209; Andreev, *Shkol'noe delo v Rossii: Nashi obshchie i spetsial'nye shkoly* (St. Petersburg, 1882), 2, 6, 80, 231–233.
25. Cited passages in Balzer, "Educating Engineers," 116; Andreev, "Doklad," 168; Andreev, *Shkol'noe delo,* 245.
26. *Zhivopisnoe obozrenie* 11 (1895): 212; *Pedagogicheskaia entsiklopediia* (Moscow, 1964), 3: 81–82; Kollontai quotation, 83. See also "A. G. Nebolsin," *Vsemirnaia illiustratsiia,* no. 1480 (1897): 552; Balzer, "Educating Engineers," 78, 87, 172–178; Kevin Donald Haukness, "Educating the Russian Worker: The School System of the Russian Technical Society in St. Petersburg, 1869–1917" (Ph.D. diss., University of Minnesota, 1994), 118.
27. A. G. Nebolsin, "Ob ustroistve periodicheskikh vystavok i s"ezdov po tekhnicheskomu i professional'nomu obrazovaniiu," in *Trudy s"ezda russkikh deiatelei po tekhnicheskomu i professional'nomu obrazovaniiu v Rossii: Doklady na obshchikh sobraniiakh otdelenii* (St. Petersburg, 1890), 3–15, quotation 3; V. I. Sreznevskii, ed., *S"ezd russkikh deiatelei po tekhnicheskomu i professional'nomu obrazovaniiu v Rossii, 1889–1890: Obshchaia chast'* (St. Petersburg, 1891), 3.
28. Andreev, *Shkol'noe delo,* 57, 62, 69, 81; Filippov, *Nauchno-tekhnicheskie obshchestva,* 169; Korol'kov, *Kratkii obzor,* 15; Tits, *Ocherk istorii Postoiannoi komissii,* 110.
29. Tits, *Ocherk istorii Postoiannoi komissii,* 38.
30. Andreev, *Shkol'noe delo,* 57, 62, 69, 81; Filippov, *Nauchno-tekhnicheskie obshchestva,* 169; Korol'kov, *Kratkii obzor,* 15; Tits, *Ocherk istorii Postoiannoi komissii,* 38, 110.
31. Geoffrey V. Sutton, *Science for a Polite Society: Gender, Culture and the Demonstration of Enlightenment* (Boulder, Colo., 1995), quotation 214;

Donald M. Scott, "The Profession That Vanished: Public Lecturing in Mid Nineteenth-century America," in Gerald L. Geison, ed., *Professions and Professional Ideologies in America* (Chapel Hill, N.C., 1983), 12–28, especially 17–21; J. N. Hays, "The London Lecturing Empire, 1800–1850," in Ian Inkster and Jack Morrell, eds., *Metropolis and Province: Science in British Culture, 1780–1850* (London, 1983), 91–119, especially 94, 97–98, 110; Bernard Lightman, *Victorian Science in Context* (Chicago, 1997), 179; Donald M. Scott, "The Popular Lecture and the Creation of a Public in Mid-nineteenth-century America," *Journal of American History* 66, no. 4 (March 1980): 791–809; Colin A. Russell, *Science and Social Change in Britain and Europe, 1700–1900* (New York, 1983), 88, 155; Jan Golinski, *Science as Public Culture: Chemistry and the Enlightenment in Britain, 1710–1820* (London, 1992), 59, 94–96.

32. "Pravila dlia ustroistva narodnykh chtenii v guberskikh gorodakh," *PSZ,* 2nd ser., 51, (1876), no. 56762. The files of the central and local authorities are filled with requests for permission for public lectures. See, for example, "O dozvolenii raznym litsam chteniia publichnykh lektsii," GARF, f. 109, 3 ekspeditsiia, op. 156 (1871), d. 9. On the many obstacles faced by organizers of public lectures and readings, see V. Devel', "K voprosu o vneshkol'nom obrazovanii naroda," *Russkoe bogatstvo,* no. 11 (1898): 178–197. The matter is also discussed in S. V. Rozhdestvenskii, *Istoricheskii obzor deiatel'nosti Ministerstva narodnogo prosveshcheniia, 1802–1902* (St. Petersburg, 1902), 562–563.

33. *Russkie vedomosti,* no. 43 (12 February 1898): 1; A. E. Gruzinskii, *Tridtsat' let zhizni Uchebnogo otdela Obshchestva rasprostraneniia tekhnicheskikh znanii* (Moscow, 1902), 5, 14, 19–20, 37, 69–76; Filippov, *Nauchno-tekhnicheskie obshchestva,* 174; *Otchet o deiatel'nosti S-Peterburgskogo Komiteta gramotnosti za 1895* (St. Petersburg, 1895), 129; P. Shestakov, "Stolichnye komitety gramotnosti," *Russkaia mysl'* (May 1896): 106–124; Shestakov (June, 1896): 107–124; Shestakov (October, 1896): 91–102, especially 97; P. V. Krotkov, "Deiatel'nost' Komissii po ustroistvu v Moskve publichnykh narodnykh chtenii," *Izvestiia Moskovskoi gorodskoi dumy,* pt. 1 (July–August 1896): 22–27.

34. A. A. Kizevetter, *Na rubezhe dvukh stoletii: Vospominaniia 1881–1914* (Moscow, 1997), 159–165, 203–214; quotation, 214.

35. Tits, *Ocherk istorii Postoiannoi komissii,* 138–141; Filippov, *Nauchno-tekhnicheskie obshchestva,* 171. For biographical information on Butlerov, see *RBS,* 3: 528–532; on Mendeleev, see *BSDET,* 2: 25–28.

36. Andreev, *Obzor prepodavaniia,* 18; Andreev, "Doklad," 205–206; Andreev, *Shkol'noe delo,* 7, 21; *Tridtsatipiatiletie E. N. Andreeva,* 17; Tits, *Ocherk istorii Postoiannoi komissii,* 4; Balzer, "Educating Engineers," 281.

37. Trudy *Vserossiiskogo torgovo-promyshlennogo s"ezda 1896 g. v Nizhnem Novgorode* (St. Petersburg) 6, no. 9 (1897): 122–123; quoted in Arcadius Kahan, *Russian Economic History: The Nineteenth Century,* ed. Roger Weiss (Chicago, 1989), 192. For more on Vyshnegradskii's role in the development of technical education, see Balzer, "Educating Engineers," 135, 141–143;

Shilov, 149–154; and *Liudi russkoi nauki: Tekhnika* (Moscow, 1965), 218–226. On the Congress of Industrialists, see Zelnik, *Labor and Society,* 302–304, 311–313.

38. Nebolsin, "Ob ustroistve," 7; GARF, f. 102 [DP], 4 d/p (1914), d. 124, pt. 20 ["O s"ezde po tekhnicheskomu obrazovaniiu"], l. 28 ob. ["Dokladnaia zapiska o s"ezdakh russkikh deiatelei po tekhnicheskomu obrazovaniiu,"]; A. V. Pogozhev, "Obzor deiatel'nosti professional'no-tekhnicheskikh s"ezdov v Rossii," *Meditsinskaia beseda,* no. 11 (1896): 328. See also Tits, *Ocherk istorii Postoiannoi komissii,* 82.

39. Abramov, *Nashi voskresnye shkoly,* 97–100; L. M. Ivanov, "Ideologicheskoe vozdeistvie na proletariat tsarizma i burzhuazii," in L. M. Ivanov, ed., *Rossiiskii proletariat: Oblik, bor'ba, gegemoniia* (Moscow, 1970), 317–355, especially 321; Susan Bronson, "Enlightening the Urban Poor: Adult Education in Late Imperial Russia, 1859–1914" (Ph.D. diss., University of Michigan, 1995), 60.

40. Nebolsin, *Istoriko-statisticheskii ocherk,* 100, 251–253; Anopov, *Opyt,* 421–422, 426–431, 438, 534–535; Korol'kov, *Kratkii obzor,* 46. According to Nebolsin's calculations, the number of pupils enrolled increased from 60 in 1870–1871 to 1,172 in 1882–1883; Anopov recorded 1,294 pupils in 1887–1888. In the five-year period 1878–1883, expenditures increased from 12,193 rubles to 24,456 rubles; the long-term average was approximately 100 rubles per pupil annually. In 1878 the Ministry of Education ran a total of 24,853 primary schools, enrolling 876,963 boys and 188,926 girls. In 1887 a total number of 6,088 pupils were enrolled in all technical schools; by 1897 this figure had risen to 10,304. For comparison, in 1877 the St. Petersburg City Council ran 22 elementary schools, enrolling 899 pupils. See also Maksin, *Ocherk razvitiia,* 45; Filippov, *Nauchno-tekhnicheskie obshchestva,* 163; Haukness, "Educating the Russian Worker," 46, 133, 143, 191, 209, 442.

41. GARF, f. 63 (1897), d. 616, l. 1 ["Ob uchilishchakh RTO"]; GARF f. 102, 4 d/p (1914), d. 124, pt. 20, l. 22 ob. ["Dokladnaia zapiska o s"ezdakh russkikh deiatelei po tekhnicheskomu obrazovaniiu,"]; "Ob uchilishchakh, uchrezhdennykh Imperatorskim Russkim tekhnicheskim obshchestvom," *PSZ,* 3rd ser., 11 (1882), no. 915; Korol'kov, *Kratkii obzor,* 11; Nebolsin, *Istoriko-statisticheskii ocherk,* 250–251; Anopov, *Opyt,* 417–418; Tits, *Ocherk istorii Postoiannoi komissii,* 53–54; Nebolsin, "Ob ustroistve," 9; Rozhdestvenskii, *Istoricheskii obzor,* 664.

42. Daniel T. Orlovsky, "Professionalism in the Ministerial Bureaucracy on the Eve of the February Revolution of 1917," in Harley D. Balzer, ed., *Russia's Missing Middle Class: The Professions in Russian History* (Armonk, N.Y., 1996), 267–292, especially 270–271; Daniel T. Orlovsky, *The Limits of Reform: The Ministry of Internal Affairs in Imperial Russia, 1802–1881* (Cambridge, 1981), 198–201; Francis William Wcislo, *Reforming Rural Russia: State, Local Society, and National Politics, 1855–1914* (Princeton, N.J., 1990), 307–308; Balzer, "Educating Engineers," 256, 271–276, 334.

43. V. Fedorchenko, *Imperatorskii dom: Vydaiushchiesia sanovniki* (Moscow, 2001), 1: 565–568. Other imperial patrons included Grand Duchess Elizaveta Fedorovna and her husband Grand Duke Sergei Aleksandrovich.
44. GARF, f. 63 (1897), d. 616, ll. 73–74 ["Zapiska MOO"]. A list of the schools founded by RTO and placed under government supervision may be found in *Uchilishcha Imperatorskogo Russkogo tekhnicheskogo obshchestva: Spravochnaia kniga Postoiannoi komissii po tekhnicheskomu obrazovaniiu za 1888/89 uchebnyi god* (St. Petersburg, 1889), 15–35.
45. Korol'kov, *Kratkii obzor,* 4, 9–10. See also V. I. Sreznevskii, "O khode dela po ustroistvu Russkim tekhnicheskim obshchestvom s"ezda russkikh deiatelei po tekhnicheskomu i promyshlennomu obrazovaniiu" *Zapiski RTO,* no. 8 (1888): 26; Tits, *Ocherk istorii Postoiannoi komissii,* 25; Nebolsin, *Istoriko-statisticheskii ocherk,* 249–254. Coverage of the opening of the Prechistenka evening and Sunday classes for workers and of the Giubner vocational school in Moscow, for example, may be found in *Russkie vedomosti,* nos. 255 and 283 (15 September and 13 October 1897).
46. *Pedagogicheskaia entsiklopediia,* 3: 82.
47. A_t, "Obshchestvo mery, vesa i chisla," *Novoe vremia,* no. 6119 (12 March 1893): 3. A-t was the pseudonym of Vladimir Karlovich Petersen, a correspondent of *Novoe vreniia* from 1879 to 1906. (I. F. Masanov, *Slovar' pseudonimov russkikh pisatelei, uchenykh i obshchestvennykh deiatelei* (Moscow, 1956), 1: 81.
48. Korol'kov, *Kratkii obzor,* 46–47; Filippov, *Nauchno-tekhnicheskie obshchestva,* 163, 168. Anopov calculated that teachers' salaries varied between 600 and 750 rubles per year (Anopov, *Opyt,* 226). Recruiting teachers prepared to teach technical subjects was the bane of vocational schooling elsewhere. See Cronin, *Technology,* 217. In the judgment of an authority on Russian technical education, the RTO schools were "among the best organized . . . and more faithful to their purpose" (Balzer, "Educating Engineers," 87).
49. Korol'kov, *Kratkii obzor,* 34–37, 41.
50. Tits, *Ocherk istorii Postoiannoi komissii,* 4.
51. Tits, *Ocherk istorii Postoiannoi komissii,* 24, 71. See also Korol'kov, *Kratkii obzor,* 91; *Russkie vedomosti,* no. 284 (14 October 1897): 3; S. Bleklov, "Obrazovatel'nye uchrezhdeniia dlia rabochikh g. Moskvy," *Russkaia mysl',* no. 5 (1904): 121–145; *Istoriia Moskvy* (Moscow, 1952–1959), 5: 372, 454–455; Thomas C. Owen, *Capitalism and Politics in Russia: A Social History of the Moscow Merchants, 1855–1905* (Cambridge, 1981), 153.
52. Sreznevskii, *S"ezd russkikh deiatelei,* 1, 16; GARF, "Dokladnaia zapiska o s"ezdakh russkikh deiatelei po tekhnicheskomu obrazovaniiu," l. 23 ob. See also V. N. Sreznevskii, "O khode dela," 2; Filippov, *Nauchno-tekhnicheskie obshchestva,* 181. Education exhibitions were covered frequently in the popular press. For example, see "Vystavka uchenicheskikh rabot tekhnicheskikh, professional'nykh i remeslennykh shkol," *Vsemirnaia illiustratsiia,* no. 1100 (17 February 1890): 129–130; "Vystavka po tekhnicheskomu i professional'nomu obrazovaniiu," *Niva,* no. 3 (1904): 57–59.

53. Haukness, "Educating the Russian Worker," 40–43, 50, 60–62.
54. Congrès international ayant pour objet l'enseignement technique, commercial, et industriel, *Compte Rendu des Travaux* (Paris-Bordeaux, 1887), 211–218. Miasoedov reported on "L'enseignement technique et professionnel en Russie," "L'association pour l'amélioration du travail national en Russie," and "Les écoles et cours pour l'enseignement général et technique des ouvriers et leurs enfants, institués à St.-Pétersbourg et ses banlieues par la Société imperial polytechnique russe," *Compte Rendu des Travaux,* 226–273. Some delegates feared language barriers, travel difficulties, and the distance of St. Petersburg from the rest of the empire would prevent the congress from accomplishing its goal of spreading technical education. Miasoedov's report to the Ministry of Education may be found in "Dokladnaia zapiska Ministerstvu narodnogo prosveshcheniia o proiskhodivshem v sentiabre 1886 g. pervom mezhdunarodnom kongresse po voprosam tekhnicheskogo, promyshlennogo i kommercheskogo obrazovaniia delegata kongressa P. A. Miasoedov," RGIA, f. 560 [Ministry of Finance], op. 22, d. 32/7, ll. 252–275.
55. GARF, f. 102, 4 d/p (1914), d. 124 pt. 20, l. 21 ["Dokladnaia zapiska o s"ezdakh russkikh deiatelei po tekhnicheskomu obrazovaniiu,"]; "P. A. Miasoedov, "Pervyi mezhdunarodnyi kongress po voprosam tekhnicheskogo, promyshlennogo i kommercheskogo obrazovaniia 1886 g. i potrebnost' Rossii v shirokom rasprostranenii sego obrazovaniia," *Trudy Komissii po tekhnicheskomu obrazovaniiu* (St. Petersburg, 1886–1887), quotation supplement, 51.
56. Sreznevskii, "O khode dela," 1.
57. GARF, f. 102, 4 d/p (1914), d. 124, pt. 20, l. 21 ["Dokladnaia zapiska o s"ezdakh russkikh deiatelei po tekhnicheskomu obrazovaniiu,"]; Nebolsin, "Ob ustroistve," 3–4; Anopov, *Opyt,* 476–477; Maksin, *Ocherk razvitiia,* 1. Education congresses are discussed in Christine Ruane, *Gender, Class and the Professionalization of Russian City Teachers, 1860–1914* (Pittsburgh, 1994), 103, and Scott J. Seregny, *Russian Teachers and Peasant Revolution: The Politics of Education in 1905* (Bloomington, Ind., 1989), 39–41.
58. RGIA, f. 90 [RTO], op. 1, d. 248, ll. 6, 364 [III S"ezd po tekhnicheskomu obrazovaniiu]; GARF, f. 102, 4 d/p (1914), d. 124, pt. 20, l. 21–24 ob. ["Dokladnaia zapiska o s"ezdakh russkikh deiatelei po tekhnicheskomu obrazovaniiu"]; Sreznevskii, "O khode dela," 3. Chairs of sections could invite additional persons to attend with voice but not vote. Sreznevskii, ed., *S"ezd russkikh deiatelei,* 17.
59. Sreznevskii, ed., *S"ezd russkikh deiatelei,* 8–9, 45. Support, sympathy *(sochustvie),* cooperation, and collaboration *(sodeistvie),* as well as animation *(ozhivlenie),* were words used constantly by the members and proponents of voluntary associations and their projects.
60. GARF, f. 102, 4 d/p (1914), d. 124, pt. 20, l. 26 ["Dokladnaia zapiska o s"ezdakh russkikh deiatelei po tekhnicheskomu obrazovaniiu"]; A. V. Pogozhev, "Obzor deiatel'nosti professional'no-tekhnicheskikh s"ezdov v

Rossii," *Meditsinskaia beseda,* no. 15 (1896): 463; Filippov, *Nauchno-tekhnicheskie obshchestva,* 182.

61. GARF, f. 102, 4 d/p (1914), d. 124, pt. 20, l. 27 ["Dokladnaia zapiska"]; S"ezd russkikh deiatelei po tekhnicheskomu i professional'nomu obrazovaniiu," *Trudy IX sektsii S'ezda* (Moscow, 1896), 5. Following the directives of the congress, Anopov wrote his study of technical education. Anopov, *Opyt,* i. See also Nebolsin, "Ob ustroistve," 3; Sreznevskii, *S"ezd russkikh deiatelei,* 3; Sreznevskii, "O khode dela," 1–4.
62. Anopov, *Opyt,* 229.
63. "Tretii s"ezd deiatelei po tekhnicheskomu i professional'nomu obrazovaniiu," *Zapiski RTO,* no. 3 (1904): 105–154; quotation, 110. For more on Vakhterov, see Ben Eklof, *Russian Peasant Schools: Officialdom, Village Culture, and Popular Pedagogy, 1861–1914* (Berkeley, Calif., 1986), 110; V. P. Vakhterov, *Vseobshchee obrazovanie* (Moscow, 1897); *Pedagogicheskaia entsiklopediia,* 1: 300–301. For more on the involvement of the St. Petersburg and Moscow literacy committees in primary education, see D. D. Protopopov, *Istoriia S.-Peterburgskogo Komiteta gramotnosti, 1861–1895* (St. Petersburg, 1897); N. M. Pirumova, *Zemskoe liberal'noe dvizhenie: Sotsial'nye korni i evoliutsiia do nachala XX veka* (Moscow, 1977), 117–120; N. M. Pirumova, Zemskaia intelligentsia i ee rol'v obshchestvennoi bor'be do nachala XX v. (Moscow, 1986), 152, 180–185.
64. "Vtoroi S"ezd russkikh deiatelei po tekhnicheskomu i professional'nomu obrazovaniiu, byvshii v Moskve v 1895–96 godu," *Zapiski RTO,* no. 5 (1897): 1–58. See also Pirumova, *Zemskaia intelligentsia,* 186; Ruane, *Gender, Class,* 105; Eklof, *Russian Peasant Schools,* 110–114.
65. Nebolsin, "Ob ustroistve," 13.
66. Pogozhev, "Obzor deiatel'nosti," *Meditsinskaia beseda,* no. 11 (1896): 327; Sreznevskii, "O khode dela," 5–6.
67. Sreznevskii, "O khode dela," 7, 28.
68. Cited passages in Pogozhev, "Obzor deiatel'nosti," *Meditsinskaia beseda,* no. 11 (1896): 327, and no. 12 (1896): 369.
69. Sreznevskii, ed., *S"ezd russkikh deiatelei,* 5, 8.
70. See the draft of rules and regulations contained in Sreznevskii, "O khode dela," appendix 4: 27–29, article 9; Sreznevskii, ed., *S"ezd russkikh deiatelei,* 35. Among the meanings embedded in the verb *khodataistvovat'* are "to intercede," "to mediate," and "to represent or act on behalf of someone." On the government ignoring resolutions, see *Itogi Vtorogo s"ezda russkikh deiatelei po tekhnicheskomu i professional'nomu obrazovaniiu v zhizni* (St. Petersburg, 1898).
71. B. B. Veselovskii, *Istoriia zemstva za sorok let* (St. Petersburg, 1909–1911), 3: 410–411.
72. Abramov, *Nashi voskresnye shkoly,* 300–301, 303–305, 312–313.
73. GARF, f. 102, 4 d/p (1914), d. 124, pt. 20, l. 28 ["Dokladnaia zapiska"]; "Vtoroi S"ezd," quotation 1. The ninth section drew up plans for model schools based on data collected from 147 officials of elementary schools. The

congress expressed the hope that there soon would be a national congress on primary education. See also Ruane, *Gender, Class,* 105.

74. GARF, f. 102, 4 d/p (1914), d. 124, pt. 20, l. 28 ob. ["Dokladnaia zapiska"]; "Vtoroi S"ezd," 42. Data compiled by the education commission of the Technical Society provided the basis for P. M. Shestakov's study of literacy at the Emile Tsindel' (Zindel) plant in Moscow, a study widely used by historians of Russian labor, an early version of which was a report at the second congress. See Pogozhev, "Obzor deiatel'nosti," *Meditsinskaia beseda,* no. 13 (1896): 393; P. M. Shestakov, *Obrazovatel'nye uchrezhdeniia i gramotnost' rabochikh na manufacture T-va Emil' Tsindel' v Moskve* (Moscow, 1904).
75. GARF, f. 102, 4 d/p (1914), d. 124, pt. 20, l. 30 ob. ["Dokladnaia zapiska"]. The government restricted other contemporaneous education congresses, such as the Congress of Primary Schoolteachers of the Moscow Education District in 1903, even more by prohibiting debate, the attendance of outsiders, and the preparation of resolutions (Ruane, *Gender, Class,* 111).
76. Cited passages in Auspitz, *Radical Bourgeoisie,* 69, 94, 103–107. On anticlericalism, see also Elwitt, *Third Republic Defended,* 235; Horvath-Peterson, *Victor Duruy,* 113. In 1867 the League of Education was denied permission to hold a congress at the Paris World Exposition.
77. Admiral A. S. Shishkov, minister of education (1824–1828), quoted in Patrick L. Allston, *Education and the State in Tsarist Russia* (Stanford, Calif., 1969), 32.
78. Orlovsky, *Limits of Reform,* 11.
79. Count Aleksandr Benkendorf, chief of the Third Section (1826–1844), quoted in Allston, *Education and the State,* 32.
80. Kropotkin, *Memoirs,* 248.
81. Kizevetter, *Na rubezhe,* 224.
82. Orlando Figes, *A People's Tragedy: A History of the Russian Revolution* (New York, 1996), 159, 162. Richard Robbins has rehabilitated the government's efforts and claims that the government tried to mobilize and coordinate the haphazard relief on the part of society in the famine year. The fact remains that the famine gave a boost to public discussion, organization, and the sense of empowerment in civil society. See Richard G. Robbins Jr., *Famine in Russia, 1891–1892: The Imperial Government Responds to a Crisis* (New York, 1975).
83. Pogozhev, "Obzor deiatel'nosti," *Meditsinskaia beseda,* no. 11 (1896): 327.
84. Bleklov, "Obrazovatel'nye uchrezhdeniia," 136.
85. GARF, f. 63 (1897), d. 616, l. 11 ob. ["Dokladnaia zapiska popechitelia Moskovskogo uchebnogo okruga"].
86. A _t, "Obshchestvo mery," 3.
87. Minister of transport and communications to Stolypin, 5 January 1907, GARF f. 102, 4 d/p (1907), d. 104 [RTO], ll. 3–4. The second letter, written on 16 December 1908, expressed concern that in doing a statistical study of railroad workers for a government commission, the Technical Society "would have an excuse to stir up the railroad workers"; the aid of the zemstvo and municipal statistical offices in the enterprise, what the society proposed,

would be "inconvenient." Shaufus, the minister of transportation after 1905, endorsed the ban on meetings of the Moscow branch in 1905 so as not "to enflame the strike movement" (GARF, f. 102, 4 d/p [1907], d. 104, ll. 96–97). A government memorandum made the same point: "Russian industry now no longer requires any help from society, while our legislation that gave these associations a special independence has remained unchanged since the 1860s" (GARF, f. 63 [1897], d. 616, ll. 73–74 ["Zapiska MOO"]).

88. GARF, f. 102 3 d/p (1905), d. 513 [Moskovskoe otdelenie RTO], l. 2; RGIA, f. 1284 [Ministry of Internal Affairs], op. 188, d. 90 ["O zakrytii Moskovskogo otdeleniia RTO"], l. 1 ["DP to DOD MVD 5 May 1905"].
89. GARF, f. 63 (1897), d. 616, l. 68 ob. ["Zapiska MOO"].
90. GARF, f. 63 (1897), d. 616, l. 13–13 ob. ["Dokladnaia zapiska popechitelia Moskovskogo uchebnogo okruga"], 67, 71–71 ob. ["Zapiska MOO"], 116.
91. Goremykin and Stasova quoted in Filippov, *Nauchno-tekhnicheskie obshchestva*, 162, 164; see also 88.
92. For example, see Andrew Verner, *The Crisis of Russian Autocracy: Nicholas II and the 1905 Revolution* (Princeton, N.J., 1990).
93. GARF, f. 63 (1897), d. 616, quotations l. 12 ["Dokladnaia zapiska popechitelia Moskovskogo uchebnogo okruga"]. See also Gruzinskii, *Tridtsat' let*, 37.
94. In addition, officials of the Ministry of Education were to be appointed to the Education Commission by the curator. The Education Commission's appointees to be teachers or school inspectors had to be approved by the ministry, and the society's vocational schools needed to be more closely supervised. The Moscow prefect made the same complaint that nothing had been done to the bylaws of RTO and of its schools. At the same time that interdepartmental correspondence was going back and forth about shutting down meetings of the Moscow branch of RTO, the society requested and received permission from the curator to organize classes for workers at the Sytin printing plant. See GARF, f. 63 (1897), d. 616, vol. 2, ll. 13–14, 128, and GARF, f. 102, 3 d/p (1905), d. 513, ll. 1–3.
95. GARF, f. 63 (1897), d. 616, vol. 2, quotations ll. 11–12, 92–92 ob. ["Ministerstvo narodnogo prosveshcheniia to Moscow Gradonachal'nik 23 January 1905"]; GARF f. 102 3 d/p (1900), d. 236, quotation, l. 12; GARF, f. 102, 4 d/p (1907), d. 104, ll. 146–153, 274–277 ob.; GARF, f. 102, 4 d/p (1914), d. 124, pt. 20, ll. 1–4 ["Khodataistvo RTO o IV S"ezde russkikh deiatelei po tekhnicheskomu obrazovaniiu"].
96. GARF, f. 63 (1897), d. 616, l. 11 ["Ob obrazovatel'nykh uchrezhdeniiakh, ustraivaemykh Imperatorskogo RTO"].
97. Memorandum of the Moscow *okhrana* to the Department of Police (26 July 1900), GARF, f. 102, 3 d/p (1900), d. 236, ll. 91 ob.–92.
98. GARF, f. 102, 3 d/p (1905), d. 513, l. 7 ob. (emphasis in original).
99. GARF, f. 63 (1897), d. 616, vol. 1, l. 1–2, 8 ob., 13; GARF, f. 102 3 d/p (1905), d. 513, l. 2; GARF, f. 102, 4 d/p (1907), d. 104, ll. 45–48, 144–145.
100. Kropotkin, *Memoirs*, 247.
101. A. G. Nebolsin, in an address to the Third Congress on Russian Technical and Vocational Education in 1904, to be discussed in Chapter 6. See "Tretii

S"ezd russkikh deiatelei po tekhnicheskomu i professional'nomu obrazovaniiu v Rossii," *Zapiski RTO,* no. 3 (1905): 131.

102. TsIAM, f. 16 [Moscow Governor General], op. 25, d. 25, vol. 2, ll. 42–50; GARF, f. 102 OO (1903), d. 2355, quotation ll. 7–8 ["Kul'turno-prosvetitel'nye organizatsii Obshchestva rasprostraneniia tekhnicheskikh znanii"].

103. Heather Hogan, *Forging Revolution: Metalworkers, Managers and the State in St. Petersburg, 1890–1914* (Bloomington, Ind., 1993), 93.

6. Advocacy in the Public Sphere

1. Randall Collins, *The Sociology of Philosophies: A Global Theory of Intellectual Change* (Cambridge, Mass., 1998), 25–26.
2. Among the studies that do recognize the importance of Russian congresses, often in the context of the liberal movement or professionalization, are N. M. Pirumova, *Zemskoe liberal'noe dvizhenie: Sotsial'nye korni i evoliutsiia do nachala XX veka* (Moscow, 1977); N. M. Pirumova, *Zemskaia intelligentsia i ee rol'v obshchestvennoi bor'be do nachala XX v.* (Moscow, 1986); Nancy Frieden, *Russian Physicians in an Era of Reform and Revolution, 1856–1905* (Princeton, N.J., 1981); Christine Ruane, *Gender, Class and Professionalization of Russian City Teachers, 1860–1914* (Pittsburgh, 1994); Scott J. Seregny, *Russian Teachers and Peasant Revolution: The Politics of Education in 1905* (Bloomington, Ind., 1989); Seregny, "Professional Activism and Association Among Russian Teachers, 1864–1905, in Harley D. Balzer, ed., *Russia's Missing Middle Class: The Professions in Russian History* (Armonk, N.Y., 1996), 169–196; and Samuel C. Ramer, "Professionalism and Politics: The Russian Feldsher Movement, 1891–1918," in Harley D. Balzer, ed., *Russia's Missing Middle Class,* 117–142.
3. Nancy Frieden, Peter Krug, and John Hutchinson have included the Pirogov congresses in their work on Russian medicine and professionalization. I treat the Pirogov congresses from the point of view of their role in the expansion of the public sphere. See Nancy Frieden, *Russian Physicians;* Peter Krug, "Russian Public Physicians and Revolution: The Pirogov Society, 1917–1920" (Ph.D. diss., University of Wisconsin–Madison, 1979); and John F. Hutchinson, *Politics and Public Health in Revolutionary Russia* (Baltimore, 1990).
4. R. Hinton Thomas, *Liberalism, Nationalism and the German Intellectuals, 1822–1847* (Cambridge, 1951), 28, 40–41, 58, 62, 87; quotation, 36. See also Thomas Nipperdey, "Verein als soziale Struktur in Deutschland im späten 18. und frühen 19. Jahrhundert," in Thomas Nipperdey, *Gesellschaft, Kultur, Theorie* (Göttingen, 1976), 200.
5. In 1822, in the wake of the Carlsbad decrees, a suspicious Prussian government "forbade university teachers to discuss political questions of the moment, under pain of dismissal" (see Thomas, *Liberalism,* quotations 31, 42). Virchow quoted in Charles E. McClelland, *The German Experience of Professionalization: Modern Learned Professions and Their Organizations from the Early Nineteenth Century to the Hitler Era* (Cambridge, 1991), 51.

6. Theodore S. Hamerow, *The Social Foundations of German Unification, 1858–1871: Ideas and Institutions* (Princeton, N.J., 1969), 339–358. See also Thomas Nipperdey, *Germany from Napoleon to Bismarck, 1800–1866,* trans. Daniel Nolan (Princeton, N.J., 1996), 440.
7. David Blackbourn, *The Long Nineteenth Century: A History of Germany, 1780–1918* (New York, 1998), 125; Alex Hall, *Scandal, Sensation, and Social Democracy: The SPD Press and Wilhelmine Germany, 1890–1914* (Cambridge, 1977), 90–91; Robert J. Goldstein, *Political Repression in Nineteenth-century Europe* (London, 1983), 49; Marven Krug, "Reports of a Cop: Civil Liberties and Associational Life in Leipzig during the Second Empire," in James Retallack, ed., *Saxony in German History: Culture, Society and Politics, 1830–1933* (Ann Arbor, Mich., 2000), 217–286, especially 272, 276. In Germany, where prevailed "not the rule of law but the power of the police," according to Hall, the political police "seriously put in question the validity of the Rechtsstaat principle," a provocative interpretation in light of common assumptions of Russia's deficiency in this regard (Hall, *Scandal,* 2, 89–90, 93). The French authorities were no less nervous than the German: Guizot feared that republicans, Saint-Simonians, and others would use scientific congresses for political ends. To avoid this, the Second Empire took the initiative, and beginning in 1861 the Ministry of Education organized congresses of learned societies, which were held annually at the Sorbonne. See Jean-Pierre Chaline, *Sociabilité et Érudition: Les sociétés savants en France XIXe–XXe siècles* (Paris, 1995), 204, 206, 209; Robert Fox and George Weisz, eds., *The Organization of Science and Technology in France, 1808–1914* (Cambridge, 1980), 259.
8. Alexander II quoted in TsIAM, f. 16 [Moscow Governor-General], op. 51, d. 133, ll. 1–3 ["O zapreshchenii sel'sko-khoziaistvennykh s"ezdov"]. In 1871 the Moscow Agricultural Society celebrated its fiftieth anniversary by convening the first of a series of congresses of rural landowners *(s"ezdy sel'skikh khoziaev).* See Joan Klobe Pratt, "The Russian Free Economic Society, 1765–1915" (Ph.D. diss., University of Missouri, 1983), 166, 230–233. In 1869 the first of a series of archaeological congresses was held in Moscow to arouse interest in local antiquities and to provide communication among the empire's archaeologists. Following the itinerant pattern established in Europe, subsequent congresses were held in St. Petersburg, Kiev, Kazan', Tiflis, Odessa, Iaroslavl', and Vilno. See "Arkheologicheskie s"ezdy," *ES,* 3: 228–229.
9. RGIA, f. 735 ["Ob uchrezhdenii periodicheskikh s"ezdov"], op. 6, d. 52, l. 2–2 ob. ["Dokladnaia zapiska o s"ezde estestvoispytatelei"]. For more on Kessler, see V. Shimkevich, "Kessler Karl Fedorovich," *RBS,* 8: 622–625; "Kessler," *ES,* 15: 15–16; and Daniel Todes, *Darwin without Malthus: The Struggle for Existence in Russian Evolutionary Thought* (Oxford, 1989), 106–112. On Norov, an Orientalist and member of RGO and the Archaeological Society, see Shilov, 467–470, and A. I. Serkov, *Russkoe masonstvo, 1731–2000: Entsiklopedicheskii slovar'* (Moscow, 2001), 597–598.

10. RGIA, f. 735, op. 6, d. 52, l. 6–6 ob. ["Dokladnaia zapiska"]. See also Frieden, *Russian Physicians*, 53–76.
11. Frieden, *Russian Physicians*, quotation 8; Ia. V. Abramov, *Nashi voskresnye shkoly,ikh proshloe i nastoiashchee* (St. Petersburg, 1900), quotation 11; Adele Lindenmeyr, *Poverty Is Not a Vice: Charity, Society, and the State in Imperial Russia* (Princeton, N.J., 1996), 117. For more on Pirogov, see, in addition to Frieden, *Liudi russkoi nauki: Biologiia, meditsina, sel'skoe khoziaistvo* (Moscow, 1963), 495–505; *Bol'shaia meditsinskaia entsiklopediia*, 2d ed. (hereafter, *BME*) (Moscow, 1956–1964), 24: 424–438.
12. There were demurs, however. The curator of the Kazan' district claimed that congresses would be too costly to subsidize, and the curators of the St. Petersburg and Dorpat districts argued that in the short run national congresses were impractical because of the absence of a railroad network. See RGIA, f. 735, op. 6, d. 52, ll. 9–11, 23–24 ["Dokladnaia zapiska"].
13. Quoted in A. V. Pogozhev, *Dvadtsatipiatiletie estestvenno-nauchnykh s"ezdov v Rossii, 1861–1886* (Moscow, 1887), 54–55. Aleksandr Vasil'evich Pogozhev was a leader of zemstvo medicine and gathered information on public health for the Moscow zemstvo from 1879 to 1885. For more on Smirnov, see *BME*, 30: 746–747.
14. Pogozhev, *Dvadtsatipiatiletie*, 55–56.
15. RGIA, f. 735, op. 6, d. 181 ["Ob uchrezhdenii periodicheskikh s"ezdov naturalistov i vrachei"], ll. 5–8 ["Proekt dokladnoi zapiski o razreshenii periodicheskikh s"ezdov russkikh estestvoispytatelei i vrachei"]; Pogozhev, *Dvadtsatipiatiletie*, 57. On Giubbenet, see *ES*, 18: 955; *RBS*, 5A: 601–604.
16. Shimkevich, "Kessler," quotation 624. Information on the Kiev congress may be found in *Izvestiia o s"ezde estestvoispytatelei v Kieve s 11go po 18go iiunia 1861 g.* [*Prilozhenie k Otchetu Universiteta za 1860–1861 g.*] (Kiev, 1861), i–xii. At the time, Bunge was president of Kiev University and a member of the commission to draw up the new university statute. Biographical information is available in *ES*, 4: 929–930, and Shilov, 99–105.
17. GARF, f. 109 [Third Section], 1 ekspeditsiia (1867), d. 64, l. 1. W. Bruce Lincoln, *The Great Reforms: Autocracy, Bureaucracy, and the Politics of Change in Imperial Russia* (DeKalb, Ill., 1990), 129–130.
18. "O vnesenii predstavleniia v Sovet ministrov o ezhegodnykh s"ezdakh," RGIA, f. 744, [Ministry of Education] op. 1, d. 24, ll. 31–33; cited passage, l. 33.
19. GARF, f. 109, 1 ekspeditsiia (1867), d. 64, quotations ll. 1–4. See also S. V. Rozhdestvenskii, *Istoricheskii obzor deiatel'nosti Ministerstva narodnogo prosveshcheniia, 1802–1902* (St. Petersburg, 1902), 600.
20. Pogozhev, *Dvadtsatipiatiletie*, 104, 112, 124; Katherine Auspitz, *The Radical Bourgeoisie: The Ligue de l'enseignement and the Origins of the Third Republic, 1866–1885* (Cambridge, 1982), 64–71, 103–107.
21. GARF, f. 109, 1 ekspeditsiia (1867), d. 64, l. 2–2 ob.
22. Cited passages in Pogozhev, *Dvadtsatipiatiletie*, 94–95. See also Obshchestvo estestvoispytatelei, *Obzor deiatel'nosti Obshchestva za pervoe dvadtsat' piat' let ego sushchestvovaniia, 1868–1893* (St. Petersburg, 1893), 1; Alexander

Vucinich, *Science in Russian Culture, 1861–1917* (Stanford, Calif., 1970), 81. It should be recognized that such tutelage was not confined to Russia. Many French scientists, as well as government officials, felt that "public debate and controversy could only ruin the reputation of real science" (Dorinda Outram, *Georges Cuvier: Vocation, Science and Authority in Post-Revolutionary France* [Manchester, 1984], 119).

23. The proceedings of the congresses were published in the multivolume *Trudy*, one example of which is *Trudy Vtorogo s"ezda russkikh estestvoispytatelei v Moskve 20–30 avgusta 1869 r. po otdelam zoologii, anatomii i fiziologii* (Moscow, 1871).
24. The organizing committee usually had help from many other scientific societies, such as OLEAE, the Society of Acclimatization, the Moscow Society of Naturalists, the Mathematics Society, the Moscow Agricultural Society, the Moscow Horticultural Society, and the Society of Russian Physicians. See Pogozhev, *Dvadtsatipiatiletie*, 63–65, 91–92, 97, 127, 151. The congresses occasionally found their way into the popular press. See, for example, "Shestoi S"ezd estestvoispytatelei v S.-Peterburge," *Vsemirnaia illiustratsiia*, no. 575 (1880): 54.
25. My understanding of science popularization has been informed by G. S. Rousseau and Roy Porter, eds., *The Ferment of Knowledge: Studies in the History of Eighteenth-century Science* (Cambridge, 1980); Larry R. Stewart, *The Rise of Public Science: Rhetoric, Technology and Natural Philosophy in Newtonian Britain, 1660–1750* (Cambridge, 1992); Thomas Broman, "The Habermasian Public Sphere and 'Science *in* the Enlightenment,'" *History of Science* 36 (1998): 123–149; E. C. Spary, "The 'Nature' of the Enlightenment," in William Clark, Jan Golinski, and Simon Schaffer, eds., *The Sciences in Enlightened Europe* (Chicago, 1999), 272–304; Jan Golinski, *Making Natural Knowledge: Constructivism and the History of Science* (Cambridge, 1998); and E. C. Spary, *Utopia's Garden: French Natural History from the Old Regime to the Revolution* (Chicago, 2000).
26. Pogozhev, *Dvadtsatipiatiletie*, 76, 80–82, 121, 212–215; RGIA, f. 735, op. 6, d. 181, l. 6 ob. ["Raport predsedatelia obshchestva Kievskikh vrachei"]; *Izvestiia o s"ezde estestvoispytatelei v Kieve*, v, vii.
27. G. E. Shchurovskii, "Ob istoricheskom razvitii estestvoznaniia v Rossii" [an address before the second congress of naturalists], *Izvestiia OLEAE* 33, no. 2 (1878): 96.
28. Shchurovskii, "Ob istoricheskom razvitii," 102. See also G. Shchurovskii, "Ob obshchedostupnosti ili populiarizatsii estestvennykh nauk" [an address before the first congress], *Zhurnal Ministerstva narodnogo prosveshcheniia* (January, 1868): 39–52; B. E. Raikov, *Grigorii Efimovich Shchurovskii: Uchenyi, naturalist i prosvetitel'* (Moscow, 1965), 61.
29. Quoted in Pogozhev, *Dvadtsatipiatiletie*, 90–91.
30. Quoted in Pogozhev, *Dvadtsatipiatiletie*, 76. Shchurovskii expressed the same idea in his address to the first congress. See B. E. Raikov, *Russkie biologi-evoliutsionery do Darvina* (Moscow, 1951), 4: 563.
31. Shchurovskii, "Ob istoricheskom razvitii," 103.

32. Pogozhev, *Dvadtsatipiatiletie,* iii–iv, 73, 87; *Izvestiia o s"ezde estestvoispytatelei v Kieve,* ix–x; GARF, f. 109, 1 ekspeditsiia (1867), d. 64, l. 4; V. Agafonov, "Nauka i zhizn': Po povodu XI s"ezda estestvoispytatelei i vrachei v S.-Peterburge," *Mir Bozhii,* no. 2 (1902): 27. Shchurovskii also states these views; see "Ob istoricheskom razvitii," 96–97.
33. Quoted in Pogozhev, *Dvadtsatipiatiletie,* 76.
34. Pogozhev, *Dvadtsatipiatiletie,* 67.
35. *Izvestiia o s"ezde estestvoispytatelei v Kieve,* vii.
36. Quoted passage in Pogozhev, *Dvadtsatipiatiletie,* 105; examples of mediation, 142, 149, 151, 170.
37. A. V. Pogozhev, *Sed'moi s"ezd russkikh estestvoispytatelei i vrachei* (Moscow, 1883), 58–59 (originally published in *Meditsinskoe obozrenie* [1883]); Pogozhev, *Dvadtsatipiatiletie,* 176. What provoked the disruptive behavior was not indicated in the sources.
38. Pogozhev, *Dvadtsatipiatiletie,* iii (emphasis added).
39. McClelland, *The German Experience of Professionalization,* 3–5, 22, 48–49.
40. Claudia Heuerkamp, "The Making of the Modern Medical Profession, 1800–1914: Prussian Doctors in the Nineteenth Century," in Konrad H. Jarausch and Geoffrey Cocks, eds., *German Professions, 1800–1950* (Oxford, 1990), 66–84, especially 77, 79, 99; McClelland, *German Experience of Professionalization,* 79.
41. Pogozhev, *Sed'moi s"ezd,* 1; D. N. Zhbankov, "Statisticheskie dannye o vrachebnykh s"ezdakh," *Zhurnal Obshchestva russkikh vrachei im. N. I. Pirogova,* no. 1 (1905): 3–24; quotation, 21; "Iz VI-ogo s"ezda russkikh estestvoispytatelei i vrachei," *Vrach,* no. 2–8 (1880): 35ff.; *Trudy chetvertogo s"ezda russkikh estestvoispytatelei po otdeleniiu statistiko-gigienicheskomu, sektsii nauchnoi meditsiny* (Kazan', 1873).
42. Quoted in L. A. Bulgakova, "Meditsina i politika: S"ezdy vrachei v kontekste russkoi politicheskoi zhizni," in *Vlast' i nauka, uchenye i vlast', 1880e-nachalo 1920-kh godov: Materialy mezhdunarodnogo nauchnogo kollokviuma* (St. Petersburg, 2003), 213–235, quotation, 217. See also RGIA, f. 1284 [Ministry of Internal Affairs], op. 188 (1900), d. 240, ll. 26–27; Zhbankov, "Statisticheskie dannye," 19; M. M. Gran, Z. G. Frenkel', and A. I. Shingarev, eds., *Nikolai Ivanovich Pirogov i ego nasledie, Pirogovskie s"ezdy* (St. Petersburg, 1911), 151; V. I. Radulevich, *Ocherk istorii russkikh meditsinskikh obshchestv, ikh tsel', znachenie i vzaimnaia sviaz'* (Orel, 1890), 27. For more on zemstvo congresses, see B. B. Veselovskii, *Istoriia zemstva za sorok let* (St. Petersburg, 1909–1911), 3: 300–307; Pirumova, *Zemskoe liberal'noe dvizhenie,* 121, 143–146, 150–154, 197–200. On teachers' congresses, see Pirumova, *Zemskaia intelligentsia,* 51–54; Seregny, *Russian Teachers,* 39–54; Seregny, "Professional Activism," 173–174, 187; Ruane, *Gender, Class,* 92, 103–104, 111–112, 172–183. For more on zemstvo medicine, see Frieden, *Russian Physicians;* Samuel C. Ramer, "The Zemstvo and Public Health," in Terence Emmons and Wayne S. Vucinich, eds., *The Zemstvo in Russia: An Experiment in Local Self-Government* (Cambridge, 1982), 279–314; and David L.

Ransel, *Mothers of Misery: Child Abandonment in Russia* (Princeton, N.J., 1988), 278–293.

43. "Meditsinskie obshchestva," BME, 17: 752–755.
44. RGIA, f. 735, op. 6, d. 181, quotation l. 6 ob. ["Raport predsedatelia obshchestva Kievskikh vrachei"]; S. Iaroshevksii, "Vrachi, kak korporatsiia," *Russkaia meditsina,* no. 6 (12 February 1895): 96–97. The article is continued in no. 7 (19 February 1895): 110–112, and no. 8 (26 February 1895): 126–128.
45. Iaroshevksii, "Vrachi," 96.
46. V. I. Radulevich, *Ocherk istorii,* 4. Radulevich's book began as a paper given at the twenty-fifth anniversary celebration of the Orel Society of Physicians. See also Obshchestvo russkikh vrachei, *Istoricheskii ocherk* (Moscow, 1875), 8. On Inozemtssev, see *RBS,* 8: 124; *BME,* 11: 507–508.
47. I. I. Neyding, *Meditsinskie obshchestva v Rossii* (Moscow, 1897), iii; this study was compiled for the Twelfth International Medical Congress, held in Moscow in 1897. See also Radulevich, *Ocherk istorii,* 4; Frieden, *Russian Physicians,* 109–113; P. Krug, "Russian Public Physicians," 4–5, 12–14, 28, 283; and Hutchinson, *Politics and Public Health,* 7–9.
48. Radulevich, *Ocherk istorii,* 9. See also Obshchestvo russkikh vrachei v Moskve, *Istoricheskii ocherk administrativnoi deiatel'nosti* (Moscow, 1909), 133–135; Neyding, *Meditsinskie obshchestva,* 14.
49. Among the founders were S. P. Botkin, V. A. Manassein, M. I. Petrunkevich, E. A. Osipov, F. F. Erisman, and A. V. Pogozhev. In 1886 the society broadened its reach and changed its name to the Society of Russian Physicians in Honor of N. I. Pirogov. See "Ob izmenenii Ustava Obshchestva russkikh vrachei v pamiat' N. I. Pirogova," *Zhurnal Obshchestva russkhikh vrachei,* no. 1 (1902): 346, 352. See also an untitled and unsigned report in GARF, f. 102, 2 d/p, d. 20.527, l. 11–11 ob. ["O s"ezdakh vrachei"]; Neyding, *Meditsinskie obshchestva,* vi, 40–41; Gran, et al., *Pirogov,* 159; and Frieden, *Russian Physicians,* 119.
50. According to a report of the Department of Police, the Pirogov Society "steadily began to be a central body to unify the nation's physicians" (GARF, f. 102, 2d/p, d. 20.527, l. 30 ob). For accounts of the society's many activities, see Gran et al., *Pirogov;* Nancy Frieden's pioneering study of Russian physicians, *Russian Physicians,* and Peter Krug's dissertation, "Russian Public Physicians."
51. Cited passages in Gran, et al., *Pirogov,* 151, 159; A. V. Pogozhev, *Pervyi s"ezd moskovsko-peterburgskogo obshchestva vrachei* (Moscow, 1886), 1; Pogozhev, *Dvadtsatipiatiletie,* 270; D. N. Zhbankov, "Meditsinskie i soprikasaiiushchiesia s vrachebno-sanitarnym delom s"ezdy v proshlom, 1861–1924," *Vrachebnoe delo,* no. 18 (1927): col. 1289–1296; Zhbankov, "Statisticheskie dannye," 4–6. On Slavianskii, see *BME,* 30: 622–623; on Zhbankov, see *BME,* 9: 1056–1057.
52. These changes paralleled similar changes in the Pirogov Society that "quickly democratized" the society, in Veselovskii's words (Veselovskii, *Istoriia zemstva,* 3: 309, 468). Pirumova also discusses the increasing role of the zemstvo

physicians, who soon became the "core" of the Pirogov congresses. See Pirumova, *Zemskoe liberal'noe dvizhenie,* 119, 122–126.

53. GARF, f. 102, 2 d/p, d. 20.527, l. 11; TsIAM, f. 179 [Moskovskaia gorodskaia duma, Moskovskaia gorodskaia uprava], op. 21, d. 849, ll. 2–6, 10; Gran, et al., *Pirogov,* 161–164; Obshchestvo russkikh vrachei, *Svod postanovlenii i rabot I-VI-go Vserossiiskikh s"ezdov vrachei,* comp. K. I. Shidlovskii (Moscow, 1899), 2; Pogozhev, *Pervyi s"ezd,* 5–6; *Svodka khodataistv Obshchestva russkikh vrachei im. N. I. Pirogova pered pravitel'stvennymi uchrezhdeniiami za 20 let, 1883–1903,* comp. K. I. Shidlovskii (Moscow, 1904), 8; N. V. Iablokov, "Pervyi s"ezd moskovsko-peterburgskogo obshchestva vrachei," *Russkaia mysl',* no. 4 (1886): 94–95, 109–110; D. N. Zhbankov, "Neskol'ko prakticheskikh predlozhenii dlia uporiadochneniia zaniatii s"ezdov russkikh vrachei," *Vrach,* no. 4 (1889): 124–125.
54. Cited passages in Iaroshevskii, "Vrachi," 96–97; G. M. Gertsenshtein, *Tretii s"ezd russkikh vrachei* (St. Petersburg, 1889), 1, quoted in Frieden, *Russian Physicians,* 106. On Gertsenshtein, see *ES Biografii,* 4: 42.
55. Quoted in L. B. Vladimirova, "Sotsial'nye problemy meditsiny i gigieny na VII s"ezde russkikh estestvoispytatelei i vrachei," *Sovetskoe zdravokhranenie,* no. 1(1984): 54–57; quotation, 55. See also Pirumova, *Zemskaia intelligentsiia,* 126.
56. GARF, f. 102, 2 d/p, d. 20.527, ll. 6–8; *Svod postanovlenii,* 20–22, 81–82; Iaroshevskii, "Vrachi," 127; Gran et al., *Pirogov,* 152. On Osipov, see *BME,* 22: 187.
57. GARF, f. 102, 2 d/p, d. 20.527, l. 19, 29 ob.; Gran et al., *Pirogov,* 169; *Svod postanovlenii,* 129–131, 138; *Svodka khodataistv,* 24–26. On Sklifosovskii, see *BME,* 30: 542–543, and *Liudi russkoi nauki: Biologiia, meditsiny, sel'skoe khoziaistvo,* 527–533. The Pirogov congresses were covered in the popular press. One example is G. S. Vol'tke, "Itogi V s"ezda Obshchestva russkikh vrachei v pamiat' N. I. Pirogova," *Niva* 9 (1894): 202–206.
58. *Novoe vremya* (8 January 1902). The article was enclosed in the files of the Ministry of Internal Affairs, whose officials were ever mindful of public opinion. See GARF, f. 1284 [Ministry of Internal Affairs], op. 188 (1900), d. 77b ["O s"ezdakh vrachei im. Pirogova"], ll. 34–34 ob. [*Novoe vremia* 8 January 1902). See also *Svod postanovlenii,* 31–32.
59. Frieden, *Russian Physicians,* 99–104; "Erisman," *ES,* 81: 24–27. See also *Liudi russkoi nauki: Biologiia, meditsina, sel'skoe khoziaistvo,* 542–549; *BME,* 35: 740–741. On the police dossier of Erisman, see Pirumova, *Zemskaia intelligentsiia,* quotation, 97.
60. GARF, f. 102, 2 d/p, d. 20.527, ll. 12–13; P. Krug, "Russian Public Physicians," quotation, 23.
61. Pogozhev, *Dvadtsatipiatiletie,* 327, 335. See also *Svod postanovlenii,* 178–179; Hutchinson, *Politics and Public Health,* 25–28.
62. GARF, f. 102, 2 d/p, d. 20.527, l. 19; *Svod postanovlenii,* 23, 130–131, 138; *Svodka khodataistv,* 24–26.
63. Radulevich, *Ocherk istorii,* 13–14.

64. John Hutchinson, "Politics and Medical Professionalization after 1905," in Harley D. Balzer, ed., *Russia's Missing Middle Class,* 89–116, especially 91, 109–110. On the issue of a ministry of public health, see Hutchinson, *Politics and Public Health* 7–9.
65. Pirumova, *Zemskaia intelligentsiia,* 186; *Vrach,* no. 2 (1889): 54.
66. Vladimirova, "Sotsial'nye problemy," 56. On Portugalov and Skvortsov, see *BME,* 26: 28–29, and *BME,* 30: 471–472, respectively.
67. GARF, f. 102, 2 d/p, d. 20.527, ll. 26–26 ob. See also *Svodka khodataistv,* quotation, 39; Gran et al., *Pirogov,* 170–171; D. N. Zhbankov, "O pomoshchi golodaiushchim ot Pirogovskogo Obshchestva russkikh vrachei," *Russkii Vrach,* no. 17 (1902): 655–656; Frieden, *Russian Physicians,* 192–199.
68. RGIA, f. 1284, op. 188 (1900), d. 77b, ll. 9–9 ob., 26–26 ob. [Kazan' Governor General]; quotation, 26.
69. GARF, f. 102, 2 d/p, d. 20.527, quotation l. 35; Gran et al., *Pirogov,* 171.
70. GARF, f. 63 [MOO] (1902), d. 173 ["O S"ezde vrachei im. Pirogova"], pt. 1, l. 8. Grand Duke Sergei Aleksandrovich was president, honorary member, or patron of many cultural and philanthropic societies. See *Al'manakh sovremennykh russkikh gosudarstvennykh deiatelei* (St. Petersburg, 1897), 7: xiv–xvi.
71. GARF, f. 102, 2 d/p, d. 20.527, ll. 22, 29; *Svod postanovlenii,* 132; D. N. Zhbankov, "Telesnoe nakazanie v Rossii," *Vrach,* nos. 28–29 (1898): 813–820, 850–852, 881–884, and no. 30 (1899): 881–887; *Moskovskie vedomosti* [19 January 1896], quoted in Veselovskii, *Istoriia Zemstva* 3: 410–411. For more on corporal punishment in Russia, see Frieden, *Russian Physicians,* 185–192, and Abby M. Schrader, *Languages of the Lash: Corporal Punishment and Identity in Imperial Russia* (DeKalb, Ill., 2002). On Iakovenko, see *BME,* 35: 1172–1173.
72. GARF, f. 63 (1902), d. 173, pt.3 ["Ob Obshchestve russkikh vrachei"], l. 73; TsIAM, f. 16, op. 95, d. 59 ["Ob Obshchestve russkikh vrachei"], vol. 1, quotation l. 42. On the eighth congress, see also Frieden, *Russian Physicians,* 232–235, and A. Skibnevskii, "Vos'moi s"ezd russkikh vrachei v pamiat' N. I. Pirogova," *Meditsinskoe obozrenie,* no. 2 (1902): 1–11.
73. TsIAM, f. 16, op. 95, d. 59, vol. 1, quotation l. 42; GARF, f. 63 MOO, (1902), d. 173, pt. 3, ll. 55, 60–63; GARF f. 102 2 d/p d. 20.527, quotation l. 35 ob.
74. TsIAM, f. 16, op. 95, d. 59, vol. 1, l. 42–42 ob.; RGIA, f. 1284, op. 188 (1900), d. 77b, l. 108 [DOD to St. Petersburg Gradonachal'nik, 24 December 1903]; GARF, f. 102, 2 d/p, d. 20.527, ll. 35–39. On Virchow, see Paul Weindling, "Bourgeois Values, Doctors and the State: The Professionalization of Medicine in Germany, 1848–1933," in David Blackbourn and Richard J. Evans, eds., *The German Bourgeoisie: Essays on the Social History of the German Middle Class from the Late Eighteenth to the Early Twentieth Century* (London, 1991), 198–223; "Virkhov [Virchow]" *ES,* 6: 525–526.
75. *Grazhdanin,* no. 3 (10 January 1902): 18; RGIA, f. 1284, op. 188 (1900), d. 77b, ll. 36, 87–88 ["Spravka DOD"]. To be fair, it must be admitted that

many scientists and physicians agreed with Russian officialdom. The program committee of the eleventh congress of scientists and physicians in 1901 rejected two paper proposals from Zhbankov, on corporal punishment and the admission of women to universities, on the grounds that these topics were not appropriate for a scientific congress. See D. N. Zhbankov, "XI-yi S"ezd russkikh estestvoispytatelei i vrachei i VIII Pirogovskii S"ezd vrachei," *Vrach,* no. 9 (1902): 334.

76. GARF, f. 102 OO (1904), d. 200 ["O S"ezde Obshchestva russkikh vrachei"], ll. 31, 41, 55; and GARF, f, 102 OO (1903), d. 1785 ["O Deviatom s"ezde russkikh vrachei"], ll. 2–3. These congresses coincided with several other important gatherings, including the First Congress of the Union of Liberation, the Organizing Committee for the 1905 Congress of Teachers' Mutual Aid Societies, and the Ushinskii Commission of the St. Petersburg Pedagogical Society. See Ruane, *Gender, Class,* 121–122; Melissa Kirschke Stockdale, *Paul Miliukov and the Quest for a Liberal Russia, 1880–1918* (Ithaca, N.Y., 1996), 107. Zhbankov claimed that the ninth Pirogov congress was "one of the most important initiators of the liberation movement that has spread all over Russia" (Zhbankov, "Statisticheskie dannye," 22).

77. GARF, f. 102, 4 d/p (1914), d. 124 pt. 20 ["Khodataistvo RTO o Chetvertom s"ezde russkikh deiatelei po tekhnicheskomu obrazovaniiu"], l. 33 ["Dokladnaia zapiska o trekh s"ezdakh deiatelei po tekhnicheskomu i professional'nomu obrazovaniiu" (hereafter, "Dokladnaia zapiska")]; "Tretii S"ezd russkikh deiatelei po tekhnicheskomu i professional'nomu obrazovaniiu v Rossii," *Zapiski RTO,* no. 3 (1904): 105-154, especially 108. Luk'ianov was a supporter of expanding educational opportunities. On Luk'ianov, see N. I. Afanas'ev, *Sovremenniki: Al'bom biografii* (St. Petersburg, 1909–1910), 1: 157–159.

78. "Itogi III-go s"ezda deiatelei po tekhnicheskomu obrazovaniiu," *Osvobozhdenie,* no. 17 [41] (1904): 310; "S"ezd deiatelei po tekhnicheskomu obrazovaniiu," *Osvobozhdenie,* nos. 15–16 [39–40] (1904): 289. On Kovalevskii, see V. Fedorchenko, *Imperatorskii dom: Vydaiushchiesia sanovniki* (Krasnoiarsk, 2001), 1: 552–553.

79. "Tretii tekhnicheskii i professional'nyi s"ezd," *Novosti i birzhevaia gazeta,* no. 357 (29 December 1903): 3.

80. RGIA, f. 1284, op. 188 (1901), d. 415 ["S"ezd deiatelei po tekhnicheskomu obrazovaniiu"], ll. 5–6; RGIA, f. 90 [RTO], op. 1, d. 251 ["Tretii s"ezd po tekhnicheskomu obrazovaniiu"], ll. 1–23; "Tretii S"ezd," 139.

81. "Tretii tekhnicheskii i professional'nyi s"ezd," 2.

82. *Rezoliutsii Tret'ego s"ezda russkikh deiatelei po tekhnicheskomu i professional'nomu obrazovaniiu* (St. Petersburg, 1903).

83. GARF, f. 124 [Ministry of Justice], op. 43 (1905), d. 1571, l. 4 ["Delo o proiznoshenii protivopravitel'stvennykh rechei na zasedanii Moskovskogo otdeleniia RTO 29 December 1904"].

84. GARF, f. 124, op. 43 (1905), d. 1571, l. 4 ob.

85. GARF, f. 102, 4 d/p (1914), d. 124 pt. 20, l. 34 ob. ["Dokladnaia zapiska"]; III S"ezd russkikh deiatelei po tekhnicheskomu i professional'nomu

obrazovaniiu 26 dekabria 1903–6 ianvaria 1904 g., *Dnevnik* (St. Petersburg, 1903–1904), various issues.

86. GARF, f. 102, 4 d/p (1914), d. 124 pt. 20, ll. 16–17, 34 ob. ["Dokladnaia zapiska"]. See a similar account in "S"ezd deiatelei po tekhnicheskomu obrazovaniiu," *Osvobozhdenie,* nos. 15–16 [39–40] (1904): 288–289. The announcement of closure appeared in the papers. See, for example, *Russkie vedomosti,* no. 7 (7 January 1904): 2. On the contribution of N. V. Chekhov to the teachers' movement, see Ruane, *Gender, Class,* 122.

87. GARF, f. 102, 4 d/p (1914), d. 124 pt. 20, ll. 33–34, 36 ["Dokladnaia zapiska"]; GARF, f. 124, op. 43 (1905), d. 1571, l. 4 ["Delo o proiznoshenii"]. See also "Dva s"ezda," *Mir Bozhii* (February 1904): 22–23.

88. RGIA, f. 90, [RTO] op. 1, d. 251, ll. 83–85 ["Ob obstoiatel'stvakh zakrytiia III-go S"ezda"].

89. *Russkaia mysl'* (February 1904): 237–238. Indeed, meetings of the Division of Technical and Vocational Education of the Moscow chapter of the Russian Technical Society discussed the congress throughout the remainder of 1904. P. I. Korzhnevskii gave a report on the congress and, in particular, on the "crude interference in the productive work of the congress" at a meeting of the newly formed Bogorodsk chapter of the Technical Society; the Bogorodsk chapter voted to express solidarity with the organizers and the resolutions of the congress. See OR RGB, f. 436 [P. I. Korzhenevskii], folder 1, article 60 ["Soobrazheniia po dokladu o Tret'em s"ezde russkikh deiatelei po tekhnicheskomu i professional'nomu obrazovaniiu"].

90. "S"ezd deiatelei po tekhnicheskomu obrazovaniiu," *Osvobozhdenie,* nos. 15–16 [39–40] (1904): 289; "Itogi s"ezda deiatelei po tekhnicheskomu obrazovaniiu," *Osvobozhdenie,* no. 17 [41] (1904): 310.

91. *Trudy IX Pirogovskogo s"ezda* (St. Petersburg, 1904), 1: 6–31; A. Skibnevskii, "Deviatyi s"ezd russkikh vrachei v pamiat' N. I. Pirogova," *Meditsinskoe obozrenie,* no. 2 (1904): 139–151; D. E. Gorokhov, "O IX Pirogovskom s"ezde," *Meditsinskoe obozrenie,* no. 5 (1904): 1–18; *Russkoe slovo,* no. 5 (5 January 1904): quotation, 2. On Gabricheveskii, see *BME,* 6: 190–191; on Kurkin, see *BME,* 14: 1058–1059; on Rein, see *BME,* 28: 207–208, and Hutchinson, *Politics and Public Health,* 78–107; on Shervinskii, see *BME,* 34: 916–917; on Shidlovskii, see *BME,* 34: 944–945.

92. Quoted in "Pirogovskii s"ezd," *Sankt-Peterburgskie vedomosti,* no. 4 (5 January 1904): 3. On Razumovskii, see *BME,* 27: 872–873.

93. GARF, f. 102, OO (1904), d. 200, l. 2 ob.; *Svodka khodataistv,* viii–ix; *Russkii vrach,* no. 38 (1904): 1296–1297.

94. Deviatyi s"ezd russkikh vrachei na pamiat' N. I. Pirogova, *Trudy* (St. Petersburg, 1904), 2: 58; GARF, f. 102, 2 d/p, d. 20.527 ["O s"ezdakh vrachei"], ll. 41–42 ob., 45; "S IX pirogovskogo s"ezda," *Osvobozhdenie,* no. 18 [42] (1904): 320–321, and no. 19 [43] (1904): 332–334; Zhbankov, "Meditsinskie s"ezdy," col. 1289. On Fal'bork's arrest, see "Itogi III s"ezda," 311. On Dril' see *ES Biografii,* 4: 812–814.

95. GARF, f. 102, 2 d/p, d. 20.527, quotations ll. 42, 44; GARF, f. 102, OO (1904), d. 200, l. 19 ob.; "Deviatyi Pirogovskii s"ezd," *Novosti i birzhevaia*

gazeta, no. 11 (11 January 1904): 5; Skibnevskii, "Deviatyi s"ezd," 3–4; *Svodka khodataistv,* viii–ix; *Russkii vrach,* no. 38 (1904): 1296–1297. Although only one-third of the seventy-two petitions of the Pirogov Society's first nine congresses were answered positively, there were eventually a few government decrees in their spirit—the establishment of the St. Petersburg Women's Medical Institute in 1895, the establishment of a standard nomenclature of diseases in 1901, and the abolition of corporal punishment of peasants in 1904.

96. A. S—n, "Pirogovtsy," *Sankt-Peterburgskie vedomosti,* no. 11 (12 January 1904): 2.
97. GARF, f. 102, OO (1905), d. 715, ll. 10–10ob.
98. GARF, f. 102, OO (1904), d. 200, l. 3 ob.
99. GARF, f. 102, 2 d/p d. 20.527, quotation, l. 42; "Deviatyi s"ezd v pamiat' Pirogova," *Russkie vedomosti,* no.9 (9 January 1904): 2.
100. GARF, f. 102, 2 d/p, d. 20.527, l. 18; GARF, f. 102, OO (1904), d. 200, l. 15.
101. GARF, f. 102, 2 d/p, d. 20.527, l. 40 ob. The presence of Jews at the congress reflected the relatively large number of the empire's Jewish physicians. See Frieden, *Russian Physicians,* 204.
102. GARF, f. 102, 2 d/p, d. 20.527, l. 40.
103. GARF, f. 102, 2 d/p, d. 20.527, quotations ll. 40–41; GARF, f. 102, OO (1904), d. 200, quotations ll. 18 ob. 19, 42.
104. GARF. f. 102, OO (1904), d. 200, quotation l. 31; GARF, f. 102, OO (1903), d. 1785, quotation, l. 2.
105. GARF, f. 102, OO (1904), d. 200, ll. 10–10 ob., 11, 16–16 ob., 20–22, 28, 55; GARF, f. 102, 2 d/p, d. 20.527, ll. 46–46 ob. To take two samples from the press, *Novosti i birzhevaia gazeta* made no mention of the disorder at the closing meeting (12 January 1904, p. 3); and *Russkie vedomosti* noted that "when the band struck up a tune, part of the audience greeted the closing with expressions of dissatisfaction." (13 January 1904, p. 2). See also "S IX pirogovskogo s"ezda," 333.
106. Gran et al., *Pirogov,* 158.
107. A. A. Sukhov, "O russkikh vrachebnykh s"ezdakh voobshche," *Meditsinskoe obozrenie,* no. 21 (1905): 650–651; D. N. Zhbankov, "VII S"ezd russkikh vrachei v Kazani: Vpechatleniia i zametki," *Vrach,* no. 22 (1899): 1–15, especially 6.
108. GARF, f. 102, OO (1904), d. 200, quotation, l. 9; and GARF, f. 102, OO (1903), d. 1785, quotation, l. 2.
109. Zhbankov, "Meditsinskie s"ezdy," col. 1288; A. A. Stakhovich, "Otgoloski IX pirogovskogo s"ezda," *Rus',* no. 58 (8 February 1904): 5, and no. 61 (12 February 1904): 5.
110. "IX-i Pirogovskii S"ezd po otzyvam pechati," *Zhurnal Obshchestra russkikh vrachei,* no. 1–2 (1904): 101–111, quotations 102, 104.
111. *Sankt-Peterburgskie vedomosti* (9, 10, and 11 January 1904), p. 4 in each issue.
112. *Zhurnal Obshchestva russkikh vrachei,* no. 1–2 (1904): 102–104.
113. Stakhovich, "Otgoloski," 5.

114. *Izvestiia Imperatorskoi voennoi-meditsinskoi akademii,* no. 1 (January 1904): 111–112, quoted in *Zhurnal Obshchestva russkikh vrachei,* nos. 1–2 (1904): 110.
115. *Grazhdanin,* no. 3 (10 January 1902): 3.
116. Collins, *Sociology of Philosophies,* 25–26.
117. Lawrence Goldman, "A Peculiarity of the English? The Social Science Association and the Absence of Sociology in Nineteenth-century Britain," *Past and Present,* no. 114 (February 1987): 133–171; quotation, 137.
118. Ibid., 171.
119. GARF, f. 102, 2 d/p, d. 20.527, ll. 46 ob.–47; TsIAM f. 184 [Moskovskaia gubernskaia zemskaia uprava], op. 5, d. 1432, l. 44 ["Kratkii otchet o poezdke na s"ezd russkikh vrachei"]. On teachers' congresses, see Ruane, *Gender, Class,* 103.
120. V. Agafonov, "Nauka i zhizn'," 271.
121. Zhbankov, "VII S"ezd," 8.
122. Ruane, *Gender, Class,* 91; Frieden, *Russian Physicians;* Harley D. Balzer, "The Problem of the Professions in Imperial Russia," in Edith W. Clowes, Samuel Kassow, and James West, eds., *Between Tsar and People: Educated Society and the Quest for Public Identity in Late-Imperial Russia* (Princeton, N.J., 1991), 183–198.
123. Pogozhev, *Dvadtsatipiatiletie,* quotation 67; Sukhov, "O russkikh vrachebnykh s"ezdakh," 650–651; *Zhurnal Obshchestva russkikh vrachei,* no. 1–2 (1904): 108.
124. A. A. Kizevetter, *Na rubezhe dvukh stoletii: Vospominaniia 1881–1914* (Moscow, 1997), quotation, 164; "Itogi IX s"ezda," Osvobozhdenie no. 19 (1904), quotation, 333. The meetings to which Kizevetter refers were the second congress on technical education, the sixth Pirogov congress, as well as an agricultural congress.

Conclusion

1. Keith Tester, *Civil Society* (London, 1992), 1–2.
2. Randall Collins, *The Sociology of Philosophies: A Global Theory of Intellectual Change* (Cambridge, Mass., 1998), 28.
3. Leonore Davidoff and Catherine Hall, *Family Fortunes: Men and Women of the English Middle Class, 1780-1850* (Chicago, 1987), 445.
4. Jürgen Habermas, *Between Facts and Norms: Contributions to a Discourse Theory of Law and Democracy,* trans. William Rehg (Cambridge, Mass., 1996), 355–356; Jean L. Cohen and Andrew Arato, *Civil Society and Political Theory* (Cambridge, Mass., 1992), 660; Craig Calhoun, ed., *Habermas and the Public Sphere* (Cambridge, Mass., 1992), 63; Ian F. McNeely, "The Intelligence Gazette *(Intelligenzblatt)* as a Road Map to Civil Society," in Frank Trentmann, ed., *Paradoxes of Civil Society: New Perspectives on Modern German and British History* (New York, 2000), 151; Katherine Auspitz, *The Radical Bourgeoisie: The Ligue de l'enseignement and the Origins of the*

Third Republic, 1866–1885 (Cambridge, 1982), 75; Stefan-Ludwig Hoffmann, "Democracy and Associations in the Long Nineteenth Century: Toward a Transnational Perspective," *Journal of Modern History* 75, no. 2 (June 2003): 276.

5. Daniel Gordon, *Citizens without Sovereignty: Equality and Sociability in French Thought, 1670–1789* (Princeton, 1994), 38; Habermas, *Between Facts and Norms*, 371; Margaret Jacob, *Living the Enlightenment: Freemasonry and Politics in Eighteenth-century Europe* (New York, 1991), 19.

Index